Puglia & Basilicata

Paula Hardy

Abigail Hole, Olivia Pozzan

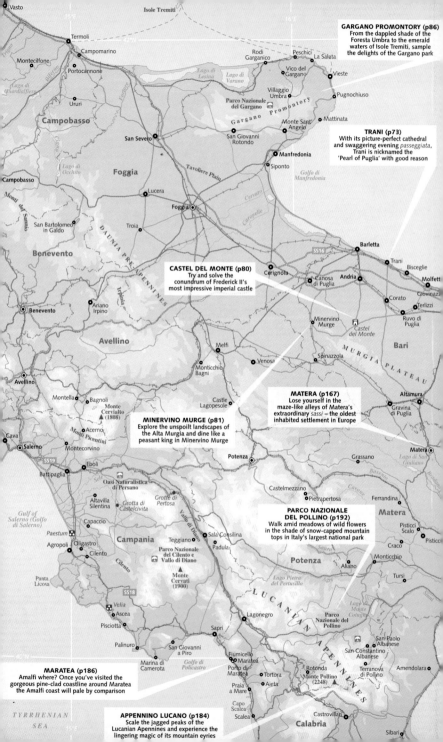

GARGANO PROMONTORY (p86)
From the dappled shade of the Foresta Umbra to the emerald waters of Isole Tremiti, sample the delights of the Gargano park

TRANI (p73)
With its picture-perfect cathedral and swaggering evening *passeggiata*, Trani is nicknamed the 'Pearl of Puglia' with good reason

CASTEL DEL MONTE (p80)
Try and solve the conundrum of Frederick II's most impressive imperial castle

MATERA (p167)
Lose yourself in the maze-like alleys of Matera's extraordinary *sassi* – the oldest inhabited settlement in Europe

MINERVINO MURGE (p81)
Explore the unspoilt landscapes of the Alta Murgia and dine like a peasant king in Minervino Murge

PARCO NAZIONALE DEL POLLINO (p192)
Walk amid meadows of wild flowers in the shade of snow-capped mountain tops in Italy's largest national park

MARATEA (p186)
Amalfi where? Once you've visited the gorgeous pine-clad coastline around Maratea the Amalfi coast will pale by comparison

APPENNINO LUCANO (p184)
Scale the jagged peaks of the Lucanian Apennines and experience the lingering magic of its mountain eyries

Highlights

In a country where every nook and cranny appears to have been explored, experienced and exhausted, Puglia and Basilicata are a charming reminder that some of travel's best secrets lie right beneath our noses. Renown for its laissez-faire atmosphere, heavenly coastline, fantastic food and authentic festivals, here are some top tips from our readers, writers and staff. Why not add to them yourself at lonelyplanet.com/bluelist.

STEFANO AMANTINI/ 4CORNERS IMAGES

1 BAROQUE & ROLL

Lecce's over-the-top architecture (p146) is pure showbiz, which would put the gaudiest movie set to shame, yet somehow it works. True style that is not afraid to show it.

Sumeet Desai, India

STEFANO AMANTINI/ 4CORNERS IMAGES

POETRY IN STONE

A drowned cathedral once made it into poetry, but what about a cathedral rising like Venus from the deep blue sea? Rising on its spit by the entrance to the harbour, Trani cathedral (p74) is the most sublime sight in all Puglia. It is dedicated to St Nicholas the Pilgrim, whose utterances were entirely limited to Kyrie Eleison (Lord have mercy) perhaps on those who dared to build so seductively to the senses.

**Anthony Quiney,
traveller, UK**

2

PASSEGIATTA IN MARTINA FRANCA

Summer *passegiatta* in the baroque centre of Martina Franca (p127) begins on the wide tree lined Piazza XX Settembre, with teens to 30-somethings swaggering their stuff, trying to outdo each other. Pressing onward (don't try turning against the flow!) funnelled into the narrow whitewashed, interlinking passageways, the individual sophisticated swagger becomes a writhing scrum, yet everyone maintaining their panache and brio finally to emerge unscathed, still preening into the Piazza Plebiscito before the wonderfully ornate baroque Basilica di San Martino. This must be repeated again and again!

John Dabney, trulli owner, UK

3

GIOVANNI SIMEONE / SIME/ 4CORNERS IMAGES

JOHANNA HUBER/SIME/4CORNERS IMAGES

4

ROLLERCOASTERS & THE REDENTORE

To reach Maratea's mountaintop statue of Christ (p188), we drove up a rollercoaster road on stilts, the tight hairpin bends getting higher and higher and giving way to thrilling views over the sparse pretty countryside and blue coast. At the top we were greeted with peace and quiet, a quaint little church and the most giant statue you could imagine. We were all alone, and it felt like any other tourists were miles away.

Kelda Bence, traveller, UK

MORNING IN MATERA

I started to explore Matera (p167) before the town got up. There were just the faintest stirrings of life and the scent of the first coffee of the day in the air. It's an extraordinary town: elegant buildings developed from caves that pock a dizzying ravine. Tinged gold by the early morning sun, it was bleary, deserted and quiet.

Abigail Hole, Lonely Planet Author, UK

5

STEFANO AMANTINI/ ATLANTIDE PHOTOTRAVEL/COR

THE CASTLE ON THE MOUNTAIN

It started as a tiny white dot high on the distant hill, slowly turning into a magic castle (p80), surrounded by trees. Its symmetry was perfect. There was no Sleeping Beauty, but sunlight threw patterns on the dark rooms. We could hear a small child's chatter echoing through them. As we came out we watched a brilliant angry sun sink over the vast plain. Long after we left, the white tower persisted in the darkness.

Tom Slater, traveller, UK

JOHANNA HUBER/SIME/4CORNERS IMAGES

6

7

TUNDRA GO

MAGIC IN THE MIST

The road zigzagged steeply uphill to the small village of Castelmezzano (p185) hidden in the mist. Magic happened that night. The mist cleared and in the spotlights I saw the needle-like teeth of rock towering above the stone houses and the darkness fall into the 1000m chasm below.

Erich Stark, traveller, Germany

BELLA FIGURA

It was on the long and windy back road to Rabatana in Tursi (p200) that we came across a friendly 80-year-old farmer attending his goats and chickens. He kindly asked us into his nearby damp 'cave' retreat, where he offered us a glass of good, local Italian wine. I asked if he would mind if I took his photograph and his tired eyes lit up. It took a couple of minutes to set up the camera and when I turned back, I discovered that he was carefully combing his hair in the mirror in preparation for his special moment. Pride. The experience was priceless.

Tundra Gorza,
photographer, Australia

MASSIMO RIPANI/SIME/4CORNERS IMAGES

(8)

TUNDRA GORZA

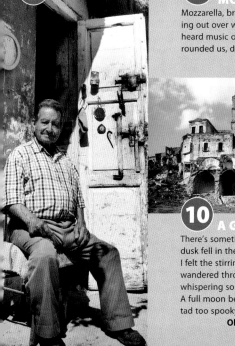

(9) **MOZZARELLA & MUSIC**

Mozzarella, bread and wine on a rocky promontory, looking out over white sand, sea and Vieste (p88). We suddenly heard music on the wind. Goats, complete with bells, surrounded us, dead keen to share the picnic.

Kirstie Walters, traveller, UK

TUNDRA GORZA

(10) **A GRIMMS FAIRYTALE**

There's something eerie about a ghost town at sunset. As dusk fell in the abandoned hilltop town of Craco (p200) I felt the stirrings of a Grimms fairytale coming on. We wandered through the ruins of collapsed memories, whispering so as not to disturb whatever wasn't going on. A full moon behind the crooked spire would have been a tad too spooky.

Olivia Pozzan, Lonely Planet Author, Australia

WILDFLOWERS & COWBELLS

Walking through Parco Nazionale del Pollino (p192) through beech-woods we came to the rocky outcrop of Monte di Grasta at 1485m, awash with colour – sheets of yellow potentilla, a haze of blue alkanet and the rosy shades of pink hawksbeard and geraniums. There were white spires of asphodel by the wood verges and woodruff in the understorey. Cuckoos called from the woods below and cowbells tinkled in the distance. Masses of orchids filled the Piano di Sopra meadow. We spent hours moving from one undulation to the next, avoiding the herd of horned cattle in shades of cream to dark brown.

Hazel Witte, traveller, Scotland

GIOVANNI SIMEONE / SIME/ 4CORNERS IMAGES

ARCANGELO PIAI /SIME /4CORNERS IMR

11 A SLICE OF THE WEST COUNTRY

The Valle d'Itria was an extraordinary revelation. It's rolling green hills and grey stone walls are just like the English West Country but the weather is much, much better. Pearly white Locorotondo (p126) was our favourite hill town. It really does seem to shine on its hill top and from the local park, where the old guys sit and smoke, you can gaze over the vineyards and the funny-looking trulli.

Sandra Haywood, traveller, UK

12

GIOVANNI SIMEONE / SIME/ 4CORNERS IM

13 SUN, SAND & SEA

Puglia in April – glorious. We hung out in Gallipoli (p156), Puglia's very own Portofino. Everyone said Torre Pizzo was the most beautiful beach on the coast, so on Sunday we went in search of it. The dirt track we headed down went on for ages. 'Do you think this is right?' we kept asking. Finally we hit the end of the track. We headed through a swathe of fragrant pines and out onto a sugar soft beach with only two other people in sight. But is was the water that I'll never forget – so blue it hurt our eyes.

Paula Hardy, Lonely Planet Author, UK

Contents

Regional Map Contents

Northern Puglia & the Gargano Promontory (p86)

Bari & the Terra di Bari (p61)

Northern Basilicata (p167)

Taranto & the Murgia (p111)

Southern Basilicata (p184)

Brindisi & the Salento (p137)

The Authors

PAULA HARDY
Coordinating Author; Itineraries; History; Bari & the Terra di Bari; Taranto & the Murgia; Brindisi & the Salento; Transport

A peripatetic childhood between various African countries and Europe led Paula inevitably to guidebook writing and to an enduring fascination with the Mediterranean, that mini-sea from which so much culture and history have evolved. For the last five years she has heroically endured thousands of dishes of pasta, braved exploding volcanoes and worshipped faithfully at the altar of the sun god in the process of researching Lonely Planet guides to Italy, Sicily, Sardinia, Andalucia and Morocco. When not struggling to work off the worst excesses of the Italian table, Paula can be found commissioning Italy books and daydreaming of southern skies in Lonely Planet's London office.

ABIGAIL HOLE
Destination Puglia & Basilicata; Getting Started; The Culture; Food & Wine; Directory

From London, Abigail moved to Hong Kong in 1997, returning in 2000 to begin a stint editing books in Lonely Planet's London office. She started to write Lonely Planet guidebooks in 2002. Two years later, she visited Rome for a month and liked it so much she stayed, working on Lonely Planet's *Best of Rome* and *Rome* guides and producing articles and podcasts on Italy. Abigail is a true Italian mamma with two *mezzo*-Pugliese sons, and *la famiglia* divide their time between London, Rome and Puglia. Her other travel journalism includes pieces for the *Guardian*, *Marie Claire*, *Wanderlust* and the *San Francisco Chronicle*.

OLIVIA POZZAN
Environment; Northern Puglia & the Gargano Promontory; Northern Basilicata; Southern Basilicata

Raised on pasta and rough red in a small Australian coastal town, Olivia didn't appreciate her Italian heritage until a discover-your-roots trip to the Veneto. Since then Italy has been a favourite destination. Having studied veterinary science she spent a few years chasing cattle in the Outback before somehow landing in the Middle East as the livestock vet for an Arabian prince. When not hiking in the world's most exotic places she lives the beach lifestyle on the Sunshine Coast, contributing to outdoor mags, writing books on alternative therapies and keeping fit as a personal trainer.

LONELY PLANET AUTHORS

Why is our travel information the best in the world? It's simple: our authors are independent, dedicated travellers. They don't research using just the internet or phone, and they don't take freebies in exchange for positive coverage. They travel widely, to all the popular spots and off the beaten track. They personally visit thousands of hotels, restaurants, cafés, bars, galleries, palaces, museums and more – and they take pride in getting all the details right, and telling it how it is. Think you can do it? Find out how at lonelyplanet.com.

Destination Puglia & Basilicata

The Italians have a way with words. They call southern Italy the *mezzogiorno* (midday), which seems to sum up both the climate and the atmosphere. In summer, the *soleone* (lion sun) beats overhead, driving towns to close shutters and shut up shop for the afternoon, ripening the olives, fruit and fresh vegetables, putting power in the local wine and meaning the best place to go is always the beach.

The south and north of this complicated country have long had a difficult relationship. The rural south has suffered economic hardship of a type unknown in the urbane north, whose residents call southerners *terroni* (literally 'of the land', less politely, 'peasants'). Unemployment today is still around 20% higher in the south than in the north. Southern Italy's history is one of invasion and emigration, though immigration is increasingly significant. As the lesser developed regions of a country whose economy is largely moribund, Puglia and Basilicata's future seems uncertain (despite the discovery of oil in Basilicata). Yet here, also, families remain stronger, traditions run deeper and people who live here speak of how good it is to know your neighbours and to have your family close at hand. Those who move away miss the sun, the sea and the slowness.

Puglia and Basilicata have powerful and distinct characters. Puglia is a lush, largely flat farming region, skirted by a long coast that alternates between glittering cliffs and long white-sand beaches. Its pipsqueak neighbour Basilicata is rocky, hilly and wild, with mountaintop villages, a dramatic stretch of coast to rival the Amalfi further north, and the extraordinary cave-town of Matera. Puglia's rustic, simple cuisine, born out of poverty, garners increasing attention and plaudits and Basilicata produces one of Italy's finest wines from its volcanic soil. Fresh, robust ingredients, seas of silver-green olive trees and winemaking vines, and a culture where food and drink are a way of expressing friendship, love and enjoying life: eating here is bound to be good.

Both regions have become achingly hip in the travel press and are gradually being discovered by foreign tourists – opened up through low-cost flights coming into Bari and Brindisi. Italian tourists have been in the know for years, swarming south every summer. In July and August Puglia hosts nightly festivals celebrating anything from snails to meatballs, parties on the beaches, concerts, events and a profusion of summery hubbub. Basilicata has attracted attention since Mel Gibson chose Matera's pock-marked hills to form the backdrop to his *The Passion of the Christ*.

But putting hype aside, people visiting Puglia and Basilicata tend to get besotted. As well as exploring the coast and the mountains, you can visit Baroque towns, seemingly goblin-built villages, powder-soft beaches, and coast through stunning scenery. Hospitality is sacred here, so you will be treated royally. Ebullient yet somehow reserved, the graceful people of the south will go out of their way to help you out and feed you up. But besides all this, you will feel like you are discovering something real – get here before anyone else finds out.

Getting Started

Italy's lesser-known south has lately become deeply fashionable in the travel press, but on the ground its increased publicity means that you're likely to meet the odd foreign tourist rather than none. Its increased popularity does mean that facilities are ever improving (though it's long been popular with Italian tourists), and there are now more and more self-catering accommodation, interesting hotels and *agriturismi* (farm-stay accommodation) – for more on accommodation, see p202. Some places in Puglia and Basilicata are extremely seasonal, so this might affect when you choose to go (see below).

Italy is not particularly cheap, though it is less costly than, for example, the UK, Germany and France, and the south is generally much cheaper than the north. Puglia in particular is extremely family friendly. Italian families head here in droves over the summer precisely because it's ideal for a family holiday. The quiet country roads are easy to drive around and don't have the mad traffic that afflicts so much of the rest of the country. There is masses of self-catering accommodation, both independent and within holiday villages and hotels, aimed at families. It's also a bargain compared to the north and there are lovely beaches and lots of great activities to tire little ones out, such as cycling, swimming, horse riding, diving, sailing and so on.

The best way to get around is by car, though there are good bus and train connections between the main towns. It's just hard to explore remote areas – the Parco Nazionale del Pollino, for example – by public transport.

WHEN TO GO

In spring (around April to June), the countryside is a multicoloured tangle of spring flowers, fields are lush and green, the weather is warm and balmy, and Puglia and Basilicata are not overcrowded. September and even October are similarly uncrowded and good weatherwise. Most Italians hit the road in July and August, so those two months – in which prices soar, tempers flare,

---

RENTING A VILLA

A fantastic way to enjoy Italy is to rent a villa, apartment or cottage for a week or so – this often works out cheaper than a hotel, means you can settle down and relax, cook your own food (visiting the wonderful local markets for ingredients) and enjoy more space and privacy than most other kinds of accommodation. It's a particularly great option for families. Puglia has lots of converted *trulli*, the pointed-roof traditional houses in the countryside, which make for a unique – verging on the fairytale – stay. Useful websites for searching for accommodation include:

Holiday Homes in Italy (www.holidayhomesinitaly.co.uk)
Owners Direct (www.ownersdirect.co.uk)
Salento Dolce Vita (www.salentodolcevita.com)
Slow Travel (www.slowtrav.com) .
Tuscany Now (www.tuscanynow.com)
Vamoose (www.vamoose.com)

Trulli specialists tend to have the worst puns and include:
Long Travel (www.long-travel.co.uk)
Trulli Italy in Puglia (www.trulliitalyinpuglia.com)
Trulli Land (www.trulliland.co.uk)

the country broils and resorts are packed – are not ideal for travel. However, if you have to travel then, don't despair, this is also the prime time for festivals and events and is incredibly lively – there are myriad nightly festivals in Puglia throughout August. Also, you can beat the heat by spending most of the day on the beach or by the pool and having long afternoon siestas. Easter and Christmas are also usually considered high season, with a mass of religious celebrations – those during Holy Week, leading up to Easter, are particularly spectacular.

Puglia and Basilicata's calendar of religious, local and food festivals, as well as cultural events, is busy year round, however; see p208 for more information.

See Climate Charts (p205) for more information.

In the low season (October to March) many hotels, B&Bs, activities operators and businesses close – towns around the Gargano coast are very quiet at this time, as are towns such as Otranto on the Salento coast and around Maratera. Ring ahead to book accommodation during these times, as your choice may not be open.

COSTS & MONEY

Puglia and Basilicata aren't cheap, although they are in the main cheaper than the north of Italy and very reasonable when compared with the UK and northern Europe. What you spend on accommodation (your single greatest expense) will depend on various factors, such as location, season (July and August see prices zoom up, particularly on the coast), the degree of comfort and luck. At the bottom end you will pay €14 to €20 at youth hostels, where meals generally cost €9. The cheapest *pensione* (small hotel) is unlikely to cost less than €40/60 for a basic single/double. You can stumble across comfortable rooms with charm and their own bathroom from €50 to €100 – particularly *agriturismi* and *masserie* (large farms or estates) in the countryside. The more expensive and luxurious converted *masserie* can easily cost from €150/200 to €200/400 for a single/double.

HOW MUCH?

Cappuccino at the bar €0.90-1

Margherita pizza €2.50

Gelato €1-3

Glass of wine €2.50-3

City bus/tram ride €1

Eating out is just as variable. On average you should reckon on €20 to €40 for a full meal with house wine. For more details see p209.

A backpacker sticking religiously to youth hostels (though there are only a few in these regions) and cheap hotels, snacking at midday, sharing rooms and travelling slowly could scrape by on €45 to €60 per day. A midrange budget, including meals out or self-catering, sightseeing, travel and car hire, might come to around €100 to €150 per day. Top-end travellers could easily spend double that, or more – the bulk of the extra expenditure going on luxurious accommodation and meals at upmarket restaurants.

If you want to limit your expenses, you can do so by camping or staying in self-catering accommodation and shopping in markets, by spending your holiday on the beach, picnicking and sightseeing by just wandering around towns (to be recommended even if you're not on a budget) and visiting churches. Pizza is always a cheap (and kid-pleasing) option for an evening meal – a *margherita* (mozzarella and tomato-topped pizza) usually costs only around €2.50.

Public transport is reasonably priced, but car hire (p223) is fairly expensive (as is petrol) and is probably best arranged before leaving home. On trains you can save money by travelling on the slower *regionale* and *diretto* trains.

TRAVEL LITERATURE

Travellers in the south of Italy have tended to strike out into the unknown far more than those in the north and the literature about Puglia and Basilicata reflects this spirit of adventure. Travelogues about these areas offer a particular insight into life here, with the older works providing a window

TOP **10**

**PUGLIA &
BASILICATA**

Alban

TOP PROVERBS

There's an endless fount of wisdom in local dialects. This is a top 10 tip of the iceberg:

1 *A ddu muti iaddri cantanu, mai giurnu luce.* If
   there are many roosters in the chicken run,
   the day never starts.

2 *Chiuù forte chiove, chiuù prima scampa.* A
   heavy shower is better than slow rain.

3 *Li guai de la pìgnata, li sape lu cuperchiu.*
   Only the lid knows the pot's problems.

4 *Cuegghi l'acqua quandu chiove.* Harvest the
   water when it's raining.

5 *Monte cu' monte 'nu se' 'cuntranu mai, omu
   cu' omu ci 'nu osce crai.* Only the mountains
   never meet each other, men sooner or
   later do.

6 *Quando lu ciucciu num 'bole 'mbive, magari
   'ca fischi.* When the donkey doesn't want to
   drink, you can whistle as much as you want.

7 *Pietre meni an' cielu, an' capu toa stessu
   catenu.* Stones thrown in the sky will fall on
   your head.

8 *La figlia muta, sulu la mamma la capisce.* The
   daughter is silent, only the mother under-
   stands.

9 *Cuscenza e turnisi, 'nu se sape ci 'nde tene.* Con-
   science and money, no-one knows who has it.

10 *Lu' purpu cu' l'acqua soa stessa se coce.* The
   octopus is cooked by its own water.

TOP PASSEGGIATE

The evening stroll. It's the best way to pass the hours from dusk. Here are 10 of the best:

1 **Matera** (p167) Anyone and everyone makes
   their way to Piazza Vittorio Veneto in the
   gracious new town.

2 **Lecce** (p143) From Piazza d'Oronzo, down
   the mostly pedestrianised Corso Vittorio
   Emanuele, a balmy bustle amid golden
   baroque.

3 **Trani** (p73) Portside is where it's at, particularly in summer.

4 **Maratea Superiore** (p186) Summertime;
   the living is easy and it's time to wander up
   and down the main street.

5 **Bari** (p60) Throngs amble up and down the
   mostly pedestrianised, designer-shop-lined
   Via Sparano da Bari in the new town.

6 **Otranto** (p161) It might take time to make
   your way along Corso Garibaldi in the old
   town in summer, as your companions will
   be the world and his *moglie* (wife).

7 **Gallipoli** (p156) Great views are just one of
   the reasons to wander around the ramparts
   in the evening.

8 **Lucera** (p106) Flat-capped elderly gentlemen,
   gaggles of girls, redoubtable matrons; they're
   all thronging around the cathedral from dusk.

9 **Martina Franca** *(p127)* It's great to sally
   along the sidewalk in this most elegant of
   towns.

10 **Polignano a Mare** (p133) An enjoyable
   hubbub in this photogenic coastal town.

TOP CDS

For a highly selective sample of Pugliese and Basilican sounds, try the following music CDs:

1 **Lontano** (2003) Sud Sound System

2 **Comu na Petra** (1996) Sud Sound System

3 **La Banda** (1996) Banda Città Ruvo di Puglia

4 **Ballati Tutti Quanti Ballati Forte** (2000)
   Canzoniere Grecanico Salentino

5 **Andamenare** (2000) Tarantolati di Tricarico

6 **Mazzatte Pesanti** (2004) Aramirè

7 **Legend of the Italian Tarantella** (2002)
   Arakne Mediterranea

8 **Il Miracolo** (2003) & **Sangua Vivo** (2004)
   Officina Zoe

9 **Skuarrajazz** (2000) Uaragniaun

10 **La Musica Rubata** (2002) Banda Città di
   Montescaglioso ospite Ettore Fioravanti &
   Belcanto Group

into a vanished or vanishing world, which nevertheless still much informs the present.

A Traveller in Southern Italy (H V Morton) Travels around toe and heel just as the Autostrade del Sole extended south from Naples to Reggio di Calabria, exploring the then little-known regions and coastline. Vivid descriptions by a venerable reporter.

By the Ionian Sea: Notes of a Ramble in Southern Italy (George Gissing) The Victorian novelist's fascinating 1897 travels from Naples to Reggio di Calabria via Taranto and Metaponto.

Christ Stopped at Eboli (Carlo Levi) A wonderful book, fascinating and enduringly relevant. This describes the poverty and pettiness of village life, and is an account of the author's exile under the Fascists.

Heel to Toe (Charles Lister) Describing Lister's trip on a clapped-out moped; there are many gems – salacious and insightful – packed in among the evidence of how well read he is.

La Bella Vita: Life, Love and Food in Southern Italy (V Adamoli) Evokes life in Torre Saraena, a small southern Italian coastal town (featuring a seaside cinema) from the 1960s to the 1980s.

Old Calabria (Norman Douglas) Gay former diplomat (he left the service due to a sex scandal) describes his travels around southern Italy in the early 20th century.

Seasons in Basilicata: A Year in a Southern Italian Hill Village (David Yeadon) Warm-spirited if uneventful and verging on smug, this has some interesting titbits on Basilicatan life.

INTERNET RESOURCES

Delicious Italy (www.deliciousitaly.com) Here's where to find that cooking course in Puglia, learn the recipe for Basilicata's walnut liqueur and indulge in fabulous food and wine without putting on any weight. Has accommodation listings too.

Ente Nazionale Italiano per il Turismo (www.enit.it) The Italian national tourist body's website has information on everything from local tourist office addresses to gallery and museum details and general introductions to food, art and history.

i-escape (www.i-escape.com) Well-researched, authoritative accommodation website – ideal for finding boutique and special places to stay.

Lonely Planet (www.lonelyplanet.com) Can get you started with summaries on Italy, links to Italy-related sites and travellers trading information on the Thorn Tree.

QuiSalento (www.quisalento.it) A useful magazine (Italian only; available at newsstands) also has online information about events (festivals, cinema, concerts etc) in the Salento and links to other good Salento sites.

Salento Summer (www.salentosummer.com) Things to do in Salento, with accommodation listings.

Salentonet (www.salentonet.it) Good general website on the Salento, with information on some out-of-the-way places and accommodation listings.

Trenitalia (www.trenitalia.it) Plan train journeys, check timetables and prices and book tickets on Italy's national railway's website.

Trova Salento (www.trovasalento.it) Events, accommodation and restaurant listings, as well as information on local tours (Italian only).

Itineraries
CLASSIC ROUTES

SUMMER IN THE SALENTO
Three Weeks / Lecce to Otranto

The pace of life in the Salento is laid-back and leisurely and your itinerary should be too. **Lecce** (p143) itself can take a good week, especially if you sign up for a cookery course at **Awaiting Table** (p149). You'll also want to incorporate a couple of day trips to **Galatina** (p153) and **La Grecia Salentina** (p153), before coasting down to **Gallipoli** (p156) to gorge yourself on fish and check out the beach scene at **Baia Verde** (p157). From here you can dawdle southwards, stopping in **Taviano** (p160), **Casarano** (p160), **Specchia** (p160) and **Patù** (p160) before you hit **Santa Maria di Leuca** (p160). You'll want to spend a couple of days with **Smarè** (p160) in its sailing school or maybe bob around in boats in some of the fantastic grottoes. In the evening head for **Gibò** (p160) for cocktails and views. Then its time to freewheel up the dramatic Adriatic Coast to **Castro** (p161), for more diving or head inland for some trekking along the macchia-covered hillsides, before finishing off in picturesque **Otranto** (p161) where you can collapse on the beautiful beaches of **Baia dei Turchi** (p164).

This itinerary meanders all over the Salento taking in its best beaches and curious towns. Ideally, try and plan your trip around a couple of festivals as these bring the small, sleepy Salentine towns to life. It's best enjoyed with your own car, especially outside summer when public transport is limited.

GHOSTS & WILD PLACES   Seven to 10 Days / Matera to Maratea

Nature-lovers can start in the cave city of **Matera** (p167). After exploring the *sassi* (stone houses), check out the *chiese rupestri* on a hike along the Gravina or cycle through the beautiful rolling hills of the Murge to the medieval hilltop town of **Montescaglioso** (p175). Bed down in one of Matera's luxury cave hotels before heading southwest on the SS7 and the SS407 passing through the quaint hill town of **Pisticci** (p201) to spend a few spooky hours in the ghost-town of **Craco** (p200). Wind your way through olive groves, citrus orchards and vineyards to **Tursi** (p200) and its ancient Saracen rabatana quarter. Indulge in a poetic feast in the Palazzo dei Poeti before heading south to the **Parco Nazionale del Pollino** (p192) and a serious nature fix in Italy's largest national park.

'Do' the east side first. From **Terranova di Pollino** (p192), hike through pine woods and beech forest to Basilicata's highest peak, Monte Pollino. Dance to the *zampogne* in the tiny Albanian villages of **San Paolo Albanese** and **San Costantino Albanese** (p194). Skirt back to the SS104 and pick the long winding road through the west side of the park towards the main hub, **Rotondo** (p193). Stay in a cosy *agriturismo* for a few days until you've had your fill of hiking, cycling, horse riding and rafting. Don't leave without eye-balling the rare Bosnian pine tree, *pino loricato*.

Take the easy road to the A3, heading northwest to the dramatic Tyrrhenian coastline and pretty **Maratea** (p186) for coastal hikes, ocean swims and seafood fests.

This 270km route through Basilicata's underbelly takes you from neolithic cave dwellings, spooky towns, wild forests and snowcapped mountains, to plunging coastal cliffs and black-sand beaches. You'll need your own car, but the roads are generally good and traffic is light. Hiking fiends might find it hard to leave the Pollino!

CASTLES, CHURCHES & CRUSADERS

Two Weeks /
Bari to Monte Sant'Angelo

Northern Puglia with its huge crusader castles and secretive caves has a very different flavour to the sunny south. Its heart is dynamic **Bari** (p60), with its ancient historic centre, huge basilica and chaotic **Festa di San Nicola** (p66). From here, the city is surrounded by historic towns like **Conversano** (p119), **Bitonto** (p71) and **Ruvo di Puglia** (p72), which boasts one of the finest archaeological museums in Puglia, the **Museo Nazionale Jatta** (p72).

Further north, elegant **Trani** (p73) sits jewel-like on the coast, the most elegant of Bari's towns. Beyond, brutish **Barletta** (p76) can't really compare, but it does have one of the biggest castles in the province and an intriguing art gallery, the **Pinacoteca di Giuseppe de Nittis** (p77), housed in the lovely Palazzo della Marra. Frederick II set off on the Third Crusade from here and not far away you'll find his most concrete imperial statement, the stunning **Castel del Monte** (p80).

Make a base for yourself at the lovely **Biomasseria Lama di Luna** (p82) where you can make your own pizza and explore the nearby vineyards and towns. More history awaits in **Canosa di Puglia** (p80), one of Rome's most important towns along the Via Appia Traiana. Along this road pilgrims and crusaders have trudged for centuries, passing under the enormous Arco Traiano. Many of them came from the Gargano, where they will have stopped at **Monte Sant'Angelo** (p95), one of the most important crusader shrines in Puglia, and still a place of thronging pilgrims today.

If that seems like a lot of sightseeing then finish off with a few lazy days on the beaches at **Vieste** (p88).

This relatively short itinerary is packed with history. There's a greater concentration of people and towns here so public transport is relatively good and you can get to most places by bus or train. To get the most out of this trip it's worth swotting up on some crusading history before you go.

TAILORED TRIPS

COLOURS OF THE GARGANO

Slip into beach gear, slop on sunscreen and you're set for the Gargano's sun-and-sand spectacular in the dazzling blue waters of the Adriatic. The spur's best beaches lay between **Vieste** (p88) and **Mattinata** (p99). Do the five-star thing at **Zagare Bay** (p100) or go au naturel at **Vignanotica** (p89). Closer to the party scene is Vieste's **Spiaggia del Castello** (p89) while **Punta Lunga** (p89) attracts

the international windsurfing crowd. Paddle a kayak along the craggy coastline and find your own secret coves and stunning sea caves or go completely under on a scuba-diving trip to the **Isole Tremiti** (p102).

After a juicy seafood platter in a *trabucco* (ancient fishing trap) near **Peschici** (p92), swap the beach-scene for an ecofriendly green scene. Hikers will find plenty of trails in the Bavarian-esque splendour of the **Foresta Umbra** (p87). Hire a mountain bike or join a bike tour and take a week to explore the national park's natural and cultural highlights, picking olives and sleeping in quaint *agriturismi*. Don't forget to pack the binoculars for an afternoon of bird-watching on the **Lesina lakes** (p95).

PRANZO WITH A DIFFERENCE

Food is serious business in the south. It's the social glue that holds everyone together. Most Italians look with nostalgia on the traditional cooking and fresh produce that you'll find here, so tuck that napkin in and get started! The Murgia Plateau with its rich history of farming harbours some of Puglia's finest restaurants, including **Il Frantoio** (p132), **Cibus** (p132) and **Falso Pepe** (p117). You'll also find they do a nice bottle of white wine around **Locorotondo** (p126), and **Noci** (p122) is well known for its endless foodie festivals.

Further south in **Manduria** (p118) you'll find the rich red Primitivo wine and across the border in Basilicata the award-winning Aglianico from **Rionero di Vulture** (p182). You'll meet it time and again in **Matera** (p167), where you should also sample the pasta with some pepperoni cruschi.

The soft peaty soil of the Parco Nazionale del Pollino yields some delicious mushrooms, game meats, salami and cheeses which you'll sample well at Ristorante Luna Rossa in **Terranova di Pollino** (p194). Other well-known centres for country cooking are **Minervino Murge** (p81) and nearby **Montegrosso** (p82), as well as **Ruvo di Puglia** (p72).

Seafood fans need not fear, however, with so much coastline you won't be missing out on the fruits of the sea. Puglia, in particular, is fish mad. **The Gargano** (p86) and **Taranto** (p111) are home to some of the best seafood restaurants in the province, although **Maratea** (p186) has a few select options as well.

History

Italy's deep south is well off the beaten track and is frequently dismissed by refined and affluent northerners as the land of *terroni* (peasants). Yet the south is terribly ancient. Its history can be traced back some 8000 years; writer Carlo Levi, exiled here, sensed its dark and enduring paganism, calling it 'that other world…which no-one may enter without a magic key'. Magical it may be, but there has been plenty to regret – invasions and conquests, feudalism and lawlessness, and a scourge of malaria that lasted centuries and effectively stunted the economic and cultural development of the south. Venture into these parts and you'll learn a lot about Italy's history that will challenge your comfortable preconceptions of just what the modern country is all about.

THE MAN OF ALTAMURA

Despite its current quiet aspect, this corner of Italy has been busy for a very long time. If you go to the De Lucia quarry, 5km outside Altamura (p82), you can see how busy from the 4000 dinosaur footprints that have been discovered there. It's the largest area of dinosaur footprints in Europe, dating back some 70 million years!

A wide-ranging general site on Italian history is available at www.arcaini.com. It covers, in potted form, everything from prehistory to the postwar period, and includes a brief chronology.

Everything else since then seems to have been concertinaed into a very short period of time indeed. The first man we know of is the man of Altamura who's currently wedged in the karst cave of Lamalunga, slowly becoming part of the crystal concretions that surround him. He's 130,000 years old now.

Apart from a few shards of pottery and engravings in the Grotta Romanelli near Castro there's not much else to fill in the blanks between then and the Neolithic period some 125,000 years later when peoples from the Levant and Anatolia were moving westwards to the Italian peninsula. Some of Puglia's grottoes bear testimony to their productive pastoral lives. The Grotta dei Cervi (Cave of the Deer; p164), near Otranto, contains nearly 3000 pictograms painted on its walls in red ochre and bat guano. Animals, people, magic symbols and hundreds and hundreds of hand prints made archaeologists exclaim that it represented a 'shrine to prehistory'. Prehistoric man must have liked it here, as all over the Salento there are dolmens, menhirs and specchie all of which had some strange magico-religious function that we no longer quite understand.

This physical evidence of human habitation slowly brought the region's long-distant history into sharper focus around 7000 BC, when the Messapians, an Illyrian-speaking people from the Balkans, were settling down in the Salento and around Foggia. Alongside them, other long-gone tribes such as the Daunii in the Gargano, the Peucetians around Taranto and the

TIMELINE

c 200,000–9000 BC	3000–1000 BC	750–600 BC
As long ago as 700,000 BC, Paleolithic men, like the Man of Altamura, lived precarious lives in caves. Painted caves like the Grotta dei Cervi and the Grotta Romanelli bear testimony to this period.	The Bronze Age reaches Italy from the eastern Mediterranean. The use of copper and bronze marks a leap in sophistication. Dolmen, menhirs and specchie start to crop up all over the Salento.	The Greeks begin to migrate, establishing cities all over southern Italy and Sicily, including Cumae, Sybaris, Croton, Metaponto, Eraklea and Taras in southern Italy. Before 600 BC, some 18 cities are established forming Magna Graecia.

Lucanians in Basilicata were starting to develop the first settled towns and by 1700 BC there is evidence that they were beginning to trade with the Mycenaeans from mainland Greece and the Minoans in Crete.

MAGNA GRAECIA

Many say the only true civilisation of the south was that of the Greeks, who founded a string of settlements along the Ionian coast in the 8th century BC. But that does a disservice to the local tribes of Puglia and Basilicata – the Messapians, Peucetians, Daunii and Lucanians – who continued to occupy the central highlands flourishing alongside the Greek coastal cities.

For a detailed run-down on Roman emperors from Caesar to Caligula, check out www.roman-emperors.org.

Nevertheless, the Greeks got all the good press and from 750 BC onwards their settlements sprang up all over southern Italy. Their major city was Taras, settled by the Spartans, which came to dominate the area now known as Magna Graecia (Greater Greece). They exploited its harbour well, trading with Greece, the Near East and the rich colonies in Sicily and so they built up a substantial network of commerce. Their lucrative business in luxury goods soon made them rich and powerful and by the 4th century BC the population had swelled to 300,000 and city life was cultured and civilised.

Although few monuments survive, the Greek era was a real golden age for the south. Art and sculpture, poetry, drama and philosophy, mathematics and science, were all part of the cultural life of Magna Graecia's cities. Exiled from Crotone (Calabria), Pythagoras spent years in Metapontum and Taras, and Empedocles, Zeno and Stesichorus were all home-grown talents. There's a small collection of ceramics, coins and jewellery at Palazza Pantaleo (p114).

Get to grips with the history, peoples and wars of Ancient Greece by logging on to www.ancientgreece.com which gives easy potted histories of all the key characters and places. It also has an online bookstore.

But despite their shared Greekness, there is no evidence that these city-states ever saw themselves as having a common identity. Deeply ingrained rivalries and parochial politics constantly undermined their civic achievements and ultimately led to damaging conflicts such as the Peloponnesian War (431–399 BC), fought by the Athenians against the Peloponnesian League (led by Sparta). It was a disastrous war that was to reshape the Ancient Greek world into a collection of warring factions and alliances that left Magna Graecia weakened and vulnerable.

During the 4th century the colonies were to come under increasing pressure from other powers with expansionist ambitions. The Etruscans began to move south towards Cumae and then the Samnites and Sabines started to capture the highlands of the Apennines in Basilicata. Then another threat arose on the southern horizon in the shape of Carthage, a new superpower on the shores of North Africa, that was beginning to look northwards. Unable to unite and beat off the growing threat, the Greeks had little choice but to make a Faustian pact with the Romans, long-standing admirers of the Greeks and seemingly the perfect ally. It was a partnership that was to cost them dearly; by 270 BC the whole of southern Italy (including all of Magna Graecia) was under Roman control.

216–201 BC	280 BC–109	300–337
The Punic Wars rage between the Romans and the Carthaginians. In 216 BC Hannibal inflicts an embarrassing defeat on the Roman army at Cannae, but ultimately the Romans defeat the Carthaginians in 202 BC.	The Romans build the Via Appia and then the Via Appia Traiana. The Via Appia Traiana covered 540km and enabled travellers to journey from Rome to Brindisi in 14 days.	After a series of false starts the Roman Empire is divided into an eastern and western half just east of Rome. In 330 Constantine moves the Imperial capital to Byzantium and re-founds it as Constantinople.

ROME VS CONSTANTINOPLE

Roman control of southern Italy was to set the tone for centuries to come. Sure they built the Via Appia (280–264 BC) and later the Via Appia Traiana (109), creating the first superhighway to the south, but they also stripped the southern landscape of its trees thus creating the conditions for the malarial scourge that the region would face centuries hence. Then they parcelled up the land into huge *latifondi* (estates) that they distributed among a handful of wealthy Romans, who established a damaging agricultural monoculture of wheat to feed the Roman army. Local peasants, meanwhile, were denied even the most basic rights of citizenship. Little wonder then that strong men like Spartacus fomented popular rebellions like the Third Servile War that were to make the 1st century BC a period of civic strife and oppression.

The other interesting feature of the Roman era was that instead of Latinising the provinces, the Roman period had the effect of reinforcing Eastern influences on the south. As it was the Romans admired and emulated Greek culture, the local populus continued to speak Greek, and the Via Appia made Puglia the gateway to the East. With the Roman army busy expanding the empire elsewhere, local communities were free to carry on pretty much as they had been prior to their arrival so long as they didn't cause any trouble. But by 245 AD, when Diocletian came to power, the empire had reached unwieldy proportions and in a radical move, he split the empire in two. Thus when his successor, Constantine, came to power in 306 the groundwork was already established for an Eastern (Byzantine) Empire and a Western Empire. And in 324 Constantinople was officially declared the capital of *Nova Roma*.

Situated between the Aegean and Black Sea, Constantinople was a Greek settlement and Constantine himself spoke fluent Greek. He was also the first emperor to legislate against the persecution of the Christians, and even today Constantine is revered as a saint in the Eastern Orthodox Church. Greekness it seems was not a thing of the past at all and with southern Italy's proximity to the Balkans and the Near East, Puglia and Basilicata were exposed to a new wave of Eastern influence, bringing with it a brand new set of Christian beliefs.

Edward Gibbon's *History of the Decline and Fall of the Roman Empire* is the acknowledged classic work on the subject of the empire's darker days. Try the abridged single-volume version.

PILGRIMS & CRUSADERS

Ever since Puglia and Basilicata's colonisation by the Greeks, multifarious myths had established themselves in the region – many were related to the presence of therapeutic waters and the practice called *incubatio,* a rite whereby it was believed that by sleeping close to a holy place one would receive saintly revelations.

In its early days the cult of the Archangel Michael, was mainly a cult of healing forces based on the saint's revelations. It started to gain currency in the early 5th century but it wasn't until the arrival of the Lombards in the 7th century that it really began to take off.

476	827-846	1059
The last Western emperor, Romulus Augustulus, is deposed. Goths, Ostrogoths and Byzantines tussle over the spoils. The result is a host of competing independent principalities, dukedoms and Byzantine territory.	In 827 a Saracen army lands at Mazara del Vallo in Sicily and proceeds to conquer the island. The mainland follows shortly: Brindisi, Taranto and Bari. In 846, the Saracens sack Rome itself.	Pope Nicholas II and Robert Guiscard sign a concordat at Melfi, investing Robert with the titles of Duke of Apulia and Calabria. Robert agrees to chase the Saracens and Byzantines out of the south.

To access a complete
list of all the popes and
biographies on each,
check out the encyclopae-
dia page of New Advent
(www.newadvent.org).
Click on Popes, List of,
and there they all are,
from St Peter Benedict
XVI.

Sweeping down from the north the Lombards found in St Michael a mirror-image of their own pagan deity, Wodan. In Michael they saw the image of a medieval warrior, a leader of celestial armies. There is little doubt that their devotion to the saint was instrumental in their easy conversion to Catholicism and they repeatedly restored and enlarged the Gargano shrine, making it the most important centre of the cult in the Western world.

Soon the trail of pilgrims along the Via Traiana became so great that the road was nicknamed the Via Sacra Langobardorum, the Holy Road of the Lombards, and dozens of churches, hostels and monasteries were built to accommodate the pilgrims along the way. You can get an idea of the scale of the cult when you visit the shrine at Monte Sant'Angelo (see p95). Medieval graffiti in Greek, Latin, Hebrew, Saxon and German illustrate the unrelenting devotion paid to the site. The earliest of these inscriptions dates back to the 6th century while the rarest are written in the ancient Runic alphabet by Anglo-Saxon pilgrims.

By the 9th century the cave in the Gargano was the Lombards' national shrine. Meanwhile, that other French tribe, the Normans, were busy conquering huge swathes of southern Italy, and familiar with the cult of St Michael they too developed strong affiliations with the shrine. As a major transit point on the route between the Byzantine Empire and Rome, Basilicata and Puglia saw a huge increase in traffic as an endless flow of pilgrims travelled to the Holy Land and the shrines of St Michael in the Gargano and St Nicolas in Bari. This intense cross-cultural traffic also saw the first dialogue between the Western and Middle Eastern worlds.

The iconoclastic policies of Byzantine Emperor Leo III (c 685–741), which sent dozens of Basilian monks fleeing to Puglia, were clearly influenced in some way by the increasing dialogue between the Byzantine and the Islamic worlds. Iconoclasm, which forbade the worship of images (and is a feature of Islam), was supported by many in the Eastern Empire and most notably in those provinces that had come under Muslim rule at one time or another. However, most Byzantine theologians and the majority of monks opposed Leo's prohibitive edict with uncompromising hostility and many fled to Puglia and Basilicata to seek refuge in their secretive ravines where they could practise their faith undisturbed in their brightly painted *chiese rupestri* (cave churches).

Kingdom of the Sun is
John Julius Norwich's
wonderful romp through
the Norman invasions
of the south leading to
their spectacular takeover
of Sicily.

By the 11th century the Seljuk Turks were threatening the borders of Byzantium and in March 1095 Emperor Alexius I called on Pope Urban II for help, thus setting the ball rolling for the First Crusade. Although the schism between the Catholic and Eastern Orthodox churches had already split the church, the pope called for a large invasion force of devoted Christian soldiers to not only defend Byzantium, but to also re-take Jerusalem.

Over the next two centuries there were at least nine crusades and Puglia's harbours were the focal point. Crusaders, the Knights Templar and the Knights Hospitaller all had bases in the port cities of the Gargano, Bari,

1189	1215	1228
William II of Sicily dies childless. His crown passes to his aunt Constance, daughter of Robert Guiscard and wife of Henry VI of Hohenstaufen who inherits the German crown of the Holy Roman Empire.	Frederick II is crowned Holy Roman Emperor in Aachen where he symbolically re-inters the body of Charlemagne in a great silver and gold reliquary. In 1220 he has a second coronation in Rome.	Frederick finally fulfils his vow to lead a Crusade. He is the first Holy Roman Emperor to wear his crown in the Church of the Holy Sepulchre in Jerusalem.

BORN TO FIGHT

In the late 10th century Norman fighters began to earn a reputation across Europe as fierce and tough mercenaries. Inheritance customs left younger sons disadvantaged so younger brothers were expected to seek their fortunes elsewhere and seek they did with remarkable success.

According to one legend, Norman involvement in southern Italy began in 1013 at the shrine of St Michael on Monte Gargano, when Latin rebel, Meles, chaffing under Byzantine authority invited the Normans to serve him as mercenaries. By 1030 what had begun as an offer of service in return for booty became a series of unusually successful attempts at wresting control from local war lords.

In the forefront of the Italian conquests were the brothers Hauteville: the eldest William 'Bras de Fer' (Iron Arm; c 1009–46) who controlled Puglia, and Robert Guiscard (the Cunning; c 1015–85) who rampaged over Calabria and southern Campania. By 1053, after six years of incessant fighting, Robert had defeated the combined forces of the Calabrian Byzantines, the Lombards and the papal forces at Civitate.

Up to this point the Normans (as mercenaries) had fought for and against the papacy as their needs had required. But Robert's relationship with the Vatican underwent a radical turn following the Great Schism of 1054, which resulted in the complete break between the Byzantine and Latin churches. In their turn, the Popes saw in the Normans a powerful potential ally, and so in 1059 Pope Nicholas II and Robert signed a concordat at Melfi, which invested Robert with the titles of duke of Apulia (including Basilicata) and Calabria. In return Robert agreed to chase the Byzantines and Saracens out of the south and Sicily and restore the southern kingdom to Papal rule.

Little could the pope suspect that Roger would go on to develop a territorial monarchy and become a ruler who saw himself as detached from the higher jurisdiction of both Western and Eastern emperor or even the pope.

Brindisi and Otranto and nearly all of Puglia's great churches were commissioned and built during this period in a fever of religious exhibitionism.

But like the Ancient Greeks before them, the Byzantine emperors were to find only betrayal in the offer of assistance from Rome. As the Papacy became increasingly paranoid and power-hungry the Pope's Christian forces were just as likely to attack and murder 'schismatic' (read Orthodox) Christians as they were to kill Muslims. Finally, in 1204, the crusading armies sacked Constantinople, in one of the worst examples of pillage and plunder in the history books. Thus the Byzantine Empire collapsed, the Islamists were in ascendancy and the deep sense of betrayal and distrust between the Eastern and Western church was firmly established.

Steven Runciman's *Fall of Constantinople 1453* provides a classic account of this bloody episode in Crusading history. It manages to be academically sound and highly entertaining at the same time.

THE WONDER OF THE WORLD

Frederick II, King of Sicily and Holy Roman Emperor presided over one of the most glamorous periods of southern history. The fact that he came to wear Charlemagne's crown at all and wield such power is one of those unexpected quirks of history.

1270–1500	1435	1516
The French Angevins and Spanish Aragonese spend the best part of two centuries fighting over southern Italy. Instability, warfare, the Black Death and over-taxation strangle the economic development of the region.	Alfonso of Aragon takes control of the region. Two hundred years of Spanish domination follow until the War of Spanish Succession sees them toppled from power.	Holy Roman Emperor, Charles V of Spain inherits southern Italy as part of his vast empire. The region is strategically important to Spain in its long-running battle with France.

He inadvertently inherited the crown of Sicily and the south from his mother Constance (the posthumous daughter of Roger I) in 1208 after William II died childless; while the crown to the Holy Roman Empire came to him through his father Henry VI, the son of Frederick Barbarossa. The union of the two crowns in 1220 meant that Frederick II would rule over lands covering Germany, Austria, the Netherlands, Poland, the Czech Republic, Slovakia, southern France, southern Italy, the rich Kingdom of Sicily and the remnants of the Byzantine world.

In *Frederick II: A Medieval Emperor* (the only notable book on the monarch in English), David Abulafia delves into the life and times of one of the most exotic Holy Roman emperors and finds that he did have a few chinks in his armour.

It was a union that caused much discomfort to the popes. For while they wanted and needed an emperor who would play the role of temporal sword, Frederick's wide-reaching kingdom, all but encircled the Papal States and his belief in the absolute power of monarchy gave them grave cause for concern.

Like Charlemagne before him Frederick controlled a kingdom so vast that he could realistically dream of reviving the fallen Roman Empire; and dream he did. Not only did he pacify Sicily and bring most of the northern Italian city-states to heel, in 1225 he married Jolanda of Brienne and gained the title of King of Jerusalem, making him the first Roman emperor to bear that title. In 1228 the Crusade he launched was not only nearly bloodless but it saw the return of the shrines of Jerusalem, Nazareth and Bethlehem to the Christian fold.

Not only was he a talented statesman, he was also a cultured man and many of his biographers see in him the precursor of the Renaissance prince. Few other medieval monarchs corresponded with the sages of Judaism and Islam; he spoke six languages and was fascinated by science, nature and architecture. He even wrote a scholarly treatise on falconry during one of the long, boring sieges of Faenza, and Dante was right to call him the father of Italian poetry.

Yet despite his brilliance, his vision for an international empire was incompatible with the ambitions of the papacy and throughout his reign he struggled to remain on good terms with increasingly aggressive popes. Finally in 1243 Pope Innocent IV formally deposed him, characterising him as a 'friend of Babylon's sultan' and a heretic. At the same time the northern Italian provinces were straining against his centralised control and years of war and strategising were finally taking their toll. Only in Puglia did Frederick remain undisputed master and throughout his reign, Puglia remained his favourite province.

In 1224 Frederick II founded the University of Naples, the third in Italy and the first in the south. It reinvigorated the region and brought many eminent scholars to its faculties.

In December 1250, after suffering a bout of dysentery, he died suddenly in Castel Fiorentino near Lucera. His heirs, Conrad and Manfred, would not survive him long. Conrad died of malaria four years later in Lavello in Basilicata, and Manfred was defeated at the Battle of Benevento in 1266 by Charles of Anjou, the Pope's pretender to the throne. This outright warfare between the emperor and the papacy consolidated the damaging divide between the Ghibellines (imperial supporters) and the Guelphs (who disliked

1647	1713	1798–99
Mismanagement on a huge scale causes the economy of southern Italy to collapse. In Naples the Masaniello Revolt breaks out. Revolt soon spreads to the provinces and in the countryside peasant militias rule.	The Bourbon claimant, Philip V of Spain is recognised as king under the Treaty of Utrecht. Southern Italy is ceded to the Austrian Hapsburgs as compensation, but barely 20 years later the Spanish re-invade.	Napoleon invades Italy and occupies Rome. Ferdinand I sends an army to evict them, but his troops flee without firing a shot. The French counter-attack and take Naples, establishing the Parthenopean Republic.

central monarchy and thus supported the church), which was to cause so much civil strife over the next few centuries of Italian politics.

By 1270 the brilliant Hohenstaufen period was over. And despite his many accomplishments, Frederick failed to leave any tangible legacies. His rule did, however, mark a major stage in the transformation of Europe from a community of Latin Christians under the headship of two competing powers (pope and emperor) to a Europe of nation states.

THE BOURBONS: LOVE 'EM OR HATE 'EM?

Assessment of Bourbon rule in southern Italy is a controversial topic. Many historians consider it a period of exploitation and stagnation. Others, more recently, have started to re-evaluate the Kingdom of the Two Sicilies, pointing out the raft of positive reforms Charles III (1735–59) implemented. These included abolishing many noble and clerical privileges, curtailing the legal rights of landowners within their fiefs and restricting ecclesiastical jurisdiction at a time when the church was reputed to own almost one-third of the land within the kingdom.

Under Charles, Naples became one of the great capital cities of Europe attracting hundreds of aristocratic travellers. On top of this, Charles was a great patron of architecture and the arts; during his reign Pompeii and Herculaneum were discovered and the Archaeological Museum in Naples was founded; he was responsible for the Teatro San Carlo, the largest opera house in Europe, and he built the huge palaces of Capodimonte and Caserta. Subsequent Bourbon monarchs, such as Ferdinand II (r 1830–59) laid the foundations for modern industry, developing southern harbours, creating a merchant fleet and building the first Italian railway line and road systems like the dramatic Amalfi drive. Even today Spanish influence is everywhere apparent in southern Italy, in its buildings, its love of Baroque art and architecture and the habits of the people.

But where Charles might rightfully claim a place among southern Italy's outstanding rulers, later Bourbon princes were some of the most eccentric and pleasure-seeking monarchs in Europe. Charles' son, Ferdinand I (b 1751–1825), was by contrast venal and poorly educated. He spent his time hunting and fishing, and he delighted in the company of the *lazzaroni*, the Neapolitan underclass. He much preferred to leave the business of government to his wife, the ambitious and treacherous Archduchess Maria Carolina of Austria, whose main aim was to free southern Italy from Spanish influence and secure a *rapprochement* with Austria and Great Britain. Her chosen administrator was the English expatriate, Sir John Acton, who replaced the long-serving Tanucci, a move that was to mire court politics in damaging corruption and espionage.

When the French Revolution broke out in 1789, Maria Carolina was initially sympathetic to the movement, but when her sister, Marie Antoinette, was beheaded she became fanatically Francophobe. The following French

Denis Mack Smith produced one of the most penetrating works on Italy's dictator with his *Mussolini*. Along with Mussolini's career it assesses his impact on the greater evil of the time, Hitler.

1805	1814–15	1848
Napoleon is proclaimed king of the newly constituted Kingdom of Italy in March. The kingdom comprises most of the northern half of the country. A year later he takes the Kingdom of Naples.	The Congress of Vienna, held after the fall of Napoleon, is held to re-establish the balance of power in Europe. The Kingdom of the Two Sicilies reverts to the Bourbons in 1815.	Revolts across Europe spark rebellion in Italy. The Bourbons are expelled from Sicily but retake the island in a rain of fire that earns Ferdinand II the uncomplimentary epithet, Re Bomba (King Bomb).

invasion of Italy in 1799, and the crowning of Napoleon as king in 1800, jolted the south out of its Bourbon slumbers. Although Napoleonic rule was to last only 14 years, this brief flirtation with republicanism was to awaken hopes of an independent Italian nation. Returning to his beloved Naples, in 1815, Ferdinand once so at ease with his subjects was now terrified of popular revolution and determined to exert his absolute authority. Changes that had been made by the Bonapartist regime were reversed causing widespread discontent. Revolutionary agitators appeared from everywhere, and the countryside, now full of discharged soldiers, became more lawless than ever.

History of the Italian People, by Giuliano Procacci, is one of the best general histories of the country in any language. It covers the period from the early Middle Ages until 1948.

But try as they might there was no putting the genie back in the box. The heavy-handed tactics of Ferdinand II only exacerbated the situation and in 1848 Sicily experienced a violent revolt which saw the expulsion of the Bourbons from the island. Although the revolt was crushed, Ferdinand's response was so heavy-handed that he earned himself the nickname Re Bomba (King Bomb) after his army mercilessly shelled Messina. From such a promising beginning, the last decades of Bourbon rule were so oppressive that they were almost universally hated throughout liberal Europe and the seeds were well and truly sown for the *Risorgimento* (Resurgence), which would finally see the whole peninsula united into a modern nation state.

THE KINGDOM OF DEATH

Although it forms no part of the literature of the development of Italy since unification, the widespread presence of malaria in the Italian peninsula during the 19th and 20th centuries is one of the most significant factors in the social and economic development (or lack of it) of the modern country. An endemic as well as an epidemic disease, it was so enmeshed in Italian rural society that it was widely regard as the 'Italian national disease'. Even the word malaria comes from the Italian *mal aria* (bad air), as it was originally thought that the disease was caused by a poisoning of the air as wet earth dried out during the heat of summer.

The scale of the problem came to light in the decades following Italian unification in 1861. Out of 69 provinces only two were found to be free of malaria; and in a population of 25 million people at least 11 million were permanently at risk of the disease. Most famously, Giuseppe Garibaldi, one of the founding fathers of modern Italy, lost both his wife, Anita, and a large number of troops to the disease. Thus stricken Garibaldi urged the newly united nation to place the fight against malaria high on its list of priorities.

The exodus of southern Italians to North and South America between 1880 and WWI is one of the great mass movements of population in modern times. By 1927 20% of the Italian population had emigrated.

In the dawning era of global competition, Italian farming was dangerously backward. As a predominantly grain-producing economy, it was tragically ironic that all of Italy's most fertile land was precisely the zones – coastal plains and river valleys – where malaria was most intense. To survive, farmworkers had to expose themselves to the disease. But disease in turn entailed suffering, days of absence and low productivity.

1861	1880–1915	1915
By the end of the Franco-Austrian War of 1859–61, Vittorio Emanuele II has Lombardy, Sardinia, Sicily, southern and parts of central Italy under his control and is proclaimed king of a newly united Italy.	People vote with their feet and millions of impoverished southerners embark on ships for the New World, causing a massive haemorrhage of the most able-bodied and hardworking southern male youths.	Italy enters WWI on the side of the Allies in order to recover Italian territories in Austrian hands. Austria offers to cede some of the territories, but the war party insists the offer is insufficient.

THE ARCHITECT OF ITALY

Count Camillo Benso di Cavour (1810–61) is seen by many as the architect of modern Italy. However, he never actually planned for the establishment of a unified country.

Cavour had been born into a well-to-do Turin family, travelled widely in Europe after an army career and in the 1830s became one of the richest men in Piedmont due to his banking and farming interests. He entered politics in 1850 and two years later was prime minister of the Savoy kingdom's parliament.

During his premiership he conspired with the French and won British support for the creation of an independent Italian state. His 1858 treaty with France's Napoleon III foresaw French aid in the event of a war with Austria and the creation of a northern Italian kingdom, in exchange for parts of Savoy and Nice.

The bloody Franco-Austrian War (also known as the war for Italian independence; 1859–61) led to the occupation of Lombardy and the retreat of the Austrians to their eastern possessions in the Veneto. Cavour immediately negotiated with Napoleon, agreeing to cede Savoy and Nice in order to annex Tuscany and Emilia-Romagna. On hearing this, professional revolutionary, Giuseppe Garibaldi, was furious to find his birthplace, Nice, had become a French city, but Cavour convinced the majority that uniting Italy would make up for these small territorial losses.

Sent south to deal with an insurrection in Palermo in April 1860, Garibaldi suddenly found himself with a real chance of sweeping up Sicily and the southern states, which he did in a military blitz with a band of volunteers (having been refused Piedmontese troops by Cavour). Cavour then tried to annex the wealthy island of Sicily for the Piedmontese, but Garibaldi wasn't having it and demanded that Cavour be dismissed.

Aware of Garibaldi's growing power and his plans to invade the Papal States, which would almost certainly cause France to declare war on Italy, Cavour marched south and took the regions of Umbria and Le Marche. This linked the Piedmontese territories with those captured by Garibaldi, enabling the king Victor Emanuele to proclaim the creation of a single Italian state in 1861.

In the same year Cavour succumbed to malaria, dying of a stroke at just 50 years of age. On hearing the news of Cavour's death, Napoleon remarked, 'The driver has fallen from the box; now we must see if the horses will bolt or go back to the stable'.

More significantly, although malaria ravaged the whole peninsula, it was pre-eminently an affliction of the south, plus the provinces of Rome and Grosseto in the centre. Of all the provinces, six were especially afflicted – Abruzzi, Basilicata, Calabria, Lazio, Puglia and Sardinia – earning the south the lugubrious epithet, 'the kingdom of death'. Furthermore, Giovanni Battista Grassi (the man who discovered that mosquitos transmit malaria) estimated that the danger of infection in the south was 10 times greater than in the north.

No issue illustrates the divide between the north and south of the country quite so vividly as the malaria crisis. Regarding malaria in the modern world the World Health Organization has defined it as a disease of poverty that distorts and 'slows a country's economic growth', in the case of the Italian

1922	1940	1943
Mussolini and his Fascists stage a march on Rome in October. King Vittorio Emanuele III, fearful of the movement's popular power and doubting the army's loyalty, entrusts Mussolini with the formation of a government.	Italy enters WWII on Nazi Germany's side and invades Greece in October. Greek forces counter-attack and enter southern Albania. Germany saves Italy's bacon in March-April 1941 by overrunning Yugoslavia and Greece.	Allies land in Sicily in July. At the same time Mussolini is replaced by Marshall Badoglio, who, after Allied landings in southern Italy, surrenders. German forces free Mussolini and occupy most of the country.

In the 17th century the Spanish learned of the ability of the bark of the cinchona (fever tree) to treat intermittent fever. The barks active ingredient quinine was a central factor in colonial expansion. Quinine, it is said, was just as important to European armies in the tropics as gunpowder.

south, malaria was a significant factor in the underdevelopment of the region at a critical time in its history. Fever thrives on exploitative working conditions, substandard housing and diet, illiteracy, war and ecological degradation, and Italy's south had certainly had its fair share by the early 20th century. As late as 1918, the Ministry of Agriculture reported that 'malaria is the key to all the economic problems of the south'. Against this background of regional inequality, fever became an important metaphor deployed by southern spokesmen *(meridionalisti)* such as Giustino Fortunato (1848–1932) and Francesco Nitti (1868–1953) to describe the plight of the south and to demand redress. Nitti attributed the entirety of southern backwardness to this single factor.

Between 1900 and 1907, the Italian parliament passed a series of laws establishing a national campaign – the first of its kind in the world – to eradicate, or at least control the disease. But it was to take the best part of half a century to bring malaria under control as two world wars and the Fascist seizure of power in 1922 were to overwhelm domestic policies, causing the programme to stall and then collapse entirely amid military defeat and occupation.

Final victory against the disease was only achieved following the end of WWII, when the government was able to re-establish public health infrastructures and implement a five-year plan which included the use of a new pesticide DDT (Dichloro-Diphenyl-Trichloroethane) to eradicate fever. The designation of 'malarial zone' was officially lifted from the entire peninsula in 1969.

Between 1944 and 1946 the German Wehrmacht systematically sabotaged the pumping systems that drained Italy's marshes and confiscated quinine from the Department of Health. The ensuing epidemic of malaria in 1946 was one of the worst the country has ever seen and is one of the great unacknowledged war crimes of WWII.

Denis Mack Smith, the most prominent English-language historian of modern Italy, wrote that the eradication of malaria was arguably 'the most important single fact in the whole of modern Italian history'. Why? Because the antimalarial campaign had lasting impacts beyond the elimination of disease. From the outset, the antimalarial warriors recognised that education and civil rights have great effects on health. The campaign played a major role in the promotion of women's rights, the labour movement and the achievement of universal literacy; and it made a major contribution to awakening a consciousness of southern conditions and to mobilising opinion to redress southern grievances.

THE SOUTHERN QUESTION

The unification of Italy meant sudden and dramatic changes for all the southern provinces. The huge upsurge in *brigantaggio* (banditry) and social unrest throughout the last decades of the 19th century was caused by widespread disillusionment about the unification project. It has to be said that it was never Cavour's intention to unify the whole country, and even later during his premiership he favoured an expanded Piedmont rather than a unified Italy.

For southerners it was difficult to see the benefits of being part of this new nation state. Naples was stripped of its capital city status (a heavy cultural and political blow); the new government carried away huge cash reserves from

1946	1950	1950s–60s
Italians vote in a national referendum in June (by about 12.7 million votes to 10.7 million) to abolish the monarchy and create a republic. The south is the only region to vote against the republic.	The Cassa per il Mezzogiorno is established to fund public works in the south. It focuses on rural areas, but due to poor management and corruption at least one-third of the money is squandered.	Soaring unemployment causes another mass migration of about two million people from the south to the factories of northern Italy and Europe. This leaves a social gap, with women, children and the elderly left behind.

the rich southern Italian banks; taxes went up and factories closed as new tariff policies, dictated by northern interests, caused a steep decline in the southern economy. Culturally, southerners were also made to feel inferior, to be southern or 'Bourbon' was to be backward, vulgar and uncivilised. From holding centre stage alongside cities like London, Paris and Vienna, the south was dramatically relegated to the political third division.

After WWI, the south fared a little better experiencing slow progress in terms of infrastructure projects like the construction of the Puglian aqueduct, the extension of the railways and the improvement of civic centres like Bari and Taranto. But Mussolini's 'Battle for Wheat' – the drive to make Italy self-sufficient in food – compounded many southern problems, destroying even more valuable pastureland by turning it over to the monoculture of wheat, while reinforcing the parlous state of the southern peasantry, who remained uneducated, disenfranchised, landless and at high risk of malaria. To escape such a hopeless future, many of them packed their bags and migrated to America and northern Europe, starting a trend that was to become one of the main features of post-WWII Italy.

In the 1946 referendum that established the Italian Republic, the south was the only region to vote no. In Naples, 80% voted to keep the monarchy. Still, change moved on apace. After the wreckage of the war had been cleared up the *Cassa per il Mezzogiorno* reconstruction fund was established in order to bring the south into the 20th century with massive, cheap housing schemes and big industrial projects like the steel plant in Taranto and the Fiat factory in Basilicata. But even this wasn't enough to enable the south to catch up with the booming business further north and a further wave of migrants moved north to the factories of Turin and Milan.

Since the 1990s, things have been steadily improving, due to the on-going nationalisation of the economy, the resurgence of tourism and the end of the *Cassa per il Mezzogiorno*, which has forced local entrepreneurs to become more dynamic. Still the average southern Italian can expect to earn only half of what their northern counterpart might command; the 10 poorest cities in Italy are all in the south; and unemployment, poor infrastructure and allegations of corrupt government continue to plague the region.

> Although much has happened since it was written, Paul Ginsborg's *A History of Contemporary Italy: Society and Politics 1943–1988* remains one of the single-most readable and insightful books on post-war Italy.

1999	2002	2005
Brindisi becomes a strategic base for the Office of the UN and the World Food Organisation and the disused military airport and hangars are converted into storage space for humanitarian aid and emergency food rations.	Italy adopts the Euro. A huge controversy about price rises follows as the south is particularly hard hit. Even today people grumble about the negative effects of the euro on their quality of life.	Nichi Vendola, representing the Communist Refoundation Party, is elected President of Puglia – a surprise victory given the conservatism of the south. He is the first gay communist to be elected president of a southern region.

The Culture

It's the end of another fabulous family lunch. Outside the sunlight dapples the ground through the fruit trees. We drink another glass of the delicious, fresh local red wine. I comment that the nearby winery resembles a petrol station, with its pumps of different wines. 'Yes,' says Marcello, 'And at 70c a litre it's cheaper than petrol! But I don't know how long these things will last. Farming is changing. For example, you take the family across the road: their grandfather was a farmer, their father was a farmer, but now the two sons tried farming for a while and didn't like it. It's too hard.'

Marcello's father too worked in agriculture, and his father's father, but he himself moved away to work in Rome, and his children work in offices, far from the fields.

'Life is good here. I would always come back,' says Luca, Marcello's son, 'But now I don't think is the right time to live here for me. Perhaps when I am older.'

Family trees here have their roots in the land. Most families will probably count a farmer among them, if not generation upon generation of them. But the tendrils of these communities also stretch out to the north of Italy and beyond, worldwide. As the saying goes, *Ogni vero Milanese ha un nonno Pugliese* ('Every true Milanese has a Pugliese grandparent').

Luca says that crime has played a part in the exodus, particularly in recent history. 'The Mafia was very strong here in the 1990s. It prevents development, stops people getting proper jobs, and makes them want to leave.'

Puglia and Basilicata host a sunbaked hedonistic summer, and are increasingly fashionable as places to visit; yet they have an elegiac sadness. Some towns are conspicuously elderly, suddenly filling with life over the summer with people coming home from the north or abroad.

The culture of the regions may seem diluted by emigration, but it's also absorbed myriad influences from outside. Just about anyone who's anyone has settled in this area at one time or another. Greeks and Romans, Christians and Muslims. The Daunians, Peucetians and Messapians were migrants from the Balkans and Crete. At the fall of the Roman Empire, Puglia became part of the Greek-speaking Eastern Empire.

'Times have changed fast here,' says Luca. 'It's only two generations ago that men and women were almost segregated. Women only used to go out on Saturdays, and they had separate beaches for men and women.' Marcello adds: 'When my father met my mother, he saw her walking along the street and tried to speak to her. Her brother said to him: 'You speak to me first.' When he was permitted to visit, my aunt sat between them and my grandmother was a chaperone.'

One thing that hasn't changed is that the family is still strong. People do come back, year after year. Those who live elsewhere yearn for the sea, the sand, the slowness and the light; for the place where it is always midday.

MEZZOGIORNO MOODS

Raffaella is in her 30s and works at Lecce university. She would never want to move away. 'Many friends of mine are desperate to return after a few years spent in northern Italy or abroad. They find life too isolated and anonymous. People don't know their neighbours. I think that the young want to experience living somewhere different, but later they grow up and understand that life is living without stress, without impossible traffic, in a beautiful ancient city.' Her friend, Deborah, a business consultant, agrees:

Ann Cornelisen arrived in 1954 to study archaeology and produced *Women of the Shadows: Wives and Mothers of Southern Italy*, a remarkable insight into the lives of five heroic women.

Torregreca: Life, Death, and Miracles in a Southern Italian Village by Ann Cornelisen – a long way from Tuscan idylls: extraordinary postwar accounts about southern village life.

Curiously for a Catholic country, Italy has one of the lowest birth rates in Europe, at 1.29 children per family.

'I'm sure that in the north there are many opportunities for my job, but I prefer to live in Lecce because I love Salento. People who live in the south are different from those living in the north. Here, family and friends are important, more important than work.'

Enzo, an older farmer who produces peaches, grapes and artichokes on his 30 hectares, paints a bleaker picture: 'The problem is that the profitability of agriculture is diminishing. There's lots of competition from Africa. This year the cost of artichokes has fallen – because in Greece and Spain people import vegetables illegally and then pass them off as EU produce. Each artichoke this year costs 5¢, but a product from Africa can cost 3¢. Then an agent can sell on for 1¢ more without any risk, while farmers suffer all the risk. The land has been exploited for so long it needs lots of fertilisers to be productive, while areas in Spain and Africa are less exploited so they can produce more cheaply. If you try to grow organic products, wind can bring fertilizers from other fields. Young people are only interested in working the land here if they love it, because it doesn't make money anymore. There is too much competition. There are two local factories and people prefer to work in these even though hours are longer and pay less. For example, in a factory you earn €3 per hour for eight hours, while in the fields you work five hours for €5 per hour. But people don't want to work in the fields because it's so much tougher. The only people who are reliable to do the farm work are Albanians and other immigrants.'

Raffaella agrees that times continue to be difficult for the young: 'If you want to work in southern Italy, you can find some job, though perhaps not the one you've studied for or dream of. You have to accept instability, short-term or freelance work.'

In 2006, unemployment in the south was 34.3%, compared with 11% in the northeast and 13.4% in the northwest.

EMIGRATION & IMMIGRATION

Severe economic problems in the south following Italy's unification and after each of the world wars led to massive emigration as people travelled in search of work. It was from 1900 to the time of WWI that most people left the south, mostly heading to America.

The breakdown of feudalism had a negative impact on the economy, as plots of land divided among local farmers were not necessarily productive or were given to people who had no experience of farming. The parcels of land also diminished as they were divided between heirs – today, several generations later, the problem of inheritance and how to divide property still frequently splits families. A lack of entrepreneurs and a glut of absentee landlords made land management unsuccessful. Farming was additionally socially despised in the south, despite being the major source of income.

Italy's highest point of emigration was in 1913, when 872,598 people left.

By 1920 around 400,000 Italians lived in New York. A government study in 1927 showed that one-fifth of the Italian population had moved abroad.

Then, in the 1980s Italy began to transform from a country of emigrants to one of immigrants. Nationwide, people have found this a difficult adjustment. Economically the country needs immigrants, particularly with the low birth rate, but social integration is very much in its nascent stages. For Puglia particularly, with its 800km coastline and geographical proximity to Eastern Europe and Africa, immigration is a lively issue. Lecce has a large immigrant population, but in other southern towns and villages the population is largely homogenous. In Basilicata there are entire Albanian villages in the Pollino, with an entirely different culture, way of worship and language.

Thus, despite the long history of invasion from outside and emigration abroad, people have little experience of mixing with other cultures. There have been cases exposed in the media of migrant Eastern European and African workers, employed for the tomato harvest around Foggia, who have been treated like slaves – though this seems less a case of racism than plain-old exploitation.

RELIGION, FOLKLORE & FESTIVITIES

The air over this desolate land and among the peasant huts is filled with spirits. Not all of them are mischievous and capricious gnomes or evil demons. There are also good spirits in the guise of guardian angels.' In *Christ Stopped at Eboli*, his book about his stay in rural Basilicata in the 1930s, writer-painter-doctor Carlo Levi depicts a mystical, half-pagan society, whose belief in witchcraft is still strong. The world he describes may no longer be recognisable, but many of the regions' celebrations come from traditions far more ancient than Christianity.

Puglia's tradition of *taranta* (or '*pizzica*', meaning bite) – a hypnotic, vigorous dance to exorcise the supposed bite of the tarantula – appears to have its origins in Ancient Greece (for more on the *taranta*, see opposite). Many festivals and traditions have been adopted and adapted by Christianity from ancient pagan customs (such as Carnival, adopted by Catholics to mark the beginning of Lent).

The most famous Holy Week celebrations are those of Taranto, where la Processione dei Misteri takes 14 hours to cover 2km.

A DAY IN THE LIFE OF A TOWN

It's just 4.30am and the first of the town's bars are open, for farmers and insomniacs. The barman serves his first caffé of the day. He likes his job, but earns only €400 per month. He's hoping to get funding from Sviluppo Italia ('Develop Italy'), the government development agency for the south, to launch a business selling beauty products.

By 8am, the truck selling vegetables has parked on the corner, and the barber's bicycle is outside his shop. He'll stay open until 11am – he's past retirement age but still keeps the shop going. He'd like to talk – he's particularly interested in local history and bemoans the town's lack of a bookshop – but he hasn't time today; he's going to see his son in the north.

At 9am traffic is at its height. The whole main road is blocked with cars. People are commuting from one end of the town to the other. The best *cornetti* are already gone from the bars. The elderly men are staged on benches in the main square, bicycles leaning against the wall in shadow.

Groups of young people, with big sunglasses, high-maintenance hair and thought-out fashion (and that's just the men) pop in for a cappuccino and *cornetto* before heading off to the beach.

At 9.15am a car drives slowly around the streets, making its recorded announcement through a rooftop megaphone, 'blade sharpening, kitchen gas repairs'. There's a queue at the shop selling mozzarella (if you don't get there early, the *burrata* sells out) and at the bread counter in the supermarket. In fields outside the town, brightly dressed workers – all women – are still toiling, picking tomatoes.

An Albanian woman hurries on her way to the shops. She's staying here looking after an elderly resident in his museum-like home. The €500 she earns each month goes further at home, but it's lonely work.

At 11am the church bell tolls in remembrance for a local man. His death is announced, like the others in town, by black-bordered notices plastered around the town centre.

The main street is lined by small clothes shops that don't do much business; two members of staff, chattering, look out onto the street, waiting for passing trade. One waves to a passing car, which swerves to a stop for a loud and cheery greeting – it's her father's cousin.

At 1pm the shops close for lunch. The main street is deserted. Houses are shuttered. It's sacred time: lunch time.

The town snoozes in the collective catatonia of a summer's afternoon.

It starts to stir at 5pm. Shops open, elderly men start to pedal slowly down the main street. The sun has moved, so they transfer their allegiance to the bar on the other side of the street, though they rarely buy anything.

From dusk the older people begin to sit outside their houses on string chairs, watching any passing traffic. The nightly *passeggiata* – where people dress up to wander; bumping into friends and relatives, checking out their fellows, stopping for a *gelato* – keeps the seafront busy until midnight or beyond.

Easter is the most lavishly celebrated of the Christian festivals, with most towns having week-long events to mark Holy Week. People pay handsomely for the privilege and prestige of carrying the various backbreaking decorations around the town – the processions are usually solemn and excruciatingly slow.

Every town also has its own saint's day, celebrated with music, special events, food and wine. Alessandro Laterza, of the famous Bari-based Laterza publishing house, urges visitors to see these, commenting that, more than any local cultural initiative, festivals are the best way into the culture of the south, 'I'd recommend the beautiful festival of Perdoni (penitents) in Taranto, the extraordinary Maggio ritual in Accettura or the Festival of San Nicola in Bari,' he says.

The church is stronger in the south than in northern Italy. Mass is often packed, though elderly ladies form the major demographic. Church features less strongly in young people's lives, but the important life stages – birth, marriage and death are usually still celebrated with a church ceremony. However, people question the church far more than they did in the past. Deborah, a young businesswoman, feels people have lost their trust in religion: 'People read negative stories about priests in the newspapers, and these things turn young people away from the Catholic church.'

However, the belief in the potential of miracles endures among the old and the young. A recent film by Eduardo Winspeare, *Il Miracolo*, explores this enduring need to believe in an otherworldly, if Christianised, magic. You will see representations of Padre Pio (see p98) – the Gargano saint who was canonised for his role in several miraculous recoveries – in churches, village squares and private homes everywhere. Around eight million pilgrims visit his shrine every year.

'How to dance the pizzica' at www.youtube .com might not be that instructive, but it'll give you a rough idea.

THE ARTS

Most festivals in Puglia and Basilicata feature music and dance: the soundtrack is either the haunting, mesmerising *taranta,* the sorrowful sound of the town *banda* (wind band) or the explosive beat of homegrown reggae. Likewise art and crafts are part of everyday life, with paintings decorating churches, *cartapesta* (papier mache) adorning festival floats and Christmas cribs, and Puglia's distinctive local pottery still very much in use at home and in restaurants. Basilicata has yielded several important poets and has inspired one of modern Italy's finest works in Carlo Levi's *Christ Stopped at Eboli,* and Bari is home to one of Italy's most influential publishing houses: Laterza.

Raffaelle Nigro, who now lives in Bari, is a journalist for RAI and is famous for his poems written in the Melfitan dialect. Read his *I Fuochi del Basento,* a prizewinning historical novel.

Music & Dance

This is a musical land, and music and dance fit its exuberant, emotional personality. Traditional music is as important as (and often combined with) contemporary sounds, and both have a powerful connection to the land.

TARANTA/PIZZICA

Black-and-white photos of tarantism ceremonies show women on the ground, their skirts flapping, their bodies tense and strange, as if having some kind of fit. You don't see this anymore, but you hear the music of *taranta,* also called *pizzica* (meaning 'pinch' or 'sting') at countless festivals, a hypnotic, bouncing rhythm that makes you want to get up and dance. Santino, now in his 60s, remembers when he was a child, 'the women who used to cut the wheat would sing songs on the way back from the fields. One woman would lead and the rest would chant the chorus.'

Taranta music was used for the ritual cure of tarantism – to dance away a tarantula's sting – and also to accompany religious celebrations. It's probable

Beppe Grillo is a popular comedian, renowned for his crusade against corruption through his searing political satire. His blog at www .beppegrillo.it (in Italian and English) is one of the 10 most-visited in the world.

that this type of dance descended from the practises of Ancient Greece. People working in the fields (particularly women, who cut the wheat) were thought to have been bitten by a spider, but were possibly suffering some sort of fit or psychological symptoms. The dance was a process of catharsis. The ritual was Christianised and St Paul (having survived a spider bite) made its patron saint, with the ability to heal the women. For more on tarantism and its origins, see the boxed text, p154.

Post-WWII, the *pizzica* became deeply unfashionable; it was associated with superstition and considered backward. It was reclaimed by local people in the 1970s and nowadays is incredibly popular, particularly among young neo-hippies and crusties. It's the theme music of the Salento, but other southern regions – such as the Gargano, Naples and Calabria – all perform forms of the tarantella.

Groups reinventing the tradition include **Arakne Mediterranea** (www.araknemediterranea.com), **Aramirè** (www.aramirè.it), **Officina Zoè** (www.officinazoe.com) and **Canzoniere Grecanico Salentino** (www.canzonieregrecanicosalentino.net).

Throughout the summer there are myriad *taranta* events, but the biggest is the Notte della Taranta at Melpignano in Puglia at the end of August, where Stuart Copeland, ex-drummer from the Police – who's been bitten by the arachnid – plays the signature pounding drums. For information on *taranta* happenings buy QuiSalento (€2.50; www.quisalento.it) from local newspaper kiosks or check at tourist offices.

> Check out local Basilican folk bands, featuring the extraordinary *zampogne* at www.totarella.it or www.terragnora.it.

SUD SOUND SYSTEM INTERVIEW

Famous all over Italy and internationally, reggae band Sud Sound System is made up of Nandu Popu, Don Rico, Terron Fabio, Papa Gianni and GGD, from Salento. Highly political, they originated a unique sound that combines reggae with the local dialect. Here singer Nandu Popu talks about their homeland and influences.

A lot of foreigners think of Italy as a land of classical music. They would probably be surprised to discover the big southern reggae scene. Why do you think this reggae movement has developed in Puglia?
I don't know if there are similarities between Jamaica and Salento, but the aspect that struck us most about this music was the link between songs and the desire to express people's aspirations where they were forgotten and exploited by progress. The south will be always the place of negated rights and stolen beauty and the *pizzica* of our grandparents also tried to remedy such evils. Maybe this is the reason why Puglia is so fertile for reggae.

Reggae and ragga seems to suit the Pugliese dialect. Why do you think singing in dialect is so important?
The first thing we did was to sing in our own language. Dialect is able to explain facts and events that official languages are not able to translate.

The dialect is an antidote. It's the antidote to the sickness of our society caused by stress, ambition and superficiality, and the idea that anything is acceptable in the name of money. The dialect remembers that it's possible to live at another rhythm: the rhythm of nature, of the sea, of the land.

Apparently young people are continuing to leave Puglia and rejecting agriculture as a career. Do you think this is a trend that will inevitably continue? What do you think the future is for Puglia?
The future of Puglia is still that of emigration! In the last 10 years there has been such a surge in tourism, creating many jobs. But many of those that manage tourism are part of that group of entrepreneurs who obliged young people to emigrate: the Mafia. The entrepreneurs need

BANDA & FOLK

In the 19th century, every village or town had its *banda* that brought the great Italian operas to rural communities. This tradition remains popular in many southern villages. Like elsewhere in the world, the bands are usually made up of working people and act as a training ground for musicians. A combination of tubas, french horns, trumpets, trombones, clarinets, bassoons, oboes, and flutes, they mainly play instrumental arrangements of famous opera songs. Today *banda* is usually heard at religious festivals. The band plays in the main town square, filling a fairylit bandstand that resembles a huge illuminated crown.

For a blog listing albums of traditional Pugliese music, with English commentary, see http://italianfolkmusic.blogspot.com/search/label/Puglia.

Like other forms of local folk music, *banda* has been reclaimed and reworked, namely by Banda Città Ruvo Di Puglia, which has produced the CD *La Banda: Traditional Italian Banda & Jazz*. Listening to it will instantly transport you to a sultry night in a village square (if you're looking for a soundtrack to transform your life into the *Godfather*, this is it).

In Basilicata, each village has a typical song or sound. Traditional folk groups play the melancholic music that the shepherds and peasants used to sing. The Albanese villages of the Pollino have an Albanian music tradition, called musica Arbresh, based mainly on female voices singing religious or satirical songs. They're accompanied by the *zampogna* – a wailing, bagpipe-type instrument, made from goatskin and somehow still goat-shaped.

'flexible' workers at their service, so they welcome Romanians, Albanians, Africans, Asians and *terroni*, who work a lot and cost little: this is the new economy.

What do you think about people from the north – such as the wine producers Antinori – buying land and operating businesses in the south?
In Jamaica, many American multinational companies bought all that was productive (beaches, hotels, supermarkets, banks…), leaving only the ghetto to the locals. Today in Jamaica the main business is weapons and cocaine. I hope the same won't happen in Salento. Also because the wine that my dad buys from his peasant friend is fantastic…not like the cheap wine sold in supermarkets!

There was a period when the Mafia was strong in Puglia – what do you think about the battle against the Mafia mentality? Can it be won?
To win against the Mafia? With our politicians? It's more likely that the *mafiosi* surrender themselves to the police. In Italy, only the people fight against the Mafia, such as Borsellino and Falcone, or activists such as the unforgettable Peppino Impastato. Unfortunately, I have doubts that the politicians would really like to get rid of the Mafia.

Part of your political agenda is the legalisation of drugs: in the light of the most recent debate in Italy, how do you think this issue will develop?
I think that it will be difficult! The leftist politicians don't have the guts to make such a law. They failed on the civil partnership law, so just imagine what they can do with legalisation. Also, the Mafia don't want legalisation, so it would cause lots of trouble.

Traditional folk music plays a part in your music. How would you say your music relates to the traditional music of Puglia?
Pizzica is the music of our grandparents, slaves of the aristocrats. Reggae is the music of Jamaicans, sons of the slaves brought to the Caribbean by our European imperialists. I hope that we will come to sing less songs of suffering and more hymns of freedom.

CLASSICAL, JAZZ & CONTEMPORARY

Venosa, in Basilicata, besides being birthplace of Horace, is famous for Carlo Gesualdo (see p179), a 16th-century composer of the *madrigali* (musical word-painting), an experimental genius and – rather less appealingly – a murderer (of his wife).

Matera has a renowned classical music school, the **Conservatorio di Matera** (www.conservatoriomatera.it), which has its own symphony orchestra and presents the **Festival Duni** (www.festivalduni.it) a classical music festival running from July to September.

There are also lots of blues and rock bands in Basilicata, such as Matera's **Le Mani** (www.myspace.com/lemaniband) and **Testata Nucleare** (www.testatanucleare.com) from Miglionico. There's been an annual jazz festival in Matera (for details see www.onyxjazzclub.it) since 1985. Big names also feature at the jazz festival in Orsara di Puglia (www.orsaramusica.it).

The contemporary music scene is not just about classical, jazz, blues and rock. Somewhat surprisingly, Puglia has a vibrant reggae and ragga scene. The grand masters are the enormously popular **Sud Sound System** (www.sudsoundsystem.com), from Salento – which plays all over Italy and abroad (for more information see the boxed text, p36). This is a band whose homeland is part of its soul. Many of the band's lyrics deal, very wittily, with the joy and sorrow of the south. The band is fantastic live, with an array of performers that fill the stage, and the music combines word-spitting ragga with bouncing reggae and searing traditional folk. Not part of this scene, but also fabulous live, are **Miranda Miranda** (www.mirandamiranda.it), a Florence-based noise/experimental-punk trio whose members are Pugliese. The band has two albums to date (the uncomfortably named *Rectal Explorations* is the latest).

> In some areas, south of Lecce towards Otranto, people still speak a form of ancient Greek, called 'Griko'.

Art

The art that most encapsulates these regions are the Byzantine frescoes: in locked, hidden chapels dotted over Puglia and Basilicata. Often 10th- and 11th-century, the art inspired and defined Christian worship in these rocky, far-flung hideaways. There is an incredible concentration in Matera (Basilicata; most fantastic of which are the monastic complex of Madonna delle Virtù (p170) and San Nicola dei Greci (p170). You can also unlock the secret monk hideaways in Puglia's Massafra and Mottola – home to the Cripta di San Nicola (p117), nicknamed the Sistine Chapel of the south.

To enter the incredible 14th-century Basilica di Santa Caterina d'Alessandria (Puglia; see p154) in Galatina is to be enveloped by captivating Renaissance frescoes. It's uncertain whether the painters were itinerant workers from the north, or well-travelled southerners, but their work resembles that of Giotto, and is delicately detailed, in jewel-like colours and spectacular in scale.

> Gianrico Carofiglio is an anti-Mafia judge in Bari. Read his *Reasonable Doubts*, a huge bestseller in Italy, about a lawyer who handles the appeal of a notorious neo-Fascist criminal.

Conversano, in Puglia, is home of the splendid works illustrating *Gerusalemme Liberata* by Italian writer Torquato Tasso. The painter Paolo Finoglio wears his admiration for Caravaggio on his sleeve.

Barletta is famous not only for its Colossus, but for Giuseppe De Nittis, the only significant Italian impressionist. After study in Barletta and Naples, he moved to Paris in 1867, and was later invited by Degas to join the first Impressionist exhibition. His later work includes portraits of Zola and Manet. His hometown has the best collection of his works, displayed in the magnificent baroque structure of the Pinacoteca Giuseppe de Nittis (p77).

Carlo Levi's large paintings, produced while he was in exile in Basilicata, are biblical in scale, while their scope is the local peasantry. You can see fine examples in Matera and Aliano, the town where he was imprisoned in the 1930s.

LITERATURE

Puglia and Basilicata are mostly renowned for the literature they have inspired. Carlo Levi's *Christ Stopped at Eboli* is an early 20th-century masterpiece, an account of his time when exiled by the Fascists to a mountain village (for more on Levi, see p168 and p184). In a completely different genre, Horace Walpole's *Castle of Otranto*, set in the Salento town, is thought to be the first ever Gothic novel, spawning a mass of imitators.

However, Basilicata has brought forth a plethora of wonderful poets, including the great Latin poet Horace (from Venosa, see p179), tragic Renaissance aristocrat Isabella Morra (1516–45), who was murdered by her brothers, and the Nobel-prize-nominated Albino Pierro (1916–95), from remote Tursi, who wrote in the archaic Tursi dialect about his hometown and life (see p200).

Bari is also the site of one of Italy's best bookshops and most venerable publishers: Laterza. Alessandro Laterza, the founder's great-grandson, told us about the local literary scene.

Your Bari bookshop is one of the best in Italy – could you tell us something about Laterza's history?
Libreria Laterza (p61) was founded in 1885 as a stationer's (cartolibreria) in Putignano, a little village between Bari and Taranto. The founder was Vito Laterza, later joined by his four brothers. The business was transferred first to Taranto and then to Bari. Between 1889 and 1901 the company acquired a printer, opened a bookshop, and launched the publishing side of the business, supported by the great intellectual Benedetto Croce. These last ventures were due to Giuseppe Laterza. Today, Laterza focuses solely on the publishing sector, even if the bookshop it is still a symbolic place for the city locally and nationally. During the Fascist period the bookshop was one of the main centres of dissent. Today, completely renovated, it's also a cultural centre, with a rich calendar of events: conferences and talks and also concerts, children's events and wine tasting. The bookshop is a reference point for the city: for people from Bari it's common to set up a meeting saying 'let's see each other at Laterza'.

Could you recommend some classic and contemporary writers and literature (in Italian or English) from Puglia and Basilicata?
Puglia doesn't have a great literary tradition – the field of nonfiction books is far more important. Laterza never published solely fiction. However, in recent years new, very talented authors, such as Gianrico Carofiglio, Giancarlo De Cataldo, Nicola La Gioia, and Andrea Piva have emerged. Carofiglio is the author of some bestsellers that have had great success at home and abroad. Basilicata has a stronger tradition, with some famous poets, and Raffaele Nigro, who is a very important writer.

Which books about these regions would you recommend to visitors (in Italian or English)?
To chose only two I would say for Puglia, *Testimone Inconsapevole* (Reasonable Doubts) by Gianrico Carofiglio and for Basilicata, *I Fuochi del Basento* (The Fires of Basento) by Raffaele Nigro.

Matera has been an inspiration to, and continues to attract, many artists, nd you'll see numerous shop-studios tucked away among the *sassi* (cave-ousing districts, see p170). Musma (p171), the new contemporary sculpture useum, taps into this artistic streak, and exhibits plenty of works by local s well as international artists. Jose Ortega is a Spanish artist and sculptor, a pil of Picasso and exponent of papier-mache, who settled in Matera – he ved the *sassi* – and whose former house there opened to the public at the d of 2007. Some of his works are displayed in Musma.

Bitonto has the best display of the work of Domenico Cantatore (1906–998), born in Ruvo di Puglia, one of Puglia's most talented 20th-century tists, influenced first by Cezanne, and then by Picasso and the Fauves.

Pino Pascali (1936–68), from Bari – but who is celebrated in Polignano a are (see p133) – was a playful, innovative artist, whose materials were old cans, fake fur, hay and dirt, and whose affiliation to the *arte povera* (poc art) movement was a direct expression of his southern roots. He died age only 32 in a car accident.

For contemporary rock art, look no further than the Gargano, when Michele Circiello creates works from sand, mosaic, clay and bronze, inspire by Neolithic art (see p107).

Crafts

Ceramics have been easing household and practical tasks since ancien times. It's believed that the ancient Greeks brought their pot- and amphora making skills with them around 2800 years ago during the Magna Greci era, though Lecce's Museo Provinciale has Messapian ceramics that sho the art was flourishing long before that. Before the advent of other material pottery was used for everything – chamber pots, wine urns, cooking pot washing linen.

The elegantly simple, rustic patterns used on Pugliese pottery are in stantly recognisable. The most familiar is a cream background with a simp decoration combining narrow blue lines with a repeated pattern of six blu dots. Traditional rustic designs also often add cockerels to the mix, show raising their wings as the lucky birds usually had their legs tied to a stic They symbolise fertility.

Grottaglie is famous for its highly elaborate, colourful ceramics. The indu try here developed into producing decorative pottery in the 18th century wi the introduction of glazing. Other ceramics centres are San Pietro in Lam Laterza, Martina Franca, Canosa, Lucera, Lucugnano and Cutrofiano.

Papier mache – *cartapesta* – is Lecce's speciality, and all over the tow you can buy religious figures made from straw, paper and glue; there is massive range of figures in all guises and sizes. If you're after a lifesize stra figure of Christ, this is where to look.

For lacework, once traditional all over Italy, Locorotondo is the place i Puglia. Otherwise the traditions of lacemaking and weaving have been im pressively maintained in the Albanian settlements in the Pollino (Basilicata The village of San Paolo Albanese also still makes *zampogna* bagpipes – ma from goatskin and somehow goat-shaped.

Matera in Basilicata is an artistic hotspot, and here you can buy we crafted decorated dishes, hand-painted terracotta whistles (known locally *cucu/cucco*) usually in the shape of a rooster, and Nativity cribs (depicting th scene as taking place in the *sassi*) often made of papier mache. The pinnac of the papier-mache oeuvre is the Madonna used during Matera's Madonn della Bruna festival, which is paraded around town then torn to pieces.

Film

Southern cinema tends to confront the 'problem of the south' but is als frequently extremely funny. It's well worth watching a few films befo you go.

The 1960s was a fertile era for film, with satire the predominant flavou In *Anni Ruggenti* (The Roaring Years; 1962), an insurance salesman wh arrives at a small town (Matera, in Basilicata) is mistaken for a Fascist o ficial sent from Rome.

Basilischi, I (The Lizards; 1964) set in Basilicata, depicts three your men with directionless, small-town lives. Capturing the mood of a sleep going-nowhere town, it was the directorial debut of Swiss aristocrat Lin Wertmuller, who had worked as Fellini's assistant.

Francesco Rosi wrote the screenplay and directed the film version Cristo si é Fermato in Eboli (1979), which is stunning, if a bit sentimentalise

Latin poet Horace coined the phrases *carpe diem* (seize the day) and *dulce et decorum est pro patria mori* (it is sweet and just to die for one's country).

Under the Southern Sun: Stories of the Real Italy and the Americans it Cre- ated, by Paul E Paolocelli is an anecdotal account of the author's exploration of his roots in southern Italy.

starring Maria Volonte as author Carlo Levi and Irene Papas as his spooky housekeeper Giulia.

More recent offerings shed sunbleached light on contemporary mores and are rich in the atmosphere and complexities of southern life, and many of them are even filmed in dialect (with Italian subtitles), indicating the new value placed on local traditions.

La Terra (2006), directed by former actor Sergio Rubini, is about a young man who's been exiled after killing his father, who returns to his Pugliese village and gets embroiled in familial conflict – unfortunately it's rich in stereotypes.

Pugliese director Eduardo Winspeare's films all pay tribute to his birthplace and are filmed in dialect. His previous experience as a documentary maker is reflected in his subtle approach, and he frequently uses local, amateur actors. *Pizzicata* is a love story set in the Salento during WWII, about an American fighter pilot who is forced to parachute into the countryside. Winspeare called the film 'a declaration of love for my country', and it's certainly the rural homeland that plays the main part, while plot and character take something of a back seat. *Sangue Vivo* (His Life Blood) explores the *pizzica* tradition alongside the relationship between two brothers, one of whom gets dragged into drug taking, while his *Il Miracolo* tells the story of Tonio, an introspective 12 year old, who is hospitalised after a car accident. When he touches a dying man in the hospital who revives, it prompts talk of miraculous healing powers. It's an interesting film about a need to believe and exploit, which has particular resonance in the south.

Prize winning *La Capagira* (The Head is Spinning; 1999), in dialect, is set in Bari during a spell of exceptionally bad weather. Exposing Bari's underbelly, the plot revolves around a mysterious package from the Balkans.

Food & Wine

The *cucina* (cuisine) of the south is born out of poverty. Pasta made without eggs, bread made from hard durum wheat, wild greens scavenged from the countryside all delicious, but driven by necessity. Food historian Luigi Sada describes *zuppa di pesce fuggito* – 'fish soup from which the fish has fled' – made from boiling seashells with vegetables, basil, oil and vermicelli. The tradition of *sopratavola* (raw vegetables such as fennel or chicory eaten after a meal) arose because people could not afford fruit.

People here take food seriously and devote time and effort to it. They eat local, seasonal produce, and many also still pickle, dry and bottle it for use in the leaner months.

The glorious sun-ripened Mediterranean diet is based on olive oil, tomatoes and the many other local vegetables. Meat was a rare treat in the past and beef is still unusual; chicken, rabbit and lamb are the traditional meats. A more recent addition clipclopping to the table is *cavallo* (horse meat).

Waves of immigration and conquest brought new foodstuffs and cooking styles. The Swabians brought radishes, the Arabs citrus fruits, juniper, raisins and almonds, and the Spanish tomatoes and potatoes. Many dishes taste distinctly Greek, such as the rich flavours of *polpo in humido* (stewed octopus).

Traditions in the south remain stronger than in the north of Italy, but the Slow Food movement also does its bit to prevent their disappearance and to promote interest in food, taste and the way things are produced. See www.slowfoodpuglia.it (in Italian), or you can look up the main website in English at www.slowfood.com.

> For extensive descriptions of regional specialities and recipes, see www.italianmade.com.

> The Slow Food movement's annually updated *Guide to Italian Wines* is an excellent resource with region-by-region profiles of producers and their wines.

THE FOOD DIARIES
January

Brrrr! This might be southern Europe, but it's cold outside and time to eat *legumes*: dried pulses or 'the protein of the poor', accompanied by winter vegetables such as cauliflower, savoy cabbage, turnip tops, chicory and fennel. Winter dishes include *orecchiette con cime di rapa* (ear-shaped pasta with turnip tops; particularly around Bari), pasta with cauliflower, which has been cooked until it resembles cream, and savoy cabbage or *orecchiete con pomodori e ricotta forte* (with tomato sauce and strong cheese).

The distinctive *lampascioni* – wild onions, actually the bulbs of a wild hyacinth – are harvested now. They have a bitter flavour and are usually pickled in oil or brine.

February

Dried or smoked meats are traditionally prepared in the darker days of the year. Basilicata has little room for grazing, so meat was previously a rare commodity, usually eaten in hearty stews, such as *cutturiddi*, made of lamb or mutton. Despite this, Basilicata is famous for its salami and sausages – pigs here are prized and fed on natural foods such as acorns. Basilicata's most renowned sausage is called *lucanica* or *lucanega*. The ancient Romans ate it and Apicio, Cicero, Marziale and Varrone remarked on it: seasoned with fennel, pepper, *peperoncino* and salt, and eaten fresh – roasted on a coal fire – or dried or preserved in olive oil.

In Basilicata you'll also find *soppressata* – pork sausage from Rivello, made from finely chopped pork grazed in pastures, dried and pressed and kept in extra-virgin olive oil, and *pezzenta* ('beggars' – probably a reference to their peasant origins) made from pork scraps and spicy Senise peppers.

> The Slow Food movement does its bit to promote interest in food, taste and the way things are produced. See www.slowfoodpuglia.it (Italian only) or www.slowfood.com.

Dried pulses saved from the summer come into their own in the cold, such as *fave nette* (dried fave purée) often eaten with raw chicory.

March

Spring has sprung and it's time to eat *mozzarella*, and fresh *fave* (broad beans) with new cheeses. Spring and Easter are also ideal for lamb and kid. Nothing goes to waste: the animal innards are used for *gnemerièdde/turciniedde* – skewered sausages grilled on charcoal fire.

Nowadays meat is more common. You'll find that the intensely flavoursome *ragu di carne* (meat sauce) that accompanies all sorts of pasta, is often prepared by using three different kinds of meat (lamb, pork and kid), cooked in a seasoned tomato sauce.

April

The strange fruit of the sea are in the ascendant. Signs emblazoned *ricci* punctuate the coast south of Bari. Sea urchins are spikily designed to be difficult to eat – known as *ricci di mare* (hedgehogs are *ricci di terra*) – but it's a testament to human resourcefulness that people manage. Once they're cracked open, you can dip bread into the delicate, dark-red roe. Now's the time to eat them, before the eggs are ejected, and restaurants all over Puglia see parties of Italians feasting on piles of the love-them-or-hate-them delicacy.

Meanwhile, the fields are nodding with *carciofi* – globe artichokes on long elegant stalks. There are many ways to eat artichokes and one of the heartiest is the lavish dish of *parmigiana*. Cut the heart of the artichoke in pieces, dip these in egg and flour batter, then fry them. Next, layer them with mozzarella, parmesan, ham and tomato sauce, bake the concoction in an oven and then eat at room temperature.

As the artichoke season ends and the *fave* one begins, you'll see fresh *fave* beans cooked with artichokes appear on the menu. People also dry the beans to tide them over in winter. Other beans are preserved in vinegar for the leaner months, such as *ceci* (chickpea).

Almonds flourish in the Valle d'Itria in spring, the caffé-latte-coloured kernel wrapped in a shell of green velvet. They're used in many sweets and cakes. A traditional Lecce sweet, made by convent nuns, is made from almond paste shaped as a fish or a lamb and stuffed with pear marmalade or creamy custard. Sweets were once the sole preserve of the church and aristocracy as poor people had no time or money for such frivolity, and they're still considered something of a special-occasion delicacy.

Look out for *nespole* (loquat), about the same size, shape and colour as apricots but with a smooth skin. They're deliciously succulent and juicy. Originally from southern China, the trees were brought back by Europeans from Japan as decoration in the 18th century.

May

By the port at Brindisi a crowd gathers as the van arrives with the fish, fresh from the sea, ready to be auctioned off. There are piles of gleaming bodies, some still jittery with life, and trays full of delicate-coloured crayfish. The whole transaction takes less than five minutes as the auctioneer reels off ascending prices and the crates are rapidly cleared. It's finished. The crowd melts. Gianni used to own a restaurant here. He explains: 'Only a couple of people are here to buy: the rest are here to look. They have nothing else to do.' He adds that now is the best time of year to eat seafood and ideal for octopus, cuttlefish and squid – it's breeding season so they're easier to catch. Dishes include *zuppa di pesce* (fish soup); *frittura di calamari e gamberi* (fried squid and prawns); and *seppie con piselli* (cuttlefish with fresh peas, sliced onion, parsley, and olive oil).

Awaiting Table (www.awaitingtable.com) Silvestro Silvestori's Lecce-based cooking school offers short, weekend or week-long cookery courses, featuring lots of visits, tastings and guest teachers.

It's said that there are 50 million olive trees in Puglia, equivalent to the Italian population.

Flavours of Puglia, by Nancy Harmon Jenkins, is the ultimate guide in English to Pugliese cooking, with background and recipes, meticulous, authentic and interesting.

INTERVIEW WITH ANTONIO CARLUCCIO, RESTAURATEUR, CHEF & FOOD WRITER

In Italy, it's said that everyone's favourite cook is their mamma. Is it the same for a famous gastronome?
My mamma inspired me as a teacher of life – I learned much of my cooking skills and passion from her – she was definitely the most important woman in my life.

As your father was a stationmaster, you travelled widely around Italy from an early age, which must have given you an amazing opportunity to experience different regional cuisines. What do you think characterises southern Italian cooking?
I am probably one of the few Italians who admires the cuisine of all the Italian regions – each one has something special and unique to offer. The south, with its sunshine and fertile land – also less industrial than the north – offers an array of produce that enables the south to cook the most wonderful food. They are major producers of olive oil, wine and many fabulous varieties of vegetables. Naturally, the vegetables are to be eaten in season but there is also a large industry for the preservation of these products as they are staple ingredients for other foods, for example, tomato sauce and pesto.

What are your favourite dishes from Puglia and Basilicata? Which do you think are the best dishes to try in order to experience these cuisines?
La cucina povera – poor man's food – is the staple cuisine in Puglia. This type of cooking was originally created by the local farmers when they were struggling. The food is certainly not so-phisticated or refined but rustic and extremely tasty. One of my favourite recipes is pan roasted peppers with almonds – served with the local bread, which is out of this world. Another local favourite using their amazing vegetables, is chicory and broad bean puree – a dish to die for, especially when drizzled with fresh olive oil. They even have an onion pie, Calzone Pugliese. I also love *orecchiette* (hand-made pasta 'ears') with broccoli and mussels. You must try antipasti: olives, capers, aubergine, artichoke, mushrooms, peppers, onions, and many other types of vegetables cooked in vinegar and then preserved in a jar with olive oil. A selection of these with fresh bread, local cheese and a good glass of wine make for an excellent meal.

Antonio Carluccio's *Southern Italian Feast: More Than 100 Recipes Inspired by the Flavour of Southern Italy*, is a splendid collection to inspire you to get cooking.

Octopus, once caught, is tenderised via a thorough bashing against the rocks. It can be eaten raw or grilled quickly over charcoal or wood, and dressed simply with lemon, oil and parsley. Never pass up an opportunity to try *polpo in umido* or *alla pignata* – one of the most punchy, tasty dishes possible, rich burgundy in colour – steamed with garlic, onion, tomatoes, parsley, olive oil, black pepper, bay leaves and cinnamon.

Mussels fill summer menus in myriad guises. Most dear to the Pugliese is *riso cozze e patate* (rice, mussels and potatoes) baked in the oven, using the juice of the mussels to cook the rice and potatoes. This is a variation of a dish known as *teglia/tiella/taieddha/tiedde*, depending on where you are. If you're in Lecce, then you might add zucchini. Baked dishes are typical of these regions, and would be popped in the oven after the bread came out.

Otherwise you may find mussels served raw, steamed with garlic, parsley and white wine or *cozze arracanate/gratinate al forno*: breaded and baked in the oven.

Fresh anchovies are also particularly delicious, often presented as an entire breaded-and-baked shoal.

June
Summer is tomato time. Time to eat them, hang them, dry them and bottle them, so that you don't miss out on them in winter. '*Pane e pomodoro*', says local housewife Anna, talking of the Pugliese favourite, 'topped with olive oil, capers and salt, it's almost a meal.'

Do you have any preferred restaurants in Puglia and Basilicata?
They have many farms in Puglia which have been renovated as restaurants and hotels called *masserie*.

The best places to eat are the *locande* and *trattorie,* never the posh restaurants, as they don't reflect the real character of the local cuisine.

What do you think is the effect of migration in Italy on cuisine?
The internal migration of Italy in the last half-century, mainly from the southern rural areas to the industrialised north, brought significant changes to the eating habits of the *polentoni* (this was the name the southern Italians jokingly called those from the north) The *terroni* were the people working the *terra* (land) who did not want to be without their beloved specialities. They transported all their favourites like olive oil, olives, oranges, lemons, fresh vegetables, fruit, salted anchovies, fresh Mediterranean fish, and, above all, the pasta made from durum wheat semolina like fusilli, spaghetti, penne, and giant penne.

Gradually, the *terroni* took on the northern habits of eating risotto, butter, *proscuitto,* Parmesan cheese and, yes, *polenta*.

However, the southerners still liked to cook using their own ingredients like *pomodorini* (cherry tomatoes) to make sauces. The northern Italians had probably never tasted those ingredients and dishes from Puglia, Sicily, Calabria and Naples. Gradually, restaurants opened all over the large northern cities selling this produce. The southern market traders promoted their local fare throughout the markets in the large towns of Milan, Turin etc which were then bought and used by the indigenous population – with the exception of Tuscany, which was still sceptical of the south!

Why do you think that food is so important in Italy?
They say that food is the second most important thing in the world – it's up to you to discover the first. Food represents a daily joy for Italians. Much time, money, thought and passion is dedicated to the enjoyment of food. A mother or father who prepares food for the family is giving love and everyone is thankful and happy.

Spaghetti with oven-roasted tomatoes, with breadcrumbs and garlic is deliciously light and summery. Soups are mainly winter fare, but you may get the odd minestrone *(zuppa di verdure stufata)*.

Fruits begin to burst into their own, with trees groaning with fat cherries, peaches, apricots, and plums. Summer vegetables include beetroot *(carrota rossa)* and *cocomeri* – stubby fat cucumbers that are startlingly crisp and sweet – sublime eaten alongside a salty pecorino cheese.

For an excellent food and travel portal, visit www.deliciousitaly.com; it also lists courses and wine tours.

July
Now the figs begin to ripen, fresh green on the outside, inside a delicate, fragrant pink. Traditionally, figs are dried here, or boiled to make a syrup that's then pressed to produce *mosto cotto,* a molasses-like syrup, poured over those special-occasion sweets, typical in the Foggia region, called *cartellate* – a sweet dough kneaded with red wine, then fried. *Anguria* (watermelon), as big as a small child, start to appear piled high by the roadside – nothing is so refreshing, served straight from the fridge in the heat of the day.

Peppers and green beans begin their long harvests. Glossy purple-black *melanzane* are also basking in the fields, and now's your chance to eat the incredible *melanzane ripiene al forno* (baked aubergine stuffed with olives, capers and tomatoes) – punchy enough to be a main course. For *parmigiana melanzane,* as in the artichoke version (see p43), aubergine is fried in batter and then layered with parmesan, mozzarella (ham) and tomato sauce (often leftover *ragù*). You'll need an afternoon snooze following this.

Summer is the best time to eat *spumone,* a mixed ice cream dessert (often chocolate and hazelnut) that's found all over Italy but with special variations here.

August

The word *melanzane* (aubergine/eggplant) – comes from 'mela insana' meaning crazy apple – in Latin it was called *solanum insanum*; it was thought to cause madness.

Red aubergines are unique to Rotonda in Basilicata – these look like tomatoes and were brought from Africa in the 19th century. The taste is spicy and bitter, and they're often dried, pickled or preserved in oil and served as antipasti – try them at Ristorante De Pepe (p196) in Rotonda, Basilicata.

Peperoncino (hot red pepper) – also known as *diavulicchiu* (little devil), *frangisello* (saddle breaker) – is more widely used in Basilicata than Puglia.

It's time for Basilicata's red fruits: strawberries and raspberries, and melons and peaches are at their best in both regions. No town is complete without its roadside vans top heavy with golden globes.

September

It's a busy month for Simona Rocco, a young Pugliese farmer. It's 11 hectares, with eight workers: 'We grow negroamaro (which is typical to Puglia) and chardonnay grapes to make red and white wine. The wine is then produced locally by *cantine*.' How has farming changed? 'Today it's all mechanised. We get help from the EU to buy machinery. Before we needed lots of people and it was more costly. What took 10 days, today takes two. Still, we depend on the weather. If it rains too much, the vineyard becomes diseased.' Grapes are also grown for eating, but the vines are really all about wine.

Wallow in the wonder of a small green fruit in the fascinating, engaging *Olives, The Life and Lore of a Noble Fruit* by Mort Rosenblum.

With the first rains, in September, the southern snail (*lumache* or *uddra-tieddri*) begins to venture above the surface. This is a mistake on their part, as it makes them easy to find. The opening of their shell is covered by a thin white seal, formed as a result of the grass they eat – this is removed during washing and preparation. You can eat them with a sauce made with onion, tomatoes and oil or fried with oil and bay leaves.

The damp ground begins to yield delicious *funghi* (mushrooms) of all shapes and sizes, particularly in mountainous Basilicata. A favourite of the ancient Romans, the small umbel oyster mushroom grows wild. Delicate and tasty, it's eaten fried with garlic and parsley or accompanying lamb or vegetables.

Look out for *cardoncelli* mushrooms in Puglia (especially the north; try them at La Traditizione Cucina Casalinga, see p81), a meaty autumnal speciality, typical of the Murge woods and so named because they grow near wild thistles.

October

The weather's still balmy but there's an occasional nip in the air, which means it makes sense to eat some soup with winter greens and meatballs (*zuppa con polpettine*).

Olive trees have become must-have additions to northern Italian gardens (ancient specimens can fetch around £8000), so Puglia has even drafted laws to protect them.

As autumn tinges the countryside gold and brown, it's also a good time to bite into pears – particularly alongside a salty *pecorino* cheese.

The first *marrons* (chestnuts) also begin to sweeten the days, best eaten roasted on the fire or the hob. You can't get much cosier than a *marron* festival, particularly in the chestnut-laden hills of Basilicata.

November

The liquid gold that oils Puglia and Basilicata's cooking is produced after the olive harvest. Most of the olive oil in Italy is produced here, with the north of Puglia being the main area of production. You'll never have seen so many gnarled, sculptural and silver-green trees, some said to be thousands of years old. Usually two types of olives make up Pugliese oil: coratina (from Corato) are faintly bitter, while ogliarola (from around Cima di Bitonto) produce a sweet, fat oil.

The best oil is made from olives picked and rushed to the mill, as olives left quickly become acidic. Pugliese farmers traditionally harvest the easy way: letting the olives drop into nets, rather than pay for labour-intensive harvesting by hand. This means the olives are too acidic and the oil has to be refined, often taken north to mix with higher quality, costlier oils. That said, more and more places here produce stunning oils at low prices; buy it at local farms such as organic Piccapane outside Cutrofiano (p156) or Il Frantoio (p132).

December

With 800km of coast and ports teeming with fresh fish it seems curious that *baccalau* (salt cod) is so popular, but this means you can eat fish even when the weather is bad. Before cooking you have to soak the dried, salted fish for around 24 hours. It's often cooked with garlic and tomato, to eat with pasta as a primo, and then on its own as a secondo.

It's time to break out the *pomodori a pendula* – hanging tomatoes – preserved to add flavour to the winter months. Hung since the summer, these tomatoes are still full of flavour, and ideal for *bruschetta* or *pane e pomodoro*.

SOUTHERN STAPLES
Pasta

'There are large companies who employ people just to taste new shapes of pasta. At least 600 different shapes exist. I love pasta in all shapes and sizes,' says Antonio Carluccio.

And doesn't everyone? The first record of this supreme comfort food is by Horace, the Latin poet born in Venosa in 65 BC. A lot has been tucked away since then: it's rare to have an Italian meal without some form of this much-loved staple.

Best known is the fresh pasta *orecchiette* (meaning 'little ears'), remarkable for the way in which they hold a sauce. You'll see countless other local shapes, such as *tapparelle* (large ears) or *troccoli* (large spaghetti), and all the other types that you find elsewhere in Italy.

Puglia produces around 80% of Europe's pasta, and per-capita consumption of bread and pasta is at least double that of the USA.

DINING DIARY

Puglia and Basilicata, like the rest of Italy, starts the day on a cappuccino and a *cornetto* (croissant) for *colazione* (breakfast), usually a quick hit taken while standing at a bar. Farmers, however, eat before going to the fields at dawn, so require something more substantial, such as *pane e pomodoro* (bread and tomatoes), and they'll take something like *friselli* (dried bread to reconstitute with water) with them as a snack.

Venture into the street at 1pm and there will be an unearthly quiet. It's sacred time: *pranzo* (lunch). Paolo, whose parents still cook in the traditional way, says, 'At home, we usually start with *primo piatto* (first course) – usually pasta or risotto – though we'll sometimes also have *antipasti* before that. Then we'll have the *secondo piatto* (second course) of meat or fish. We often follow with some cheese, plus fruit. Occasionally we have *dolce* (sweets) too. After this it's time for a big sleep.'

Most shops and businesses close for three to four hours every afternoon for the meal and the traditional siesta – the streets remain quiet and empty before beginning to stir again at 5pm. This is a necessity in the summer months, when it's too hot to do much in the afternoon.

Cena, the evening meal, was traditionally a more simple affair, but now usually also follows the *primo*, *secondo*, *dolce* pattern.

Carlotta, a young Pugliese woman who lives near Brindisi, describes making traditional pasta: '*Orecchiette* is made with durum wheat flour, water and salt. It has to be worked hard. Then you make strands of pasta, cut them into pieces, and shape these into the form of an ear, using your thumb. *Orecchiette* are usually accompanied with another type of pasta, called *strascinati* or *cavatelli,* made by using an iron rod. You roll the pasta around it two or three times, then extract the iron and divide the pasta into 2cm pieces. At one time all the women knew how to make these varieties. They would sit outside in the street with their tables and make pasta while chatting with their neighbours. Now few people know how.'

Antonio Carluccio's *Italia* celebrates Italy's regional cuisine and love of convivial living.

Cheese

You thought mozzarella was delicious and creamy, but when you taste *burratta* – the variety invented in Andria near Bari – you move onto an entirely different level of deliciousness. Best eaten when freshly made that morning, it's a large porcelain-white mozzarella with a distinctive top knot, and when you slice into it, luscious, buttery cream floods out. It's a relatively recent invention, produced from around the 1950s.

Mozzarella also originated from southern Italy. This famous plastic cheese is usually made from cow's milk in Puglia; buffalo mozzarella comes from around Foggia as here there are the big swampy fields that buffalo so like.

Scamorza (from dialect – referring to how the cheese appears strangled at the neck) is a creamy close relative of mozzarella, a bit dryer, with a stringy texture (but much better than it sounds).

Ferula Viaggi (www .ferulaviaggi.it) In Matera, this excellent agency offers food-themed tours and tastings, where you can, for example, see mozzarella being made and taste local wines.

There are some superb sheep's-milk cheeses to be had in the south, and Basilicata is famous for its strong, salty Lucanian pecorino, a blend of sheep and goat's milk which is aged from a few weeks to 18 months. Canestrino – from Foggia – is another semi-hard form of pecorino, with added peppercorns.

Caciocavallo is a renowned southern cheese. Don't panic: despite the name 'horse cheese', it's made from cow's milk. It has a distinctive gourd-shaped, pale-mustard exterior, and the name is thought to have arisen either because it was once made from mare's milk, or because it would be hung from the horse's back when transported. When it's young it tastes *dolce* (sweet), after two month's aging it's *piccante* (spicy) or *affumicato* (smoked). Most prized is *Podilico Caciocavallo*, made from the especially good milk of the Basilican Podolico cow.

Cacioricotta is made with sheep's and goat's milk and has a fresh, creamy, somewhat acidic taste, and is eaten in slices or grated on pasta.

Spiciest of all is *ricotta forte* (a double-fermented cheese, eaten sprinkled on pasta dishes), which kicks like a mule.

Bread & Baking

Eating a meal in Puglia and Basilicata without bread is like playing tennis without a racquet. You'll need it to wipe up the sauce (a practise fondly called *fare scarpetta* 'to make a little shoe'). Bread here is usually made from hard durum wheat (like pasta), has a russet-brown crust, an almost eggy-golden interior and distinctively good flavour. It's baked in a wood-burning oven, and keeps well. Puglia's most famous bread comes from Altamura, is thrice-risen and even gets better with time.

Many recipes call for breadcrumbs, made from stale bread – in Italian it's *pane rafferme* (firmed-up bread), which is a much more glass-half-full way of looking at it.

Friselli – bagel-shaped rolls that have been dried – are another Pugliese delicacy born out of practicality, ideal for labourers on the move. These you douse in water to soften and then dress with tomatoes, olive oil and oregano.

Taralli – hard little savoury biscuits, also bagel-shaped, are something of an Italian pretzel. In Bari they're traditionally plain, in Taranto sprinkled with fennel seeds, and in Lecce have a touch of chilli; they're sometimes even caramelised.

When deciding on your morning *cornetto* (croissant) consider biting into a *bocconotto* (big mouthful) also commonly known as *pasticciotto* (big pastry). This is a crispy sponge cake filled with tepid custard cream and is a unique regional morning pick-me-up. Another local (and this author's) favourite are *cornetti* filled with *crema merena* – custard cream and sour cherry.

Check out http://wine country.it for a useful overview of Puglia and Basilicata's wines.

WINE

Winemaking in Puglia and Basilicata dates back to the Phoenicians, with Puglia important enough as a wine-producing region to be called Enotria (Wineland) by the Greeks.

The different characteristics of the regions' wines reflect their diverse topography and terroir. In Puglia there are vast flat acreages of vineyards, while Basilicata's vineyards tend to be steep and volcanic.

Until the 1980s, the strong Puglia wine, made so by the long hot summers, was used mainly for providing strength and body to the wines of northern Italy and other European countries. Now producers have understood that the conditions are perfect for top-quality winemaking. Italian wine houses, such as Antinori and Avignonesi, and Australian and American winemakers have invested heavily here. Pugliese wine families such as Candido, Garofano and Vallone have upped their game by employing stricter and more modern winemaking practices.

Puglia is the sixth-biggest wine-making region in the world.

It's the Pugliese reds that gain most plaudits. The main grapes grown are the Primitivo (a clone of the Zindafel grape), Negroamaro, Nero di Troia and Malvasia. The best Primitivi are found around Manduria, while Negroamaro reaches its peak in the Salento, particularly around Salice, Guagnano and Copertino. The two grapes are often blended to derive the best from the sweetness of Primitivo and the slightly bitter, wilder edge of Negroamaro.

Almost all Puglia reds work perfectly with pasta, pizza, meats, and cheeses. Puglia whites have less cachet; however, those grown on the Murge,

TABLE MANNERS

The Puglia and Basilicata book of etiquette:

- Cardinal sins: skipping or being late for lunch.
- *Salutè!* (cheers!) is the toast used for alcoholic drinks. *Buon appetito* is the thing to say before eating.
- Unless you have hollow legs, don't accept a second helping of that delicious *primo* – you might not have room for the *secondo, dolce, sopratavola* and fruit.
- Devour everything to the last olive and you'll be endeared to your hosts' hearts forever.
- *Scarpetta* (meaning 'little shoe') the practice of wiping up your remaining sauce with bread is perfectly acceptable.
- End your meal with a short sharp *caffè* (espresso); ordering anything else is just not on.
- Don't drink cappuccino or other milky coffee after breakfast – that would be weird.
- If invited to someone's house, bring a tray of *dolcetti* from a local patisserie.

THE FAMOUS FIVE

What we consider to be some of the regions' best eating experiences:

Falso Pepe (see p117) A small brilliant white *casa* with sublime food.

Il Frantoio (see p132) A 10-course lunch and a foodie paradise.

Masseria Barbera (see p81) One of Puglia's most wonderful farm restaurants.

Porta di Basso (see p93) Superb ocean views and Dolce Guida's Young Chef of the Year.

Ristorante Tipico Luna Rossa (p196) Breathtaking views and ancient recipes turned into exquisite masterpieces.

---

particularly Locorotondo and Martina, are good, clean, fresh-tasting wines, while those from Gravina are a little weightier. They are all excellent with fish.

In Basilicata, the red wine of choice is made from the Aglianico grape, the best being produced in the Vulture region. It is the volcanic terroir that makes these wines so unique and splendid. Basilicata, like Puglia, has seen a renaissance in recent years with much inward investment, such as that of oenologist, Donato d'Angelo at his eponymous winery at Rionero in Vulture.

Our top-10 best-value wines:

Puglia (Andria) Rivera, 'Il Falcone', Nero di Troia/Montepulciano, 03. Intense garnet red, full-bodied, dry, robust, rich flavour.

Puglia (Bari) Tormaresca, 'Masseria Maime', Negroamaro, 04. Coffee, oak and black berry fruits.

Puglia (Cellino San Marco) Cantina Due Palme, 'Brindisi Rosso', Negroamaro/Malvasia, 02. Good-value red from well-run Cantina Sociale.

Puglia (Guagnano) Cantele, 'Amativo', Primitivo/Negroamaro, 04. Forest fruits, figs, tar and oak with long finish.

Puglia (Guagnano) Cosimo Taurino, 'Notarpanaro' Negroamaro/Malvasia, 02. Dry, slightly bitter, rich finish. Great value from producer of more expensive 'Patriglione'.

Puglia (San Donaci) Candido, 'Capello di Prete', Negroamaro, 01. Good quality and value.

Puglia (Guagnano) Cantele, 'Teresa Manara', Chardonnay, 05. Fine Puglia white, slightly oaked with tropical fruits.

Basilicata (Rionero in Vulture) D'Angelo, 'Vigna Caselle Riserva', Aglianico, 01. Classic, cherry and liquorice on the nose. Elegant velvety richness.

Basilicata (Rionero in Vulture) 'Terra dei Re', Divinus, Aglianico, 03. New vineyard producing fine Aglianico, especially this deep rich beauty.

Basilicata (Barile) Tenute Le Querce, 'Rosso di Costanza', Aglianico, 04. Lively, balanced wine with dense complex fruit.

Buy them at Il Cucco (see p127), a great *enoteca* – and super restaurant – for wines from Puglia, Basilicata and other Italian regions.

FOOD FESTIVALS

Food is celebrated with as much fervour as religion, with local festivals marking the seasons and harvests. In summer there are nightly events – called *sagre* – exalting a particular local foodstuff, from snails to sausages. They're all lively and fun, with foodstalls, drinks, complex ticket-coupon arrangements and live music. To find out what's on in Salento, get a copy of *QuiSalento* (€2.50; www.quisalento.it); elsewhere, you could ask at the tourist office.

EAT YOUR WORDS

Get behind the cuisine scene by getting to know the language. For more on pronunciation guidelines, see p51.

Useful Phrases

I'd like to reserve a table.

Vorrei riservare un tavolo.

vo-*ray* ree-ser-*va*-re oon *ta*-vo-lo

I'd like the menu, please.

Vorrei il menù, per favore.

vo-*ray* eel me-*noo* per fa-*vo*-re

Do you have a menu in English?

Avete un menù (scritto) in inglese?

a-*ve*-te oon me-*noo* (*skree*-to) een een-*gle*-ze

What would you recommend?

Cosa mi consiglia?

ko-za mee kon-*see*-lya

I'd like a house/local speciality.

Vorrei una specialità di casa/
di questa regione.

vo-*ray* *oo*-na spe-cha-lee-*ta* dee *ka*-za/
dee *kwe*-sta re-*jo*-ne

Please bring the bill.

Mi porta il conto, per favore?

mee *por*-ta eel *kon*-to per fa-*vo*-re

Is service included in the bill?

Il servizio è compreso nel conto?

eel ser-*vee*-tsyo e kom-*pre*-zo nel *kon*-to

I'm a vegetarian.

Sono vegetariano/a. (m/f)

so-no ve-je-ta-*rya*-no/a

I'm a vegan.

Sono vegetaliano/a. (m/f)

so-no ve-je-ta-*lya*-no/a

Food Glossary

acciughe	a-*choo*-ge	anchovies
agnello	a-*nye*-lo	lamb
calamari	ka-la-*ma*-ree	squid
capretto	ka-*pre*-to	kid (goat)
carciofi	kar-*cho*-fee	artichokes
cavolo	*ka*-vo-lo	cabbage
ciambotta/	cham-*bo*-ta/	a 'mixture' – sometimes fish and
ciambotella	cham-bo-*te*-la	vegetable mix, some just vegetables
ciliegia	chee-lee-*e*-ja	cherry
coniglio	ko-*nee*-lyo	rabbit
cozze	*ko*-tse	mussels
fagiolini	fa-jo-*lee*-nee	green beans
finocchio	fee-*no*-kyo	fennel
merluzzo	mer-*loo*-tso	cod
ostriche	*os*-tree-ke	oysters
peperoncino	pe-pe-ron-*chee*-no	chilli
peperoni	pe-pe-*ro*-nee	capsicum; peppers
pera	*pe*-ra	pear
pesca	*pe*-ska	peach
pesce spada	*pe*-she *spa*-da	swordfish
piselli	pee-*ze*-lee	peas
polpi	*pol*-pee	octopus
sarde	*sar*-de	sardines
seppia	*se*-pya	cuttlefish
sgombro	*sgom*-bro	mackerel
tonno	*to*-no	tuna
uovo/uova	*wo*-vo/*wo*-va	egg/eggs
uva	*oo*-va	grapes

Environment

If Italy is a boot, Basilicata forms the high-arched instep, a chaotic landscape of concertinaed mountain ridges and steep forested valleys, while Puglia thrusts its spur and heel firmly into the Adriatic and Ionian seas. At 19,348 sq km, Puglia is double the size of Basilicata and has an 800km coastline (10% of the entire Italian coastline). The terrain in this part of southern Italy's *mezzogiorno* (land of the midday sun) varies considerably; the tail of Italy's 1350km backbone (the rugged Apennine mountain range) cuts through densely wooded forests, cultivated pastures, and dry sunbaked plains stretching to sandy coves and craggy coastal cliffs.

THE LAND

Aside from a narrow coastal plain along the Ionian Sea's Gulf of Taranto, Basilicata is completely mountainous. The peaks aren't particularly high, the highest is Monte Pollino (2267m) in the Parco Nazionale del Pollino. For the most part the mountains are barren and flinty, with small localised pockets of dense forest in the national parks and around Monte Vulture's extinct volcano. South of Potenza, wind and water has shaped weird karstic formations and carved deep gorges in the sandstone rock of the Apennines. In this surreal landscape, remote stone villages cling precariously to the high needles of the Lucanian Dolomites, a perfect setting for folkloric legends of shape-shifters and werewolves.

Twenty-one of Puglia's and Basilicata's beaches are currently listed as 'blue flag' beaches – a criteria based on environmental management and water quality. Visit www.blueflag.org.

Geologically, the rocks that make up Italy's mountain ranges began life more than 100 million years ago on the Tethys sea bed. About 40 million years ago when the African continental plate butted up against the European land mass, the Apennine and Alpine mountain chains were born. A fault line corresponding to this collision runs through the length of the Apennines from Sicily to Genoa and has resulted in some massive earthquakes in Basilicata, including the 1980 quake that rocked Potenza.

Along the Ionian coast improved drainage and irrigation has converted the once malarial marshlands into fertile vineyards and citrus and olive groves. In the hinterland, white limestone hills form the arid and lunar landscape of the Murge. Water has eroded sinkholes and caves in the limestone bedrock, some of which (like the famous *sassi* of Matera) have been inhabited since prehistoric times. In Puglia, the Murge tableland covers a central, roughly rectangular area 50km wide and 150km long. At times it's a harsh, rocky landscape where olive and almond trees fight for a hold in the thin loamy soil, at others a rolling, grassy and picturesque plain, the undulating hills of the Murge gently slope down into the vineyards and farm lands of the Itria Valley.

Unlike Basilicata, Puglia's landscape is virtually flat. The highest peak is Monte Cornacchia (1161m), which lies in the narrow stretch of the Daunia mountains, part of the Apennine chain on the northwestern border with Campania. Except for the Gargano Promontory, the provinces of Puglia blend into each other with very little contrast. The tablelands of the Salentine are intensely cultivated as are those of the once malaria-infested marshlands of the Tavoliere (Foggia's large chequerboard plain of golden wheatfields). The Gargano Promontory, a mountainous and heavily forested spur jutting bluntly into the Adriatic, hogs most of Puglia's meagre 5% of forested land. White limestone cliffs, sandy beaches and small seaside villages surround the densely wooded interior of Aleppo pines, oak and beech trees. The entire promontory is a national park, one of the most beautiful in Italy.

Many of Italy's popular northern beach resorts strain under the volume of the holidaying summer hordes and don't always reflect the sparkling blue seas of the tourist brochures, but the clean and unpolluted clear waters of Puglia's and Basilicata's beaches deserve a gold star. The Adriatic coast is a sun-drenched fringe of hidden coves, long sandy beaches and craggy cliffs nowhere more dramatic than in the Gargano Promontory.

Puglia's Mediterranean climate of mild, wet winters and hot, dry summers extends to the long sandy beaches and low-lying hinterland of Basilicata's Ionian coast whereas deep in the Apennines, in the heart of the Parco Nazionale del Pollino, the peaks are often covered in winter snows.

WILDLIFE

Basilicata's inhospitable interior and scattered human population (only 61 inhabitants per sq km in the Lucanian Dolomites) has proven to be a protective blessing to its wildlife, some of which is rare and unique to this forgotten corner of Italy. The fertile land around the Monticchio Lakes to the north and the pockets of national parks and forests (only 8% of Basilicata is forested) are packed with thick timber wood trees including oak, beech, pine and maple.

Since Roman times, deforestation for timber and farming has left its mark on southern Italy but environmental awareness, reforestation and appropriate land management has remedied some of the damage. Not all human intervention is a bad thing – notable man-made improvements include damming the Bradano River near Matera to form the San Giuliano Lake, a protected area for wildlife and birds; draining silted river mouths in both Basilicata and Puglia, robbing malarial mosquitoes of their swampy breeding grounds thus opening the way for arable farming; and the salt pans of Margherita di Savoia, which attract water and feed up to 50,000 birds each year.

In *Seasons in Basilicata*, David Yeadon evocatively describes the bizarre lunar landscape of the calanchi, eerie cliff-top villages in the Lucanian Dolomites, and the *sassi*, Matera's neolithic cave-dwellings.

Animals

Basilicata was once known as Lucania (from the Latin *lupus* for wolf) and although werewolves belong to the myths of Basilicata's dark side, the endangered Apennine wolf is alive and making a comeback. In numbers once large enough to cause havoc to sheep and goat farmers along the entire length of Italy's backbone, the wolf was hunted almost to extinction, only managing a claw-hold on survival in Basilicata's rugged interior. Now, Italy's wolf population has reached 500.

La caccia (the hunt) fed the table for many years but in the past decades environmental protection laws have seen a healthy growth in the number of wild cat, marten, deer, fox and boar. The WWF-protected Italian roe-deer (*Capreolus capreolus italicus*) inhabits Basilicata's forests as well as Puglia's Parco Nazionale del Gargano while the rare otter *Lutra lutra* lives in the Agri and Noce river streams.

The Gargano Promontory's high rainfall, rounded mountains and thick forests are filled with more different species of animals and birds than are found throughout the rest of Puglia. As well as the usual suspects – boar, marten, wild cat and fox – the Gargano is home to 170 of Italy's 237 different species of birds. A convenient green perch on the European–African migratory route, the national park's two large lakes (Lago Varano and Lago Lesina) and the Margherita di Savoia salt pans attract large sea birds including osprey, heron and flamingo as well as duck, wader, cormorant and crane. Of particular importance is the endangered slender-billed curlew.

The predominant cattle breed in Basilicata is the Podolico, a hardy breed able to survive difficult environmental conditions. From its milk comes the famous *caciocavallo* cheese – best eaten after a three-year maturation.

Plants

For a modern-day reminder of southern Italy's once close geographical attachment to the Balkans, look no further than the rare and unusual *pino loricato* (the Bosnian Pine). Only found in the Balkans and the Parco Nazionale del Pollino the trees form weird arboreal sculptures on the windswept mountain peaks. They are hundreds of years old as are the Aleppo pines in the Foresta Umbra of the Parco Nazionale del Gargano.

Another unusual geographical quirk, the *Fraxinus oxycarpa*, an ancient plant of Balkan-Asian origin grows in an isolated pocket in the north of Basilicata. The tree attracts a nocturnal moth, *Bramea europea*, which is usually only found in Asia. In 1971 the Grotticelle Nature Reserve was created to protect the habitat of this rare night butterfly.

Orchidee spontanee nel Parco Nazionale del Gargano by Angela Rossini and Giovanni Quitadamo describes the amazing orchid species found in the Gargano (85 of Italy's 90 different species). Find out more at www .orchideedelgargano.it

Turkey oaks, beech, maple and fir trees are common at higher altitudes but at slightly lower altitudes the mountain slopes are populated with hornbeams, downy oaks, walnut and ash trees. In spring, orchid-hunters flock to the Gargano, home to 70% of Europe's orchid species.

Along the flat coastal lands is the typical Mediterranean *maquis* – low brush of juniper, lavender, myrtle, strawberry and wild herbs including thyme, mint, sage and oregano. In southern Puglia giant fleshy-leafed prickly pear *(Opuntia)* and native carobs fill gaps between vineyards and olive groves. Olives and grapes dominate the landscape of the *mezzogiorno* and it's not surprising that some of the country's best olive oil comes from Puglia or that Basilicata's Aglianico del Vulture wines are becoming increasingly popular. Of Puglia's 50 million olive trees the secular olive trees *(Olivi secolari)* in the heart of the Murgia between Ostuni and Lecce are some of the oldest. A recent law has put an end to the commercial sale of centuries old trees, some of which fetched prices up to €12,000 to adorn northern Italian gardens.

NATIONAL PARKS

Basilicata boasts two national parks, two regional parks and a number of nature reserves. The Parco Nazionale del Pollino (p192) is Italy's largest national park, covering an area of 1960 sq km divided equally between Basilicata and Calabria. The terrain is wild and isolated, home to the rare Bosnian Pine, Monte Pollino (2267m) and tiny Albanian villages that are linguistic islands in the mountains.

For information on the Parco Nazionale del Pollino visit www .viaggiarenelpollino .com. Giuseppe Cosenza is an official guide of the park and his website has loads of information on the nature, history and culture of the Pollino.

The Parco Nazionale della Val d'Agri-Lagonegrese runs south of Potenza along the Lucanian Dolomites to the Parco Nazionale del Pollino. Its rugged stream system makes this a verdant area and a bird-watcher's dream.

The centrally located Parco Naturale Gallipoli Cognata e Piccole Dolomiti Lucane (p186), straddling the provinces of Potenza and Matera, highlights the contrast between the heavily forested Gallipoli Cognata Forest and the rocky spires and sandstone peaks of the Lucanian Apennines, which dominate the Basento Valley.

Bird-watchers might want to check the marshy reserves in the hinterland of the Ionian coast – the Bosco di Policoro and Lake San Giuliano.

Of Puglia's two national parks, the Parco Nazionale del Gargano (p86) is a geographic idiosyncrasy. The park covers the entire Gargano Promontory and the marine reserve of the Isole Tremiti. The biodiversity of the region reflects a varied landscape of sandy beaches, low-lying marshlands, dramatic rocky coastlines and a heavily forested mountainous interior. At its heart, the Foresta Umbra (Forest of Shadows) is the last remnant of the ancient forest that once covered the entire promontory. The Parco Nazionale del Gargano includes the delicate wet areas (the Zone Umide) of the Fratterolo and the Daunia Resi marshlands and the Lesina and Varano lagoons.

Covering a roughly rectangular 900 sq km area in the Murge west of Bari, the Parco Nazionale dell'Alta Murgia was formed in 2004. More than half the park is hard, rocky ground, the rest is cultivated farmland and hard wood forest.

RESPONSIBLE TRAVEL

Leave nothing but footprints. Be an eco-friendly traveller:

- Fly less, go overland wherever possible.
- If you fly, compensate for carbon emissions by donating to a carbon offset scheme.
- Minimise environmental damage, hike on marked trails.
- Pack it in, pack it out. Never leave rubbish in the woods.
- Wildflowers are more beautiful alive. Don't pick them.
- Opt for hiking or cycling trips over driving holidays.
- Save energy: turn off the air-conditioning and lights when you leave a hotel room.
- Stay in eco-friendly and locally run accommodation.
- Buy local produce.

Marine Parks

Puglia's pull is a tie between its excellent pasta and its pristine coastline. Relatively uncrowded, except at the height of summer, the long sandy beaches and intimate coves are perfect for swimming, sailing and a range of water sports – something holidaying Italians have somehow managed to keep to themselves. But with a soaring profile on the international beach-scene the risk of tarnishing its beautiful natural resource has rung an environmental alarm bell. Three small marine reserves along Puglia's 800km coastline might not seem like much of a response, but it's a start.

Riserva Marina della Isole Tremiti (p102) is a marine reserve covering the three islands clustered together 22km off the Gargano Promontory. Part of the Parco Nazionale del Gargano the islands have distinctly different characters. San Domino is the largest of the islands, San Nicola has the only sandy beach and San Capraia is merely a rocky outcrop.

The Riserva Marina di Torre Guaceto (p135) is a 12 sq km rectangle along the Salento coast south of Brindisi. Its name is derived from the Arabic *gaw-sit* meaning freshwater place. The reserve covers an umbrella area of sand dunes, marshland and *maquis* and although it is fed by freshwater springs the water along the short 6km stretch of coastline is decidedly brackish.

The smallest reserve, Riserva Marina Porto Cesareo (p155), near the town of Porto Cesareo (p155), is considered to be one of the most beautiful spots on the western Salentine coast. In its waters lives the rare and protected gastropod, *Mitra zonata*, prized worldwide by shell collectors. Also on the Ionian coast is the Parco Regionale Porto Selvaggio (p156), established in 1980. The 516 hectare reserve has dense forests of Aleppo pines planted in the 1950s, as well as eucalypts and *maquis*, and the rocky coastline is dotted with sea caves.

When planning a trip to the Gargano Promontory make sure to visit www .parks.it/parco.nazionale .gargano, the official site of the Parco Nazionale del Gargano.

ENVIRONMENTAL ISSUES

Southern Italy's predisposition to natural disasters such as earthquakes and landslides is not the region's only environmental concern. The Italian government's record on ecological and environmental issues has been consistently inconsistent. Currently in the spotlight is the Enel power station in Brindisi, ranked by WWF as Europe's ninth biggest producer of carbon dioxide in 2006. In fact, Puglia has the dubious honour of housing the top three carbon dioxide producing sites in Italy. Carbon dioxide is a prime culprit in global warming, and the toxic industrial waste product, dioxin, is a harmful carcinogenic chemical and 30% of Italy's dioxin is produced in

OUTDOOR ACTIVITIES

Except for the bitter winters in the Parco Nazionale del Pollino, southern Italy has a Mediterranean climate of hot, dry summers and mild, wet winters. Take this into account when planning your trip.

What to do	Where to do it	Experience	When to do it	Find out more
hiking	Adriatic coast	coastal views; Porto Badisco; sea caves; dolmens and menhirs; medieval watchtowers; *maquis*-covered hillsides; pagliare (shepherds' huts); translucent sea	spring, autumn, winter	p161
	Gallipoli Cognata Forest	Oak forest; springs; picnics	year-round	p186
	Lucanian Dolomites	cliff-hugging villages; Tyrolean traverse across the Caperrino gorge; raptors; star-gazing	spring, summer, autumn	p186
	Matera Gravina	Rupestrian cave-churches; neolithic sites; *maquis*; shepherds retreats	year-round	p176
	Murgia	shepherds' tracks through vineyards; almond groves; *trulli*; 300-year-old olive trees; farmers markets; picnics	year-round (although can be hot in summer)	p167
	Parco Nazionale del Gargano	Aleppo pines; roe deer; rare orchids; unique flora and fauna; Monte Calvo; sandy beaches; pilgrimage sites	year-round (spring for orchids)	p86
	Parco Nazionale del Pollino	1000-year-old Bosnian pines; Apennine wolf; roe deer; otter	late spring, summer, early autumn (cross-country skiing in winter)	p192
	Parco Regionale delle Gravine dell'Arco Jonico	Rupestrian cave-churches; ravine trekking; bird-watching; shepherds' retreats; rural restaurants	year-round	p116
	Tyrrhenian coast	dramatic cliffs; secluded coves; *caciocavello* cheese	year-round	p186
	Vulture area	Brahmea moth; brigands pathways; Aglianico wines; olive oil; castles	year-round	p182
water sports	Castro	boat trips to grottoes; scuba-diving	summer	p161
	Isole Tremiti	scuba-diving	spring and summer	p102
	Parco Nazionale del Gargano	windsurfing; kayaking; marine caves; ferry trip to Isole Tremiti or Croatia	spring and summer	p86
	Parco Nazionale del Pollino	white-water rafting	late spring and summer	p192
	Parco Regionale Porto Selvaggio	protected rocky coastline; scuba-diving; sea caves; kite-surfing	February to October	p156
	Porto Cesareo	boat trips; scuba-diving	spring and summer	p155
	Santa Maria di Leuca	boat trips to grottoes; scuba diving; sailing	May to September	p160
	Tyrrhenian coast	deep-sea fishing; kayaking; sea caves	late spring, summer and autumn	p186

What to do	Where to do it	Experience	When to do it	Find out more
cycling	Adriatic coast	spectacular coastal views; challenging grades between Santa Maria di Leuca and Castro; coastal towns; Otranto; Grecia Salentina villages; inland roads through fields of wild flowers; Polignano a Mare; ruins of Egnazia	spring and autumn	p161
	Appennino Lucano	tight hairpin bends and steep hills; sandstone spires; eerie mountain villages; *calanchi*; 'Il Maggio' festival; Aliano	spring, summer, autumn	p184
	Daunia Pre-Apennines	medieval hill towns; castles; rolling hills; neolithic sites	year-round	p108
	Ionian coast	easy riding; cultivated flat lands; Puglia's best sandy beaches; ancient Greek ruins; the ghost-town of Craco; Porto Selvaggio marine park; Gallipoli	year-round (but summer can get hot)	p196
	Murgia	baroque market towns; off-road cycling along farm tracks; long lunches at *masserias*; Via Verde routes around Ostuni	year-round	p167
	Parco Nazionale del Gargano	Aleppo pines; *agriturismi*; sandy beaches; olive groves; *trabucci*; cultural tours	year-round	p86
	Parco Nazionale del Pollino	Bosnian Pine; Albanian villages; 'festa dell'abete'; off-road cycling; major ups and downs; red eggplant feast	late spring, summer, autumn	p192
	Parco Regionale delle Gravine dell'Arco Jonico	Rupestrian cave-churches; off-roading down Laterza ravine; bird-watching	year-round	p116
	Riserva di Torre Guaceto	cycle tracks through marshy lagoons; haven for migrating birds and turtles; zone of sandy dunes	year-round	p135
	Tyrrhenian coast	Redentore; dramatic coastline; Grotta delle Meraviglia; ocean swims	year-round	p186
	Vulture area	Brigands pathways; medieval hilltowns; castles; Lagopesole; vineyards; Aglianico wines; ride across undulating hills to Venosa (Roman ruins)	year-round	p182
horse riding	Murgia	hacks through olive groves and vineyards; *masseria* lunches; picnics and riding on the beach	year-round	p119
	Parco Nazionale del Gargano	sandy beaches; forest trails; Aleppo pines; Lesina lakes	year-round	p86
	Parco Nazionale del Pollino	pines and forest; rivers; picnic lunch; Serra dei Crispi	late spring, summer, autumn	p192
	Terra d'Otranto	Capo d'Otranto; swimming at Porto Badisco; Cave di Bauxite; coastal views; Valle d'Idro	late spring, summer, autumn	p161
	Vulture area	castles and medieval hilltop towns	year-round	p182

Taranto. But it's not all gloom. As a signatory to the Kyoto Protocol, Italy has agreed to reduce greenhouse gas emissions by 6.5% below 1990 levels by the 2008–12 timeframe. And at the 2007 G8 summit in Heiligendamm, Italy (along with other country members) agreed to consider at least halving global CO_2 emissions by 2050. The regional Ministry for the Environment in Puglia is pushing for a 25% reduction in electricity generation at two power stations in Brindisi over the next 10 years to meet the Kyoto Protocol guidelines, and is fighting Britain's BG Group plan to build a liquefied natural gas (LNG) terminal in the port of Brindisi.

Legambiente is an Italian nonprofit association geared towards safeguarding the environment, promoting sustainable living, and environmentally-sound management and use of resources. Find out more at www.legambiente .com.

Puglia produces more electricity than it needs and this has caused mixed reactions to the environmentally friendly wind farms around the small hilltop town of Alberona in the northern province of Foggia. Sixty windmills were erected in the late 1990s and although a visual eyesore they are an effective and clean energy source. However, the government has no plans to build further wind farms until the region creates a better general energy program to 'avoid uncontrolled wild wind farming'. This hasn't stopped the proposed installation of an off-shore wind farm 20km off the coast of Tricase from going ahead. It should be operational by mid-2007 and will be the first off-shore deepwater wind energy farm in the world – with an installed capacity of 90 MW, enough to cover 75,000 households.

Along the coastline, southern Italy has managed to escape the degradation, pollution and over-development affecting the northern beaches, but environmental concerns are mounting. The Gargano Promontory's spectacular marine caves are a major tourist attraction, but boat traffic is steadily damaging the fragile limestone grottoes. Numerous boats enter the caves each summer creating air pollution and wave erosion, prompting discussions on further speed restrictions and tour operations. Until now the waters of the southern coastline have remained relatively clean, but with an increasing tourist tide the potential for environmental pollution and over-development are real concerns.

Bari & the Terra di Bari

Bari may still be considered the Bronx of southern Italy, but that old reputation is wearing thin these days. Michele Emiliano, the city's tough anti-mafia mayor is convinced that Bari is the next Barcelona: a city on the sea attracting big business and tourists alike. Okay, so it is a stretch of the imagination to see Bari as the new Barcelona, but you can't deny that things are looking up these days and Bari airport is certainly seeing lots of traffic with all those Ryanair and Easyjet flights.

Really, Emiliano is right, Bari should be much better than it is. This region has the richest architectural heritage on the Adriatic after Venice and the magnificent Terra di Bari cathedrals embody its impressive and lengthy history. Pilgrims and princes have always been partial to it, and in the past it was the centre of an extensive network of *castra* (camps) and castles that rise along the coast like a massive curtain wall.

More than that, Bari and its *terra* are utterly authentic, and the rural and religious traditions of the region have deep, deep roots. Just spend a day in Bari during the Festa di San Nicola or visit Italy's oldest country fair in Bitonto and you'll experience a sense of community and an almost pagan sense of celebration that seems to belong to another era. It may not be Barcelona, but Italian enthusiasts should watch this space.

HIGHLIGHTS

- ▪ Join the crush at the **Festa di San Nicola** (p66) and pay your respects to the relics of Father Christmas in the **Basilica di San Nicola** (p64) in Bari

- ▪ Acquaint yourself with the Greek myths by studying a few of the 2000 artefacts housed in the **Museo Nazionale Jatta** (p72) in Ruvo di Puglia

- ▪ Puzzle over the medieval mysteries of the **Castel del Monte** (p80), Puglia's most famous and frenzied tourist sight

- ▪ Tour the finest examples of Puglian Romanesque architecture in **Bitonto** (p71), **Ruvo di Puglia** (p72), **Trani** (p73) and **Barletta** (p76)

- ▪ Ride bikes across acres of olive grove or make pizza in a wood-fired oven at the eco-friendly **Biomasseria Lama di Luna** (p82)

- ▪ Join the weekend walkabout in unspoilt **Minervino Murge** (p81) and then sit down to a long and lazy lunch at **Masseria Barbera** (p81)

BARI

pop 328,500

Anyone wanting proof that Bari is no longer the region's capital of crime and car theft should sample a beer in the renovated old town centre, where restaurants, shops and cafés now abound. The city council has ambitious plans for the place and, since the civic renaissance of the late 1990s, the old town has gone from looking like a ghetto to a modestly glamorous *citta vecchia*.

But despite the changes, Bari's still a far cry from a tourist-friendly city. It may be Puglia's capital, the market of the south and one of the busiest ports on the Adriatic, but most people take one look at its concrete carapace and high hotel rates and head straight for the ferry or the station. Still, the drab exterior hides a prosperous and lively university town, second only to Naples in the south. You won't be disappointed by the fine restaurants or the boisterous Barese who certainly know how to have a good time.

HISTORY

Bari is an old city, dating back 3500 years before the Bronze Age. It started life as an Illyrian village; a small collection of farmhouses on a limestone promontory which is now the Bari Vecchia.

Looking eastwards it wasn't long before Bari was trading with the Greeks. But it was under the Romans that it really started to develop as a city, situated as it was in a strategic position on the Via Traiana. In AD 465 it was elevated to an episcopal see and in the early Middle Ages it became the seat of the 'catapan' or Byzantine governor.

With the advent of the Normans, Bari was to see a huge cultural shift from the Byzantine East to the Latin West. In 1025 the city became attached to the see of Rome, and a few decades later it fell to Robert Guiscard, a Lombard mercenary and strong-arm of the Pope. In short succession the relics of San Nicola of Myra landed in the city making it the focus of Bari's first pilgrim tourists, and a few years later, in 1095, Peter the Hermit preached the first crusade here.

Assuming the cloak of Holy Roman Emperor and defender of the Faith, Frederick II of Swabia elevated Bari to a regional capital and granted it many privileges, which allowed the city to expand and flourish. But the death of Frederick in 1250 and the fall from power of the Swabians ushered in a centuries-long period of decline. When Isabella of Aragon set up her court here in the 15th century there was a brief period of respite, but on the death of her daughter, Bona Sforza, in 1558, Bari became part of the Kingdom of Naples and sank into decline. Disinterested government and successive bouts of famine and civil unrest brought the city to its knees. By 1657, after a devastating plague, the population had shrunk to just 3000 inhabitants.

When the Bourbons came to power in the 18th century Bari was a shadow of its former self. The city was suffocating within its own walls, so an ambitious plan of expansion was conceived. Under the guidance of Joachim Murat (Napoleon's brother-in-law), Bari once again became the most important port in the region.

Today Bari sits at the centre of a metropolitan area that encompasses some 1.5 million people, taking in 44 municipalities. Despite the vagaries of WWII, it has retained its pre-eminent position as southern Italy's commercial heart. In 1930 the Fiera del Levante was inaugurated, confirming Bari as the main market of the south, and even now its September trade fair is second only to Milan's. To all intents and purposes it is a thriving urban area. But even with a balanced economy the city has its share of problems. Cigarette smuggling has now given way to drug trafficking, and illegal immigration continues to cause problems.

ORIENTATION

Orient yourself from Piazza Aldo Moro in front of the main train station. From the square, it's about 1km northwards to Bari Vecchia, the old town where all the major monuments are located. The main thoroughfare running north–south is Corso Cavour, which is intersected by Corso Vittorio Emanuele II, the east–west axis that separates the old and new town, and which heads northwest out of town towards the ferry terminal and the Fiera di Levante.

INFORMATION
Bookshops

Libreria Feltrinelli (☎ 080 520 75 11; Via Melo 119; ☯ noon-9.30pm Mon, 10am-9.30pm Tue-Fri, 10am-10pm Sat, 10am-1.30pm & 5-9.30pm Sun) Bari's largest

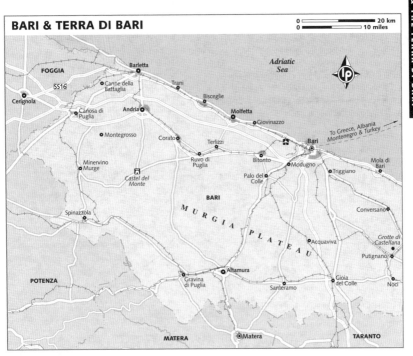

BARI & TERRA DI BARI

0 ————— 20 km
0 ————— 10 miles

bookshop has a fairly good selection of maps and tourist literature on the city.

Libreria Laterza (☎ 080 521 17 14; www.librerialaterza.it; Via Sparano da Bari 136; ⏰ 9am-8.30pm Mon-Sat) A designer bookstore with plate glass windows and bookshelves arranged like an art gallery. It also hosts literary talks.

Libreria Mondadori (☎ 080 521 83 43; Via Sparano da Bari 158; ⏰ 9am-8.30pm Mon-Sat) A convenient bookstore catering mainly to the university. It also stocks some maps and tourist literature if you can't find everything you need in Feltrinelli.

Emergency
Ambulance (☎ 118)
Police station (☎ 080 529 11 11; Via Gioacchino Murat 4) The main police station.

Internet Access
Netcafé (☎ 080 524 17 56; Via Andrea da Bari 11; per hr €4; ⏰ 9am-10pm Mon-Fri, 9am-1.30pm Sat) An efficient internet café with eight fast computers.

Medical Services
Pharmacies operate a rotation system for night services. This changes every six months so check with the tourist office or the nearest large pharmacy for out-of-hours services.

Guardia Medica (☎ 080 543 70 04) A 24-hour emergency call-out service.

Hospital (☎ 080 547 31 11; Piazza Giulio Cesare)

Money
There are plenty of banks in town, including one with an ATM at the station. There's a currency-exchange booth at the ferry terminal, but exchange rates are better in town.

Post
Post office (Piazza Cesare Battisti; ⏰ 8am-6.30pm Mon-Fri, 8am-12.30pm Sat)

Tourist Information
Regional Tourist Office (☎ 080 524 23 61; www .pugliaturismo.com; 1st fl, Piazza Aldo Moro 33a; ⏰ 8am-2pm Mon-Fri, 3-6pm Tue & Thu) The regional tourist board.
Tourist Info Point (☎ 080 990 93 41; Piazza Aldo Moro; ⏰ 10am-1pm & 3-6pm Mon-Sat, 10am-1pm Sun) Service here is erratic and depends on the person behind the desk. They hold all the necessary information on transport and sights, so if at first you don't succeed, persevere!

BARI & THE TERRA DI BARI

BARI

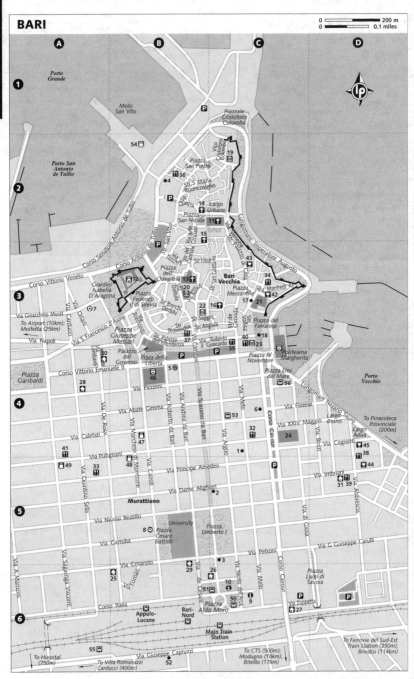

Porto Grande

Molo San Vito

Porto San Antonio de Tullio

54

Piazzale Cristoforo Colombo

19

36

4

St S Maria Buoncosiglio

14 Largo Urbano

Piazza San Pietro

11 Piazza San Nicola

Lungomare Imperatore Augusto

15

Corso Senatore Antonio de Tullio

Corso Antonio de Tullio

Corso Vittorio Veneto

Via Gioacchino Murat

Giardini Isabella D'Aragona

12

7

Piazza Federico il di Svevia

Piazza dell'Odegitria 13 20

43

34

42

Bari Vecchia

Piazza Mercantile

17 21

22 16 23

Via S Francesco d'Assisi

Via Napoli

Piazza Giuseppe Massari

Str Stravecchia

Str Angiola

Str Saggese

Piazza del Ferrarese

37 40 18

35

30

Palazzo del Governo

Piazza della Liberta

5 46

Piazza IV Novembre

Politeama Margherita

Piazza Garibaldi

Corso Vittorio Emanuele II

28

Piazza Eroi del Mare

56

Porto Vecchio

Via Piccinni

Via Abate Gimma

53

6

Via Fiorese

Largo Bruno

Via Calefati

32

Via XXIV Maggio

24

Largo Adua

45

41

47

1

38

49

33

48

Via Principe Amedeo

31 39

44

Via Imbriani

2

Murattiano

Via Dante Alighieri

Via Nicolai Beatillo

8 Piazza Cesare Battisti

University

Piazza Umberto I

Via Garruba

Via Petroni

Via G Giuseppe Carulli

29

3

26

Piazza Luigi di Savoia

25

10

50

9

27

Corso Italia

Appulo-Lucane

Bari-Nord

51

Piazza Aldo Moro

Via Zuppetta

55

Main Train Station

52

To Hospital (750m)

To Villa Romanazzi Carducci (400m)

Via Giuseppe Capruzzi

To CTS (500m); Modugno (10km); Bitetto (17km)

To Ferrovie del Sud-Est Train Station (250m); Brindisi (114km)

0 ——— 200 m
0 ——— 0.1 miles

Travel Agencies

Bari is littered with travel agents where you can book both onward train and ferry tickets.

CTS (☎ 080 555 99 16; Via G Postiglione 27) Good for student travel and discount flights.

Morfimare Travel Agency (☎ 080 578 98 11; Corso Antonio de Tullio 36-40) Represents American Express.

DANGERS & ANNOYANCES

Bari has long had a reputation for crime, a situation not helped by some of the city's more unsavoury drug trafficking and illegal immigration problems. However, in recent years the city council has done much to clean up the old town and there is a high police presence, especially at night. Petty crime and car theft can still be a problem, so take all the usual commonsense precautions: park in one of the local garages, don't leave anything valuable on display and avoid the dark streets of Bari Vecchia at night.

SIGHTS

Bari is a large but manageable city with three distinct parts. To the north, Bari Vecchia, the old town, occupies a tiny peninsula between the harbours of Porto Vecchio and Porto Grande. To the south extends the Murattiano district, the heart of the modern city, laid out on a neat grid system with a fine *lungomare* (promenade) and even finer shopping streets like Via Sparano da Bari (pedestrianised). Across the tracks (literally the railway tracks), and beyond the tourist radar, extends the chaotic development of the modern suburbs which, spreads in a vast semicircle around the centre and now incorporates the small towns of Modugno and Bitetto.

Bari Vecchia

Covering the narrow peninsula adjacent to the port, Bari Vecchia is an atmospheric labyrinth of tight, uneven alleyways. Squeezed into this small area are 40 churches and more than 120 shrines – if you can find them. Bari Vecchia's town plan is famous throughout Italy for its mazelike effect.

PIAZZA DEL FERRARESE & PIAZZA MERCANTILE

Piazza del Ferrarese, named after the Ferrara merchant Stefano Fabri who lived here in the 17th century, provides an elegant entrance to the old town. On your left are the rounded arches of **Sala Murat** (☒ 10am-1pm & 6-9pm Tue-Sat), which holds minor contemporary art exhibitions, and on your right is the old indoor **fish market** (☒ 6am-noon).

The piazza is lined with bars and cafés, an old section of roman road roped off in the middle. To the north it merges imperceptibly into another set-piece piazza, Piazza Mercantile, historically the political centre of the old town and an important public space. It contains the **Palazzo del Sedile** (much altered over time), the medieval headquarters of Bari's Council of Nobles, and the **Colonna della Giustizia** (Column of Justice), to which debtors were tied and lashed.

PALAZZO SIMI

Since 1999 Bari's Archaeological Operations Centre has been housed in **Palazzo Simi** (☎ 080 527 54 51; Strada Lamberti; admission free; ⏰ 9.30am-1pm & 4-6.30pm Mon-Fri), and until the new archaeological museum opens its doors in Santa Scolastica (see opposite), the small archaeological exhibition here provides a reasonable idea of the city's history. Arranged over the ground floor it takes you through the early days of the city's foundation, from a model of what the initial settlement would have looked like, to fragments of prehistoric pottery and some rare Italo-Mycenaean ceramics, which show the extent of Bari's trading network in the eastern Mediterranean.

The palace itself is something of museum piece given there are remains of a 9th- to 10th-century church you can visit in the basement. The three apses are clearly distinguished, as are the remains of the altar and some fragments of fresco depicting the Fathers of the Church.

CATTEDRALE SAN SABINO

Just north of Strada Lamberti the tortuous alleyways open out into Largo San Sabino where you're faced with the huge construct that makes up the Museo Diocesano and the **Cattedrale San Sabino** (Piazza dell'Odegitria; admission free; ⏰ 9am-noon & 4-7pm).

Most people assume that the Basilica of San Nicola is Bari's main cathedral but this pearly white church dedicated to Bishop San Sabino is really the main seat of worship. Like the Basilica, the cathedral was begun during the Byzantine era (1034), but when the city revolted against William II of Sicily, he razed it to the ground. It was rebuilt between 1170 and 1178 in a simple Romanesque style with a wide nave and shallow transepts and a 35m-high cupola. Typical of the style, deep arcades run along each side and the elegant eastern window retains a richly decorated canopy sporting animal and vegetal reliefs.

Thirteenth- and 14th-century frescoes adorn the north apse and recent excavations have brought to light the remains of the original mosaic pavement, which can now be seen in the south apse. The cathedral's most valuable treasure, however, is the 11th-century *Exultet*, a lavishly illuminated scroll of Easter prayers, which is housed in the sacristy.

Other treasures – carved stone fragments, icons, paintings and silver objects and reliquaries – can be found in the **Museo Diocesano** (☎ 080 521 00 64; Via Dottula; admission free; ⏰ 9.30am-12.30pm Thu, Sat & Sun, 4.30-7.30pm Sat, or by reservation).

BASILICA DI SAN NICOLA

Heading north up Strade del Carmine will bring you to the doorstep of the **Basilica di San Nicola** (☎ 080 573 71 11; www.basilicasannicola.org; Piazza San Nicola; admission free; ⏰ 8am-12.30pm & 4-7.30pm Mon-Fri, 8am-12.30pm & 5-8.30pm Sat & Sun), the first great Norman church in the south and the template for the restrained Puglian-Romanesque style that informed the architecture of so many of the region's churches. Its solid hulk sits astride four piazze known as the Corti del Catapano, as it's thought that the Byzantine governor's (catapan's) palace was once sited here. The building of the Basilica over the remains of the Byzantine palace may well have been intentional – a symbol of the victory of the Latin church over Eastern Orthodoxy.

At first site the façade seems shockingly plain, its odd triangular shape rearing up before you in white limestone blocks, flanked by two stunted towers (destroyed by earthquakes). It has a massive solidity and spareness about it, although here and there are some delightful ornamental details like the sculpted **Porta dei Leoni** (Lion Door) on the north side, which depicts a series of chivalric scenes in bas relief.

Inside, the same decorative minimalism prevails, the huge transverse arches soaring to lofty heights above elaborately carved capitals. The stone tabernacle (canopy) over the altar dates from 1150 and is a unique piece of medieval sculpture, as is the Bishop's Throne otherwise known as the **Cattedra di Elia** (Elia's Pulpit). Supported on the backs of three groaning caryatids and two lions, it hides behind the altar and was created in 1098 for the Council of Bari.

Despite its obvious sophistication, the basilica was built at a feverish pace to house the relics of St Nicholas, better known to you and me as Father Christmas, which were stolen from Myra (in modern-day Turkey) in 1087 by Baresi fishermen. His remains still lie in the cathedral crypt amid a forest of marble columns. Said to exude a miraculous manna, his relics remain an important point of pilgrimage for both Catholics and Greek Orthodox pilgrims.

Upstairs in the 'women's gallery' you'll find the basilica's treasures, gold relics, icons and paintings – many donated by bishops, popes and kings over the centuries.

TEATRO PETRUZELLI

Of all the grand theatres it is the Teatro Petruzelli that dominates the hearts of the Barese opera-going public. It was conceived and commissioned by the Petruzzelli brothers, Onofrio and Antonio, traders and shipowners originally from Trieste, who felt that the city had outgrown Teatro Piccinni. The city authorities liked the proposal and granted the family some land in perpetuity if they agreed to construct and manage the theatre.

The result was a gorgeously grand Art Noveau music hall, with an enormous frescoed cupola, velvet seats, cherry-wood stage and golden cherubs. The opening night in February 1903 squeezed in an ecstatic crowd of 3200 people, and there was 'not a theatre box, not a seat, not a single empty place in the loggia' the newspapers reported the next day. In the decades that followed, the theatre established itself as one of the great opera houses of Italy alongside La Scala in Milan, Teatro San Carlo in Naples and Teatro Massimo in Palermo. Aside from the works of Italian composers such as Mascagni and Respighi, the Petruzzelli saw an illustrious list of performers over the years, including the likes of Frank Sinatra, Rudolf Nureyev, Liza Minnelli, Riccardo Muti, Luciano Pavarotti and even Freddie Mercury. It was the pride and joy of the city, its cultural compass and most dashing landmark.

But on the evening of 26 October 1991 the city's most beautiful building suffered from a devastating fire, which reduced all the seats, carpets, balconies and putti to ash, leaving the skeleton of the cupola yawning aloft like a giant spider web.

Before long there were accusations of arson, bribery and gangsterism. In July 1993 Ferdinand Pinto, the manager of the theatre, was arrested following accusations that he set the building alight having failed to pay off a loan to a local crime syndicate. The theory was that the theatre could be rebuilt with the insurance money and Pinto could then pay off his debts. Gangsters Antonio Capriati and Vito Martiradonna were also arrested as was the caretaker Giuseppe Tisci. The public muttered that it was all a symptom of the city's parlous degeneration into criminality and commercialism.

Now, 16 years after the terrible fire the theatre still stands derelict, despite plans approved in 1998 for its reconstruction and some 20 billion euros earmarked to cover the costs. Part of the problems have been design related, but the main issue is the city council's insistence that the family sell the theatre back to the city before funds can be released for its renovation. The family maintain that the sum proposed is not enough and so the theatre's rehabilitation remains on hold despite a promised completion date of 2010.

MUSEO ARCHEOLOGICO PROVINCIALE

Housed in the Palazzo Ateneo since 1880, Bari's **Museo Archeologico** (☎ 080 521 15 76; Via Venezia 5; admission free; ☾ currently closed) now has a new location in the ex-monastery of Santa Scolastica right at the tip of the old town. There is currently no date set for its opening, but the collection, once assembled, will cover the history of city from the pre-historic period (Paleolithic, Bronze and Iron Age finds) through the ceramics and *objet d'art* of the Classical era to the early Middle Ages, including a massive collection of some 12,000 coins.

CASTELLO SVEVO

Just beyond the western perimeter of Bari Vecchia broods the sprawling **Castello Svevo** (Swabian Castle; ☎ 080 528 61 11; Piazza Frederico II di Svevia; adult/concession €2/1; ☾ 8.30am-7.30pm Thu-Tue), just one of a whole string of castles that dominate Apulian towns and ports.

It started life as a Roman fort, but was quickly incorporated by the Byzantines into a more complex system of fortification in the 11th century. As usual, it is located just outside the old city walls, which it would have shielded from attack, but under the Normans Puglia's castles gained another function, that of keeping wayward towns in check and impressing on them the might of Norman imperial power. When the city revolted in 1156 William 'the Bad' razed them all to the ground with the exception of the Basilica of San Nicola.

The structure that you see today – the low broad ramparts, drawbridge and internal quadrangular courtyard – all date from the early 16th century when Isabella of Aragon made it the centre of her court, giving it a Renaissance update.

BARI & THE TERRA DI BARI

Today the castle houses the **Gipsoteca** (included with admission to castle), a permanent gallery that features plaster copies of Romanesque monumental sculpture between the 12th and 13th centuries. It includes a copy of Bishop Elias' Throne from the Basilica di San Nicola, slabs and capitals from the cathedral of Bitonto, bas reliefs of Trani's bronze doors and the ambo (pulpit) and Bishop's throne from the sanctuary of Monte Sant'Angelo.

The rest of the castle is given over to temporary exhibitions, some of world-class standard.

OTHER SIGHTS

Part of the real pleasure of Bari Vecchia is wandering around its narrow alleys and chancing upon vignettes of local life – vendors selling artichokes off the back of their trucks, men debating on the best way to lay cobbles or women yelling at kids on street corners. The winding streets are full of dead ends and tiny courtyards and there are a dozen or more smaller churches to admire, although many of them are firmly shuttered awaiting renovation.

The more interesting of these are the **Chiesa di San Gregorio** (Piazzetta 62 Marinai), once a Byzantine temple with a fine façade and a Romanesque interior, and the Venetian **Chiesa di San Marco** (Strada San Marco 7), with its rose window sporting a Venetian lion at its centre. The **Chiesa di Santa Teresa dei Maschi** (Strada Incuria) is one of the few baroque examples.

Borgo Nuovo

The Borgo Nuovo (New Town), or Murattiano, is a typical 19th-century city beneath the grime. Its wide boulevards, arrow-straight roads, sculpted balconies and elegant wrought-iron work are all classic Art Nouveau. Via Imbriani retains some fine examples of the genteel townhouses that once lined the city streets, although the grand theatres of **Teatro Petruzelli** (scheduled for restoration), **Politeama Margherita** (currently undergoing restoration) and **Teatro Comunale Niccolò Piccinni** (see p69), as well as the **Palazzo del Governo**, provide some of the grandest examples of Murat's famous neoclassical 'curtain' buildings.

PINACOTECA PROVINCIALE

A short walk along the Lungomare takes you past more neoclassical façades, the most impressive of which is the Palazzo della Provincia which now houses the **Pinacoteca Provinciale** (☎ 080 541 24 22; Lungomare Nazario Sauro 27; adult/concession €2.60/0.50; ⏰ 9.30am-1pm & 4-7pm Tue-Sun) on the 3rd floor.

The collection focuses firmly on southern Italian artists and the works range over a huge period of time from fragments of 11th-century sculpture, blown off churches from the old town during WWII, through 13th-century icons and 15th-century Venetian altarpieces, right up to huge canvases from the 17th- and 18th-century Neapolitan school and finally a smattering of 19th-century pieces. In all there are 16 rooms to wander through, but although the collection is comprehensive in its local coverage there are really only a few pieces here and there to wow an art lover. In particular, Bartolomeo Vivarini's (c 1440–99) lustrous altarpieces in Room 2; Giovanni Bellini's (c 1430–1516) St Peter Martyr in Room 3; Andrea Vaccaro's (1604–70) Caravaggio-inspired works in Rooms 7 to 9, particularly his almost black canvas with the luminous St Catherine of Alexandria; Luca Giordano's (1634–1705) St Peter of Alcantara in Room 13; and some lighter, more frivolous pieces by Francesco Netti (1832–94) in Room 16 stand out.

FESTIVALS & EVENTS

Festa di San Nicola (Festival of St Nicholas; 7-8 May) Bari's biggest festival celebrating the arrival of St Nick's relics in Bari. The delivery of the saint's bones to the Dominican friars is re-enacted. The following day a fleet of boats transports a statue of the saint along the coast and the evening culminates with an impressive fireworks display.

Premium Città di Bari (July) A home-grown festival of literature and poetry featuring up-and-coming southern writers. A selection of work is judged by a panel.

Fiera di Levante (2nd Sunday in September) The second-biggest trade fair in Italy held in a specially constructed fairground north of the city centre.

Time Zones (November) A music festival showcasing both Italian and international bands, which play at several venues around the city.

SLEEPING

Bari is a commercial town and most of its hotels cater to the business clientele. This generally means good service, bland decor and relatively high prices. Amazingly there are still no B&Bs in the old town, so you'll have to settle for one of a handful of hotels in the Borgo Nuovo.

Budget

Pensione Fiorini (☎ 080 554 07 88; Via Imbriani 89; s/d €20/40) Probably the best budget accommodation in Murattiano, the Fiorini is located in a grand Art Noveau building with sculpted balconies overlooking stylish Via Imbriani. Rooms are large and light, and some of them retain the original tiled floors. The eclectic retro bric-a-brac of the owner lends the place great charm.

Hotel Pensione Giulia (☎ 080 521 66 30; www.hotel pensionegiulia.it; Via Crisanzio 12; s/d €45/60, with bathroom €55/70; ☒) A family-run *pensione*, the Giulia is near the train station. It's plainly furnished, but there are some nice personal touches – pictures, faux flowers and plants which lend the place a homey feel. For an extra €10 you can have air-con in your room.

Albergo Moderno (☎ 080 521 33 13; www.moderno bari.com; Via Crisanzio 60; s €45-70, d €65-105; P ☒) The Moderno verges on the very edge of the budget category, both in terms of price and home comforts. It's an efficient hotel in a well-maintained *palazzo*, although it's debatable whether the rooms are 'modern' or simply spartan. Still, outside high season it's good value for money. They also offer apartments for rent.

Midrange

ourpick Hotel Adria (☎ 080 524 66 99; www.adriahotel bari.com; Via Zuppetta 10; s €70-80, d €90-110; P ▯ ☒) Although a small hotel, the Adria competes favourably with some of the larger and more expensive hotels in Bari. It's located in a pink *palazzo* and offers comfortable, modern rooms with every mod con. Parking costs €12 in the garage across the road. Via Zuppeta is one way and should be accessed from Corso Cavour.

Hotel Boston (☎ 080 524 68 02; www.bostonbari.it; Via Piccinni 155; s €95, d €135; P ▯ ☒) The best thing about Hotel Boston is the helpful reception and the location, just a few blocks south of Bari Vecchia. The rooms are bland beyond belief, decked out in a dreary shade of green that could do with an overhaul. Parking costs €17.

Grand Hotel Leon d'Oro (☎ 080 523 50 40; www .grandhotelleondoro.it; Piazza Aldo Moro 4; s €95, d €145; P ▯ ☒) Despite it's big, grey '70s exterior, Leon d'Oro has been radically transformed inside, boasting try-hard modern rooms with wood panelling, white blinds, stripy bedspreads and gleaming bathrooms. Parking is an additional €13 per day.

Top End

Villa Romanazzi Carducci (☎ 080 542 74 00; www .villaromanazzi.com; Via Capruzzi 326; s/d €116-136/170-180; P ☒ ☒) The one hotel in Bari daring to show some flare, the Villa Romanazzi is housed in the pastel pink, 19th-century Villa Rachele. Rooms are a mixture of old and new, although the décor in the villa rooms is more characterful. Add to this an enormous fitness centre, pool and huge verdant park and this is probably Bari's best hotel.

Palace Hotel Bari (☎ 080 521 65 51; www.palacehotel bari.it; Via Lombardi 13; s/d €175/235; P ☒ ▯) Despite its sinfully ugly concrete exterior, Palace Hotel is an oasis of hushed luxury in a chaotic city. However, you will pay a premium price for the plush comfort of its quiet rooms. Its rooftop restaurant, Murat, is one of the best in the city (see p68).

EATING

As a true-blue portside town, the Barese table has a strong seafood bias, including favourites like mussels, oysters, clams, cuttlefish, prawns and anchovies, all of which are baked, fried, boiled or served up *crudo* (raw).

Bari is also famous for *orecchiette,* an ear-shaped pasta usually served with a tomato and basil sauce, or more particularly with turnip tops.

In the evening things start to get going around 9.30pm, although in summer people tend to dine even later.

Budget

ourpick Al Focolare da Emilio (☎ 080 523 5887; Via Principe Amedeo 173; meals €15-20, pizza €6-8; ☺ lunch Tue-Sun) An unobtrusive restaurant that attracts a crowd of lunching families and local bigwigs. The décor is plain, but the food is something to shout about, especially the homemade pasta dishes. When ordering pasta it's best to order the same dish as it's all cooked on the spot and can take some time. The tagliatelle with mussels is the signature dish.

Pizzeria Enzo e Ciro (☎ 080 553 41 96; Via Cardassi 70; meals €15-20; ☺ Tue-Sat) The most celebrated pizzeria in town, tucked away down elegant Via Cardassi. The pizzas are wafer thin, the atmosphere boisterous and the beers as cheap as chips. Start with the mushroom antipasti – large frilly mushrooms grilled with a light cheese-and-breadcrumb topping.

Osteria al Gambero (☎ 080 521 60 18; Corso Antonio de Tullio 8; meals €20-25; ☺ Mon-Sat) Also highly recommended; this is a good fish restaurant close to the port.

Osteria delle Travi (☎ 080 561 71 50; Largo Chiurlia 12; meals €25; ☽ Tue-Sat, lunch Sun) This rustic old town *osteria* has great traditional cooking, with a splendid antipasti buffet as well as delicious pasta containing all things fishy and lots of fried delicacies. Book ahead at weekends.

Midrange

our pick **Terranima** (☎ 080 521 97 25; Via Putignani 213; meals €20-25; ☽ 7-11pm Mon-Sat, lunch Sun) Peep through the lace curtains into the cool interior of this rustic trattoria. Worn flagstone floors and period furnishings make you feel like you're dining in someone's front room. The menu features earthy offerings like *capocollo* (thin slices of lard), potatoes and cardoncelli mushrooms, and *sporcamusi* (lemon custard in filo pastry).

La Taverna sul Mare (☎ 080 523 18 18; Via Vallisa 50-51; meals €25; Mon-Sat, lunch Sun) A good fish place tucked in one of the busiest alleys of Bari Vecchia.

La Locanda di Federico (☎ 080 522 77 05; Piazza Mercantile 63-64; meals €25-30; ☽ Tue-Sun) An elegant restaurant in the corner of Piazza Mercantile. Its pseudo-medieval décor – colourful canvases of crusading knights – is tasteful and the service is impeccable. The focus is on simple seasonal dishes, including risotto with potatoes and mussels, horsemeat in a tomato *ragu*, as well as fresh fish.

PerBacco (☎ 080 558 01 79; Via Abbrescia 99; meals €25-30; ☽ Mon-Fri, dinner Sat) Ring the bell to enter this intimate dining room, where romancing couples murmur over PerBacco gnocchi (with a tomato and cream of aubergine sauce and rucola) and bell-sized glasses of wine. Other treats include the codfish and slices of fillet in a sweet balsamic vinegar.

Ristorante Alberosole (☎ 080 523 54 46; Corso Vittorio Emanuele II 13; meals €30-40; ☽ Tue-Sun Sep-Jul) A first-rate restaurant where Barese in Brioni suits come to dine on pea-pod-shaped pasta with anchovies, pine nuts and mint. The dining room has a modern-rustic feel that marries well with the vaulted ceiling and old stone-flagged floor.

Top End

Murat (☎ 080 521 65 51; Via Lombardi 13; meals €35-45; ☽ Mon-Sat) Dine in style on the roof terrace of the Palace hotel with a picture postcard view

over Bari Vecchia. The menu is baroque in its offerings: sea-urchin mousse in a crust basket with herb toast, consommé of sole with seafood profiteroles and crêpes with scorpion fish fillet.

Ai 2 Ghiottoni (☎ 080 523 22 40; Via Putignani 11; meals €45-55; ☽ Mon-Sat) For a euro-busting blow-out sit down at Bari's premier fish restaurant, where the evening's slivery offerings (delivered fresh for lunch and dinner) literally flip-flop around in the ice-counter. From every imaginable crustacean to a host of white and oily fish, the menu and methods of cooking are encyclopaedic.

DRINKING

The centre of student nightlife and the haunt of romancing couples is undoubtedly Piazza Ferrarese and Piazza Mercantile in Bari Vecchia. Via Manfredi Re and Strada Vallisa, both off Piazza Mercantile, are full of late-night bars, and more crowds congregate along Corso Vittorio Emanuele II. Your best bet is to grab a beer wherever and join in.

The older crowd tend to hide out in small bars in the new part of town, although you'll always find a good group of people at the bars around Largo Adua like the cosy pub **Premiata Norcineria** (Largo Adua 16; ☽ 8pm-3am).

our pick **La Vineria** (☎ 080 558 34 89; www.lavineria .eu; Via Imbriani 78; ☽ 8pm-midnight Tue-Sun) A cool place for serious samplers of vino. Minimalist décor is accompanied by a grown-up wine list offering excellent local varieties alongside other regional favourites. The simple menu of cheese, charcuterie and grilled meat is the perfect no-frills side order.

Gargà (☎ 333 277 13 77; Strada Palazzo di Città 58; ☽ 9pm-late Wed-Sun) This rustic-chic American bar in the old town is the only place where you'll find live music and DJ sets. It starts to fill up around midnight. There's live music on Thursday and Sunday and DJ sets on Friday and Saturday night.

Barcollo (☎ 080 521 38 89; Piazza Mercantile 69/70; cocktails €6; ☽ 8-3am) One of the chicest (or most pretentious) bars on Piazza Mercantile, Barcollo is the haunt of the beautiful people. Lounge on blood-red banquettes, supping a cocktail and nibbling exquisitely presented aperitivi.

ENTERTAINMENT

Since the destruction of Teatro Petruzzelli, Bari's cultural life has undoubtedly constricted, but the Piccinni theatre still puts on a lively programme of dance and opera. There are a couple of other minor theatres such as Teatro Kursaal and Teatro Kismet Opera.

Teatro Comunale Niccolò Piccinni (☎ 080 521 08 78; www.teatropubblicopugliese.it; Corso Vittorio Emanuele II 84) This is the oldest theatre in Bari (built in 1854), and is the cultural hub of the city hosting local and international opera, music and dance seasons.

SHOPPING

Bari is a good place to shop as it's not really a tourist city. It also boasts some smart shopping streets, in particular the pedestrianised Via Sparano da Bari, which is lined with big brand names. Via Argiro is another shopping hotspot, while Corso Cavour is dedicated to the cheaper high street brands. In Piazza Umberto and at the top end of Corso Cavour you will find local traders working behind bargain stalls.

De Carne (☎ 080 521 96 76; Via Calefati 128) For some fine regional produce head for the venerable delicatessen De Carne. Its well-stocked halls offer a huge range to choose from, as well as some tasty takeaway dishes.

Il Germoglio (☎ 080 524 27 72; Via Putignani 204) Opened in 1987, Il Germoglio (the Bud) is a serious organic shop selling a good variety of Pugliese specialities from jams and cheeses to fresh veg and *taralli* biscuits, bread and wine.

Enoteca de Pasquale (☎ 080 521 31 92; Via Marchese di Montrone 87) Pick up a rare Nero di Troia or a full-blooded Mandurian Primitivo from this well-stocked *enoteca* (wine store) where you can sample the wine before you buy.

GETTING THERE & AWAY
Air

Bari's **Palese airport** (BRI; ☎ 080 583 52 00; www .seap-puglia.it) is located 10km west of the city centre. It is serviced by a host of international and budget airlines including Alitalia, British Airways, Hapag-Lloyd Express, Lufthansa and Ryanair.

Alitalia, AirOne and Alpi Eagles run a range of domestic services to and from Bologna, Catania (Sicily), Florence, Milan, Palermo, Rome and Venice. Ada Air flies daily to Tirrana in Albania.

For more information on tickets and routes, both international and domestic, see p218.

Boat

Bari's **port** (www.porto.bari.it) is the principal port in the Adriatic. Ferries run from Bari to Greece (Corfu–Igoumenitsa–Patras), Albania (Durazzo), Croatia (Dubrovnik) and Montenegro (Bar). The port is also a staging point for cruise ships sailing in the eastern Mediterranean.

All boat companies have offices at the ferry terminal although you can purchase ferry tickets at any travel agent in town as well as on most internet sites. To reach the ferry terminal catch the AMTAB bus No 20/ from the main train station at Piazza Aldo Moro. Note that you need to catch the bus with the '/' as the No 20 will take you to a city suburb.

Once you have bought your ticket and paid the embarkation tax (per person or car €4) you'll get a boarding card, which must be stamped by the police at the ferry terminal. Tariffs can be as much as one third cheaper outside the peak period of mid-July to late August. Bicycles normally travel free.

The main companies and the routes they served at the time of writing are as follows:

Blue Star Ferries (☎ 080 52 11 416; www.bluestarferries.com) To Patras (8pm) and Igoumenitsa (8pm).

Jadrolinija (☎ +385 51 666 111; www.jadrolinija.hr) To Dubrovnik in Croatia.

Montenegro Lines (☎ 080 578 98 27; www.morfimare.it) Reservations via Morfimare Travel Agency (see p63); to Bar in Montenegro (10pm Sunday to Friday April to September), Cephalonia (6.30pm every few days July to September), Igoumenitsa (6.30pm daily April to September) and Patrasso (6.30pm daily April to September).

Superfast (☎ 080 528 28 28; www.superfast.com) To Igoumenitsa and Patras (Patrassa) in Greece. Daily departure at either midday or 8pm year-round. Superfast is the only company that accepts Eurail, Eurodomino and Inter-Rail passes (port taxes and a high-season supplement may apply).

FERRY CROSSINGS FROM BARI

Destination	Cost return high season (€) seat/cabin/car	Duration (hr)
Bar, Montenegro	55/116/78	9
Cephalonia, Greece	134/200/122	15½
Corfu, Greece	137/202/127	11
Durrës, Albania	48/89/87	8
Igoumenitsa, Greece	134/202/122	10-12
Patras, Greece	137/202/127	16½

Tirrenia (☎ 199 12 31 99; www.tirrenia.it) To and from Durazzo in Albania (11pm daily year-round).
Ventouris Ferries (☎ 080 521 76 09; www.ventouris .gr) Regular ferries to Igoumenitsa, Patras and Corfu. Also daily ferries to and from Durazzo (Albania).

Bus

Puglia has a complicated network of private bus companies servicing different areas of the province, with intercity buses leaving from several locations around town.

The main point of departure, however, is from Via Capruzzi, on the south side of the main train station. From here **SITA** (☎ 080 579 02 11; www.sitabus.it in Italian) covers local destinations like Canosa (€5.10, two hours). This is also the departure point for the Sunday service of the **Ferrovie Appulo-Lucane** (☎ 080 572 52 29; www.fal-srl.it in Italian) serving Matera (€4, 1½ hours), plus **Marozzi** (☎ 080 579 01 11; www .marozzivt.it in Italian) buses for Rome (€30, 5½ hours, day departures only, the overnight bus departs from Piazza Aldo Moro). Other bus lines like Marino and Etna Linea service long-distance destinations like Naples and Messina in Sicily. You can purchase tickets at **ATS Viaggi** (☎ 080 556 24 46; www.atsviaggi.com; Via Capruzzi 224/c), which you'll find opposite the bus stops.

Piazza Erio del Mare is the terminal for **STP** (☎ 800 091 155; www.stpspa.it in Italian) buses serving Andria (€3.35, one hour, seven daily) and Trani (€2.85, 45 minutes, frequent). Tickets are available at the tabacchi cabin on Corso Cavour. **Ferrotramviaria** (☎ 080 578 95 42; www .ferrovienordbarese.it in Italian) buses also leave from here for Andria and Ruvo di Puglia. On Sunday they leave from Piazza Aldo Moro in front of the main train station.

Buses operated by **Ferrovie del Sud-Est** (FSE; ☎ 080 546 21 11; www.fseonline.it in Italian) leave from Largo Ciaia, south of Piazza Aldo Moro, for Brindisi (€6.80, 2½ hours, four daily) and Taranto (€5.10, 1½ hours, six daily). They also run frequently to Alberobello (€3.40, 1½ hours).

Car & Motorcycle

Bari is on the A14 *autostrada* (motorway), which heads northwest to Foggia, south to Taranto and connects with the A16 to Naples at Canosa di Puglia. Exit at Bari-Nord to reach the centre of town.

The main route south is on the SS16, a good state road, which connects Bari with Brindisi and also extends north to Foggia if you don't want to take the *autostrada*. To reach Taranto and Matera take the SS100.

Train

The train system out of Bari is terribly confusing due to the various private and state railway services that operate.

On Piazza Aldo Moro you'll find the **main train station** (☎ 080 524 43 86; www.trenitalia.com) which is serviced by mainline trains connecting Bari with the major cities to the north. Eurostar trains operate from Milan (1st/2nd class €82/61, eight to 9½ hours) and Rome (€35, five hours), and there are frequent services to other main cities in Puglia, including Foggia (€10.40, 1½ hours), Brindisi (€6.80, 1¼ hours), Lecce (€11.60, 1½ to two hours) and Taranto (€6.80, 1¾ hours).

Of the private train services, the **Ferrovia Bari-Nord** (☎ 080 578 95 42; www.ferrovienordbarese .it in Italian) services a string of towns north of Bari, stopping first at the airport (€0.80 at least 20 daily) and then continuing on to Ruvo di Puglia (€2.30, 35 minutes), Andria (€3.40, one hour) and Barletta (€4, 1¼ hours). Services are roughly hourly and run from Monday to Saturday. On Sunday the railway line operates buses (Ferrotramviaria) instead which depart from in front of the station.

As its name implies, the **Ferrovie Appulo-Lucane** (☎ 080 572 52 29; www.fal-srl.it in Italian) links Bari with Basilicata (Lucania), servicing Altamura (€2.60, one hour, hourly), Matera (€4, one hour 20 minutes, 10 daily), Gravina (€3.40, one hour 10 minutes, hourly) and Potenza (€8.60, 3½ hours, four daily). Again these services only run Monday to Saturday and there's a bus service, leaving from Via Capruzzi, on Sunday.

The south of Puglia is serviced by the **Ferrovie del Sud-Est** (☎ 080 546 21 11; www.fseonline.it in Italian). Every hour its tiny trains head for some of the most touristed towns in Puglia like Castellana Grotte (€2.60, one hour 10 minutes), Alberobello (€4, one hour 50 minutes) and Martina Franca (€4.60, two hours 10 minutes). It also services Taranto (€6.80, 2½ hours, six daily). The station is on the other side of the mainline tracks (Via Oberdan). To reach it cross under the train tracks south of Piazza Luigi di Savoia or through the underpass in the main train station and head east along Via Giuseppe Capruzzi for about 500m.

GETTING AROUND

Central Bari is quite compact – a 20-minute walk will take you from Piazza Aldo Moro to he old town. For the ferry terminal take bus No 20/ from Piazza Aldo Moro.

o/From the Airport

To get to the airport take the Cotrap bus €4.15), which leaves the main train station 80 minutes before most flight departures. It also calls by the Alitalia office at Via Calefati 37.

There are plenty of taxis outside the airport and the trip into town costs around €20. All the major car-hire companies are represented at the airport including Hertz, Avis and Maggiore.

Bus

Bari's city buses are frequent and efficient ,but you won't really need them as everything is within easy walking distance. For the ferry terminal take bus No 20/ from Piazza Aldo Moro. A single journey costs €0.80 and a day pass is €1.80.

Car & Motorcycle

Street parking is hell in Bari and the city has a reputation for car theft. There's a large free parking area just south of the main port entrance, otherwise there is a large multistorey car park between the main and Ferrovie del Sud-Est train stations. There are plenty of small private garages in town, which charge between €12 and €17 for a day's parking.

AROUND BARI

To escape the noise and drama of Bari *centro* you could consider one of two worthwhile day trips, 18km northwest to **Giovinazzo** or 22km outheast to **Mola di Bari**. Both places have super quaint old town centres and ports full of bobbing boats. Mola di Bari, like Polignano a Mare, is characterised by whitewashed houses, while Giovinazzo's old town is situated on a fortified promontory much like Bari Vecchia, with gleaming limestone houses and an elegant Duomo built by the widow of Prince Boemondo I.

You can eat well in both towns so if you're travelling up or down the coast stop for lunch. In Giovinazzo you should try the rustic **Osteria dei Poeti** (☎ 080 394 65 54; Piazza Meschino; meals 40), where you would do well to order the risotto with clams. In Mola di Bari try **Van Westerhout** (☎ 080 474 69 89; Via de Amicis 3/5; meals 35; ☟ Wed-Mon).

NORTH OF BARI

Unlike the Grecian influences further south, Bari province represents the heartland of Norman and Swabian power, strung together with massive castles and impressive cathedrals – physical and spiritual bulwarks against the heresies of the East. Crowning it all, the Castel del Monte, occupies a lonely hill, testimony to the absolute rule of the Holy Roman Emperor Frederick II who once loved to hunt in Puglia's verdant countryside.

BITONTO
pop 56,420

Like nearly all the towns circling Bari, Bitonto was once a Peucetian settlement later made over into a Roman municipium called Buntuntum. These days it's famous for the top-quality olive oil that it produces and its magnificent **cathedral** (Piazza Cattedrale; admission free; ☟ 8am-noon & 5-8pm). Built between the 12th and 13th centuries it is dedicated to St Valentine. In many ways it has greater aesthetic merit than other Puglian cathedrals due to its external decoration. Its façade is divided into three parts, with three portals, the central one sculpted with vegetal designs and scenes from the Old Testament. Above, four mullioned windows break up the blank wall, and are surmounted by a rose window flanked by sculptures of animals on slender columns. Inside, the cathedral's prized possession is the sculpted ambo (pulpit) by Nicolaus Sacerdotus dating from 1229. Downstairs in the crypt you'll find Byzantine frescoes and some mosaic flooring.

Other interesting stone fragments from the cathedral are now housed in the **Museo Diocesano** (☎ 080 375 13 59; Via Corte Vescovado; ☟ 10am-noon Thu & Fri), which also acts as the town's very modest art gallery. The **Museo Civico E Rogadeo** (☎ 080 375 18 77; Via Rogadeo 52; ☟ 9.30am-1.30pm Mon-Fri, 3.30-6.30pm Tue & Thu) is another small museum housing archaeological finds and paintings. More interesting is the 16th-century *palazzo* itself, which is typical of the grand Renaisssance and baroque palaces that once graced the centre of Bitonto.

Aside from some lavish Easter festivities, Bitonto hosts **San Leone**, the oldest country fair in Italy, on the 6th April, with a medieval pageant and much revelry. But the biggest festival is the **Intorciata** (third Sunday in October) which celebrates the cult of St Cosmas and St

Damiano, brother doctors, who healed the poor for free and were beheaded by Diocletian in the 4th century.

To get hold of some of Bitonto's olive oil head for the **Oleificio Cooperativo Cima di Bitonto** (☎ 080 375 17 03; www.oleificiocimadibitonto.it; Via Modugno; ☻ 9am-1pm & 4-6pm Mon-Fri, 8.30am-1pm Sat). They speak both English and French there.

Regular trains service Bitonto from Bari (€1.10, 20 minutes) and Ruvo (€1.10, 15 minutes), with bus services on Sunday. By car, take the SS98 from Ruvo or head north out of Bari on SS16 and turn off south at Santo Spirito.

RUVO DI PUGLIA
pop 25,920 / elevation 260m
Situated on the eastern slopes of the Murge plateau, surrounded by olives and orchards, Ruvo is one of the most attractive country towns in the province. The Greeks established its famous 3rd-century potteries, where they produced those fine black-and-red Attic vases and minted their own coins. When the Romans came to town, Ruvo prospered even more by trading goods along the Via Traiana.

These days, Ruvo di Puglia is a quiet agricultural centre with a famous cathedral, sumptuous museum (one of the best in Puglia) and a smattering of good restaurants. You'll find the **Pro Loco** (☎ 080 361 54 19; Via V Veneto 48; ☻ 9am-12.30pm & 4-7.30pm Mon-Sat, 9am-12.30pm Sun) just off Piazza Bovio, housed in a tower that was once part of the old city walls.

Sights
During the 19th century it was common practise for antique dealers to trawl southern Italy to see what treasures local peasants may have uncovered while working in the fields, such was the number of tombs and grave goods going begging. Appalled by the pillage, the Jatta family in Ruvo determined to rescue their dwindling heritage by offering to buy many of the artefacts themselves. As a result they amassed a huge collection of over 2000 vases and craters, coins and cups, which are now proudly displayed in the **Museo Nazionale Jatta** (☎ 080 361 28 48; www.palazzojatta.org; Piazza Bovio 35; admission free; ☻ 8.30am-1.30pm Sun-Wed, 8.30am-7.30pm Thu-Sat). Laid out in a wing of their huge neoclassical mansion (still occupied by the family), the museum is now universally acknowledged to hold one of the most complete collections of ceramics in Puglia. The most

famous piece in the gallery is a vase dating from the 5th century BC showing the death of the bronze giant Talos at the hand of the Argonauts (Room 4).

The other very worthwhile museum in town is **Palazzo Caputi** (☎ 080 362 80 82; Via A de Gasperi 26; admission free; ☻ 9am-noon & 5-7pm Mon-Sat, 10am-noon Sun), which houses the work of Michele Chieco and Domenico Cantatore (1906–98), one of Puglia's most talented 20th-century artists. Influenced by the Impressionists (particularly Cézanne and Daumier) and later Picasso, Domenico's work is striking for its geometric solidity, strong colours and dramatic Van Gogh–like brushstrokes. At the time of research the museum was closed for renovations, but hopefully this interesting collection will soon be on display again.

From Palazzo Caputi you can weave your way up Via Cassano Nicola to Ruvo's 13th-century **duomo** (Largo di Cattedrale; ☻ 8am-noon Mon Sat), with its steeply gabled facade and huge wagon-wheel rose window. It has a classic Puglian-Romanesque design. Its central portal is guarded by two sharp-beaked griffons balanced precariously on slender columns borne by two weather-worn lions. According to legend, St Peter preached the gospel here and appointed Ruvo's first Bishop, St Cletus. Inside recent renovations have restored the interior to its original state, exposing some of the 16th century frescoes that once covered the walls.

Just north of here you'll find the **Chiesa del Purgatorio** (Via Cattedrale 120), beneath which is the **Grotta di San Cleto**, a frescoed cave that was once a Roman cistern. Again, the grotto was closed for further archaeological work at the time of research but is certainly worth a visit once it reopens.

Festivals & Events
Easter Holy Week A big occasion including three days of processions – the 'Eight Saints' on Thursday, Christ bearing the Cross on Friday and the resurrected Christ on Sunday when the allegorical figures of Lent are finally blown up with fireworks.
Talos Jazz Festival (1-10 September) Showcases a mixture of modern jazz, contemporary and ethnic music from local names like Pino Minafra, to international groups from as far afield as South Africa.

Sleeping
There is a real dearth of B&Bs in the historic centre of Ruvo although the council is currently looking to promote this type of ac-

commodation in the future. In the meantime you'll have to make do with the following two options.

I Girasoli (☎ 080 361 49 54; bedgirasoli@libero.it; Arco Melodia 6; s/d €35/70) A small B&B with a couple of rooms in the impressive Palazzo Camerino and two more at Via Crocifisso 27. Accommodation is simple, but there is a good continental breakfast.

Hotel Pineta (☎ 080 361 15 78; www.hotelpinetaruvo .it; Via Carlo Marx 5; s/d €45/70; **P**) The only other option close to the centre of town, this single-storey hotel is well situated amid a cluster of pines on the edge of town.

Eating

L'Angolo Divino (☎ 080 362 85 44; Corso Giovanni Jatta 11; meals €20-25; ☺ 8-11pm Tue-Sun) With over 200 of the finest Puglian and international wines, L'Angolo Divino is a serious *vineria* although you won't go hungry here either. Fine cuts of *capocollo* (lard), slices of tangy pecorino and dollops of creamy *burrata* cheese sit comfortably beside large glasses of wine, which Giulio is happy to recommend.

ourpick Hostaria Pomponio (☎ 080 362 99 70; Vico Pomponio 3; meals €25; ☺ Wed-Mon) If U.P.E.P.I.D.D.E is the rich-man's version of rusticity, Pomponio is the real thing: a one-room restaurant with an open fire serving up soups and sundries in terracotta dishes. The food is thoroughly local: Murgia cheeses, vegetable soups and grilled meats including local staples like *gnumeridd'* (a roulade of lamb giblets).

U.P.E.P.I.D.D.E (☎ 080 361 38 79; www.upepidde .it; Via Sant'Agnese; meals €30-40; ☺ Tue-Sun) Sit beneath rough-hewn barrel vaults, tuck your heavy linen napkin into your shirt and dine on hearty country fare at this well-known restaurant. Dishes include homemade pastas with rich meat sauces or mussels and beans, and lip-smacking grilled meats. The wine list is impressive and the service friendly.

Getting There & Away

Ruvo is on the Ferrovie Nord Barese line so you'll find frequent trains to Bari (€2.30, 35 minutes) from Monday to Saturday. On Sunday buses leave from outside the train station. STP buses also service Trani and depart from Corso Cotugno near Piazza Matteotti. You can buy tickets from Tabacchio Michel on Piazza Cavallotti. Metered parking is available outside the historic centre and costs €0.60 per hour.

TRANI

pop 53,520

With its prime position and magnificent portside cathedral it's no wonder that Trani is known as the 'Pearl of Puglia'. Fashioned from gleaming limestone blocks and sited on the curve of an elegant port, it has an easy seaside allure and is deservedly popular with weekending Pugliese who come to parade around the *porto* and furiously lick ice-creams in the park.

It's always been a prosperous place, during the Middle Ages the town even rivalled Bari in importance, and it became a major embarkation point for merchants travelling to and from the Near East. In fact, its business interests grew so large that the town devised the very first maritime code, the Ordinamenta Maris (1063), much to the chagrin of the Venetians.

At only 40km from Bari, Trani is an ideal base for exploring this part of Puglia – Barletta, Minervino, Ruvo and the Castel del Monte are all within easy reach.

Orientation

Trani is a compact town laid out on a neat grid system. The train station is situated at the southern edge of town while the cathedral and the castle are located at the northern extremity overlooking the sea. From the station, Via Cavour leads through tree-lined Piazza della Repubblica, the main square, to Piazza Plebiscito and the public gardens. Turn left for the small picturesque harbour and the cathedral.

Information

EMERGENCY

Accident & emergency (☎ 0883 48 21 11)
Municipal police (☎ 0883 58 80 00; Corso Imbriani 119)

INTERNET ACCESS

Centro Servizi (☎ 0883 50 85 69; Via Giovanni Bovio 22; ☺ 9.30am-1.30pm & 5-9pm Mon-Wed, Fri & Sat, 10am-1pm & 6-9.30pm Sun) Handy, but small with only three computers. It's also a phone centre

MEDICAL SERVICES

Farmacia de Nicolo (☎ 0883 58 34 65; Corso Vittorio Emanuele 126)
Ospedale San Nicola Pellegrino (☎ 0883 48 31 11; Viale Padre Pio)

MONEY

You'll find the main banks clustered around Piazza della Repubblica

POST

Post office (Via Giovanni Bovio 115; ⊗ 8am-6pm Mon-Sat)

TOURIST INFORMATION

Tourist office (☎ 0883 58 88 30; www.traniweb.it; 1st fl, Palazzo Palmieri, Piazza Trieste; ⊗ 8.30am-1.30pm Mon-Fri, 3-6pm Tue & Thu) A well-organised and friendly tourist office with all the necessary info and a small town map.

Sights

Trani has one of the best preserved medieval centres of Bari's coastal towns, a neat nucleus of churches and *palazzi* that reflect its prosperous past.

Undoubtedly, for many tourists the main draw is the photogenic **cathedral** (☎ 0883 58 24 70; Piazza del Duomo; admission free; ⊗ 8am-noon & 5-7pm daily Jun-Sep, 8.15am-12.15pm & 3.15-6.30pm Mon-Sat, 9am-12.45pm & 4-7pm Sun Oct-May) with its backdrop of blue, blue sea. It is unusually tall for a Puglian cathedral (the cathedrals of Ruvo and Bari look positively squat by comparison) and that's because it's constructed on top of an older Byzantine church, the Chiesa di Santa Maria della Scala, which itself sits on the Ipogèo San Leucio, a chamber believed to date from the 6th or 7th century.

Constructed between the 11th and 13th centuries, it boasts all the classic Puglian Romanesque features, a steep gabled façade, blind arcades and richly sculpted portals and windows. The interior is stunningly plain, the result of restoration work which stripped away

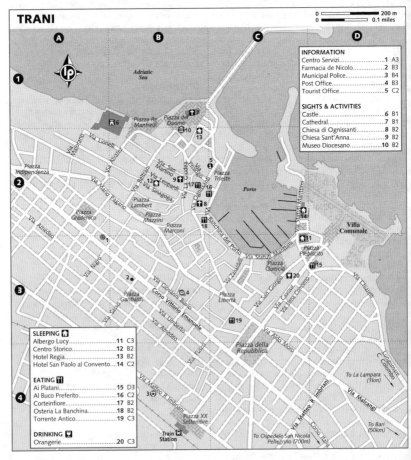

TRANI

0 _____ 200 m
0 _____ 0.1 miles

Adriatic Sea

Porto

INFORMATION
Centro Servizi....................1 A3
Farmacia de Nicolo...........2 B3
Municipal Police................3 B4
Post Office........................4 B3
Tourist Office....................5 C2

SIGHTS & ACTIVITIES
Castle................................6 B1
Cathedral..........................7 B1
Chiesa di Ognissanti..........8 B2
Chiesa Sant'Anna..............9 B2
Museo Diocesano............10 B2

SLEEPING 🛏
Albergo Lucy....................11 C3
Centro Storico..................12 B2
Hotel Regia......................13 B2
Hotel San Paolo al Convento....14 C2

EATING 🍴
Ai Platani.........................15 D3
Al Buco Preferito..............16 C2
Corteinfiore.....................17 B2
Osteria La Banchina.........18 B2
Torrente Antico................19 C3

DRINKING 🍷
Orangerie.........................20 C3

an elaborate baroque scheme grafted onto the original interior in 1837.

Inside the church you can view the original bronze doors, cast by Barisano da Trani, who also created the doors for the cathedral at Ravello and Monreale, while near the main altar fragments of the original mosaic floor remain – large-scale naive images of Adam and Eve, and Alexander the Great. Like Otranto's cathedral (p162), this mosaic would once have carpeted the entire floor with rich patterns and medieval iconography. The crypt below contains the relics of St Nicholas and sports some vibrant 15th-century frescoes ascribed to the Venetian artist Giovanni di Francia.

To get a closer look at the ingenuity of Puglian-Romanesque sculpture its worth a quick trip to the **Museo Diocesano** (☎ 0883 49 19 38; Piazza del Duomo 9; adults/concession €2/1; ⊙ 10am-12.30pm & 4-7pm Jun-Sep, 10am-12.30pm & 5-7pm Oct-May) where you'll find a fantastic collection of friezes, architraves, tombstones and capitals alongside archaeological finds and more typical church furnishings.

About 200m west of the cathedral is Trani's other major landmark, the vast 13th-century **castle** (☎ 0883 50 66 03; Piazza Re Manfredi 16; admission €2; ⊙ 8.30am-7.30pm) built by Frederick II. It was the favourite residence of his son Manfred, but after years of service as a prison there is little of interest to see and its currently undergoing restoration.

More interesting is a wander through the tiny streets of Trani's historic centre, lined as they are with grand *palazzi*. Strike off Via Beltrani down Via Leopardi and you'll lose yourself in the old Jewish Ghetto, one of Trani's powerful immigrant communities. The **Chiesa Sant'Anna** (Via La Giudea; ⊙ closed for restoration) is only one of four synagogues that once serviced the community. They were all converted to churches in the 14th century, but there has been talk of re-converting Sant'Anna into a Jewish cultural centre.

Wandering down Via Prologo to the port will bring you to Via Ognissanti. Here you'll find another Trani curiosity, the **Chiesa di Ognissanti** (All Saint's Church; admission free; ⊙ for services only). It was once an important Templar church, where Norman knights swore allegiance before setting off on the First Crusade, and it contains much of the decorative symbolism made famous in Dan Brown's *Da Vinci Code*.

In the early evening the *passeggiata* will be in full swing around the port. Join the crowds and make your way around to the **Villa Comunale**, Trani's lovely public park. It has absolutely gorgeous views of the cathedral with the sun setting behind it.

Sleeping

With such a well-developed tourist scene, Trani doesn't want for B&B's and hotels although really good midrange options are a bit thin on the ground.

Albergo Lucy (☎ 0883 48 10 22; www.albergolucy.com; Piazza Plebiscito 11; s/d €36/50) This charming hotel in a restored 17th-century *palazzo* offers huge rooms full of character. The vaulted ceilings are high, letting in plenty of light, and the décor is unobtrusive. It's ideally located close to the port and the park. They don't do breakfast.

Centro Storico (☎ 0883 50 61 76; www.bbtrani.it; Via Leopardi 29; s/d €40/50) With pots of character, this B&B inhabits an old backstreet monastery and is run by an elderly couple. There's a courtyard filled with orange and lemon trees, where you can have breakfast. Accommodation is old-fashioned and simple.

Hotel San Paolo al Convento (☎ 0883 482 949; www.sanpaoloalconvento.traniweb.it; Via Statuti Marittimi 111; s/d €120/140, with seaview €130/150; 🅿) Trani's finest hotel is located in the old Barnabiti monastery across the bay from the cathedral. Its grand proportions make for impressive suites and formal dining rooms, although the décor is rather uninspired. It also has an onsite gym and spa facilities.

Hotel Regia (☎ /fax 0883 58 44 44; hotelregia@tiscali.it; Piazza del Duomo 2; s/d €130/150; 🅿) The Regia has a front row view of the cathedral and bags of style, housed as it is in the 18th-century Palazzo Filisio. The rooms are understated and stylish, with parquet flooring and perfectly suited elegant furniture. What's more, there's a good restaurant (meals €27).

Eating

Fish in all its forms is a staple of the Trani table, but simple *grigliata di pesce misto* (grilled mixed fish) is a favourite alongside *baccalà* (salted cod). You'll also find *maccarun-o furn* (baked maccaroni) and pasta with cabbage (rather than the typical chicory).

Al Buco Preferito (☎ 0883 50 60 83; Via Banchina del Porto 4; meals €12-15; ⊙ Thu-Tue) It doesn't look much, but Al Buco has a port side location and is frantically busy due to the fact that it serves up myriad different varieties of wafer thin pizza on wooden boards. Most folk sink a few cocktails at the nearby Caribbean Bar and then try and cajole the staff to find them a seat amid the crowded tables.

Ai Platini (☎ 0883 48 24 21; Via Elena Commeno 16; meals €25-30; ☺ Tue-Sun) Away from the buzz of the portside, Ai Platani is a nice retreat with a more intimate and romantic atmosphere. The décor is rustic-chic and although the food is still very much focused on the sea, the homemade gnocchetti and ragu (tomato sauce) is a nice alternative.

Osteria La Banchina (☎ 0883 58 47 47; Via Banchina del Porto 16/18; meals €30; ☺ Thu-Tue) Packed amid a host of other restaurant hopefuls overlooking the port, La Banchina is a cut above the competition with a shaded outdoor eating area in the shadow of the Ognissanti church. Fresh fish is the order of the day – grilled, baked in a salt crust or fried in a light batter.

ourpick Corteinfiore (☎ 0883 50 84 02; Via Ognissanti 18; meals €35; ☺ Tue-Sun) Here it feels like you are eating outside even though you're not, with a kind of marquee-conservatory arrangement, wooden decking and sunny yellow tablecloths. Melas are delicious, with dishes such as pasta with monkfish and clams. Bevies of friendly waiters keep the show on the road, and wines are excellent.

Torrente Antico (☎ 0883 48 79 11; Via Fusco 3; meals €45; ☺ lunch Tue-Sun, closed Jan & Jul) Also recommended is Torrente Antico, which has an inventive menu and an excellent wine list.

Drinking & Entertainment

Bars line the portside and are crammed with drinkers at the weekends. During summer the bars down the *lungomare* also fill up.

Orangerie (☎ 0883 48 52 77; Via San Giorgio 16; meals €30; ☺ noon-2am Tue-Sun) Drink with the beautiful people in Piazza Quercia with a front row view of the port. Although this place is primarily a bar it also has a good restaurant upstairs where trad dishes get an interesting makeover at the hands of Luca Depalo.

La Lampara (☎ 0883 48 25 73; Viale de Gemmis 1; ☺ 1-3pm & 9-late Tue-Sun) The nearest thing Trani has to a club. Although it has a fairly fancy restaurant, it's best to stick to the neon-tinged bar and dancing, which takes place on Thursday, Friday and Saturday night. For popular gigs you have to book.

Getting There & Away

Buses operated by **Bari STP** (☎ 0883 49 18 00; www .stpspa.it in Italian) connect Trani with points along the coast and inland, including Andria (€0.90, 20 minutes, eight daily), Barletta (€0.90, 20 minutes, hourly) as well as Canosa and Ruvo di Puglia. Services depart from in front of **Bar Stazione** (☎ 0883 58 88 26; Piazza XX Settembre 23a), where timetables and tickets are available.

In July and August, a bus departs from Trani at 8.30am and connects with the 9am service from Andria to Castel del Monte. The first return run to Andria leaves the castle at 3pm.

The SS16 runs through Trani, linking it to Bari and Foggia, or you can hook up with the A14 Bologna–Bari *autostrada*.

Trani is on the main train line between Bari (€2.60, 45 minutes, hourly) and Foggia (€4.60, one hour, hourly) and is easily reached from towns along the coast.

AROUND TRANI

An easy day-trip from Trani is a run down the coast to **Molfetta** (17km), another pretty seaside town with a tawny historic centre on the waterfront. It is the main fishing port on the Adriatic so you can be sure to eat well at local restaurants like **Bufi** (☎ 080 3971597; Via Vittorio Emanuele 15; meals around €60; ☺ Tue-Sat & lunch Sun Sep-Dec & Feb-Jul). Then wander down to the waterfront to gawp at the three-domed **Duomo San Conado** (Largo Chiesa Vecchia; admission free; ☺ 9am-noon & 4-8pm), and finish off with a coffee in front of the port. There ends another perfect day!

BARLETTA
pop 93,100

Barletta's crusading history is a lot more exotic than the modern-day town, although the historic centre is pretty enough with its cathedral and fine castle. The history of the town is closely linked with the nearby archaeological site of Canne della Battaglia where the Carthaginian pin-up, Hannibal, whipped the Romans and 40,000 men lost their lives. After the Carthaginians, the Crusaders came to town and Richard the Lionheart is said to have had a hand in the building of Barletta's cathedral. Frederick II proclaimed his son, Henry, king here and then set off on the Third Crusade. It was also the principal seat of the Archbishop of Nazareth for some 600 years (1291–1891) and in 1459 Ferdinand I of Aragon was crowned King of Naples here. In

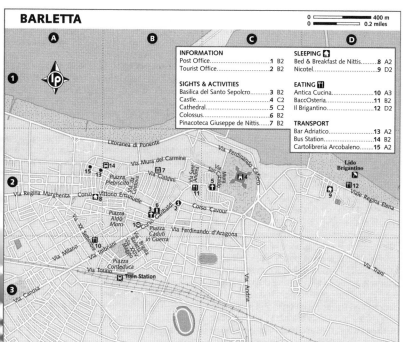

BARLETTA

INFORMATION		SLEEPING	
Post Office.................................1 B2		Bed & Breakfast de Nittis........8 A2	
Tourist Office............................2 B2		Nicotel....................................9 D2	
SIGHTS & ACTIVITIES		EATING	
Basilica del Santo Sepolcro..........3 B2		Antica Cucina.........................10 A3	
Castle......................................4 C2		BaccOsteria............................11 B2	
Cathedral.................................5 C2		Il Brigantino...........................12 D2	
Colossus..................................6 B2			
Pinacoteca Giuseppe de Nittis.....7 B2		TRANSPORT	
		Bar Adriatico..........................13 A2	
		Bus Station.............................14 B2	
		Cartolibreria Arcobaleno........15 A2	

the 1940s the Barlettans were fighting again, this time instigating the first Italian resistance to the Nazi's for which the town was awarded the Gold Medal of Military Valour.

These days swords and sandals have given way to shades and swim suits as Barletta boasts some of the nicest beaches along the north coast.

Orientation & Information

From the train station, go down Via Giannone and through the municipal gardens. Turn right along Corso Garibaldi to reach Barletta's centre where you'll find the tourist office at the junction with Via Cavour. Continue a bit further and you'll eventually hit Via Duomo which will take you into the historic centre.

There is a helpful **tourist office** (☎ 0883 33 13 31; Corso Garibaldi 202; ❂ 9am-1pm & 5-7pm Mon-Fri, 9am-1pm Sat) in the town centre with plenty of information on Barletta and the surrounding area, but no English is spoken.

Sights & Activities

Despite its wonderful museum, fancy churches and enormous castle, Barletta is best known for the not-so-colossal **Colossus** that stands beside the **Basilica del Santo Sepolcro** (❂ services only) on Corso Vittorio Emanuele. No-one knows who the guy in the funny frilly crown really is although he's definitely a Roman Emperor of some sort – Theodosius, Valentinian, Marcian – they just can't decide which one.

The statue was stolen by the Venetians in 1203 after the sacking of Constantinople, but the ship foundered off the coast and it washed ashore. In 1309 Charles of Anjou thought he'd use a bit of the bronze to make some bells for the Palazzo del Sedile so his arms and legs were melted down and only later restored in a very clumsy job that's left him looking like he's wearing wellies.

Much more interesting is the newly restored Palazzo della Marra, now the **Pinacoteca Giuseppe de Nittis** (☎ 0883 57 86 15; www.pinacotecad enittis.it; Via Cialdini 75; adult/concession €4/2; ❂ 10am-8pm Tue-Sun). It exhibits a comprehensive selection of de Nittis' works, which were donated to the city by his wife, Léontine Gruvelle, after his premature death in 1884 (see boxed text, p79).

From Via Cialdini you can wander straight down into the shady alleys of the *centro storico*, at the heart of which you'll find Barletta's 12th-century **cathedral** (Via Duomo 52; ☯ 8.30am-noon & 4-8pm). It's another classic Puglian-Romanesque church, although the interior displays some Gothic influences in the polygonal apse. Aside from anything else it has a lovely location on the edge of the old town and if you wander across to the castle it makes a very fetching photograph. You can also visit the **castle** (☎ 0883 57 83 20; Piazza Corvi; adult/concession €4/2; ☯ 9am-1pm & 3-7pm Tue-Sun), but since the removal of the de Nittis collection to Palazzo della Marra there isn't a great deal to see. On the ground floor one of the rooms contains sculptural fragments, the most interesting of which is the bust of Frederick II, the only contemporary portrait of the emperor.

The castle moat has been laid to grass and there's a large area of public park which is usually full of families and ice-cream toting children, while in the evening the whole area is given over to open-air bars and cafés. More bars and restaurants can be found along Barletta's stretch of sandy **beaches** to the southeast of the town. They are within easy walking distance from the castle although they only get busy in summer.

Festivals

The **Disfida di Barletta** (Challenge of Barletta) is one of Italy's best-known medieval pageants. Held twice a year in February and July, it re-enacts a duel fought between 13 Italian and 13 French knights on 13 February 1503 when the French were besieging the town. The home side won and the chivalrous French decamped.

Sleeping & Eating

Most hotels cluster along Viale Regina Elena opposite the beaches.

Bed & Breakfast De Nittis (☎ 0883 57 13 10; www .bbdenittis.it; Vico del Lupo 9; s €30-45, d €45-60; ☒ ☐) Don't be put off by the exterior of the building or the dingy stairwell, as this is the best B&B in Barletta, with welcoming rooms decked out in bright primary colours. It's also well located for the town centre, and the young couple who run it are friendly and full of suggestions.

Nicotel (☎ 0883 34 89 46; www.nicotelhotels.com; Viale Regina Elena; s €90-100, d €130-150; P ☒) The best option along the seafront is the modern Nicotel with its cool marble reception and low-key

rooms. The buffet breakfast is sumptuous and the price includes parking and free access to the Brigantino Lido (beach) which makes it very good value.

BaccOsteria (☎ 0883 53 40 00; Via San Giorgio 5; meals €30; ☯ lunch Tue-Sun, dinner Tue-Sat) It might be small in size, but BaccOsteria is big on taste. Sit beneath the cool barrel vaults and sample the tiny tasters – swordfish *carpaccio*, sardines in lemon and mussels – before moving to fish wrapped in aubergines, *tagiolini* with cuttlefish or lobster and courgettes. You know you'll drink well because you can see the well-stocked wine cellar through the glass floor.

Antica Cucina (☎ 0883 52 17 18; Via Milano 73; meals €35; ☯ Wed-Sun) You have to ring the bell to gain entry to this superbly pretentious little restaurant and you'd better come looking the part. Slow jazz, crystal wine glasses, suited and booted waiting staff and a menu as florid as a romantic poem are all par for the course, but you can't argue with the tuna stuffed with capers and marinated in zibbibo wine.

Also recommended is **Il Brigantino** (☎ 0883 53 33 45; Viale Regina Elena; meals €30), which overlooks the beach.

Getting There & Away

Barletta is a main transport hub serviced by mainline Trenitalia trains and long-distance bus companies. From the bus station located on Via Manfredi, **Ferrovie del Gargano** (☎ 0881 58 72 11; www.ferroviedelgargano.com) buses link Barletta with Foggia (€4.60, two hours, hourly) and Margherita di Savoia (€1, hourly); there are regular **STP** (☎ 0883 49 18 00) buses to Trani (€0.90, 20 minutes) and Bari (€3.35, one hour). **Marino Autolinee** (☎ 199 800 100; www .marinobus.it) also runs services to Naples (€24.15, one daily).

Buy tickets for Ferrovie del Gargano services from **Bar Adriatico** (Via Manfredi 53) and all other tickets at **Cartolibreria Arcobaleno** (☎ 0883 52 07 96; Via Manfredi 73).

Barletta is on both the Bari-Foggia Trenitalia coastal train line and the Bari-Nord train line. It's easily accessible from Trani and other points along the coast, as well as inland towns. The ticket office is on platform 6 to 7.

AROUND BARLETTA

Nine kilometres from Barletta down a series of very windy country roads is the archaeological site of **Canne della Battaglia** (☎ 0883 51 09 93; adult,

THE PAINTER OF HAPPINESS

Despite the fact that Impressionism is on the curriculum of almost every school-age artist, barely anyone can name an Italian Impressionist. So a visit to the de Nittis exhibition in Barletta is something of an eye-opener on this artistic cul-de-sac. Like their French counterparts the Italian Impressionists shared the same desire to capture their 'impressions' of the world 'en plein air'; in other words, they sought to free painting from the restrictions of the easel and immerse themselves in nature itself. The play of light, sun, air, the reflections on the clouds and sea, these were their preoccupations. De Nittis himself modestly wrote 'I know all the colours, all the secrets of the air and the sky in their intimate nature'. And when you look at his *Primavera* (1883) canvas, with its subtle sugar-pink almond blossom and white-blue sky, or the rolling cloud of steam and mossy, muddy-coloured countryside in *Passa il Treno* (1869), you have to agree.

Giuseppe de Nittis (1846–84) was one of the few Italian impressionists to make an international name for himself. He moved to Paris, where he met and married Léontine Gruvelle and began exhibiting alongside the likes of Edgar Degas, Paul Gauguin and Camille Pissaro. Technically brilliant and devoted to his work, de Nittis swiftly excelled in the styles and techniques of the period. As the art critic Vittorio Pica famously remarked of the multifaceted artist, he was 'a southerner in the South, French in Paris, [and] a Londoner in London'.

Although he painted prolifically and across the spectrum of Impressionist subjects, his best work is devoted to his much-loved wife. Like many Impressionists he devoted much time to exploring the feminist ideal, but unlike Renoir's rosy-cheeked society ladies, de Nittis' portraits of women are strikingly 'real'. His female subjects, in many cases his wife, stare directly out of the canvas to hold the viewer's gaze. They are arresting and, as in the case of *Passeggiata Invernale* (1879) and *Signora de Nittis e Figlio* (1876), the women fill the canvas with their strong, dramatic stance. These aren't the typical bourgeoisie women of Impressionist painting, those reassuringly feminine creatures that Renoir, Degas and Morisot specialised in; no, these are more the women of Flaubert and Balzac's social commentary, strong personalities, full of sharp wit and grace.

The most famous, and beautiful, painting in the collection is undoubtedly *Figura di Donna* (1880), another portrait of Léontine in a full, gathered skirt, with coiffed hair and flowers at her lapel set against a golden background. Barely four years later, de Nittis died from pneumonia at the absolute peak of his success.

concession €2/1; ☼ 8.30am-7.30pm). It is gorgeously sited amid rolling countryside which gives little indication of the terrible battle that was fought here between the Romans and Carthaginians in 216 BC during the 2nd Punic War. Trapped in a classic pincer movement, the Roman forces were decimated on the banks of the River Ofanto (the ancient Aufidus), earning Hannibal a reputation as a master tactician and a ruthless opponent. Only a handful of men escaped, including Consul Gaius Varro, who returned to Rome gripped by terror while Hannibal marched on Capua.

Nothing remains of the site of the battle and the remains of the ancient town of Cannae have barely been excavated, revealing only the medieval remains of the village and the large necropolis. Finds from the necropolis are housed in the antiquarium (same hours as the archaeological site) and include some of the oldest painted ceramics in Puglia.

The site is well sign-posted off the main SP93. Once you turn off the main road it's a further 5km to the site.

ANDRIA

pop 97,380

Despite its regional importance and long history, there is little to hold one's interest in Andria. However, it is the main hub for buses to the Castel del Monte.

It was one of Frederick II's favourite towns due to its stalwart loyalty, a fact that is commemorated in an inscription on the Porta Sant'Andrea, one of the old city gates. It was in Andria that his son Conrad IV was born and two of his wives, Jolanda of Brienne and Isabella of England, are buried in the crypt of Andria's Gothic **cathedral** (Piazza Duomo 25), although this was closed for restoration at the time of research. In 1266, when Manfred was finally defeated at Benevento, his sons were brought to Andria and imprisoned in

THE CROWN OF STONE

The **Castel del Monte** (☎ 0883 56 99 97; adult/child €3/free; ☼ 9am-6pm) is Puglia's most prominent and talked-about landmark. Rising from a hilltop (540m), it is visible for miles around and is now a Unesco World Heritage site.

Nobody really knows why Frederick II built it in 1240 or why he adopted such a peculiar octagonal design. As far as anyone knows, nobody has ever lived there and there is no town or strategic crossroads nearby. Nor does it have any of the typical defensive features of a castle; there is no moat or drawbridge, no arrow slits or trapdoors for boiling oil. It's full of annoying brain-teasers.

And then there's the 'look' of it – its 25m-high blind walls and octagonal Gothic towers, its Italianate windows, Islamic floor mosaics and Roman triumphal entrance as well as all the decorative details. What was it all for?

Some people take the Dan Brown approach and claim that its geometry is rooted in mid-13th-century hocus-pocus, the octagon representing the union of the circle (God) and the square (man) and is therefore symbolic of the Emperor's divine right to rule. Others take a scientific approach, stating the castle was built in Neapolitan spans, an ancient rule of measurement and so-called golden number which was studied by Fibonacci who lived in the Swabian court. Most likely the castle was a propaganda tool for Frederick, a physical means of conveying his imperial might, a literal crown of stone. The fact that Charles I of Anjou chose to imprison Frederick's descendants in the castle for 30 years, gives some hint of its symbolic nature, and just looking at it you can't fail to be impressed by its size and solidity.

In the years that followed it was mostly used as a prison and a refuge – many families sought shelter here during the plague of 1656 – until it was abandoned in the 18th century and plundered by shepherds and bandits. In 1876, when the castle had fallen to ruin, the Italian state bought it for 25,000 lira and its restoration has taken nearly a century to complete. There are free tours of the castle (in English and German). Ask at the information hut in the car park.

The car park (car/caravan €4/5) is over 1km from the castle entrance. A free shuttle bus runs between the two.

Without a car, travelling to the Castel del Monte is a real pain. The least difficult way is by bus from Andria (p79).

the Castel del Monte – a symbolic gesture which spoke clearly of the total defeat of the Swabian monarchy.

STP buses for Trani leave from Corso Cavour opposite the Hotel dei Pini. Buy tickets in **Tabacchi Sinisi** (Corso Cavour 190), opposite. There are buses from Andria to Castel del Monte at 9.15am, 12.15pm and 4pm. Buses return to Andria from the castle at 11.35am, 1.30pm and 6pm. The Andria–Spinazzola bus also passes close by – ask the driver to let you off.

For Barletta (€1.10), its best to take one of the frequent Bari-Nord trains. From Andria you can connect to the main Foggia–Bari *autostrada* (A14), while the SS98 links up with Ruvo and Bitonto.

CANOSA DI PUGLIA
pop 31,450

An ancient Daunian town, dating back to the 7th century BC, Canosa has a fascinating history

but a less impressive present. Despite being a flourishing agricultural centre, the modern town is rather drab and sprawls down the hillside to the Tavoliere plain. It's certainly not Pompeii, but Canosa is the main archaeological centre in Puglia and every summer groups of students still arrive to excavate a few more metres of earth.

Ancient Canusium was a rich and powerful city allied with Rome who it supported loyally in the face of Carthaginian attack, even sheltering the survivors of the Battle of Cannae. It prospered further when the Via Traiana opened in the 2nd century and eventually became capital of the region. The massive **Arco Traiano** and the **Roman Bridge** are scant testimony to the prosperity of this period.

Subsequently it became the first diocese in Puglia (AD 343), so they converted the local Roman temple (the biggest in southern Italy) into the **Basilica di San Leucio** between the 4th and 5th centuries. Only the floor, with a few fragments of mosaic and sculpture remains, but at nearly 50 sq metres you can imagine its size and grandeur.

Equally grand is the **Cattedrale di San Sabino** (Piazza Vittorio Veneto; ☽ 9am-noon & 5-7pm), with it's five domes and echoing interior. Like Bitonto, the cathedral boasts an ambo (pulpit) by the 11th-century master craftsman Acceptus, whose decoration is strangely reminiscent of modern fascist designs. Other treasures include Pope Pasquale II's gloves(!), Roger of Melfi's bronze doors from Bohemond's tomb and a Bishops Throne sculpted out of white marble by Romualdo, who must have had a good sense of humour as he gave his lions extravagant swirling moustaches. A door in the south transept leads out to the **Tomba di Boemondo**, with its smooth white marble walls and oriental design.

From the cathedral it's a short walk to the **Museo Civico Archeologico** (☎ 0883 66 47 16; Via Kennedy 18; admission free; ☽ 9am-1pm Tue-Sun, 5-7pm Tue & Thu) and its extensive collection of grave goods dating back to the 4th century BC. The most unique pieces are the polychrome *askoi* (vases) which sport over-the-top figurines and faces, mainly of women with large bouffant hairdos and wide-eyed expressions. There are over 42 tombs in the Canosa area, although you can only visit three or four of them. The largest of all the tombs is the **Ipogeo Lagrasta**.

Most of the sights mentioned above are dispersed in impossible-to-find locations around Canosa, and many of them – the tombs, the Basilica di San Leucio – can only be visited with a guide. The helpful people at **Dromos** (☎ 0883 66 40 43; www.campidiomedei.it; Via Kennedy 18) hold the keys to the sights and can accompany you around town.

Beyond the sight-seeing there's little to detain you in Canosa. You can have a good lunch at **Ristorante Boemondo** (☎ 0883 61 41 11; Corso San Sabino 92; meals €18; ☽ daily) or even better at **Locanda di Nunno** (☎ 0883 61 50 96; Via Balilla 2; meals €35; ☽ lunch Tue-Sun).

STP buses connect Canosa with Barletta (€1.40, 30 minutes) and Bari (€5.10, two hours), and the main bus stop is on Piazza Terme in the centre of town. You can buy tickets and check timetables at the newsagent, **Edicola Sinesi** (Via Kennedy 28). You can also access the Foggia–Bari *autostrada* at Canosa.

MINERVINO MURGE
pop 9900

Perched on the crest of the Parco Nazionale dell'Alta Murgia (High Murge), Minervino Murge is a medieval throwback that feels like it's been lost in time. It commands sweeping views over the far-flung expanses of the plateau and its roots are firmly planted in the rural heritage of the area. From the 15th to the 18th century it was a feudal estate, the property of powerful families and it retains an insular, tight-knit community feel.

The Scesciola, the sleepy historic centre, has an austere character with its grey limestone houses and narrow alleys. But at weekends the streets fill up with strolling Minervese and vegetable stalls, and the place exudes a great sense of rural contentment. There is the ubiquitous castle, a small museum, some fancy churches and a wonderful *belvedere* (viewpoint) crowned by a war memorial. But the real pleasure of Minervino is wandering through its streets and then settling in for a long lunch.

There is a small **Pro Loco** (☎ 0883 69 12 91; Via Dante Alighieri 69) with information on the town but phone ahead to check it's open.

Eating

Eating in Minervino is an experience in itself, totally authentic with fresh, honest food from the surrounding countryside.

our pick Masseria Barbera (☎ 0833 692095; www .masseriabarbera.it; SS97, km5.850; meals €35; ☽ lunch Tue-Sun) Masseria Barbera is one of the most wonderful farm restaurants in Puglia, and the enormous white-washed dining room provides a fitting stage for the epic procession of food. In brisk succession come plates of antipasti: ricotta with *vinocotto*, courgette- and ricotta-plumped fritters, deep-fried veal balls and tiny mint omelettes. Then come homemade pastas with turnip tops or warm vegetable soups followed by succulent grilled meats. Afterwards, stroll around the gorgeous garden and buy lots of goodies from the farm shop.

La Traditizione Cucina Casalinga (☎ 0883 69 16 90; Via Imbriani 11; meals €25; ☽ Fri-Wed) The Dinoia brothers, like many Minervese, have an almost religious regard for food and their commitment to the cuisine of the Upper Murge is plain to taste in every plate. Seasonal treats like sausage and peppers, snails and cardoncelli mushrooms keep the menu varied, as do

---

PRINCIPLED PLEASURE

Stunningly situated on a gentle hill overlooking 190 hectares of olive trees, vines and orchards is the **Biomasseria Lama di Luna** (☎ 0883 56 95 05; www.lamadiluna.com; s/d €100/130; P ✷), an 18th-century working farm near the tiny village of Montegrosso. It's a classic *masseria*, a forti-fied compound that was originally home to 26 tenant farmers who once occupied the now cosy guestrooms.

Sure there are lots of *masserie* in Puglia, so what's so special about this one? Well, it's probably Puglia's only real eco-hotel. The building has been renovated according to the principles of feng shui and the farm is cultivated along strict eco-friendly lines, the olives harvested to make the farm's own range of soaps and creams. Solar panels feed the computer-operated heating system and at night you sleep amid unbleached cotton sheets on some of the most comfortable mat-tresses in Puglia. If they arrange an evening meal, be sure to join in, they're such good fun. You get to make your own pizza in the wood-fired oven.

During the day, take out the mountain bikes and cycle around the immense farm or head down to Montegrosso to eat at **Antichi Sapori** (☎ 0883 56 95 29; Piazza San Isidoro 10; meals €35; ✷ lunch Mon-Sat), one of the most highly recommended restaurants in the region.

---

real local specialities like *troccoli alla murgese* (pasta with Marzotica ricotta and cherry to-matoes) and *cutturid con cime di rape* (lamb stew with turnip tops).

SOUTH OF BARI

Nestled between the southern side of the Murge plateau and the rising Lucanian Apen-nines to the southwest, Altamura and Gravina di Puglia seem remote and cut off, more tied to Basilicata than to the Puglia. It really makes most sense to visit them in combination with Matera, as the history and character of the towns are closely related.

ALTAMURA
pop 66,600

OK, it has history, it has churches and it has a very good museum, but best of all Alta-mura has bread. And not just any old bread – famous bread. The people in Matera say the recipe is really theirs and the Altamuran's just stole the idea and made an international busi-ness out of it. Whatever the story, Altamura is more famous for its bread than for anything else so you absolutely have to visit one of the old bakeries in town. You can do this in the historic centre in one of the atmospheric tra-ditional bakeries.

Forno Antico Santa Caterina dal 1724 (Via Ambrogio del Giudice 2) is just off the main drag and there's another one on Via S Caterina. Having bought a loaf of bread big enough to feed a family of 10, wander around to Frederick II's Palatine

cathedral (Piazza Duomo; admission free; ✷ 7am-noon & 4-8pm daily) and try and guess what the vignettes of Christ's Life are around the fabulously carved portal. It's difficult to conceive how the sculp-tors were able to make the scenes so intricate and involved – just look at that Last Supper in the lunette above the door. Opposite the cathedral the small **Chiesa di San Niccolo dei Greci** (Corso Federico II di Svevia; ✷ services only), originally a church dedicated to the celebration of the Greek rite, has a similarly ornate door, with scenes from the Old and New Testament – the best one is of a sinner being boiled in a large pot surrounded by grinning devils.

The other site worth visiting is the well-organised **Museo Archeologico** (☎ 080 311 76 79; Via Santeramo 88; adult/concession €2/1; ✷ 8.30am-7.30pm). It displays a good collection of grave goods dat-ing from the 8th to the 5th century BC. There is also a selection of locally painted ceramics from the 6th to 5th centuries, and for once there are labels with explanations in English.

Despite its size, Altamura does not have a tourist office, but there is a small **Pro Loco** (☎ 080 314 39 30; Piazza Repubblica 11; ✷ 10am-1pm & 5.30-8pm Mon-Sat, 10am-1pm Sun), with some limited information and a map of the city.

Although Altamura has one good hotel, **Hotel San Nicola** (☎ 080 314 4752; www.hotelsannicola .com; Via L de Samuele Cagnazzi 29; s €85-110, d €130-150; P), it's probably best to stay elsewhere, either down the road in Gravina or in Matera.

The Ferrovie Appulo–Lucano line runs between Bari and Basilicata and has regular services Monday to Saturday from Matera (€1.70, 25 minutes), Gravina (€1, 10 minutes) and Bari (€2.60, one hour). On Sunday there is a replacement bus service. A shuttle bus runs from the station to the town centre.

GRAVINA DI PUGLIA
pop 43,550

Barely 10km from Altamura, Gravina is the more scenic of the two towns, perched as it is on the edge of a precipitous ravine. Riddled with caves, the ravine has been inhabited for thousands of years. It really came in use during the Barbarian invasions, which sent the inhabitants scurrying into the caves where they remained long after the new (now old) town, Fondovico, began to take shape around the 5th century.

There isn't a tourist office as such in Gravina, but the **Associazione Culturale Benedetto XIII** (☎ 338 567 80 17; Piazza Notar Domenico; ☼ 9am-12.30pm & 3-sunset) is an organisation of volunteers who hold the keys to all the churches and offer free guided tours in numerous languages.

Sights

For a long time Gravina was pretty much the personal property of the Roman Orsini family. The town was given to them by the Normans in 1420 and it remained their fee until 1807, and as such it benefited from their wealth and patronage. The massive **Chiesa del Purgatorio** (Piazza Notar Domenico; ☼ only with guide) was actually their family church and mausoleum, the columns embellished by bears a subtle allusion to their family name (orso means 'bear'). It is stuffed with treasures like the polychrome marble altar and picture frames designed by Cosimo Fansago and the huge organ, possibly the finest in Puglia.

Equally ornate is the **duomo** (Piazza Benedetto XIII; ☼ 9am-noon & 5-7pm), with is baroque ceiling, walnut-wood choir stalls and acres of polychrome marble. But despite the pomp and splendour, Gravina's most famous church is the rock-hewn **Chiesa di San Michele di Grotti** (Rione Fondovico; ☼ only with guide), now a pale shadow of its frescoed past. It was the first cathedral of Gravina, but its fame comes from the ossuary that was once piled high with the bones of martyrs murdered by the Saracens. They're gone now, moved during the restoration to a more peaceful place, although there is talk of returning them to the sanctuary one day.

From the grotto you can see the **Parco Archeologico di Botromagno** (☎ 080 325 25 73; SS96, km86,400) on the other side of the ravine. It's currently closed due to investigations into recent spending of EU money, which will hopefully be resolved soon so that the park can reopen. You can see items from the site in the fascinating **Museo Civico** (☎ 080 322 10 40; Piazza Benedetto XIII; admission free; ☼ 9am-1pm & 4-8pm Tue-Sun). The best displays are the reconstructed tombs of two Peucetian warriors complete with their weapons and treasures and a complete walk-in family tomb dating from the 3rd century BC.

Also well worth a visit is the **Palazzo Pomarici Santomasi** (☎ 080 325 10 21; Via Museo 20; adult/concession €3/0.50; ☼ 9am-1pm & 4-7pm Mon-Sat, 9am-noon Sun), mainly to see the reconstruction of the Byzantine crypt of San Vito Vecchio with a complete set of 13th-century frescoes of local

---

GOURMET BREAD

Altamura's D.O.P. (Denomination of Origin of Production) bread is the best of the best, made with ingredients and techniques almost unchanged since the baker's guild was formed in the Middle Ages. What results are large, heavy wheels of bread with burnished brown crusts that have been baked in 300-year-old wood-fired ovens. 'Using a wood-fired brick oven with a stone surface is about the most difficult way to bake bread,' Giuseppe Barile, President of the Bread Consortium of Altamura, tells me, 'But it's also the best way'.

In the Forno Antico Santa Caterina, I watch as bakers shape huge rounds of fragrant country bread made with high-quality hard wheat flour. It is given three risings, then baked slowly at gradually decreasing temperatures to allow the moisture to evaporate and the bread to cook through without burning the crust. The loaf will last for several days and even improves with time. Of course, there is more than one type of bread, there's the *ciambella*, a large bread ring with a small hole that is cut open after it is baked, and a variety of hearth-baked focaccia. There is also an infinite variety of toppings – everything from simple olive oil and salt, herbs and garlic to onions, tomatoes, peppers and cheese. It really is impossible to choose.

workmanship. It gives you just some idea of what the grotto of San Michele would once have looked like.

Sleeping & Eating

Trattoria Zia Rosa (☎ 080 325 63 69; www.trattoriazia rosa.it; r €25; 🗶) There isn't a great selection of hotels in Gravina, but the rooms here are neat and comfortable and it is well located just inside the entrance to the old town centre.

`our pick` **Osteria Cucco** (☎ 080 326 18 72; Piazza Pellicciari 4; meals €30; 🕙 Tue-Sat) Opposite Trattoria Zia Rosa, you'll find this Slow Food restaurant. A cheerful place with a serious kitchen turning out delicate aubergine *millefeuille* (literally 'a thousand leaves' to describe the numerous layers of wafer-thin pastry) and artichoke heart *carpaccio*. The cured meats and local cheeses are also noteworthy.

Madonna della Stella (☎ 080 325 63 83; www.madon nadellastella.org; Via Fontana la Stella; meals €30; 🕙 Wed-Mon) If you'd rather have a view, you can try this place on the other side of the ravine. In summer you can eat out on their terrace and look straight down into the green gorge.

Getting There & Away

Gravina is on the same Ferrovie Appulo–Lucano line as Altamura from where you can connect with Bari and Matera.

Northern Puglia & the Gargano Promontory

Crowning Italy's boot, the northern province of Foggia (the *capitanata*) is an attractive land of contrasting geographical bands, from the mountainous rocky spur of the Gargano Promontory to the vast flat tablelands of the Tavoliere and the gentle rolling hills of the Daunia Pre-Apennines. The Tavoliere is the wheatbowl of southern Italy, covering half of the *capitanata* in a 3000-sq-km geometric chequerboard of golden fields. Tracks across the plains bear witness to the centuries-old transhumance routes, the ancient droving trails or *tratturi* along which sheep and cattle were moved from Abruzzo to Puglia. The wheatfields surrounding the provincial capital of Foggia gently give way to the wetlands and salt works of Margherita di Savoia on the southeast coast, a region famous for its prolific birdlife.

To the west, the Tavoliere merges into the undulating foothills, shallow valleys and wooded slopes of the beautiful Daunia mountains. Here, castles and towers of the medieval hilltop towns watch over Foggia's Pre-Apennine border.

Puglia's only mountainous zone is the stunning Gargano Promontory, a blunt spur of limestone cliffs and dense forest jutting into the blue Adriatic Sea. Its landscape, flora and fauna are a geographical anomaly in Puglia's Mediterranean *mezzogiorno*, more Croatian than southern Italian. Millions of years ago the Gargano was separated from the mainland by a thin strip of ocean. Now its unique beauty and summer seaside resorts are a favourite with Italian and German tourists.

HIGHLIGHTS

- Worship the gods of sun, sand and sea in the attractive seaside resort of **Vieste** (p88)
- Explore the dramatic coastal road between Mattinata and Peschici, stopping at a **trabucco** (boxed text, p93) for a fresh seafood lunch
- Hike or mountain bike in the uniquely Bavarian-esque **Foresta Umbra** (p87)
- Brave the pilgrims for a spiritual experience in the atmospheric **Santuario di San Michele** (p97) in Monte Sant'Angelo
- Drive through the rolling hills and medieval hilltop towns of the stunning **Daunia Pre-Apennines** (p108)
- Dive the incredibly clear blue waters of the **Isole Tremiti** (p102)

★ Isole Tremiti

Mattanata-Peschici Coastal Road ★

Vieste ★

Foresta Umbra ★

Monte ★ Sant'Angelo

Daunia Pre-Apennines ★

THE GARGANO PROMONTORY

The Gargano Promontory (Promontorio del Gargano) is one of the most beautiful areas in southern Italy, rising from the sea to tower 1000m above Puglia's flat tablelands. Characterised by white limestone cliffs, calcareous grottoes, a crystal-clear green sea and ancient forests, the 'spur' of the Italian boot has more in common with Dalmatia than the rest of Italy. A winding drive along the coastal road affords breathtaking views of the Adriatic Sea and the secluded sandy coves and long beaches

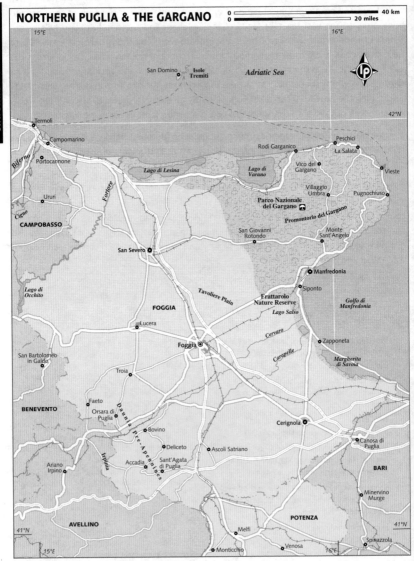

NORTHERN PUGLIA & THE GARGANO

THE GARGANO PROMONTORY

NORTHERN PUGLIA & THE GARGANO PROMONTORY

that attract summer sun-worshippers to its attractive seaside towns, especially Vieste and Peschici.

The peninsula is also a place of creeping urbanisation, which was thankfully halted in 1991 by the creation of the Parco Nazionale del Gargano, which encompasses the entire promontory and its island off-shoots, the Isole Tremiti. Aside from its magnificent display of flora and fauna in the primeval forests of Quarto, Spigno and Umbra, and its whitewashed coastal towns, the park takes in the no-holds-barred miracle town of San Giovanni Rotondo and the historic pilgrimage destination of Monte Sant'Angelo. Outside the summer tourist season the Gargano is a quiet and tranquil nature retreat.

FORESTA UMBRA

Although the Parco Nazionale del Gargano takes in most of the peninsula, only a small portion of this, the Foresta Umbra (Forest of Shadows), is truly wild. The forest is the last remnant of Puglia's ancient forests, and shades the peaks of the promontory's mountainous interior with a blanket of Aleppo pines, oak and beech. Rare orchids, fantastic birdlife, and endemic fauna and flora define this geographical island. Hikers and mountain bikers will find plenty of well-marked trails within the forest's 15,000 hectares, and there are several picnic areas.

At the Villagio Umbra, in the heart of the forest, the **Corpo Forestale dello Stato** (☎ 0884 56 54 44; admission €1.20; 9am-7pm Apr-Oct) runs a visitors centre housing a small museum and nature centre. Here you can see photographs of the Gargano's endemic plant life and over 200 stuffed animals. Hikers can pick up a *Carta dei Sentieri*, a handy map with pictures of the park's flora and fauna and a description of 15 hiking trails (in English and Italian).

Specialist tour operators within the Gargano Promontory also organise excursions in the Foresta Umbra and throughout the Gargano. **Explora Gargano** (☎ 340 713 68 64; www .exploragargano.it; Via Santa Maria di Merino 62, Vieste; 9.30am-12.30pm & 6-10.30pm May-Sep) offers mountain-biking and hiking tours and jeep safaris. **Gargano Bike Holidays** (☎ 339 717 53 34; www.garganobike.com; Localita Defensola, Vieste; 4-7pm) offer specialist mountain-biking

expeditions. **Ecogargano** (☎ 0884 56 54 44; www
.ecogargano.it; Largo Roberto Giuscardo 2, Monte Sant'Angelo;
⊗ 9am-1pm & 2.30-7pm summer, 9am-1pm & 2.30-6pm
winter) offers tours with official guides of the
national park. For horse-riding tours contact
Anello Equestre del Gargano (☎ 0884 53 04 00; www
.postaruggiano.com; Locanda Ruggiano).

VIESTE
pop 13,600 / elev 43m

Vieste is an attractive whitewashed town
jutting off the Gargano's easternmost rocky
promontory into the Adriatic Sea. Of its
spectacular beaches the Spiaggia del Castello
is a wide yellow-sand strip backed by sheer
white cliffs and overshadowed by the towering
Scoglio di Pizzomunno, an enormous rocky
monolith. This popular seaside resort is the
commercial and tourist capital of the Gargano
and the staging point for ferries to the Isole
Tremiti. In summer Vieste is a lively spot on
and off the sand, but it can get overcrowded
in July and August. In winter, it more or less
closes down.

With its range of restaurants and accommodation options, Vieste is an ideal base from
which to explore the Gargano.

Orientation
Intercity buses terminate at Piazzale Manzoni.
A 10-minute walk east along Via XXIV Maggio
leads to Corso Fazzini and the old town with its
attractive promenade of Marina Piccola. You'll
find the tourist office at Piazza Kennedy.

Vieste sits on two promontories. From the
old town on the easternmost promontory the
promenade leads north to the port.

Information
Banca Apulia (☎ 0884 70 56 89; Viale XXIV Maggio 37)
Banca Carime (☎ 0884 70 22 09; Viale XXIV Maggio 92)
Guardia Medica (☎ 0884 71 12 22)
Internet point (InfoTraining; ☎ 0884 70 22 65; Viale
XXIV Maggio 11; per hr €2; ⊗ 9.30am-1pm & 5-9pm
Mon-Sat)
Police (☎ 0884 70 80 14; Via Petrone)
Post office (☎ 0884 70 80 00; Piazza Vittorio Veneto)
Tourist office (☎ 0884 70 88 06; Piazza Kennedy;
⊗ 8am-2pm & 3-9pm daily in summer, 8am-8pm Mon-
Sat in winter) The pink tourist office is at the southern end
of the Marina.

Sights
Pizzomunno, the unmistakable white rocky
tower jutting out of the sea as you approach

Vieste from the south, is a natural landmark
with a tale to tell. If legend is to be believed,
underneath that hard rocky exterior lies the
heart of a romantic. Pizzomunno, so the story
goes, was a humble fisherman in love with the
beautiful Cristalda. Jealous sirens, unable to
tempt him with their wily charms, dragged
Cristalda to the bottom of the sea and turned
the heartbroken Pizzomunno into a rock. But
the sirens weren't completely wicked. Every
100 years the rock breaks free and the lovers
are reunited for one wild night.

Vieste is primarily a beach resort and has
only a few sights of interest located in the
winding medieval streets of the historic centre. From the **Chiesa di San Francesco** (a former
monastery, closed for restoration) at the tip of
the promontory walk up Via Carlo Mafrolla
where boutique craftshops selling ceramics
and local handicrafts have replaced hippy
market stalls. The **Chianca Amara** (bitter stone; Via
Cimaglia) is where the Turkish pirate Dragut
Rais allegedly beheaded 5000 local inhabitants
in the raid of 1554.

Nearby is the Puglian-Romanesque **cathedral** (☎ 0884 70 80 78; Via Duomo; ⊗ 7.30am-noon &
4-11pm), built in the 11th century but altered
in the 18th century. It houses a wooden statue
of the Santa Maria di Merino, one of Vieste's
two patron saints. At the town's highest point
is the **castle** (Piazza Castello) built by Frederick II.
It's now occupied by the military and closed
to the public.

The **Museo Malacologico** (☎ 0884 70 76 88; Via Pola
8; admission free; ⊗ 9.30am-noon & 4.30-9pm) showcases 14,550 seashells from around the world.
Look for the *Epitonium scalare*, the collector's
favourite.

At 9km north of town, off the SP52 towards
the Hotel Gabbiano Beach, is a palaeochris-
tian graveyard dating from the 4th to the 6th
centuries AD, **La Salata** (☎ 0884 70 66 35; www
.agenziasinergie.it; admission €5; ⊗ 5.30-6.15pm Jun-Aug,
4-4.45pm Sep, Oct-May on request). The cave burial
chambers are found in marshland close to
the sea, in an area dense with typical Mediterranean *maquis*. Inside the caves tier upon tier
of narrow tombs are cut into the rock wall;
others form shallow niches in the cave floor.

Activities
There's plenty of sun and sand for beach wor-
shippers. The best **beaches**, such as Baia di San
Felice and Baia di Campi, are south of Vieste.
However, if you don't have your own trans-

port, Spiaggia del Castello (of Pizzomunno fame) is easily accessible only 1km south of town, while the Spiaggia di San Lorenzo is just north of the port. The beaches are lined with lidos where you can hire umbrellas, sunbeds, canoes and pedalos. **Punta Lunga**, 2km north of Vieste, is a renowned windsurfing hot spot. Hire a windsurfer from **Gargano Surf'n'kite Centre** (☎ 0884 70 14 33; www.garganosurf .com; Cala Azzurra, Litoranea Vieste-Peschici km5; half-day hire €25, 1hr lesson €35).

From May to September hop on one of the fast boats and day-trip it to the **Isole Tremiti** where you can learn to dive. From July to September you can go as far afield as Croatia with **Navigargano** (☎ 0884 70 84 09; ✆ weekends only). It takes two hours and costs €55.

Closer to home, you can cave-hop on a two-hour boat trip to the Gargano's fabulous **marine caves**. Tickets are available at the port kiosks and cost €12 to €15. The boats follow the craggy coastline south to Mattinata so you can scope out the Gargano's best beaches (and maybe more – Vignanotica attracts nature-loving nudists). Before booking consider the environmental impact of fast boats and splashback on the fragile limestone caves (see p55).

To get off the beach for a day or two, take one of the many tours on offer. As well as hiking and mountain biking in the Foresta Umbra, **Explora Gargano** (☎ 340 713 68 64; www .exploragargano.it; Via Santa Maria di Merino 62; ✆ 9.30-12.30pm & 6-10.30pm May-Sep) offers quad tours

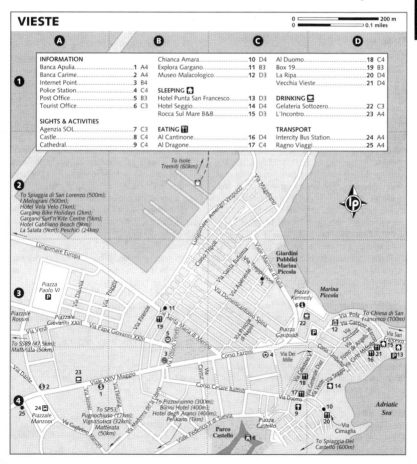

VIESTE

INFORMATION	Chianca Amara...........10 D4	Al Duomo...................18 C4	
Banca Apulia..................1 A4	Explora Gargano...........11 B3	Box 19.......................19 B3	
Banca Carime.................2 A4	Museo Malacologico......12 D3	La Ripa.....................20 D4	
Internet Point................3 B4		Vecchia Vieste............21 D4	
Police Station.................4 C4	**SLEEPING**		
Post Office.....................5 B3	Hotel Punta San Francesco...13 D3	**DRINKING**	
Tourist Office..................6 C3	Hotel Seggio...............14 D4	Gelateria Sottozero........22 C3	
	Rocca Sul Mare B&B.......15 D3	L'Incontro..................23 A4	
SIGHTS & ACTIVITIES			
Agenzia SOL..................7 C3	**EATING**	**TRANSPORT**	
Castle.........................8 C4	Al Cantinone...............16 D4	Intercity Bus Station.......24 A4	
Cathedral.....................9 C4	Al Dragone.................17 C4	Ragno Viaggi...............25 A4	

(half-day from €70) and jeep safaris (per day from €50). **Gargano Bike Holidays** (☎ 339 717 53 34; www.garganobike.com; Localita Defensola; ☒ 4-7pm) specialise in cultural and scenic mountain-bike tours, exploring the Gargano on half-day to weekly trips. The itineraries are graded from easy to difficult and the guides are multilingual. **Agenzia SOL** (☎ 0884 70 15 58; www.solvieste.it; Via Treppiccioni 5; ☒ 9am-1pm & 5-9pm) also arranges a host of walking and cycling opportunities in the Foresta Umbra. It hires out mountain bikes and cars (per day from €58) and organises 25hp motorboat (per day €80) and 11.8m sailing boat (per day €600) hire. Francesca Toto from **Agenzia Sinergie** (☎ 0884 70 66 35; www .agenziasinergie.it; Via Saragat 3; ☒ 9am-2pm & 4-8pm Mon-Fri) is a helpful and informative *Guida Ufficiale del Parco Nazionale del Gargano* (Official Guide of the Gargano National Park).

Sleeping

The most attractive place to stay is the historic centre, although resort-style hotels and *pensioni* stretch along the beachfront north and south of town. Camping villages are another plentiful and economical option.

BUDGET

Rocca Sul Mare B&B (☎ 0884 70 27 19; Via Carlo Maf-rolla 32; s €25-60 d €50-120; ☒ ⌨ P) In a former convent in the old quarter, this recently re-furbished B&B has high-ceilinged rooms and steep staircases. The bathrooms are small and cramped but the old-fashioned hospitality makes you feel right at home. The terrace has magnificent views over the port.

Hotel Punta San Francesco (☎ 0884 70 14 22; www .hotelpuntasanfrancesco.it; Via San Francesco 2; s €30-60, d €60-120; ☒) Also in the old quarter on the promontory and with the same magnificent views, this small hotel occupies a good position close to the action.

Hotel Vela Velo (☎ 0884 70 63 03; Lungomare Europa 55; s €40-110 d €60-120; ☒ P) A great base 1.5km from the town centre, this friendly and unpretentious hotel overlooks the northern end of San Lorenzo beach. It has sunrise views of the port, a sundeck on the roof, a private stretch of beach and a pleasant breakfast terrace. Mountain bikes are free for guest use.

MIDRANGE

Hotel Seggio (☎ 0884 70 81 23; www.hotelseggio.it; Via Veste 7; s €40-70, d €75-140; ☒ Apr-Oct; ☒ ⌨ P ☒) A lemon-yellow *palazzo* in the historic centre of Vieste. It has a seafront location and its pretty pool and sunbathing terrace are right at the sea's edge. Also runs a bar and *gelateria* in the small square overlooking the bay.

Hotel Gabbiano Beach (☎ 0884 70 63 76; www.gab bianobeach.com; Localita Santa Maria di Merinum; half-board per person €46.50-106.50; ☒ Apr-Oct; ☒ ☒ P) Set in tranquil woodland 9km north of Vieste, this well-maintained hotel is right on the beach. The rooms are airy and spacious with large bathrooms and private terraces. There's a tennis court, and a beachfront pool bar for partying. The hotel also has 50 self-contained bungalows (minimum stay one week).

Bikini Hotel (☎ 0884 70 15 45; www.bikinihotelvieste .it; Via Massimo D'Azeglio 13; s €60-98, d €120-196; ☒ Apr-Oct; ☒ ⌨ P ☒) Built in 2003, this modern 32-room hotel is a good choice – a short walk from the town centre and from the main beach. Ocean-facing rooms have a view of Pizzomunno while all rooms display fascinating pieces from local artist Circiello.

TOP END

Hotel degli Aranci (☎ 0884 70 85 57; www.hotelaranci .com; Piazza Santa Maria delle Grazie 10; s €58-160, d €93-240; ☒ Mar-Nov; ☒ P ☒) Excellent service in this large modern hotel makes for a comfortable stay. The private beach with its lido and water toys is a short walk away. In summer the hotel hosts a weekly gala dinner and performances. This is one of the few hotels to serve a large buffet breakfast. Ask for a room with a jacuzzi and a hydro-massage shower.

I Melograni (☎ 0884 70 10 88; www.imelograni.it; Lun-gomare Europa 48; half-board per person €59-122; ☒ Apr-Oct; ☒ ⌨ P ☒) Set on 11 hectares, this huge complex has two hotels, 100 bungalows (minimum stay one week from €240 per person) and camping facilities (person/site per day €4/10). The hotel rooms are stock standard but the village atmosphere (with nightly outdoor entertainment around the two pools) makes this a happening scene. To reach the private beach on Spiaggia San Lorenzo walk through a tunnel beneath the busy esplanade road.

Eating

There are plenty of restaurants to choose from in the old town and around Piazza Kennedy.

BUDGET

Box 19 (☎ 0884 70 52 29; Via Santa Maria di Merino 13; meals €20-30; ☒ lunch & dinner daily summer, Tue-Sun winter, closed Nov) You might feel like a fish in a tank dining in a box on the street but Box 19 is renowned for its excellent seafood. Tuck into a plate of *linguine all'astice* (linguine with lobster) while the crowds surge around you.

Al Cantinone (☎ 0884 70 77 53; Via Carlo Mafrolla 26; meals €25; ✆ lunch & dinner Thu-Tue Easter-Oct) The menu comes in a wooden book but otherwise this is an unpretentious restaurant that offers good, simple fare. Recommended dish is the *troccoli alla zappatora*, as is the seafood antipasto and local desserts.

MIDRANGE

Al Duomo (☎ 0884 70 82 43; Via Alessandro III 23; meals €25-30; ✆ noon-midnight Mar-Dec) Tucked away in a narrow alley in the heart of the old town, this restaurant has a cosy cave interior and outdoor seating under a shady arbour. Homemade pastas with seafood sauces feature prominently. Try the *cavatelli con ceci polipetti e rughetta* (pasta with chickpeas, octopus and rocket).

La Ripa (☎ 0884 70 80 48; Via Cimaglia 16; meals €25-30; ✆ lunch & dinner Mar-Oct) Near the Chianca Amara, this family-run restaurant in a converted stable has lots of character – and plenty of half-melted candles that would do a goth proud. The meat and vegetables are home-grown and organic (as is the podolico cheese). For a pasta mouthful try the *foglie d'ulivo con gamberi, rucola, ricotta e julienne di zucchini* (olive-leaf shaped pasta with prawns, zucchini and rocket).

Vecchia Vieste (☎ 0884 70 70 83; Via Carlo Mafrolla 32; meals €30; ✆ lunch & dinner daily summer, Thu-Tue winter) Where better to serve *tipico antiche* traditional recipes than in a converted stable? If you haven't yet tried sea-urchin pasta now's your chance. Order *troccoli con polpa di riccio della scogliera* and be prepared for a taste sensation.

TOP END

ourpick Pelikano (☎ 0884 70 24 89; Lungomare E Mattei 9b; meals €35; ✆ lunch & dinner daily, Wed-Mon in winter) Opening directly onto Vieste's main beach, this restaurant is beach-chic at its best. Cane chairs, wooden tables and palm trees on the beachfront gives a Polynesian feel but the cuisine is typical Pugliese with fresh seafood and homemade pasta dishes. Also has an extensive pizza menu (€7 to €8).

Al Dragone (☎ 0884 70 12 12; Via Duomo 8; meals €35; ✆ lunch & dinner Mar-Nov) Colourful palaeo-lithic pieces from local artist, Circiello add a distinctly stone-age touch to this intimate cave restaurant. The chef uses local seasonal products with an innovative twist. A recommended dish is *orecchiette con cime di rape e acciughe rosse* washed down with a bottle of Puglian wine.

Drinking

L'Incontro (☎ 0884 70 26 64; Viale XXIV Maggio 82; panini €2.50; ✆ 6am-midnight summer, Wed-Mon winter) A funky bar whose name, The Encounter, promises a fun night out or at least an interesting time puzzling over the symbolic artwork and stitched-iron plates in the back room. Has a legendary *aperitivo* – after 11am a complimentary plate of homemade hors d'oeuvres is served with your drink.

Gelateria Sottozero (☎ 0884 70 14 44; Piazza Kennedy 9; gelati €1.50-3; ✆ 8.30-2am Jul & Aug, 8.30am-1.30pm & 3.30-11pm Sep-Jun) Dawdle over a coffee or *prosecco* while checking out the chic-elite in town but don't leave without indulging in the best ice cream in Vieste. For a rich, fat, chocolate fix drown in the *amarena*.

Getting There & Away

There are no train services in the Gargano Promontory; trains stop at San Severo. Although buses link the coastal towns in summer it is difficult to explore the Foresta Umbra and the Gargano's numerous bays and inlets without your own transport.

BUS

SITA (☎ 0881 77 31 17) buses connect Vieste with towns to the south of the promontory. Frequent services from Foggia (€5.70, 2¾ hours) travel along the Gargano's southern coast road via Manfredonia (€3.40, two hours).

Ferrovie del Gargano (☎ 0881 72 51 88) buses connect Vieste with towns to the north of the promontory. Frequent services operate between Vieste and Peschici (€1.50, 30 minutes) during the summer.

Buses terminate at Piazzale Manzoni and timetables are posted outside **Ragno Viaggi** (☎ 0884 70 15 28) on the square.

CAR & MOTORBIKE

From Foggia take the SS89 to Manfredonia and follow the southern coastal road to Vieste. Alternatively, take the SS16 to San Severo turning onto the SS89 to follow the northern coastal road around the promontory.

NORTHERN PUGLIA & THE
GARGANO PROMONTORY

TRAIN

Trains from Foggia stop at San Severo (€1.80, 20 minutes, five daily). From here Ferrovie del Gargano buses link to Vieste (€6.80, 3½ hours, three daily).

Getting Around

The local yellow council buses (€0.50) run frequently (almost hourly) in summer along the coast road from 11km north of Vieste to 11km south of Vieste. In winter services are virtually nonexistent.

In summer several companies, including **Adriatica** (☎ 0884 70 85 01; www.adriatica.it) and **Navi-gargano** (☎ 0884 70 84 09) run boats to the Isole Tremiti. The companies run at least one boat daily (€31.60 return; 1½ hours) and tickets can be bought at the port or from **Agenzia SOL** (☎ 0884 70 15 58; www.solvieste.it; Via Treppiccioni 5; 🕑 9am-1pm & 5-9pm).

PESCHICI

pop 4317 / elev 90m

A little smaller than Vieste, but possibly even more picturesque, Peschici has whitewashed houses (some topped with Byzantine cupolas) that cascade down a rocky outcrop to a beautiful sandy cove. Originally built by the Normans to guard against maritime invasions, Peschici is now a fast-developing resort town, but remains relatively unspoilt. The town is another good base from which to explore the Gargano or to visit the Isole Tremiti.

Orientation & Information

The medieval and more interesting part of town clings to the clifftop at the point of the bay, while the newer parts extend inland and around the bay. In winter, buses terminate beside Chiesa di San Antonio. For the rest of the year, the terminal is beside the sports ground, 200m uphill from the town's main street, Corso Garibaldi. Turn right into the *corso* and walk straight ahead to reach the old town.

Agrifoglio Tour (☎ 0884 96 27 21; www.agrifoglio tour.it; Piazza Sant'Antonio 3; 🕑 9am-1pm & 5.30-10.30pm summer, times may vary in winter) has a helpful English-speaking travel agent who can organise cultural tours, trips to the Isole Tremiti and jeep safaris in the park.

Sights & Activities

After a day lounging on the beach a stroll through Peschici's labyrinthine medieval

heart is a pleasant way to start the evening. In an impressive clifftop position is the 11th-century **castle** (☎ 0884 96 40 78; Via Castello; adult/child €3/2; 🕑 10am-1pm & 7.30-10pm May-Sep). It is privately owned and houses a small museum.

Also situated in the town centre is the **Chiesa di Sant'Elia** (Largo Chiesa Madre; 🕑 10am-12.30pm & 3.30-8pm) with some interesting Bauhaus-style paintings of the Via Crucis by Alfredo Bortoluzzi.

A little way out of town, 1.5km along the coast road to Vieste, stands the small **Chiesa di Madonna di Loreto** (☎ 0884 96 40 64; 🕑 by appointment) erected where the Virgin Mary supposedly appeared before a ship caught in a storm. Built in the 16th and 17th centuries, the whitewashed chapel has the same dimensions as the lucky ship. Model boats hang from the inside walls.

As you drive between Peschici and Vieste look out for the trabucci (see the box text, opposite) jutting out over the water.

Sleeping

Peschici has several hotels and *pensioni* but many insist upon a minimum of half board. Numerous camp sites dot the coast east and west of Peschici.

La Torretta (☎ 0884 96 29 35; www.latorrettapeschici .it; Via Torretta 15; half board per person €42-80; 😺) The views alone are worth the stay in this no-frills but clean and new *pensione* where all rooms face the bay of Peschici. It's close to the centre of town and has a pizzeria with a view.

Agriturismo Torre dei Prati (☎ 0884 96 30 66; www .torredeiprati.it; Località Vale Croci; half board per person €50-90; Apr-Oct; 😺 🖳 🅿 🐾) A tranquil retreat set in a 26-hectare olive grove 2km north of Peschici, this stylish *agriturismo* makes a great base away from the tourist frenzy. The 16th-century tower has four rooms on four floors while seven cottages are scattered among the olive trees in the grounds. The restaurant serves typical dishes from the region using home-grown olive oil.

Locanda al Castello (☎ 0884 96 40 38; Piazza Castello 29; half/full board per person €55/70; 😺 🅿) Arriving at this cheerful place is kind of like entering a family home. The welcome is genuine and the atmosphere unstuffy. Situated right on the cliffs, it is definitely the pick of the old quarter. It also runs a decent restaurant (meals €20) and a neighbouring pizzeria (evenings only).

La Chiusa delle More (☎ 330 54 37 66; www.lachiusa dellemore.it; Vallo dello Schiaffo; half board per person €55-

FISHERMEN & AERIAL ACROBATS

The *trabucco* is an ancient fishing trap (possibly Phoenician in origin) consisting of a wooden platform on stilts, long wooden poles, ropes and winches. On first sight they look like abandoned and half-collapsed fishing shacks but they are remarkably practical and efficient implements. The poles (antennae) jutting over the water are attached with ropes to a large net suspended underwater and the man on watch literally 'walks the plank' like an aerial acrobat to check on fish activity. When a school of fish swims over the net, the watcher gives the word and the whole thing is hoisted up to the platform. This system of fishing is unique to the Gargano and probably has a lot to do with the clear coastal waters and easy visibility of what goes on beneath the surface.

115; ⌗ Ⓟ ⏚) also lets you get away from the cramped coast and escape to an attractive stone-built *agriturismo* where you can dine on home-grown produce and enjoy the panoramic views from your poolside lounger. In August weekly stays are obligatory.

Eating

There's no shortage of restaurants and bars in Peschici and you can't go wrong with the seafood.

Ristorante Fra Stefano (☎ 0884 96 41 41; Via Forno 8; meals €20; ☽ lunch & dinner Apr-Oct) This low-key restaurant in the heart of town serves up typical Garganico dishes with an emphasis on local seafood. The house wine is served from a barrel by the door. It feels like a bit of a tourist trap but the *capistrelli* (pasta with white beans and seafood) is good and the prices are reasonable.

Ristorante Vecchia Peschici (☎ 0884 96 20 53; Via Roma 31; meals €20-25; ☽ lunch & dinner Apr-Oct) In a perfect position for a sunset aperitif overlooking the Baia di Peschici, this family-run restaurant offers a menu based on fresh seafood and inland meats. The menu isn't fixed and depends on seasonal availability, but the signature dish is *la vecchia peschici* (a stew of clams, beans, tomato and rucola).

Il Trabucco (☎ 0884 91 10 08; Località Punta Manaccora; meals €20-25; ☽ lunch & dinner Easter-Oct) About 6km further down the road on the point of Manaccora you descend a steep flight of steps to reach this rustic and unpretentious *trabucco* restaurant. The menu depends on what comes up in the nets, but if cuttlefish is on the go order the *seppia ripiene* (stuffed cuttlefish). A cave tunnel traverses the point and if you're lucky you might get to see the owner's private museum.

Il Trabucco da Mimi (☎ 0884 96 25 56; Località Punta San Nicola; meals €25-35; ☽ 12.15-2pm & 6.30-9.30pm Easter-Oct, weekends only Nov-Mar) For the ultimate in fresh fish you can't beat dining in a *trabucco*, the traditional wooden fishing platforms lining the coast. Watch the process in operation then dine on the catch. In this family-run restaurant 2.5km south of Peschici, you're surrounded by all things fishy and fishing. A signature dish is *orecchiette al nero di seppia* (black orecchiette made by stirring fresh squid or cuttlefish ink through the uncooked pasta dough). Son Mario has added a new musical dimension to the *trabucco* experience, hosting a regular jazz night every second Friday in summer.

ourpick Porta di Basso (☎ 0884 91 53 64; Via Colombo 38; meals €30-40; ☽ lunch & dinner Wed-Mon Mar-Dec) Superb views of the ocean drop away from the floor-length windows beside the intimate alcove tables in this elegant clifftop restaurant. With Domenico Cilenti, Dolce Guida's Young Chef of the Year, in charge of the kitchen you know you're in for a treat. The menu of fresh local seafood changes daily.

Getting There & Away

Ferrovie del Gargano buses service all the northern Gargano towns from Peschici to San Severo (€5.30, two hours). Frequent services link to Vieste (€1.50, 30 minutes) and a daily service operates from Pescara (€11.30).

In summer frequent local mini-buses (every 20 minutes, €1) connect the town with the beach.

VICO DEL GARGANO

pop 8017 / elev 445

With St Valentine as its patron saint, this hilltop town on the edge of the Foresta Umbra is a charming inland retreat and a welcome break from the crowded beaches. Its medieval heart is a maze of narrow lanes, steep stepped pathways and elegant archways while the surrounding area is covered in citrus trees and

THE GARGANO'S BEST BEACHES

The best beaches are found in secluded coves along the craggy coastline between Vieste and Mattinata:

Baia delle Zagare

Baia di Campi

Pugnochiuso

Vignanotica

TOP 10 CAMPING VILLAGES

Forget roughing it in the bush, most camping villages in the Gargano comprise a hotel, self-contained bungalows and tent sites with a range of facilities including a mini-market, restaurants, bars, pool, private beach, lido and water-sports.

Vieste

Baia di Campi (☎ 0884 70 00 01; www.baiadicampi.it; Località Campi) 10km south of Vieste.
Baia degli Aranci (☎ 0884 70 65 91; www.baiadegliaranci.it; Lungomare Europa 48) 1km north of Vieste.
Gabbiano Beach (☎ 0884 70 63 76; www.gabbianobeach.com; Località Santa Maria di Merino) 7km north of Vieste.
Punta Lunga (☎ 0884 70 60 31; www.puntalunga.it; Località Defensola) 2km north of Vieste.

Peschici

Baia di Manacora (☎ 0884 91 10 17; www.baiadimanaccora.it; Località Manaccora) 7km south of Peschici.
Baia San Nicola (☎ 0884 96 42 31; www.baiasannicola.it; Località San Nicola) 2km south of Peschici.
Internazionale Manacorra (☎ 0884 91 10 20; www.gruppoaccia.it; Località Manaccora) 10km south of Peschici.
Parco degli Ulivi (☎ 0884 96 34 04; www.parcodegliulivi.it; Località Padula) 1km north of Peschici.

Rodi Garganico

Villaggio Ripa (☎ 0884 96 53 67; www.villaggioripa.it; Contrada Ripa) 1.5km north of Rodi Garganico, this is the only 5-star camping village in the Gargano.

Mattinata

Camping Vignanotica (☎ 0884 55 06 40; www.vignanotica.it; Località Vignanotica) 18km north of Mattinata.

---

olive groves. During the **Festa di San Valentino**, celebrated on February 14 (of course), a statue of the saint decorated with locally grown oranges and orange blossoms is paraded around town.

Hikers might find Vico del Gargano a more convenient base from which to explore the natural delights of the Foresta Umbra.

Orientation & Information

Vico del Gargano is 5km inland from San Menaio and 13.5km from the Corpo Forestale in the Foresta Umbra. The town's main sights are clustered together in the medieval centre.

Sights & Activities

The 13th-century **castle** with its large round tower was built by Frederick II and has re-

cently undergone restorations. It's not open to the public. Nearby is the **Museo Trappeto Maratea** (☎ 0884 99 46 66; Via Castello; 4-10pm in summer, otherwise by appointment), an 'olive-oil museum' set in an underground 14th-century *frantoio* (olive mill) outlining the various stages of olive-oil production through grinding, pressing and draining.

There's a statue of St Valentine in the 17th-century **Chiesa Matrice** (☎ 3388 80 68 93; phone to visit). Before leaving town squeeze through **Vico dei Baci** (Kissing Alley or Lover's Lane), where stolen kisses supposedly bring good fortune. The lane is opposite the church of San Giuseppe in Via San Giuseppe.

Northeast of town is the **Convento dei Cappucini** (☎ 0884 99 10 49; Viale Cappucini 47), built in 1556 and renovated after the 1646 earthquake. Inside the church are paintings by Neapolitan

Andrea Vaccaro and the *Milk Madonna* by Ippolito Borghese. Take a moment to admire the majestic holm oak out the front, planted in 1646.

Sleeping & Eating

Hotel Maremonti (☎ 0884 99 14 18; Via della Resistenza; s €30-45, d €50-80; ✹ P) The only hotel in town. There's nothing particularly distinctive or appealing about the place, but the rooms are large and clean and it's close to the town centre.

If you don't mind a 5km drive you could stay on the beach at San Menaio.

Hotel Sole (☎ 0884 96 86 21; Lungomare 2; s €40-75 d €80-150; Apr-Oct; ✹ P ♨ ♿) A pink palace built in the 1920s and once favoured by the wealthy elite, is now looking a little tired. The rusty rail tracks beside the hotel are an eyesore, but the hotel bags a private stretch of the longest beach in the Gargano.

Pizzicato (☎ 0884 99 12 45; Via Risorgimento 14; pastries €1-2, cocktails €5; ✹ 5am-late) A sweet stop here is mandatory. This bar/*pasticceria*/*gelateria* has a megalithic assortment of mouth-watering pastries and cakes. Try the *cannolo siciliano* (tough choice between the chocolate, custard and ricotta centres) washed down with a glass of the deliciously sweet and refreshing *latte di mandorla* (almond milk). In summer catch a band and hit the cocktails.

ourpick Il Trappeto Cantina Ristorante (☎ 0884 96 10 03; Via Casale 168; meals €20; ✹ lunch & dinner Wed-Mon) is an artfully renovated 14th-century *frantoio* (olive mill). The cave setting is atmospheric and intimate, the décor half museum with a modern twist. Home-grown vegetables, especially chicory and fava beans, feature in a menu of typical Garganico dishes.

Getting There & Away

Ferrovie del Gargano buses connect to the train station at San Severo, and also to Peschici (€0.90) and Vieste (€2.40).

RODI GARGANICO

pop 3690 / elev 42m

Rodi Garganico's oranges have been famous since the year AD 1000 so it's not surprising to find this small town west of Peschici nestled amongst citrus orchards and olive groves. It was originally settled by the Greeks and for centuries it was a popular trading port and fishing village. Rodi's string of white sandy beaches are becoming increasingly popular and in August the town can get quite busy.

Rodi is home to the only five-star camping village in the Gargano, **Villaggio Ripa** (☎ 0884 96 53 56; www.villaggioripa.it; Contrada Ripa; hotel s €25-50, d €50-100, bungalows low/high season from €210/630, tent site per person high/low season €8/13; ✹ Jun-Sep), a large complex set among olive trees and bougainvillea overlooking a long sandy beach. With its own mini-market, ATM, restaurants, bars, entertainment, private beach and water-sports, there's no need to leave the grounds.

Every second Saturday Rodi's street markets sell local foods and produce. If you prefer your meals prepared, **Pino's Caffè Restaurant** (☎ 340 557 80 95; Corso Madonna 69a; meals €25; ✹ 7am-10pm) serves fresh seafood and home-made pasta on its shady outdoor terrace. It's the place for passing cyclists to refuel with an espresso and a brioche.

Heading west out of town along the coast road are the Lesina lakes, **Lago di Varano** (10km long and 8km wide) and **Lago di Lesina** (20km long and 3km wide). A narrow sand bar (the Bosco Isola), covered with Mediterranean *maquis* and holm oak, pine and elm trees, separates the lakes from the Adriatic Sea and makes for an interesting drive. The area is a designated nature reserve, the lakes are full of fish (eels are a local favourite), and birdwatchers can feast their binos on curlews, warblers, cormorants and other species flitting by on the annual Africa–Europe migratory route. Although the lakes are not on the usual tourist beat the beaches are polluted with rubbish and debris and a number of unattractive camping villages and hotels have sprung up along the lake shores, especially around Lago di Varano.

Ferrovie del Gargano buses connect Rodi Garganico with Peschici (€0.90), Vieste (€2.40) and San Severo, but the Lesina lakes can only be reached with private transport.

MONTE SANT'ANGELO

pop 13,759 / elev 796m

Pilgrim routes are not meant to be easy, so it's appropriate that one of Italy's most important pilgrimage sites is a long steep zigzag uphill to the highest town in the Gargano Promontory. From its 800m perch Monte Sant'Angelo has stupendous views of the bay of Manfredonia and, whether you're a pilgrim or not, the picturesque town is worth a visit for a wander through its medieval quarter. Of course modern-day pilgrims flock here in cars and buses, but once a year on 29 September the dedicated wind their way on foot from Vieste, 50km away. In the wake of the faithful, hustlers have moved in, pushing everything from car-parking space to kitsch religious souvenirs.

History

The town sprang up around the Santuario di San Michele where, in 490, St Michael the archangel is said to have appeared in a grotto before the Bishop of Siponto. For centuries, pilgrims (including crusaders on their way to the Holy Land) have trudged up the hill to the spot where the archangel appeared a total of four times (see p23). In AD 999 the Holy Roman Emperor Otto III made a pilgrimage to the sanctuary to pray that prophecies about the end of the world in the year 1000 would not be fulfilled. The sanctuary's fame grew after the widely predicted apocalypse proved to be a damp squib.

Orientation

From the bus stop in Piazza Duca d'Aosta follow Corso Vittorio Emanuele uphill to Via Reale Basilica in the old town where the tourist office and all the sights are located.

Coming from Manfredonia or the from coast, follow the Strada Panoramica around the old town to the large car park next to the castle.

Information

Banco di Napoli ATM (Corso Vittorio Emanuele 40)
Banco Popolare di Milano (☎ 0884 56 10 06; Piazza Roma)
Ecogargano (☎ 0884 56 54 44; www.ecogargano .it; Largo Roberto Guiscardo 2; ☽ 9am-1pm & 2.30-7pm summer, 9am-1pm & 2.30-6pm winter) A cooperative dedicated to promoting cultural and natural tours in the Gargano National Park. Based at the castle.
Ente Parco Nazionale del Gargano (☎ 0884 56 89 11; Via Antonio Abate 121; ☽ 8am-2pm Mon-Fri, 3-6pm Tue & Thu) The official office of the Gargano National Park is not very helpful. A better source of information can be found in Ecogargano.
Guardia Medica (☎ 0884 56 59 29)
Hospital (☎ 0884 56 12 10; Via Cimitero 1)
Police (☎ 0884 56 10 08; Piazza Roma 2)
Post Office (☎ 0884 56 10 09; Via Reale Basilica 10; ☽ 8am-1.30pm Mon-Sat)
Tourist Office (☎ 0884 56 55 20; Via Reale Basilica 40; ☽ 9am-8pm summer)

MONTE SANT'ANGELO

INFORMATION	
Banco Popolare di Milano	1 C3
Banco di Napoli ATM	2 D2
Ecogargano	(see 6)
Police Station	3 C3
Post Office	4 C2
Tourist Office	5 B2

SIGHTS & ACTIVITIES	
Castle	6 A2
Chiesa di San Pietro	7 B2
Chiesa di Santa Maria Maggiore	8 B2
Ecogargano	9 B2
Museo di Arti e Tradizioni	10 B2
Santuario di San Michele	11 B2
Tomba di Rotari	12 B2

SLEEPING	
Casa del Pellegrino	13 B2
Hotel Michael	14 B2

EATING	
Gusto	15 B2
I Templari	16 B3
La Jalantuùmene	17 B2
Medioevo	18 B2

TRANSPORT	
Bus Stop	19 D2

Sights & Activities

The pilgrim route culminates at the **Santuario di San Michele** (☎ 0884 56 11 50; Via Reale Basilica; admission free; ☻ 7.30am-7.30pm Jul-Sep, 7.30am-12.30pm & 2.30-7pm Apr, Jun & Oct, 7.30am-12.30pm & 2.30-5pm Nov-Mar) where an octagonal 13th-century campanile stands at the entrance to the sanctuary. Cross the courtyard to the two portals and as you descend the long flight of stone steps note the graffiti, some of it the work of 17th-century pilgrims. St Michael is said to have left a footprint in stone inside the grotto so it became customary for pilgrims to carve outlines of their feet and hands and leave accompanying messages. At the foot of the stairs magnificent Byzantine bronze and silver doors, cast in Constantinople in 1076 (depicting scenes from the Old and New Testaments), open into the grotto where the archangel first appeared. Inside, a 16th-century white marble statue of the archangel covers the site of his footprint. Other religious objects include a 17th-century bishop's throne and a silver cross donated by Frederick II.

Once outside, head down the short flight of steps opposite the sanctuary to the **Tomba di Rotari** (admission €0.60; ☻ 9.40am-1pm & 3-7.30pm Apr-Oct) reached through the façade of the **Chiesa di San Pietro**. The façade (and its intricate rose window) is all that remains of the church, destroyed in a 19th-century earthquake. The Tomba di Rotari, at one time thought to be the tomb of 7th-century Lombard chieftain Rothari, is more likely a 12th-century baptistry. Inside the domed tower is a deep basin sunk into the floor for total baptismal immersion. The Romanesque portal of the adjacent 11th-century **Chiesa di Santa Maria Maggiore** (Largo Tomba di Rotari; ☻ 7am-12.30pm & 3-7pm) has some fine bas-reliefs. Inside are some well-preserved frescoes including a Byzantine fresco of the archangel.

The Norman **castle** (☎ 0884 56 54 44; Largo Roberto Guiscardo 2; admission €1.80; ☻ 9am-7pm Jun-Sep, 9am-1pm & 2.30-7pm Oct-May) commands the highest point overlooking the medieval town and the valleys and villages beyond. The impressive Torre dei Giganti (the Giants' Tower) dates to AD 837–38.

The serpentine alleys and jumbled houses of the medieval quarter, the **Rione Junno**, are perfect for a little aimless wandering. The *cappelletti* (chimney stacks) on top of the neat whitewashed houses come in interesting designs and shapes. Models of the *cappelletti*

can be found in the **Museo di Arti e Tradizioni** (☎ 0884 56 20 98; Piazza San Francesco 15; admission €1.50; ☻ 9am-1pm & 2.30-7pm), also known as the Museo Tancredi after its founder Giovanni Tancredi. Located in the former monastery of San Francesco, the museum displays agricultural equipment, handicrafts and artefacts and depictions of daily life in the Gargano, including plenty of photographs of pilgrims.

The isolated **Abbazia di Santa Maria di Pulsano** (☎ 0884 56 10 47; Localita Pulsano; ☻ 9am-8pm), 9km southwest of town, sits on the edge of the vast Pulsano gorge overlooking the bay of Manfredonia. Originally built at the end of the 6th century, it was destroyed in 952 by the Saracens and rebuilt by the Benedictines in 1129. Well-preserved 12th-century Apulian art can be seen in the cave chapel. Look for the hermit cells and caves in the cliff face.

Sleeping

Surprisingly, in a place that teems with visitors, the accommodation here is limited.

Casa del Pellegrino (☎ 0884 56 23 96; Via Carlo D'Angio; s/d €33/45) This is the pilgrims' lodge and is an institutional but intriguing place, with around 50 rooms right above the sanctuary. The atmosphere veers somewhere between a private hospital and *The Shining*, but the rooms are comfortable (pilgrims don't have to suffer) and many have views down across the valley. There's an 11pm curfew and it's a 9.30am checkout.

Hotel Michael (☎ 0884 56 55 19; www.hotelmichael .com; Via Reale Basilica 86; s/d €45/75) A small hotel with shuttered windows on the main street leading away from the sanctuary in the old town, this traditional place has spacious rooms with extremely pink bedspreads. Ask for a room with a view.

Eating

Gusto (☎ 032 02910711; Via Reale Basilica 111; panini €2, meals from €14; ☻ 9am-10pm daily summer, 9am-10pm Sat & Sun only Jan-Mar) For a quick bite to eat this handy bar in a converted rock stable is close to the Santuario di San Michele. After all that religious fervour relax with a glass of wine and a platter of mixed local cheese (€7) at the tables and chairs in the piazza out front.

I Templari (☎ 0884 56 49 06; Via del Torrione 10/12; pizza €5-7; ☻ noon-2pm & 8pm-late Tue-Sun) A pizzeria/restaurant/music bar in a prime position overlooking the bay of Manfredonia. On a clear day you can see along the coast all the

NORTHERN PUGLIA & THE
GARGANO PROMONTORY

> **MARCELLO BLASI MEETS PADRE PIO (1968)**
>
> A retired military officer, Marcello Blasi recalls the day he and a group of officers met Padre Pio.
> 'We arrived just as they were starting to say the mass. At that time Padre Pio no longer said the mass, as he was very ill. It was a couple of weeks before he died. Padre Pio appeared at a small balcony with some assistants and another monk officiated. The women there were praying and inside the church there was a very strange feeling, like hysteria, in waiting to see the padre. As time went on their prayers became more and more intense and some women fainted from the tension and stress. After the mass we went upstairs to meet him with the soldiers. I remember that his eyes seemed very alive, but I had the impression of a man who was very tired.'

way to Bari. In summer the bar has live music nearly every night.

Medioevo (☎ 0884 56 53 56; Via Castello 21; meals €25; lunch & dinner daily summer, Tue-Sun winter) An elegant restaurant with a matching menu focusing on locally grown ingredients. House specialties include home-made pasta *orecchiette medioevo* (orecchiette with rucola, pecorino cheese and lamb ragu) and pancotto with cabbage, potatoes and fava beans.

La Jalantuùmene (☎ 0884 56 54 84; Piazza de Galganis 5; meals €35-40; lunch & dinner daily summer, lunch only Wed-Mon winter) This restaurant is justifiably recommended by everyone who visits it. It serves excellent fare, accompanied by a long, select wine list, in picturesque surroundings. In summer, tables spill into the petite piazza.

Getting There & Away

From Foggia take the SS89 towards Manfredonia and Vieste, exiting at the sign for Monte Sant'Angelo. From Vieste head south along the SS89, turning off to Monte Sant'Angelo after Mattinata.

Monte Sant'Angelo can be accessed by **SITA** (☎ 0881 77 31 17) bus from Foggia (€4, 1½ hours, five daily), Manfredonia (€1.80, 20 minutes, frequent services) and Vieste (€4, two hours).

SAN GIOVANNI ROTONDO

pop 26,469 / elev 566m

Once a tiny, isolated medieval village in the heart of the Gargano, San Giovanni Rotondo underwent a miraculous transformation after the arrival of Padre Pio, a humble and pious capuchin priest 'blessed' with the stigmata and a legendary ability to heal the sick. Pio (1887–1968) was canonised in 2002, and immortalised in the vast numbers of prefabricated statues to be found throughout the Gargano. Unless you're one of the eight million pilgrims that pile into town each year

there's only one reason to visit – to marvel at the grand-scale exploitation and blatant commercialisation religious 'devotees' can wring out of one man's self-sacrificing life.

If you escape the frenzy around the *santuario* and the touts flogging high-priced religious souvenirs and miniature statuettes of the good saint, the pedestrianised Corso Umberto I in the heart of town is actually quite pleasant. Nearby Piazza Europa has a few cool bars and hang-outs that have nothing to do with pilgrims or pilgrimages.

Orientation & Information

The sights are grouped around Piazza Santa Maria delle Grazie at the west end of town where Viale Cappuccini merges into Viale Padre Pio. The **pilgrim reception office** (☎ 0882 41 75 00; Piazza Santa Maria delle Grazie; 8am-8pm summer, 8am-6pm winter) has all the information you need regarding maps, tours and all things Padre Pio.

Sights & Activities

The **santuario** (☎ 0882 41 75 00; Piazza Santa Maria delle Grazie; 5.30am-8pm summer, 6am-8pm winter) is a vast complex comprising the **Chiesa di Santa Maria delle Grazie** (built in 1959), the **Chiesa Antica** (built in 1540) and the **Convento di Cappuccini**. If you don't know where to start, shuffle along behind the queues. The major points of interest are Padre Pio's **cell** (a spartan room with a single bed, a wash-stand and blood-stained cloths from his stigmata wounds), his **crypt** (open until 7pm) and the **crucifix** in front of which he received the stigmata in 1918. Viewing hours for Padre Pio's cell and crucifix are 7am to 7pm in summer, 7.30am to 6.30pm in winter.

At the back of the complex, behind the pilgrim reception office, is the architecturally controversial **Nuova Chiesa di San Pio** (☎ 0882 41 75 00; 8am-8pm summer, 8am-6pm winter) and the

Open Sky Church (6am-8pm summer, 6am-7pm winter). Designed by Renzo Piano and inaugurated in 2004, the new church is a strikingly modern half-dome resembling an auditorium. Behind the painted glass windows, space-age lighting and an enormous hanging cross shaped like a spiral helix furnish the interior while out the front olive trees, running streams, an outdoor pulpit and marble eagles decorate the Open Sky Church. The innovative concept has polarised opinions but love it or hate it, it's a must-see.

Across the road and east of the Chiesa di Santa Maria delle Grazie is the **Casa Sollievo della Sofferenza** (Home for the Relief of Suffering; 0882 41 02 02; Viale Cappuccini), a hospital established by Padre Pio in 1947.

Next to the hospital is the **Via Crucis** (Viale Padre Pio; 6am-6pm summer, 6am-5.30pm winter), a well-planned winding pathway in a landscaped garden. The 14 bronze stations of the cross were sculpted by Francesco Messina. Note the fifth station where Padre Pio is helping Christ to lift the cross. Also note the number of donation boxes along the way. Subtlety is not San Giovanni Rotondo's strong point.

Sleeping & Eating

There's no lack of accommodation in this money-making town. From basic digs to kitsch splendour you'll find it all.

Albergo Soire San Giuseppe (0882 45 11 21; Viale Cappuccini 111; s/d €31/53) Pilgrims will feel right at home in this spartan hotel run by three nuns. With a chapel and a 10.45pm curfew guests are bound to be pious. It's only 100m from the *santuario* and doors open at 6.30am.

Grande Hotel degli Angeli (0882 45 46 46; www .grandhoteldegliangeli.it; Prolungamento Viale Padre Pio; s/d €100/130; Mar-Nov;) As soon as you see the Padre Pio statue rising out of a spray of coloured lights at the entrance fountain you know you've reached the other end of the spectrum from the simple Albergo Soire San Giuseppe. Chandeliers and leather lounges rub shoulders with crucifixes and religious icons.

I Santi (0882 45 61 16; Via Forgione 10; meals €14; lunch only, bar 6am-10pm) All that religious fervour can work up a thirst. Fight your way through the hustlers to this bar 20m down the road from the *santuario* for a saintly drop of *vino* (if the name of the bar is any indication). Those wallowing in religious piety can opt for a *gelato*.

Osteria Antica Piazzetta (0882 45 19 20; Via Al Mercato 13; meals €25; lunch & dinner Thu-Tue) Once a cinema, this cosy restaurant near Corso Umberto I is a welcome haven. The menu is typical Garganico with oven-roasted meats, home-made pasta with *rape* (turnips) and fresh seafood from Manfredonia. Ask for a table in the upstairs gallery.

For a taste of secular nightlife wander down to the bars in Piazza Europa. **Open Gallery Cafe** (320 565 79 42; Piazza Europa 98; 7am-1am Mon-Sat) is a happening scene with mod lighting, cane lounges and funky music.

Getting There & Away

From Foggia take the SS89 towards Manfredonia, exiting onto the SS273 for San Giovanni Rotondo. From Monte Sant'Angelo follow the SS272 west. From Vieste follow the SS89 south, turning off for San Giovanni Rotondo before reaching Manfredonia.

SITA runs frequent services from Foggia (€2.70, 1¾ hours), and Vieste (€3.40) via Manfredonia (€1.90, 20 minutes).

MATTINATA

pop 6445 / elev 75m

As the only south-facing town in the Gargano, Mattinata is sheltered in a wide protected bay. It is a quiet village attracting a smattering of beachgoers but its main industry revolves around agriculture and fishing, the climate favouring olives, almonds and fig trees. The area around Mattinata is an orchid-hunters' paradise as 70% of Europe's orchid genus population is found in the Gargano and over 80 different orchid species are found here. Archaeological finds around Mattinata have dug up an ancient Roman villa near the harbour and Daunia Bronze Age relics on nearby Monte Saraceno. Many of these finds are showcased in Manfredonia's museum, but you'll also find a selection in town at the rarely open **Museo Civico Archeologico** (0884 55 01 55; Via Giuseppe di Vittorio; admission free; 9.30-11.30am Tue, Thu & Sun, 4-7.30pm Wed, Fri & Sat). A new **Paleoworking division** (9am-1pm & 4-8pm) under the museum is due to open in late 2007 and will display reproductions of prehistoric weapons and equipment found throughout the region.

The local pharmacy **Farmacia Sansone** (0884 55 08 36; Corso Matino 114; admission free; 8am-12.30pm & 5-8.30pm Mon-Sat, 8am-12.30pm Sun) dishes up more than cough drops. The private collection in the pharmacy, begun in the 19th century, displays over 2700 archaeological finds from the Daunia civilisation as well as ancient Roman and Greek pieces, old medical books, ethnographs and other curiosities.

Sleeping & Eating

About 16km north of Mattinata along the coast is the beautiful **Zagare Bay**, arguably the Gargano Promontory's most picturesque bay and the location of its only five-star hotel.

ourpick Baia dei Faraglioni Beach Resort (☎ 0884 55 95 84; Litoranea Mattinata-Vieste km16; s €180-260, d €280-390; ☼ May-Sep; ✷ **P** ☲) An exclusive resort set on a cliff in the Mount Barone woods with stunning views of the azure blue waters of the Adriatic. An elevator in the cliff face takes you down to the dazzling white shingle beach. No luxury has been spared throughout the rooms or gardens but to really pamper yourself ask for a suite with a private pool (€1030 per night).

Agriturismo Madonna Incoronata (☎ 0884 58 23 17; Località Madonna Incoronata; apt from €75, minimum 2-night stay) A little more down to earth and 1km from Mattinata. Old farm buildings on this tranquil 60-hectare olive grove have been converted into comfortable and rustic-styled self-contained apartments. The old *frantoio* (olive mill) on the grounds is a mini-museum and you're likely to get a passionate run-down on olive-oil production from the owner. It's a great base from which to explore the Gargano's southern coast and the pilgrim towns of Monte Sant'Angelo and San Giovanni Rotondo. The park bench under the 500-year-old carob tree is perfect for meditation and contemplation.

Trattoria della Nonna (☎ 0884 55 92 05; Mattinata Mare; meals €30; ☼ lunch & dinner Tue-Sun) The waves ripple along the beach a stone's throw out the window in this small seaside restaurant near Mattinata. The prices are high but the sea-food is fresh (the seafood antipasto is highly recommended) and the service attentive, but the attached *pensione* does not live up to the restaurant's standards.

Getting There & Away

Mattinata is 18km north of Manfredonia. SITA buses have frequent connections with Manfredonia (€1.10, 30 minutes) and Vieste (€2.30, one hour 25 minutes).

MANFREDONIA

pop 57,424 / elev 5m

This rapidly developing industrial town in the bay of the same name owes its birth to the Swabian king Manfred (1231–66), Frederick II's illegitimate son. In 1256, Manfred and his subjects abandoned the earthquake-prone and malaria-ridden ancient port of Siponto to move a few kilometres to safer ground. As the gateway to the Gargano Promontory Manfredonia is a convenient transport hub and once you get through the heavy industry on its outskirts it has a pleasant town centre in front of the port.

The town spreads down the coast to envelope Siponto and its long white sandy beaches, the site of an ancient Daunia settlement and now a burgeoning seaside resort.

Orientation & Information

Trains from Foggia terminate at the station in Piazza delle Libertà. Turn right out of the station and walk down Viale Aldo Moro to Piazza Marconi where the intercity buses terminate. From here, a 300m walk along semipedestrianised Corso Manfredi leads to Piazza del Popolo and the very helpful **tourist office** (☎ 0884 58 19 98; Piazza del Popolo 1; ☼ 9am-1pm Mon-Fri winter, 9am-1pm & 5-8pm Mon-Fri, 10am-noon Sat summer).

From June to August a daily ferry service leaves the port for the Isole Tremiti (€46.20,

---

THE PILGRIMS ROUTE

As the cult of St Michael (for more information see p23) became more widespread, spiritual seekers, pilgrims and crusaders beat a well-trod path from Foggia and San Severo in the west to San Giovanni Rotondo and Monte Sant'Angelo and on to Manfredonia on the coast. Along this *Via Sacra Langobardorum* the **Santuario di San Matteo** (☎ 0882 83 11 51; www.santuariosanmatteo.it; ☼ 9am-1pm & 3-8.30pm Apr-Oct, 9am-1pm & 4-8pm Nov-Mar), 3km east of San Marco in Lamis, became a designated stopover. Built in the 6th century, the monastery passed from the Lombards to the Benedictines and finally to the Franciscans in the 16th century. The monastery was dedicated to St Matthew because, apparently, the Franciscans had one of his molars. A 12th-century statue of the saint stands above the altar in the church. The 100-year-old library is worth a visit.

two hours 20 minutes). Buy tickets from **Agenzia Galli** (☎ 0884 58 25 20).

Sights & Activities

Guarding the far end of the *corso* is the town's **castle** (☎ 0884 58 78 39; Corso Manfredi; adult/concession €2.50/1.25; ☼ 8.30am-7.30pm, closed 1st & last Mon of month). Manfred built it, Charles of Anjou finished it and the Aragonese reworked it. Climb up the stairs for a panoramic view of the port. The **Museo Archeologico Nazionale del Gargano**, within the castle, displays finds from local excavations. Of particular interest are the Daunia stele (stone grave slabs from the 6th to the 7th century BC), carved with images of warriors, hunters, animals and scenes of daily life. The tombstones are gender specific: stele with round heads and square shoulders represent men; those with pointed heads and square holes in the collars represent women. Little is known of the Daunia race but archaeological finds point to a rich and cultured Bronze Age civilisation.

Inside the 17th-century **cathedral** (☎ 0884 53 26 33; Piazza Papa Giovanni XXIII; ☼ 9am-noon & 5-8pm) is a wooden image of the Madonna di Siponto carved in cedar, a 12th-century crucifix from the Abbazia di San Leonardo and a 12th-century Byzantine painting of the Madonna.

The small **Chiesa di San Domenico** (☎ 0884 58 18 44; Piazza del Popolo; ☼ by appointment) next to the tourist office was built in the late 13th century. It has a Gothic doorway, the highest arch of all Puglia's churches, the ruins of the *cappella della Maddalena* (the Magdalena's chapel) and some beautiful frescoes, including Mary Magdalene helping the Christ, and the genealogical tree, *albero genealogico di Jesse*. The hole in the base of the alcove beside the frescoes was to drain post-mortem fluids from the dead.

About 3km south of town is the last remaining building of old Siponto, the distinctly Byzantine-looking Romanesque **Basilica di Santa Maria Maggiore di Siponto** (☎ 0884 54 14 70; SS89km3; ☼ 10am-noon & 3.30-5pm Wed-Mon). The church was built in the 11th century on the site of a pagan temple probably dedicated to Diana, and is one of the most interesting examples of Roman architecture in Puglia. It has a fine 13th-century portal, an altar made from an early Christian sarcophagus and a crypt to the left of the church.

Another 7km along the SS89 towards Foggia is the 11th-century Romanesque-Apulian **Abbazia di San Leonardo** (☎ 0884 58 18 44; SS89km10;

☼ by appointment). In 1261 Pope Alexander IV gave the abbey to the Teutonic Knights who built a hospital to treat crusaders returning ill and wounded from the Holy Land. Another important stopover for pilgrims on the way to Monte Sant'Angelo, the small chapel is all that remains of the complex. The church has a Romanesque portal, one of the most impressive in Puglia. At noon on the summer solstice (June 21) a ray of light penetrates through the rosette window in the ceiling to light a precise point on the floor between the two columns in the central nave. No-one seems to know the exact significance of this solar phenomenon, but some helpful character has marked the spot with a cross.

Sleeping & Eating

Manfredonia has a few stock-standard but expensive business hotels while Siponto's accommodation follows the beach.

Hotel Gabbiano (☎ 0884 54 25 54; www.albergogabbiano.it; Viale Eurostides 20, Siponto; s €65-80, d €75-96; ⚡ 🅿 ♿) This clean, modern and friendly hotel nestled in a quiet street is 150m from the beach and only 2km from the port. The pizzeria is a lively spot and the outdoor garden café is the perfect place for a morning coffee and a good book.

Ristorante Coppolarossa (☎ 0884 58 25 22; Via dei Celestini 13; meals €25-30; ☼ lunch & dinner Tue-Sat, lunch only Sun) This jovial family-run restaurant comes highly recommended. Specialising in seafood, it grills, fries and boils with panache, producing dishes of high quality. As a starter the seafood buffet is difficult to top.

Ristorante Il Porto (☎ 0884 58 18 00; Via del Porto 8/10; meals €30; ☼ lunch & dinner Tue-Sun) In a prime spot opposite the castle and overlooking the port, this restaurant serves up seafood (of course) and oven-roasted Garganico meats. There's a buffet of antipasti and the menu is in English. The outside terrace resembles a ship deck complete with slanted wooden floorboards.

Il Baraccio (☎ 0884 58 38 74; Corso Roma 38; meals €30; ☼ lunch Fri-Wed) Despite its modern décor, Il Baraccio is an unpretentious, traditional *trattoria* serving up local specialities such as octopus salad, squid-ink pasta and seafood soup. It has a good reputation that it lives up to.

Getting There & Away

Trains connect Manfredonia with Foggia (€3, 30 minutes, five daily). Both **SITA** (☎ 0881 77 31 17) and **Ferrovie del Gargano** (☎ 0881 72 51 88) have regular buses connecting to Foggia (€1.10, 20 minutes), while SITA has buses daily to and from Vieste (€3.40, 1¾ hours, eight daily). There are also frequent buses daily to and from Monte Sant'Angelo (€1.80, 20 minutes) and San Giovanni Rotondo (€1.90, 20 minutes). Get tickets and timetable information from Bar Impero on Piazza Marconi; all services leave from there.

AROUND MANFREDONIA

On the coast road south of Manfredonia the landscape is flat and intensely cultivated. The wetlands which start south of Siponto and extend to Margherita di Savoia are some of the most important in southern Italy, attracting 20,000 to 50,000 wintering birds each year on the annual Europe–Africa migrations. An extensive canebreak and a series of marshland ponds mark the start of **Lago Salso** and the **Frattarolo** nature reserve. Along the beach paralleling the road, small clusters of buildings mark new developments, while towards the Tavoliere tablelands isolated farmhouses overlook wheat fields, cereal and vegetable crops, red poppies and yellow wildflowers. Soon after passing Zapponeta, Italy's largest salt works stretch along the coast for 20km to Margherita di Savoia (a quiet and relatively uninteresting township).

The **Margherita di Savoia salt works** are no more than 4km wide, cover an area of 40 sq km and have been around since the 3rd century BC. The man-made salt works occupy the site of a former coastal lagoon, Lago Salpi, that probably first attracted attention from the salt crusts left behind after periodic seawater flooding. The number and the varying depths of the salt pans and their differing salinity levels create ideal ecological niches for a variety of aquatic birds. Birdwatchers can have a field day panning their binos over a host of avian species including ducks, coots, herons, egrets, plovers, oystercatchers, gulls, and the largest population of Greater Flamingos in Italy. Of particular importance is the slender-billed curlew, which has the dubious honour of being the bird most at risk of extinction in Europe.

Further information on the wetlands can be obtained from the **tourist office** (☎ 0884 58 19 98; Piazza del Popolo 1; ☺ 9am-1pm & 5-8pm Mon-Fri, 10am-noon Sat summer, 9am-1pm Mon-Fri winter) in Manfredonia or from the National Park office in Monte Sant'Angelo, **Ente Parco Nazionale del Gargano**

(☎ 0884 56 89 11; Via Antonio Abate 121; ☺ 8am-2pm Mon-Fri, 3-6pm Tue & Thu).

ISOLE TREMITI

pop 413 / elev 146m

It's always an adventure to float out to an island, and this beautiful archipelago of three, 36km offshore, makes for a splendid trip. The hour-long boat ride takes you to raggedy cliffs, sandy coves and thick pine woods, surrounded by glittering dark-blue sea. Unfortunately this is no secret, and in July and August some 100,000 holidaymakers descend, somewhat masking the islands' natural beauty and tranquillity. Out of season they are magical, if strange. Most tourist facilities close down, and the few permanent residents resume their quiet and isolated lives.

The islands' accommodation and facilities are on **San Domino**, the largest, lushest island, formerly used to grow crops. It's ringed by sandy bays, rocky caves and limestone cliffs, and covered in tall pine forests and thick *maquis* flecked with rosemary and foxgloves. The centre harbours a nondescript small town with several hotels.

Easily defensible, the small island of **San Nicola** was always the administrative centre – a castle-like cluster of medieval buildings rise up from the rocks. The third island, **Caprara**, is uninhabited.

Orientation & Information

Most boats arrive at San Domino. Small boats regularly make the brief crossing to San Nicola (€5 return) in season – from October to March a single boat makes the trip after meeting the boat from the mainland.

Sights & Activities

Head to San Domino for walks, grottoes and coves. It has a pristine, marvellous coastline and the islands' only sandy beach, **Cala delle Arene**. There are several small coves where you can swim in amazingly clear waters. You can also take a boat trip (€10 from the port) around the island to explore the grottoes: the largest, **Grotta del Bue Marino**, is 46m long. A tour around all three islands costs €16. Diving in the translucent sea is another option, with **Blue Space** (☎ 0882 46 32 29; www.tremitidiving.com; Villaggio San Domino).

There's an undemanding but enchanting walking track around the island, starting a the far end of the village. Alternatively, you could hire a bicycle from **Jimmy Bike** (☎ 338 897 09 09) at Piazzetta San Domino.

Medieval buildings thrust out of San Nicola's rocky shores, the same pale-sand colour as the barren cliffs. In 1010 Benedictine monks founded the **Abbazia e Chiesa di Santa Maria** here, and for the next 700 years the islands were ruled by a series of abbots who accumulated great wealth. Although the church retains a weather-worn Renaissance portal and a fine 11th-century floor mosaic, its other treasures have been stolen or destroyed throughout its troubled history. The one exception is a painted wooden Byzantine crucifix brought to the island in AD 747 and a black Madonna, probably transported here from Constantinople in the Middle Ages.

The third of the Isole Tremiti, Caprara, is uninhabited. Birdlife is plentiful, with impressive flocks of seagulls. There is no organised transport, but you can negotiate a trip with a local fisherman.

Sleeping & Eating

In summer you'll need to book well ahead. Out of season, phone to check that your chosen hotel is open. In the high season many hotels insist on full board.

Pensione Ristorante-Bar Belvedere (☎ 0882 46 32 32; Via Garibaldi 6, San Domino; low season d €50) Across the road from Gabbiano, above a café that's the only eatery open in the low season, this guesthouse has nice, plain, pretty rooms with tiled floors and sea views.

Hotel Gabbiano (☎ 0882 46 34 10; www.hotel-gab biano.com; Piazza Belvedere, San Domino; half board per person €55-105) This San Domino hotel, run for over 30 years by a Neapolitan family, has smart pastel-coloured rooms with balconies overlooking San Nicola and the sea. Its renowned terrace restaurant with similarly splendid views offers straight-from-the-sea fish.

Il Pirata (☎ 0882 46 34 09; Cala delle Arene, San Domino; Apr-Oct) A class act with a terrace on the beach, this specialises in – what else? – fresh fish.

Getting There & Away

In summer, boats for Tremiti depart from Manfredonia (€46.20, two hours 20 minutes), Vieste (€31.60, one hour), Peschici (€31.60, one hour), and Termoli in Molise (€32, one hour).

You can take a helicopter (€50, 20 minutes, two daily) from Foggia courtesy of **Alidaunia** (☎ 0881 61 96 96).

IL TAVOLIERE

The 'breadbasket of Italy' derives its title from the vast wheat-covered tablelands stretching from the Gargano Promontory to the foothills of the Daunia Pre-Apennines. The neat chessboard squares of land, originally gifted to pensioned-off Roman centurions, produces a lot of Italy's wheat and, arguably, its best pasta and bread. But the land wasn't always fertile – before the irrigation schemes of the early 1900s it was a diseased malarial swampland, rocked by earthquakes (see p28). Now it is a landscape of changing colours – lush green in spring, golden yellow in summer. Other cultivated cereals and crops include barley, beets and tomatoes; olives and grapes from the Tavoliere produce quality oils and wines.

Foggia rules the vast wheat-bowl from its centre, its hazy outline of tall buildings dominating the plains and the medieval towns of the Tavoliere just as it once dominated the transhumance routes, the shepherd's tracks traversing southern Italy from Abruzzo to Puglia. The largest Neolithic settlement in northern Europe was discovered near Foggia, and the neolithic Daunia (a cultured Illyrian people) have left numerous traces of their once thriving civilisation.

FOGGIA

pop 154,780 / elev 76m

The modern city of Foggia rises from the flat plain of the Tavoliere, spreading a tentacle-like network of roads through its famous wheat belt. Dating to around AD 1000 and linked to near the ancient village of Arpi, Foggia flourished under the reign of Frederick II (1194–1250). It was one of his favourite towns; his heart remained in Foggia (literally) in a casket until the massive earthquake of 1731 that devastated the town and everything in it. Later, Foggia became a strategic airbase in WWII, suffering extensive bomb damage that further destroyed many of its historical sites.

Wheat farming is nothing new to Foggia; its name is derived from *fovea* (hole) for the underground wheat silos beneath the town. Aside from its agricultural and commercial importance Foggia is an important transport hub and the main gateway to northern Puglia and the Gargano. With its modern boutiques, wide streets and lively evening *passeggiata*, a stopover here can be quite pleasant.

NORTHERN PUGLIA & THE GARGANO PROMONTORY

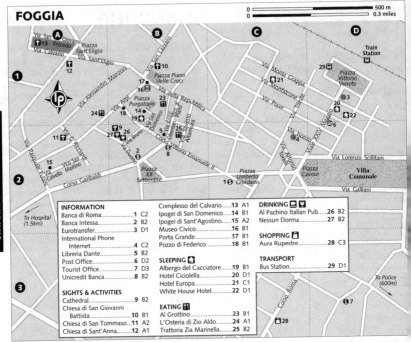

INFORMATION			Complesso del Calvario......13 A1	DRINKING 🍷 🎵
Banca di Roma.................1 C2			Ipogei di San Domenico....14 B1	Al Pachino Italian Pub.....26 B2
Banca Intessa..................2 B2			Ipogei di Sant'Agostino....15 A2	Nessun Dorma...............27 B2
Eurotransfer....................3 D1			Museo Civico..................16 B1	
International Phone			Porta Grande..................17 B1	SHOPPING 🛍
Internet....................4 C2			Pozzo di Federico.............18 B1	Aura Rupestre.................28 C3
Libreria Dante.................5 B2				
Post Office......................6 D2			SLEEPING 🛏	TRANSPORT
Tourist Office..................7 D3			Albergo del Cacciatore......19 B1	Bus Station....................29 D1
Unicredit Banca...............8 B2			Hotel Ciciolella................20 D1	
			Hotel Europa...................21 C1	
SIGHTS & ACTIVITIES			White House Hotel..........22 D1	
Cathedral.......................9 B2				
Chiesa di San Giovanni			EATING 🍴	
Battista...................10 B1			Al Grottino.....................23 B1	
Chiesa di San Tommaso...11 A2			L'Osteria di Zio Aldo........24 A1	
Chiesa di Sant'Anna........12 A1			Trattoria Zia Marinella......25 B2	

Orientation

Train and bus stations face Piazza Vittorio Veneto, on the north rim of town. Viale XXIV Maggio leads south into Piazza Cavour and its impressive fountain. On or around the *viale* are several hotels, restaurants and shops, as well as the post office. From Piazza Cavour, Via Lanza leads to Corso Vittorio Emanuele II and what remains of the old quarter.

Information

Banco di Roma (Piazza Umberto Giordano)
Banco Intessa (Corso Garibaldi)
Emergency (medical ☎ 118, police ☎ 113)
Eurotransfer (☎ 0881 70 90 79; Viale XXIV Maggio 82; per hr €2; ☻ 9am-9pm Mon-Sat) Internet access.
Guardia Medica (☎ 0881 73 20 30)
Hospital (☎ 0881 73 20 30; Via Luigi Pinto)
International Phone Internet (☎ 0881 71 50 57; Via Isonzo 25; per 30 minutes €1; ☻ 8am-10pm)
Libreria Dante (☎ 0881 72 51 33; Via Oberdan 9-11; ☻ 8.30am-1pm Mon-Sat & 4.30-8.30pm Mon-Fri)
Police (☎ 0881 33 15 11; Via Gramsci 1)
Post Office (☎ 0881 56 37 15; Viale XXIV Maggio 26; ☻ 8.30am-6.30pm Mon, Tue, Thu & Fri, 8.30am-2pm Wed)

Tourist Office (☎ 0881 72 31 41; www.viaggiarein puglia.it; Via Emilio Perrone 17; ☻ 9am-2pm Mon-Fri, 3-6pm Tue & Thu)
Unicredit Banca (Corso Garibaldi)

Sights

The **cathedral** (☎ 0881 77 34 82; Piazza de Santis; ☻ 7am-12.30pm & 5-8pm) was built in the 12th century and its lower section remains true to the original Romanesque style. The top half, exuberantly baroque, was grafted on after the earthquake in 1731. Most of the cathedral's treasures were lost in the quake but you can see a Byzantine icon of the Madonna preserved in a chapel inside the church. Legend has it that in the 11th century, shepherds discovered the icon lying in a pond over which burned three flames. These flames became the symbol of the city. Wrapping the icon in a sheet, the shepherds carried it back to an inn and it quickly became known as the *Madonna delle sette vele* (Madonna of the seven veils). Foggia's oldest church, the **Chiesa di San Tommaso** (☎ 0881 74 59 29; Via G Ricciardi), baroque after many restorations, was built over the site of the inn.

After leaving the cathedral turn right into Via Arpi, the ancient arterial road with its elegant *palazzi*, passing the **pozzo di Federico** (a fountain built in 1931 over the site of an ancient well) in the Piazza Federico II, on your way to the museum. The **Museo Civico** (☎ 0881 02 62 45; Piazza Nigri; 9am-1pm Tue-Sun, 4-7pm Tue & Thu) in Palazzo Arpi showcases archaeological finds from the surrounding area including those from excavations at the Neolithic village of Herdoniae and Arpi. Fascinating relics of the Daunia civilisation include 4th- to 6th-century BC stele, vases, ceramics, iron and bronze ornaments, and a *serpente* road decorated with a sinuous snake-like mosaic pattern. The Daunia were an animistic people; note the dolphin motif in many of the mosaics and statues. The museum also houses ancient Roman and Greek finds and an art gallery with 18th- and 19th-century paintings.

The bricked-in arch on the side of the museum building, the **Arco di Federico II**, is all that remains of Frederick II's original palace. Next to the museum are three arches – the middle one, **Porta Grande**, is an ancient city gate leading out of the old town onto Via della Repubblica.

Before leaving the old town visit the **Ipogei di San Domenico** (☎ 0881 72 13 08; Piazza Purgatorio; 10am-1pm & 6-10pm Wed, Thu & Sat 20 Aug-15 Sep) and **Ipogei di Sant'Agostino** (☎ 0881 72 13 08; Via Calvello; 10am-1pm & 6-10pm Wed, Thu & Sat 20 Aug-15 Sep) if you want to see some of the underground caverns that connected many parts of the city. They are both open by appointment outside of the usual hours.

The **Chiesa di San Giovanni Battista** (☎ 0881 72 27 81; Piazza Piano della Croci; 9.30-11.30am & 6-9pm), a baroque church of the 17th century, has a statue of the Madonna dell'Addolorata that supposedly performed a miracle in 1837, shedding tears to end a cholera epidemic. In front of the church is the **Piano delle Fosse**, a large underground silo once used to store wheat.

The **Complesso del Calvario** (☎ 0881 72 27 81; Piazza Sant'Eligio; 9am-12.30pm & 6-8pm Mon-Sat, 9am-noon Sun), a short walk down Via Sant'Eligio, is an architecturally interesting national monument. Built between 1693 and 1742, the baroque complex comprises a monumental triumphal arch and five small chapels leading up to the Chiesa delle Croci. Legend has it that Palestinian soil is buried beneath each of the five chapels and another legend has a splinter of the original cross inserted in the wooden cross inside the church. The crypt has piles of skulls and bones and a small collection of religious vestments and relics.

Opposite the complex is the **Chiesa di Sant'Anna** (☎ 0881 71 44 28; Piazza Sant'Eligio 34; 9am-1pm & 5-8pm), connected to the Capuchin friary in Palazzo Sannicandro. Padre Pio, canonised after his death in 1968, lived here for six months before moving to San Giovanni Rotondo (p98). Apparently he relocated for health reasons, and because his nocturnal battles with demons kept the other brothers awake. You can visit his bedroom – a spartan affair comprising a narrow cot, a writing desk, and cloths and gloves stained with blood from his stigmata wounds. There's even a vial of his pleural fluids on show.

Sleeping

Considering its size there aren't a lot of hotels in Foggia but it's easy enough to find a room – except during the agricultural fair at the beginning of May.

Albergo del Cacciatore (☎ 0881 77 18 39; Via Arrigotti 4; s/d €40/80; P) This small hotel and restaurant is a basic, no-frills, family-run affair centrally located in the old town near the theatre. The restaurant has filling homemade pasta dishes. It's close to everything so it can get quite noisy. Watch the leaky bathrooms.

Hotel Europa (☎ 0881 71 10 57; www.hoteleuropafog gia.com; Via Monfalcone 52; s/d €90-135;) About 50m from the train station, this place has comfortable rooms even if the common areas are cold and imposing. For a few euros more you can enjoy the suites, which are larger and decked out in some style.

White House Hotel (☎ 0881 72 16 44; Via Sabotino 24; s/d €95/120;) Close to the train station and the Hotel Ciciolella, this is one of the better choices although the mirrored walls are a bit OTT. The staff are friendly and efficient and can help point out the major sights.

Hotel Ciciolella (☎ 0881 56 61 11; www.hotelcicolella .it; Viale XXIV Maggio 60; s/d €135/190;) This rust-coloured Foggia landmark, founded more than 100 years ago, is a delightful blend of old-world charm spiced with contemporary efficiency, but is in desperate need of a makeover. The restaurant serves excellent local cuisine.

Eating

You'll eat well in Foggia, so don't be afraid to explore.

Al Grottino (☎ 0881 77 13 31; Vico Teatro 13; pizza €4-9; 9.30am-3.30pm & 5.30pm-late Tue-Sun) Since 1918 Al Grottino has been dishing up pizzas and is one of the best pizzerie in town. See if you can name the famous Italian actors in the photo montage on the wall. If the pizza was good enough for them…. Try the house special *pizza quatro formaggi con salsiccia piccante*. Pizza is only served at night.

Trattoria Zia Marinella (☎ 330 654510; Via Saverio Altamura 23; meals €25-30; ⏰ 12.30-4.30pm & 8.30pm-midnight) In this cosy *trattoria*, once a stable, you're surrounded by wine bottles – and over 150 varieties of wine. The menu changes daily but specialises in fresh seafood from Manfredonia.

L'Osteria di Zio Aldo (☎ 0881 70 81 04; Via Arpi 62; meals €40; ⏰ lunch & dinner Mon-Sat) A candle flicker from the cathedral, this *osteria* is overseen by ebullient Aldo Massimo, who seems a celebrity chef in the making. Passion and eccentricity produce some memorable dishes where traditional antique plates are given a unique interpretation. There's no menu – the waiters give you the low-down. Ask for red wine with fish at your peril.

Drinking

After the evening *passeggiata* along Corso Vittorio Emanuele it's time to hit the cathedral, or rather, the streets and piazze out front. Music and tables and chairs from the many bars spill into Piazza Duomo and Piazza de Santis, the action hot spot for Foggia's university crowd. Have a drink in a street box at **Nessun Dorma** (☎ 0881 72 70 38; Via Duomo 12; ⏰ 8pm-late) or check out the **Al Pachino Italian Pub** (☎ 337 3470719; Via Bruno 26; ⏰ 8pm-late), so un-Italian with its laid-back lounges and chill-out music.

Shopping

Via Arpi has been a commercial zone since the days of ancient Rome. Note that the archways beneath the old palaces don't have doors. Artisans and craftsmen once sold their wares in these open portals where jewellery and souvenir stores, boutiques and clothes shops have taken over. Shopping continues down the main drag, Corso Vittorio Emanuele. For a fascinating and artistic interpretation of the Daunia stele and Gargano's rock art pay a visit to local artist Michele Circiello's gallery Aura Rupestre (see the boxed text, opposite).

Getting There & Away

BUS

Buses depart from Piazzale Vittorio Veneto, from in front of the train station, for towns throughout the province of Foggia.

SITA (☎ 0881 77 31 17; www.sitabus.com) runs buses to Vieste (€4.90, five daily) via Manfredonia (€1.80, 50 minutes), Monte Sant'Angelo (€3.60, 1½ hours, five daily), San Giovanni Rotondo (€2.60, one hour, half-hourly) and Lucera (€1.30, 30 minutes, five daily).

Ferrovie del Gargano (☎ 0881 72 51 88; www .ferroviedelgargano.com) has frequent services to Manfredonia (€1.80, 45 minutes) and Troia (€1.50, 50 minutes).

Tickets for both companies are available from the tobacconist at the train station or from the bar opposite, under the Cinema Ariston sign.

CLP (in Naples ☎ 081 531 17 06) runs direct buses connecting Foggia with Naples (€9, two hours) – they're a faster option than the train. Buy your ticket on board.

CAR & MOTORCYCLE

Take the SS16 south for Bari or north for the Adriatic coast, Termoli and Pescara. The Bologna–Bari A14 also passes Foggia. For Naples, take the SS655 which links with the east–west A16 and to Rome.

TRAIN

There are frequent train services from Foggia to Potenza (€6), Bari (€15, 1¼ hours) and Brindisi (€22.50, 2½ hours). Northwards, up to 10 trains daily head for Ancona (€27, 3½ hours) and Bologna (€40, five hours), with fewer services going to Milan (€54, seven hours, six daily).

Getting Around

The train station and the intercity and local bus terminals are in Piazzale Vittorio Veneto. Look for the ATAF logo. Tickets cost €0.90 and are valid for an hour.

LUCERA

pop 35,036 / elev 219m

Lucera has a curious history. Founded by the Romans in the 4th century BC, the settlement had pretty much run out of steam by the 13th century and was practically abandoned. Then, following his excommunication by his bitter rival Pope Gregory IX, Frederick II decided to bolster his support base in Puglia by importing some 20,000 Sicilian Arabs into town, simultaneously diminishing the headache Arab bandits were causing him in Sicily.

It was an extraordinary move by the Christian monarch, even more so because Frederick

---

AURA RUPESTRE

'I draw inspiration from nature, from the colours of the Gargano, from the Daunia and primitive man.' Michele Circiello's rupestrian, or rock art, evocatively captures the essence of the neolithic civilisations that once inhabited this land. Born in a small town near Foggia, Circiello studied figurative art in Rome and Milan before moving to the Gargano where he underwent an epiphany. Fascinated by primitive rock graffiti, he spent years contemplating and imagining the long-dead Neolithic artists. In the silent emotional traces left in the rock he feels the same deep-seated impulses affecting past and present civilisations. 'The rock tells me what to do,' he says, tracing the cracks and lines of the stones he uses in his rupestrian sculptures. His art is powerful; a mix of sand, rock, mosaics, clay and bronze shaped into lunettes, round shields and modern Daunia stele, decorated with cave-man images of warriors, animals and patterns in the bold primal colours of the Gargano. Circiello sees himself as a medium, expressing the timeless primitive core within us all. 'I feel close to primitive man,' he says simply. Get in touch with your inner cave-man at **Aura Rupestre** (☎ 0881 71 36 74; www.michelecirciello.it; Corso Roma 81; ☼ 5-8.30pm or by appointment). Circiello also has a gallery in **Vieste** (Via Battisti 51; ☼ 8pm-midnight summer).

NORTHERN PUGLIA & THE GARGANO PROMONTORY

allowed the new Muslim inhabitants of Lucera the freedom to build mosques and practice their religion freely a mere 290km from the Holy See at Rome. It was an unprecedented act of liberalism and Frederick was mightily pleased with himself. He spent considerable time in Lucera, handpicking his famous Saracen bodyguard from its inhabitants. Famous for their loyalty, they even accompanied him on his Crusade to the Holy Land in 1228.

History, however, was not so kind; when the town was taken over by the rabidly Christian Angevins in 1269, every Muslim who failed to convert was slaughtered.

Orientation & Information

The bus station in Piazza del Popolo is in front of the Arco di Troia, the medieval city gate facing Troia. Walk under the arch down Via Gramsci to the cathedral. Close by is the **tourist office** (☎ 0881 52 27 62; Piazza Nocelli 6; ☼ 9am-2pm Tue-Sun, 3-6pm Tue-Fri). The castle is 500m northwest of town, the amphitheatre a similar distance to the east.

Sights

Frederick II built the **castle** (☎ 0881 52 27 62; Piazza Matteotti; admission free; ☼ 9am-2pm & 3-8pm Tue-Sun), the largest in southern Italy after Lagopesole (p178), but only ruins remain of his handiwork. However, the 900m-long fortress walls and 24 towers surrounding the ruins are an impressive Angevin addition. From the Queen Tower spectacular views of the Tavoliere stretch from the Gargano in the east to the Apennine foothills in the west.

The banqueting table from the castle has found its way into the **cathedral** (☎ 0881 52 08 80; Piazza Duomo; ☼ 6.30am-noon & 4-7pm), where it does duty as an altar. The cathedral was originally Lucera's Great Mosque but Charles II of Anjou remodelled it in 1300 into Puglia's only Gothic cathedral. The small Gothic-Byzantine **Chiesa di San Francesco** (Piazza Tribunali; ☼ 8am-12.30pm & 4-8pm) was erected at the same time and incorporates numerous recycled materials from Lucera's 1st-century BC **Roman amphitheatre** (currently closed for restoration), which seated 18,000 spectators.

The **Museo Civico Giuseppe Fiorelli** (☎ 0881 54 70 41; Via dei Nicastri 36), currently closed for restoration, exhibits finds from the Neolithic to medieval period, including a fine bust of a Roman Venus, 3rd-century BC terracottas and a 1st-century BC mosaic pavement.

Sleeping

B&B Mimosa (☎ 0881 54 60 66; www.mimosalucera.it; Via de Nicastri 36-40; s €38-45, d €60-70) In a backstreet behind the cathedral, Mimosa offers cute arched studios and two-room apartments – the newest addition is a fabulous arched space adjoining the city museum (unfinished).

Villa Imperiale (☎ 0881 52 09 98; www.villaimperialehotel.com; s/d €50/75; ☒ ☐ ℗) Lucera's only hotel is just outside the old city gate. It's a business-like affair with standard rooms and has a decent restaurant. The hotel also has slightly cheaper rooms to rent next door in La Balconetta. The rooms are modern and comfortable but the set-up (in a residential apartment block) is slightly disconcerting.

Eating

Il Saraceno (☎ 0881 52 09 50; Piazza Duomo; ⏱ 6.30-1.30am) A top-notch stand-up cafè opposite the cathedral, this bar is central for breakfast or an aperitivo, and also sells quality Italian wines.

Al Federiciano Ristorante Pizzeria (☎ 0881 54 94 90; Vico Caropresa 9; pasta €6, pizzas €4; ⏱ lunch & dinner) If you can stand the fluoro lighting, blaring TV and total lack of ambience, follow the locals to this recommended pizzeria in the old town. Quality, crispy pizzas at reasonable prices make up for many faults including noisy Italian families.

Il Cortiletto (☎ 0881 54 25 54; Via de Nicastri 26; meals €30-35; ⏱ lunch & dinner) This quaint restaurant near the Museo Civico serves up vegetarian meals as well as traditional Pugliese and typical Luceran dishes. Only local products are used and most of the wines are regional. A good choice.

Getting There & Away

Lucera is connected with frequent SITA and Ferrovie del Gargano buses to Foggia (€1.30, 30 minutes).

TROIA

pop 7367 / elev 439m

Ironically, this small town with the unfortunate name (*troia* means 'slut') has an impressive religious presence – five patron saints and a magnificent **cathedral** (☎ 0881 97 00 64; Piazza Cattedrale; ⏱ 8.30am-1pm). Begun in 1093, it is one of the oldest in Puglia and gracefully combines Arab-inspired Byzantine artistry with the blind arcades and lozenge motifs of Pisan Romanesque. The 13th-century rose window is one of the finest in Italy. Influenced by the highly developed sense of geometry in Islamic art, it resembles a delicately carved piece of ivory. The simplicity of the blind arcading around the base is in marked contrast to sculpted gargoyles above and the finely wrought 12th-century bronze doors with their dragon handles.

The interior is divided into three narrow aisles lined with columned arches topped with sculpted capitals, and the pulpit is superbly worked. The rich treasury, the **Tesoro** (adult/concession €3/1.50), has silver chalices, vestments, statues and parchments including three famous medieval Exultet codes. To visit the Tesoro see the **tourist office** (☎ 0881 97 00 20; Piazza Giovanni XXVIII 1; ⏱ 9.30am-12.30pm & 4.45-7.45pm Mon-Sat Jun-Apr, also open Sun in May), opposite the cathedral.

Troia's location on a gentle hill surrounded by a crinoline of emerald-green fields only 20km from Foggia makes it a convenient and easy base from which to explore Lucera and the Daunia towns – but don't expect a thriving nightlife.

ourpick **San Basilio B&B** (☎ 0881 97 73 29; Piazza Sabato 4; apt €25-35; P) is a charming self-contained apartment centrally located near the Chiesa di San Basilio. The living room is large and comfortable with French doors opening onto a tiny balcony. Filmy curtains, fluffy towels and a tastefully decorated bedroom make you feel right at home.

Just off the main thoroughfare and in a converted stable, **Ristorante Pizzeria D'Avalos** (☎ 0881 97 00 67; Piazza della Vittoria 9; meals €30; ⏱ Tue-Sun) serves traditional Pugliese cuisine and homemade *crema all'arancio* (orange liqueur).

Regular Ferrovie del Gargano buses link Troia and Foggia (€1.50, 45 minutes).

DAUNIA PRE-APENNINES

Southwest of Foggia the Tavoliere spreads in a long flat wheat belt towards the rolling hills, medieval castles and hilltop towns of the Daunia Pre-Apennines. Narrow roads cut solitary lines through fertile fields, past isolated stone farmhouses with red-tiled roofs and patches of the dense forest that once covered the land. This is big-sky country, where you breathe space and see for miles. In this tranquil landscape, rows of tall metallic windmills suddenly appear like invading aliens. The best way to explore the Daunia's beauty is on a day trip, stopping where and when the mood strikes.

Orsara di Puglia

pop 3197 / elev 650m

Fifteen kilometres south of Troia, the town of Orsara di Puglia has seen a few changes since its early days of Lombard lords and bear hunts. Now summer entertainment in Orsara spells jazz with a six-day international jazz festival at the end of July. Even when the music isn't playing this medieval hill town, with its maze of alleys, steep steps and fountains, is a treat to explore. Worth a visit is the **Complesso Abbaziale dell'Angelo** (☎ 340 5717620; Piazza Mazzini; ⏱ by appointment) a complex of three churches; one dating to the 11th century, one from the 16th century and a 15th-century cave church 6m below ground dedicated to St Michael the archangel.

ourpick **Peppe Zullo** (☎ 0881 96 47 63; Piano Paradiso; meals €30, d with breakfast €90; ⏱ 1-3.30pm Dec-Oct) located at the base of the hill, is one of Orsara's major highlights. Peppe's passion for food and wine shines through in the details – he only cooks in a wood-fired oven, uses organic home-grown herbs and vegetables, makes his own olive oil and wines, and has designed and artfully decorated a number of private dining rooms in the cellar. To make the most of summer jazz (and the fabulous night views of Orsara) stay in one of the five suites perched on top of the hill above the restaurant.

Ascoli Satriano
pop 6318 / elev 410m
The picturesque woodland countryside around Ascoli Satriano was the site of a bloody battle in 279 BC when Pyrrhus defeated the Romans and again in 1041 AD when the Normans conquered the Byzantines. The **Parco Archeologico dei Dauni** (☎ 0885 5662186; Largo Maria Teresa di Lascia 1; ☺ 8am-2pm Tue-Sun) has ancient Daunia ruins dating from the 4th to the 6th centuries BC. There's not much else to see in town apart from the 12th-century Romanesque-Gothic **cathedral** (☎ 0885 65 17 76; Via Duomo 2; ☺ by appointment) in the main *piazza* which has 18th-century Neapolitan paintings on the ceiling.

Sant'Agata di Puglia
pop 2292 / elev 795m
A number of switchbacks take you up to Sant'Agata di Puglia and its **castle** (closed for restoration at the time of research) for a panoramic view of the windmills sprouting like alien antennae from the surrounding hilltops. Two churches are of interest: the **Chiesa di Sant'Andrea** (☎ 0881 98 44 33; ☺ by appointment) originally built in the 7th century and reworked in the 16th century, and the **Chiesa di San Nicola** (☎ 0881 98 44 33; Via de Carlo 20; ☺ 10am-2pm Mon-Sat & 4-9pm daily Aug & Sep, otherwise by appointment) built in the 14th and 15th centuries and housing a 17th-century wooden choir and altar and a 16th-century stone crib. It's hard to get lost in this little town; all the steps and laneways lead back to the main piazza.

Accadia
pop 2608 / elev 650m
From the Frugno River, pine trees and thick woods cover the slopes up to Accadia. The new town was built after the 1930 and 1962 earthquakes damaged most of the medieval quarter. Park your car at the **Fontana Monumentale**, a fountain resembling a mini-pantheon with its four stone columns. The bronze panel depicts the 19-day siege of 1462 when the townsmen withstood an attack by the Aragonese. The spring water is potable. Opposite the fountain is the medieval quarter, the **Rione Fossi**, built on the ancient site of Eca. Some reconstruction is underway in the maze of abandoned cave houses and medieval buildings.

Deliceto
pop 4057 / elev 621m
Deliceto's most impressive sight is its monumental 12th-century Norman **castle** (closed for restoration at the time of research), a national monument since 1902 and best appreciated from a distance. The 15th-century **Convento della Consolazione** (☎ 0881 96 34 64; ☺ by appointment) 2km south of town is famous for housing two saints in its time, one of whom, St Alfonso Maria dei Liguori, composed the Christmas carol *Tu scendi dalle stelle* (You come down from the stars). If you visit on the second Sunday in August, hog into some local pork dishes during the **Black Pig Day** celebrations.

Bovino
pop 3820 / elev 646m
Another monumental **castle** best appreciated from a distance dominates the medieval hilltop town of Bovino. Built in 1045, the castle underwent a series of alterations over the centuries, but the imposing cylindrical tower is the Norman original. It is currently closed for restoration but it's worth a drive for the panoramic views of rolling hills, isolated farmhouses, patchwork fields and dense forests. The Romanesque-Apulian **cathedral** (☎ 0881 96 62 36; Piazza Duomo; ☺ 9am-1pm & 4-9pm Jul-Sep) dates to the 10th-century and is now a national monument. In the late 1800s bandits hid in the surrounding forests and woods.

Faeto
pop 704 / elev 820m
A long winding drive on a narrow, rough road brings you to the small linguistic island of Faeto, the highest town in the Daunia hills. In the 13th century a garrison of French soldiers settling in a nearby Benedictine Abbey provided the Provencal base for the unique dialect that is spoken to this day. Faeto is a tiny town of 700 inhabitants and it takes only a little time to wander through its cramped alleys and lanes. Be sure to sample its famous prosciutto and salamis.

Taranto & the Murgia

Between the Ionian and Adriatic coast, rises the great limestone plateau of the Murgia (473m). It has a strange karst geology; the landscape is riddled with holes and ravines through which small streams and rivers gurgle, creating what is in effect a giant sponge. The ancient tribes of Puglia, the Messapians and the Peucetians, found it an ideal location to set up home and since then the Murgia has been cultivated and moulded by generations of farmers.

The fertile land and strategic location made cities like Taranto, Brindisi, Martina Franca and Conversano rich and content. The Roman roads Via Appia and Via Appia Traiana, criss-crossing the plateau bringing all those ideas, history and art from Greece to Rome engendering a period of change and development. Feudal estates sprang up across the plateau, taking advantage of this cultural and commercial superhighway. Communities of peasant farmers created the bedrock of farming traditions in wine-making, olive-oil production and stock-breeding that made this one of the most productive rural regions in Italy.

Even today the Murgia and its two coastlines is the most populus area in Puglia, and it's certainly the most highly touristed area – although that only means you'll bump into a few foreigners as opposed to none at all. Small farms, clusters of *trulli* (houses with conical tiled roofs) and large *masseria* (fortified estates) dot the landscape, providing some of Puglia's finest and most distinctive accommodation.

TARANTO & THE MURGIA

HIGHLIGHTS

- Get the merest taste of Taranto's Grecian treasures in the **Palazzo Pantaleo** (p114) and then feast on its famous mussels at **Trattoria Gesù Cristo** (p115)

- Go fresco-hunting in the rock churches of **Massafra** (p117) and **Mottola** (p117)

- Rent a **trulli** (boxed text, p125), visit local markets and immerse yourself in country life in the **Valle d'Itria** (p122)

- Relax on a quilted bedspread at **Il Frantoio** (p130), and gear yourself up for one of the finest meals you'll eat in Puglia

- Passeggiata in **Martina Franca** (p127) amid some lavish baroque architecture and then lunch in beautiful **Locorotondo** (p126)

TARANTO & THE TARANTINE MURGE

Once the jewel in the crown of Magna Graecia, Taranto and its environs has now been well and truly eclipsed by the port cities of the Adriatic Coast. However, it is an area rich in history, the landscape is scored with frescoed caves and lost-in-time towns, and the deep ravines that score the landscape make for some dramatic trekking.

TARANTO

pop 199,000

Break through the industrial horror show that Taranto presents to visitors and you will find a vivacious city centre, with a large palm-planted piazza and an elegant pedestrianised *corso*. But the air of bourgeois prosperity disguises a very troubled city, declared bankrupt in October 2006 due to fraud and mismanagement on a tragic scale with debts running to €357 million. The newspapers shrieked, 'how can a city, once the capital of Magna Graecia, sink so low?' and 'the local council shouldn't be allowed to go bankrupt in the midst of indifference', but somehow it has and the Tarentines feel bewildered and betrayed.

It is all a far cry from the city's exotic past as a Spartan stronghold and the greatest city of the south. With such a history, and a hinterland dotted with early Christian cave churches, Taranto deserves more tourists than it sees, but until the corruption scandal subsides and the city's parlous financial problems are resolved it's unlikely that things will improve any time soon.

History

Founded in the 8th century BC by exiles from Sparta, the city was christened Taras and grew to become one of the wealthiest and most important colonies of Magna Graecia, with a peak population of 300,000. It traded in wine, wool, figs and purple murex shells (from which the imperial purple dye was extracted), which minted a fine profit on the open market. Such prosperity spawned intellectuals like the mathematician Archytas and the musician

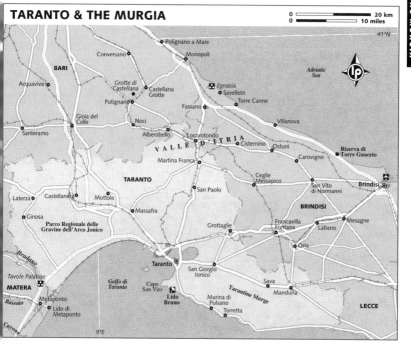

TARANTO & THE MURGIA

Arixtoxenes, and even the likes of Plato, Horace and Virgil spent some time here.

After such a bright beginning, Taranto has had nothing but bad luck. It was conquered by the Romans in 272 BC, then conspired with Hannibal in 209 BC, for which the city was severely punished when the Romans finally got their hands back on it. The advent of the Normans and later the Swabians brought a brief period of respite before various members of the Italian and Spanish nobility played tug-of-war with it during the 15th and 16th centuries. In 1734 it came under Bourbon rule and during the 19th century it proved one of Napoleon's most stalwart bases.

Its cultural heyday may be over but Taranto remains an important naval base, second only to La Spezia, and the presence of young sailors is emblematic of a city that has always sought its fortune on the sea.

Orientation

Taranto splits neatly into three distinct areas. The industrial centre, including Italy's largest steel plant, and the train station are on the mainland to the northwest. The Città Vecchia occupies an island, which was once the Roman citadel. It's linked to the mainland to the northwest by a bridge and to the southeast by a causeway. Over the causeway to the southeast is the Città Nuova, the main city centre and residential area. The tourist office and most of the hotels, banks and shops can be found here.

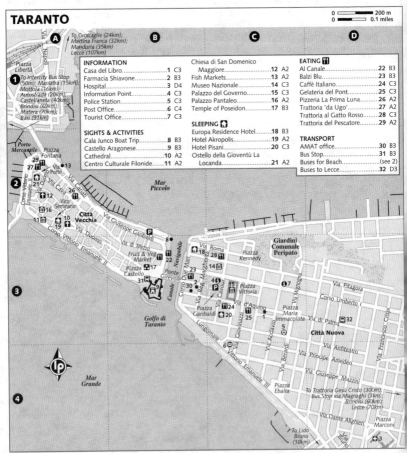

TARANTO

0 — 200 m
0 — 0.1 miles

INFORMATION
Casa del Libro................................1 C3
Farmacia Shiavone.......................2 B3
Hospital..3 D4
Information Point..........................4 C3
Police Station.................................5 C3
Post Office.....................................6 C4
Tourist Office................................7 C3

SIGHTS & ACTIVITIES
Cala Junco Boat Trip...................8 B3
Castello Aragonese.......................9 B3
Cathedral.....................................10 A2
Centro Culturale Filonide........11 A2

Chiesa di San Domenico
  Maggiore..................................12 A2
Fish Markets.................................13 A2
Museo Nazionale.......................14 C3
Palazzo del Governo..................15 C3
Palazzo Pantaleo........................16 A2
Temple of Poseidon..................17 B3

SLEEPING
Europa Residence Hotel...........18 B3
Hotel Akropolis..........................19 A2
Hotel Pisani.................................20 C3
Ostello della Gioventù La
  Locanda....................................21 A2

EATING
Al Canale......................................22 B3
Balzi Blu..23 B3
Caffè Italiano..............................24 C3
Gelateria del Pont.....................25 C3
Pizzeria La Prima Luna.............26 A2
Trattoria 'da Ugo'......................27 A2
Trattoria al Gatto Rosso...........28 C3
Trattoria del Pescatore.............29 A2

TRANSPORT
AMAT office................................30 B3
Bus Stop.......................................31 B3
Buses for Beach.....................(see 2)
Buses to Lecce...........................32 D3

Information

BOOKSHOPS

Casa del Libro (☎ 099 452 05 04; Via d'Aquino 142; 9am-1pm & 5-8pm Mon-Fri) An independent bookshop selling books on Taranto, alongside maps and guides in Italian.

EMERGENCY

Ambulance (☎ 118)
Police station (☎ 099 454 51 11; Via Anfiteatro 8)

MEDICAL SERVICES

Farmacia Shiavone (☎ 099 452 19 04; Via Regina Margherita 46/48; 9am-1pm & 5-8.30pm Mon-Sat) A large pharmacy in the centre of town.
Guardia Medica (☎ 099 452 19 97) A 24-hour emergency call-out service.
Hospital (☎ 099 453 49 38; Via Bruno)

MONEY

Banks are located in the new town along Via d'Aquino and Corso Umberto. In the Città Vecchia there is an ATM in Piazza Fontana.

POST

Post office (☎ 099 470 75 91; Lungomare Vittorio Emanuele III)

TOURIST INFORMATION

Tourist office (☎ 099 453 23 92; Corso Umberto I 113; 9am-1pm & 5-7pm Mon-Fri, 9am-noon Sat) With the city administration in turmoil, the tourist office is a bit beleaguered with unpaid staff soldiering on during erratic hours.
Information Point (Piazza Garibaldi; 9am-1pm Mon-Fri) At the time of research this information point was closed. If it reopens it is the most convenient information point in the city.

Dangers & Annoyances

The Città Vecchia looks terribly rundown and at night there is no street lighting. It's actually a lot less sinister than it looks and the two main streets, Via Duomo and Via Garibaldi, are generally busy during the day. At night when things are quiet it's worth being more careful and avoiding any unlit alleys.

Sights

Until the Museo Nazionale reopens, the majority of sites are located in the atmospheric Città Vecchia, which is accessed over the swing bridge from the modern town centre. In the evenings the flow of people moves in the opposite direction as everyone makes their way to the bars and cafés that line Corso Due Mare.

CITTÀ VECCHIA

Just like Naples and Palermo, Taranto has an old town that retains a gritty atmosphere of deep decay and, at the same time, an irrepressible energy. It may be temporarily down at heel but it certainly isn't down and out, as private individuals slowly rehabilitate its old palaces and monuments.

Castello Aragonese

Taranto has a curious city plan where the old town is perched on a small island dividing the Mar Piccolo (Small Sea; an enclosed lagoon) and the Mar Grande (Big Sea). It's a peculiar geography that provides the old town with a self-contained atmosphere. Guarding the swing bridge that joins the old and new town, the 15th-century **Castello Aragonese** (☎ 099 775 34 38; admission free; by appointment 9am-noon Mon-Fri) is quite an impressive structure, its sturdy bulwark jutting out to sea. It's occupied by the Italian navy and can only be visited providing you book one of the guided tours, which take you through its echoing halls and finishing on the ramparts. Opposite the castle you can see the remaining columns of what was once Taranto's **Temple of Poseidon**. Legend has it that his son, Taras, founded the city when he rode into its harbour on the back of a dolphin.

Duomo

Via Duomo is the main thoroughfare of the old town, lined with boarded-up 15th- and 16th-century *palazzi*. In the centre it opens up into a small cobbled piazza in front of the 11th-century **cathedral** (Piazza Duomo; 8am-noon & 4.30-7pm), which is dedicated to the Irish Saint Cataldo, who settled in Taranto after his pilgrimage to the Holy Land in the 7th century. Although it's essentially a three-aisled basilica the building has been burnt down and modified several times and now sports a whole mixture of styles from its baroque façade by Mauro Manieri to its Byzantine and Romanesque décor. The main feature is the stunning Cappella di San Cataldo, which is an absolute riot of polychrome marble inlay, 18th-century statuary and a richly frescoed ceiling by Paolo de Matteis. The altar holds the relics of St Cataldo and is surmounted by a huge silver bust of him.

TARANTO & THE MURGIA

Palazzo Pantaleo

Carry on down Via Duomo and take a left onto Corso Vittorio Emanuele II. Here you'll find the **Palazzo Pantaleo** (☎ 099 458 17 15; Corso Vittorio Emanuele II; admission €2; ⊙ 8.30am-7.30pm), the temporary home of the city's archaeological collection. We say 'temporary', but the edited selection of artefacts on display has actually been here for seven years now. Still, it's certainly worth the visit as it exhibits the most sophisticated works of Magna Graecia that you're likely to see anywhere in Puglia.

Particularly fine are the ceramics, which Taranto developed in its potteries during the 4th century and sold throughout the Greek world. There are lots of Corinthian and Laconian ceramics, but the best pieces are the superb black-and-red Attic vases, most of them decorated with mythical stories showing thick-thighed heroes and thin-legged horses. At the end of the exhibit you'll come to the highlight of the show, the gold jewellery, which is mainly of Tarentine workmanship of the 4th century BC. There are earrings, belts, a delicate crown of laurel wreathes and rings with engraved bezels and scarabs – it's a stunning collection. The most famous piece is a bronze nutcracker in the shape of two clasped hands, the bronze arms adorned with gold spiral bracelets.

Other Sights

After the palace you won't feel like doing much more but you might wander past the **Chiesa di San Domenico Maggiore** (Via Duomo; ⊙ 8.30am-noon & 4.30-7.30pm), with its high baroque double staircase, and head down to Piazza Fontana, once the commercial heart of the city but now a scruffy roundabout. Here you'll find the small **fishing port**, along Via Cariati where you can buy piles of *ricci* (sea urchins) or shiny-looking mussels harvested from the Mar Piccola.

Another fun place to visit is the **Centro Culturale Filonide** (☎ 099 476 43 74; www.filonidetaranto.it; Corso Vittorio Emanuele II 39; ⊙ by appointment only), an eccentric non-profit-making cultural centre located in a renovated 17th-century palace. Its painted salons are full of old furniture and interesting bric-a-brac that gives a fascinating glimpse into how grand the old town must once have been.

CITTÀ NUOVA

Taranto's new town is a pleasant surprise. It has a truly urbane atmosphere, with sleek shopping streets shooting off the impressive palm-planted Piazza Garibaldi which is dominated by the gigantic rust-red 1920s **Palazzo del Governo**.

The **Museo Nazionale** (☎ 099 453 21 12; www.museotaranto.it; Corso Umberto I 41) is also located on the piazza and tourism officials are promising a grand re-opening in 2008.

A short walk down Via Cavour will bring you to the **Giardini Comunale Peripato** (Piazza Kennedy; ⊙ 8am-11pm Jun-Sep, 9am-8pm Oct-May), a formal 18th-century garden that now makes a lovely city park complete with a children's play area and great views over the Mar Piccola.

Activities

Southeast of Taranto the coast begins to unfurl in one long series of sandy **beaches** and coves. The closest beach to town is the Lido Bruno, but you'll need to head beyond that to get to the better beaches like the ones at Marino di Pulsano and Toretta. You can reach some of the closer beaches by public transport but, you really need a car to get the best out of beachcombing.

Festivals

Le Feste di Pasqua (Holy Week) On Holy Thursday thousands of people gather to witness the Procession of the *Addolorata* (the Sorrowful) and then the Procession of the Mysteries on Good Friday. Huge effigies of Christ and the Madonna are carried by barefoot *penitente* (penitents), shrouded from head to toe in white robes.

Festa di San Cataldo (8-10 May) The silver effigy of the city's patron saint is carried on a warship followed by fishing boats; there are fireworks at the castle and everyone eats *carteddate* (fried pastry made with wine).

Sleeping

In the past, Taranto's hotels were confined to the southeastern edge of the city on the road to the beaches, but many of these have since closed due to the absence of any real tourist trade and only a smattering remain in the centre of town.

CITTÀ VECCHIA

Many people are put off by the decrepit appearance of the old town, but since the opening of the Akropolis in 2004 more and more people are considering it as an option.

Ostello della Gioventù La Locanda (☎ 099 476 00 33; www.ostellolalocanda.it; Vico Civitanova; dm €20, €30/60) Taranto now has its own youth hostel tucked in a tiny alley near Piazza Fontana

There are 24 beds in total and rooms are very spartan. It also has a restaurant serving a very cheap meal for €12.

ourpick **Hotel Akropolis** (☎ 099 470 41 10; www .hotelakropolis.it; Vico I Seminario 3; s €95-105, d €135-160; ✿ 🖳) Located in the old town, the Akropolis has got it all right, from the tremendous view from its rooftop terrace to the hushed comfort of its rooms, many of which still sport the original majolica tiled floors.

CITTÀ NUOVA

As the majority of bars and restaurants are located in the new town, where the main *passeggiata* takes place, you may want to be located here.

Hotel Pisani (☎ 099 453 40 87; fax 099 470 75 93; Via Cavour 43; s/d €30/50) Taranto's best budget option is the Hotel Pisani, although that isn't saying much. Despite the promising entrance in a pleasant apartment block, the rooms tend to be a bit gloomy, a fact not helped by the odd assortment of dated furniture. Still, it's busy and the reception is friendly.

Europa Residence Hotel (☎ 099 452 59 94; www.hotel europaonline.it; Via Roma 2; s €80-105, d €135; ✿) If you don't want to be in the old town, this is the next best thing. The Europa is located right on the edge of the Mar Piccola overlooking the traffic going to and fro beneath the swing bridge. Inside, the hotel is bland but comfortable and lots of rooms have sea views.

Eating

Come to Taranto to eat, if for nothing else. It has been famous for its seafood since antiquity, the speciality being its shellfish and sinfully fleshy oysters.

CITTÀ VECCHIA

The old town is a great place to eat, especially during the Easter festivities (when you definitely need to book). The main drag is Via Garibaldi, where lots of people simply hang out drinking or buying pizza and grilled meat from the hole-in-the-wall joints.

Pizzeria La Prima Luna (☎ 099 471 52 50; Via Garibaldi 74; meals €25-30; ✷ Wed-Mon) Ring to enter this furiously popular pizzeria. The candlelit tables and vaulted dining room are full of character and the atmosphere is as Neapolitan (read noisy) as the pizzas. Reservations are essential on Saturday.

Al Canale (☎ 099 476 42 01; Discesa Vasto; meals €35; ✷ Wed-Mon) Gaze dreamily out of the floor-to-ceiling windows over the canal, then turn your attention to the orgy of seafood you've ordered: mussels au gratin, grilled octopus, carpaccio of bream, pappardelle with scampi and grilled mixed fish. You'll barely be able to squeeze in the lemon sorbet at the end.

ourpick **Trattoria 'da Ugo'** (☎ 329 141 58 50; cnr of Via Cataldo de Tulio & Via Fontana; meals €10-15; ✷ Mon-Fri, lunch Sat) A typical Tarantine trattoria that's stuck close to its roots with a menu consisting entirely of fish. Feast on grilled mussels, octopus flavoured with oil and lemon, and fried prawns and squid. It also serves homemade pastas like tubettini with beans and mussels. Great value for money.

Also recommended is **Trattoria del Pescatore** (☎ 099 470 71 21; Piazza Fontana; meals €25; ✷ Mon-Sat).

CITTÀ NUOVA

Restaurants in the new town may not share the same quaint atmosphere, but there's plenty of variety and Corso Due Mari is crammed on summer evenings.

Balzi Blu (☎ 347 465 32 11; Corso Due Mari 22; meals €10-15; ✷ Tue-Sun) The Balzi Blu is the most popular restaurant on the corso. The secret of its success is the delicious pizza, apparently made from a mixture of 13 different types of flour. The main menu simply isn't as good, so stick to pizza.

Trattoria al Gatto Rosso (☎ 099 452 98 75; Via Cavour 2; meals €25; ✷ Tue-Sun) A relaxed and unpretentious trattoria with a real touch of class – heavy tablecloths, deep wine glasses and the like. It is located in the new town and is very popular with discerning businessmen.

ourpick **Trattoria Gesù Cristo** (☎ 099 477 72 53; Via Battisti 8; meals €30; ✷ Tue-Sat, lunch Sun) It's a bit of a hike to get to this restaurant, but its sterling reputation keeps the punters coming. The family owns the fish shop next door so you can be sure that the fish is super fresh. The grilled fish cooked on an open-flame grill is delicious. It's an old-fashioned place with long tables full of big families.

CAFÉS & GELATERIE

Taranto has an impressive *passeggiata* along the pedestrianised Via d'Aquino, where you'll find lots of cafés and *gelaterie*, catering to the hungry walkers.

Caffè Italiano (☎ 099 452 17 81; Via D'Aquino 86a; salads €4, meals €10) A stylish modern café that does the job of restaurant/café/bar. It has a good deli counter serving *foccacie*, salads, calzone and sandwiches. In the evenings it transforms itself into a cocktail bar.

Gelateria del Ponte (Via d'Aquino 110; ice cream €2.50) A tiny parlour with mountainous tubs of ice cream piled high with real fruit and nuts, and even cake (the Tiramisu flavour is sublime). Indulge in the *semifreddo fetta al latte* or the *torrone*.

Getting There & Away

Due to its location, it's easier to travel in and out of Taranto on the bus services, unless you are taking the train to Metaponto. Buses heading north and west depart from Porto Mercantile; those going south and east leave from Via Magnaghi in the new city.

BUS

FSE (☎ 800 07 90 80) buses connect Taranto with Bari (€5.10, two hours, eight Monday to Saturday, one Sunday), leaving from the Porto Mercantile, as well as to smaller towns in the area. Infrequent **SITA** (☎ 099 32 52 04; www.sitabus.it) buses leave from Porto Mercantile for Matera (€4.60, 1½ hours, two daily) and Metaponto (€2.70, two daily). **STP** (☎ 0832 22 44 11) and FSE buses connect Taranto with Lecce (€6.80, two hours, three Monday to Saturday), departing from Via di Palma.

Marozzi (☎ 080 579 90 111) has express services to and from Rome's Stazione Tiburtina (€39.50, six hours, three daily), leaving from Porto Mercantile. **Autolinee Miccolis** (☎ 099 470 44 51) runs daily to and from Naples (€16, four hours, three daily) via Potenza (€8.40, two hours). The **ticket office** (🕐 7am-1.30pm & 3-9.30pm) for all three companies can be found at Porto Mercantile.

CAR

Taranto is accessible from Bari (SS100) and Brindisi (SS7). The SS7 and SS100 also connect Taranto with Massafra and Mottola. Just after Massafra you'll also find the turning to Matera. To travel southwest along the coast there is a good, but heavily trafficked dual carriageway, the SS106.

TRAIN

Train travel is really only more convenient when travelling to Metaponto (€2.60 to €5.60, 50 minutes, six daily) up the coast. There are services to all the main destinations but it's more than likely that you'll have to change somewhere en route.

Frequent **Trenitalia** (☎ 89 20 21) and **FSE** (☎ 099 471 59 01) trains connect Taranto with Brindisi (€4, one hour 10 minutes) and Bari (€6.80, 1¼ hours). The Brindisi train stops at Grottaglie, Francavilla Fontana and Oria.

To travel further afield you'll need to make a connection at either Bari (for Naples or Rome) or Brindisi (for Lecce).

Getting Around

AMAT (☎ 099 4 52 67 32; Via d'Aquino) buses 1/2, 3 and 8 run between the train station and the new city. Buses 14, 15 and 16 head out towards the beaches.

For a taxi, call ☎ 099 7 30 47 34. There is metered parking in Piazza Garibaldi (€0.80 to €1 per hour).

PARCO REGIONALE DELLE GRAVINE DELL'ARCO JONICO

The countryside to the northwest of Taranto is popularly known as the Anifteatro delle Murge (the Amphitheatre of the Murge), a nickname it has earned due to the particular geography of the landscape, which is riddled with fossil rivers. Perched on the vertical edge of many of the ravines are a series of small rural towns – Massafra, Mottola, Palagiano, Palagianello, Castellaneta, Ginosa and Laterza – built on top of caves that were once inhabited by Basilian monks and hermits.

Massafra
pop 31,200

The largest of the Jonico towns, Massafra sits on a terrace overlooking the coast and the Calabrian mountains. From a distance it looks like a kasbah, with the high white walls of the town's perimeter rising above the plain in a protective circle. At its centre it straddles the ravine of San Marco, the Terra (old town) on the western side and the Borgo Santa Caterina (new town) on the eastern side. It is a spectacular location, with the two halves of town linked together by lofty bridges.

INFORMATION

To visit the churches you'll need to take a guided tour as the caves are locked. You can book tours at the **tourist office** (Cooperativa Nuova Hellas; ☎ 099 880 46 95, 338 565 96 01; Via Vittorio Veneto 15; 🕐 9am-noon Mon-Fri), which you'll find in the old town. For €5 you can take one of two tours (usually at 10am and 3pm from September to April, and 9.30am, 11.30am and 4pm or 5pm from May to August), one of which takes you to the crypts in the old town and the other to the Sanctuary of the Madonna della Scala. Both tours take about 1½ to two hours. For English- or French-speaking guides you'll need to phone in advance.

SIGHTS

From Piazza Vittorio Emanuele in the centre of the new town, Corso Italia leads you to the Ponte Vecchio, from where you have the best views of the ravine and, to the north, the **Norman castle**. The most spectacular ravine is the Gravina Madonna della Scala, which is located on the outskirts of town. It stretches for 4km and is famous for its fragrant flowers and herbs, which the Basilian monks used in their medicines. There are around 30 cave churches here, including the **Farmacia del Mago Greguro** (Pharmacy of the Wizard Gregory), a series of 12 interconnecting caves with over 300 *loculi* (niches) where Gregory is supposed to have stored his lotions and potions. The cave churches date from between the 11th and the 15th centuries, the most famous being the **Santuario di Madonna della Scala**, which contains an unusual 12th- to 13th-century fresco of the Madonna and Child with two kneeling deer. The church over it was built later in 1731 and is still a site of pilgrimage. The adjacent **Cripta di Bona Nuova** has a wonderful Christ Pantocrator.

There are 125 steps down into the ravine. If you don't feel up to that you should take the second tour, which covers the **Cripta di San Leonardo** and the **Cripta di San Marco**. Both have equally good frescoes; the latter contains two unusual images, one depicting Jesus as a small boy walking beside the Madonna and the other known as the *Madonna della Dolcezza* (Sweet Madonna) because of her heavily kohled, oriental eyes.

SLEEPING & EATING

There is no accommodation in Massafra itself, only the sinfully ugly Hotel Appia located just off the SS7. If you want to stay in the area it's preferable to seek out accommodation in one of the surrounding farmhouses.

Masseria La Brunetta (☎ 099 880 09 42; www.masserialabrunetta.it; Via per Chiatona; s €70-80, d €140-160; P 🍴 🐾) A classic whitewashed manor house set in manicured lawns between Massafra and its beaches. The interior is a cool haven of smooth limestone barrel vaults, with pared-

back décor in the bedrooms. In summer it's heavenly, in winter it can be a bit chilly.

ourpick Falso Pepe (☎ 099 880 46 87; www.falsopepe.it; Via II SS Medici 45; meals €35; 🕑 7.30-11pm Thu-Tue, lunch Sat & Sun) In this small brilliant white *casa*, beneath the shade of the pepper tree they named it after, you'll eat some of the most sublime food in Puglia. Local goat's cheese with sweet Tropea onions, homemade wild boar salumi, carpaccio of tuna with a bitter orange compote and intensely flavoured bucatini with three meat sauces (veal, lamb and pork) are just some of the options on the accomplished menu.

GETTING THERE & AWAY

Massafra is located just off the SS7, 17km from Taranto. To get to get there take the FSE bus from Piazza Castello in Taranto (€1.10, 30 minutes, seven Monday to Saturday).

Mottola
pop 16,500

Just 6km from Massafra, Mottola shares the same characteristics – a whitewashed town, perched on a hill surrounded by rock churches. Again, you'll need to be accompanied by a guide to visit them and you can arrange tours at the **tourist office** (☎ 099 886 69 48, 338 565 96 01; Via Vanvitelli 2; 🕑 9am-1pm & 4-8pm). It costs €30 for the guide and a further €3 per person.

The **Grotte di Dio** (Caves of the Gods), as they are nicknamed, date from between the 5th and 15th century and although there are about 30 in total you can only visit four of them – the crypts of Sant'Angelo (with a unique two-storey construction containing a necropolis in the lower half), Santa Margherita, San Gregorio and the stunning **Cripta di San Nicola**. Otherwise known as the Sistine Chapel of the south, it contains a cycle of 24 frescoes, depicting full-length images of popular saints like the Archangel Michael, St Nicholas, St John the Baptist and St George, which fan out from the central altar, above which there is a magnificent Christ Pantocrator. They date from between the 11th and 14th centuries and are the most complete set of frescoes in southern Italy. Some of the saints, like St Pelagia, are almost unheard of in the Catholic canon but are still venerated in the Balkans, and so the church remains an important site of pilgrimage for Greek Orthodox Christians.

Through the tourist office you can also arrange treks down the Petruscio ravine,

TARANTO & THE MURGIA

although you'll need a group of at least two or three people for safety reasons.

To reach Mottola take the FSE bus from Piazzo Castello in Taranto (€1.10, 30 minutes, seven Monday to Saturday). It is located just 6km further west from Massafra on the SS100.

Ginosa, Laterza & Castellaneta

Although Massafra and Mottola are undoubtedly the stars of the show when it comes to cave churches, the other towns in the Jonico arc have other things to recommend them. Like Matera, **Ginosa** has a ravine full of *sassi*, although here they remain eerily abandoned, giving you just a glimpse of what Matera was like barely 10 years ago. The town also holds a great *tableaux vivant* of the life of Christ (the **Passio Cristi**) in the ravine during the Easter weekend. To book tours contact the **tourist office** (☎ 099 829 48 84; Via Aloisie 3).

Alternatively, if you prefer walking to gawping, then head for **Laterza**, perched on one of the biggest ravines in Europe, which runs some 12km in length. It contains a magical microclimate and is home to pellegrine falcons and imperial eagles. The Italian bird organisation **Lipu** (www.lipu.it) has created trekking trails within the ravine and you can head out with a guide, on foot or on mountain bikes. To book a guided trek contact the **Centro Visite** (☎ 339 331 19 47; Via Selva San Vito; ⏰ 9am-1pm & 4-6pm Thu-Fri, 9am-6pm Sat & Sun, closes 8pm Jul & Aug). The trips take between two to four hours so you'll need at least half a day.

For a real 'lost in time' feeling spend a day exploring the historic centre of **Castellaneta**, a brilliant white tangle of tiny streets that end in a precipitous drop into a spectacular ravine. The ravine at Castellaneta is the only one where water still flows so it's only accessible during the summer months. To book trips to the cave churches here contact the **tourist office** (☎ 099 849 21 70; Via Pietro Nenni 28). You can also ask to see the **Museo Rodolfo Valentino** (☎ 099 849 72 57; Via Municipio 19; ⏰ on request) – the great love god was apparently born here.

THE TARANTINE MURGE

To the east of Taranto lies the Tarantine Murge, a sunny plain just south of the main Murgia plateau with some once-prosperous Bourbon towns. Grottaglie, Francavilla Fontana, Manduria and pretty Oria are relatively off the beaten track for most travellers, but

if you're looking for wine or ceramics you'll want to make a detour.

Grottaglie
pop 32,500

Of all these towns, Grottaglie is probably the most well known, and is considered by those in the know to be the ceramics capital of the south. You've probably seen Grottaglie pottery before in your local branch of Habitat or Ikea, but shop here and you'll be able to snap it up for half the price straight from the potter.

The town's ceramics tradition dates back to the Middle Ages. The **Museo della Ceramica** (☎ 099 562 02 22; www.museogrottaglie.it; Largo Maria Immacolata; admission free; ⏰ 9.30am-12.30pm & 4-7pm, to 8pm in summer), housed in the Castello Episcopio, exhibits over 400 ceramics dating from between the 14th and 20th centuries. It is arranged in chronological order so you can see how the techniques got better and the colours brighter as they went along.

Having seen the best head down to *Li cammen're*, the potters' quarter, where around 60 studios, many of them caves carved out of the tufa rock, produce thousands of pots, plates and vases all stacked in colourful piles around the town. The **'del Monaco' studio** (☎ 099 566 10 23; Via S Sofia 2/4) is one of the more distinguished, specialising in sophisticated designs along a rustic theme. The studio is now run by Giuseppe – have a look at some of his work at www.ceramistidigrottaglie.it.

If you're shopping in Grottaglie then you'll probably need a car. To reach the town take the SS7 from Taranto. If you don't have a car the easiest way to get there is by train from either Taranto (€1.30, 15 minutes) or Brindisi (€3.40, 50 minutes).

Manduria
pop 31,800

If ceramics aren't your thing, then maybe you fancy some wine? In which case you'll jump back in your car and head for Manduria; this faded Bourbon town with its mouldering baroque *palazzi* and churches is the centre of production for the Primitivo grape.

The central piazza is impressive (a nice place to have ice cream if you can elbow your way through all those flat-capped blokes at the counter of the local ice-cream shop), with the 18th-century **Palazzo Imperiali** (Town Hall) dominating the eastern end of the square and hiding behind it a warren of streets that once constituted the **Jewish ghetto**. Its medieval layout is pretty much perfectly preserved and if you wander around you'll find any number of wine merchants and the odd winebar or two, like the **Enoteca del Primitivo** (☎ 099 971 15 23; Vico I Senatore G Lacaita 6; meals €20; 10am-1pm & 6pm-midnight Wed-Mon). You might also chance upon the **cathedral**, originally a Romanesque building (spot those lions at the portal), but later remodelled in Gothic and Renaissance forms. The other excellent venue for sampling wine is **Vivavino** (☎ 099 971 29 20; Via Roma 75E; Fri-Wed), a franchise of the **l'Accademia dei Racemi** (www .accademiadeiracemi.it) run by Gregory Perrucci and Elisabetta Gorla. It's a large, light, modern winebar-cum-shop with hundreds of bottles to choose from alongside oil, balsamic vinegar and various jams and preserves.

Manduria also boasts the fine remains of its Messapian **fortifications** (☎ 099 979 50 76; www.messapi.it; Via Sant'Antonio Abate; adult/concession €5.50/4, guide €3; 8am-4.30pm Tue-Sun Nov-Mar, 8am-8.30pm Tue-Sun Apr-Oct). They are ridiculously old, the inner ring dating as far back as the 5th century BC. There are three concentric circles varying from the 2m-thick inner wall to the 5m-thick outer wall, which says something for the lengths the Messapians were prepared to go to, to ward off their archenemies the Greek Tarantines. At the heart of the archaeological area is Pliny's Well, which he wrote about in the *Natural Histories*, and along the Viale Panoramico you can see some of the 1200 rock-cut tombs, which have yielded many a treasure for Taranto's archaeological museum. You can find the walls on the outskirts of town along the SS7 heading in the direction of Lecce.

It is difficult to reach Manduria without a car. You can take a train from both Brindisi and Taranto but you'll have to change at Francavilla Fontana. By car, you'll need to take the SS7t, a provincial road that is nevertheless the main connection between Taranto and Lecce.

Oria
pop 15,400

Barely 6km from Manduria down a pretty rural road is picturesque Oria. It's way off the beaten track and it's really quite difficult to understand why as it has a lovely historic centre and a lively local scene.

It used to be called Hyria, and was the capital of Messapia, dominating surrounding towns like Ceglie Messapica and Manduria. Like Siena it is still divided into legally chartered communities, called *contrade*, which pre-date the Roman period. This makes for lots of fun during local festivals like the **Corto Storico di Frederico II**, a medieval procession which takes place on the second weekend of August with a tournament between the town's four quarters.

Like Manduria it has a Jewish ghetto, which still retains its medieval character and is topped off by an impressive **castle** (☎ 0831 84 00 09; adult/concession €5/2.50; 9.30am-12.30pm & 5-8pm Jul & Aug, 9.30am-12.30pm & 3.30-6.30pm Sep & Oct & Mar-Jun) built by Frederick II in 1227–33. Amazingly it is still in private hands. To book a tour of the castle contact **Nuova Hyria** (☎ 335 726 16 16, 349 553 93 79; guide €15).

Further up the hill on the Colle del Vaglio is the **cathedral** (Piazza Cattedrale; 9am-noon & 4-7pm), perched on what was once the ancient acropolis. It was built in 1743 to replace the previous church, which fell down in an earthquake. The rococo tastes of the day inform the whole interior but what's more intriguing is the **Cripta delle Mummie** (Crypt of the Mummies), where a number of mummified corpses are still preserved. Across the square is the **Museo Diocesano** (☎ 0831 84 50 93; Piazza Cattedrale 9; voluntary donations; 9.30am-12.30pm & 4.30-6.30pm).

Oria is on both the main Trenitalia line and there are frequent services from both Brindisi (30 minutes, seven Monday to Saturday) and Taranto (40 minutes, eight Monday to Saturday). From Brindisi you can also connect with Ostuni. Heading in the other direction, you can change at Francavilla Fontana for Martina Franca. The train station is 1.5km outside the city centre. Buses to the station depart from Piazza San Domenico.

THE MURGIA

The well-watered limestone plateau of the Murgia rises up between the Adriatic and Ionian coasts, providing some of the richest farming area in the region. It extends from medieval Conversano, southeast of Bari, to just beyond Ceglie Messapica, where it tapers off towards the Salentine peninsula.

CONVERSANO
pop 24,400

The Counts of Conversano sound like something from a James Bond film, and if you read a brief history of the town it's not a surprise to find that the original counts were from that extraordinary Norman clan that included William 'Bras de Fer' (Iron Arm; c 1009–46) and Robert Guiscard (c 1015–85), conqueror and King of Sicily and the south (see p25). But that's not to say that they were a happy family; in fact the Conversano branch, headed by Geoffrey the Elder, was to cause interminable trouble for Robert, refusing to pay homage and repeatedly conspiring with other family members in an attempt to outfox Robert and make a grab for power.

In the Middle Ages the town ended up in the hands of the Acquaviva d'Aragona family who kept it in fee right up until 1806. They enriched the town with noble palaces, churches and monasteries, which remain charmingly unspoilt today.

Orientation & Information

From the train station head south up Via Golgota until you reach the main road, Viale dei Paolotti, from where you should be able to see the castle and the old town centre above you.

You'll find the **tourist office** (☎ 080 495 12 28; Piazza Castello 13; ☼ 9am-1pm & 5-7pm Mon-Fri, 9am-1pm Sat) in the west wall of the castle. It is staffed by volunteers who have limited information although they're friendly enough. They only have a map of the historic centre, which is very unhelpful considering the size of the new town. Around the corner is **Armida** (☎ 080 495 95 10; www.cooparmida.org; Piazza Conciliazione 5), a private tourist organisation which has more information. A useful website, in Italian, is www.conversano.com.

Sights

Conversano's historic centre is a gem of medieval architecture and the town has a quiet and austere atmosphere. At its northern edge, the **castle** commands views over the coastal plains all the way to Bari. Troublesome Geoffrey built it on the old megalithic walls during the 11th century when he was busy fighting with his brother Robert, but in the 13th century it was taken over by the counts of Acquaviva who tailored it into a more elegant, private residence. The main entrance can be found in Piazza della Concilizione from where you access the **Pinacoteca Comunale** (☎ 080 495 95 10; Piazza della Conciliazione; admission €2.50 incl Museo Civico; ☼ 9am-noon & 4.30-7.30pm Tue-Sat, 10am-1pm & 4.30-7.30pm Sun). It houses just some of the 400

paintings from the Acquaviva collection, including Paolo Finoglio's 10 canvases, *Gerusalemme Liberata* (Jerusalem Liberated), which are the most important non-religious Italian paintings of the 17th century and are clearly influenced by Caravaggio.

Included in the price of the ticket is entrance to the **Museo Civico** (☎ 080 495 19 75; Via San Benedetto 18; ☼ 9am-noon & 4.30-7.30pm Tue-Sat, 10am-1pm & 4.30-7.30pm Sun), which is located on the ground floor of the **Convento dei Benedettini**. It houses a small collection of archaeological finds from the Conversano area. Built in the 10th century, the enormous convent and majolica-domed church illustrate the size and power of the monastic orders in medieval Puglia.

The episcopal counterpoint to the monastery is Conversano's lovely Romanesque **cathedral** (Largo Cattedrale; ☼ 9am-noon & 4-7pm), built between the 9th and the 14th centuries. It has a typical graven portal, large rose window and pointy gabled roof. It houses the 13th-century Byzantine icon, the Madonna della Fonte, the patroness of Conversano. At the other end of the decorative scale is the **Chiesa di SS Cosma e Damiano** (Largo San Cosma; ☼ 9am-noon & 4-7pm), another Paolo Finoglio baroque fantasy, with an incredibly ornate frescoed ceiling.

At the time of research the Pinacoteca, Museo Civico and the Benedictine convent were all closed for restoration. Armida should be able to give you an update on reopening times.

Sleeping

Conversano has some nice accommodation in the historic centre.

ourpick **Corte Altavilla** (☎ 080 495 96 68; www.cortealtavilla.it; Vico Goffredo Altavilla 8; d €85-115, ste €110-140; P ⌘ ▯) A lovely hotel hidden at the end of a flower-filled alley in the historic centre. The old houses, where the rooms are located, have been renovated to an extremely high standard and are decorated with subtle style. Once they've completed the rooftop restaurant there'll be a very good reason to eat here too.

Agriturismo Montepaolo (☎ 080 495 50 87; www.montepaolo.it; Contrada Montepaolo 2; s €52-90, d €79-121; P ☛) Perched on a hill above the surrounding countryside, Montepaolo must have been the perfect hunting lodge when the Counts of Acquaviva d'Aragona rode down here for the weekend. Now you, too, can enjoy its rustic elegance, acres of olives, cherries and almonds, and enormous pool.

Eating

Despite its proximity to the coast, the cuisine of Conversano is closely wedded to the earth – in the past this was prime hunting territory.

our pick **I Pasticcioni** (☎ 080 495 91 02; www.ipasticcioni.it; Via Palmiro Togliatti 39; meals €20-25; ☺ Thu-Tue) The location on the outskirts of town may not seem encouraging, but I Pasticcioni is the real deal. The interior is modern – an open kitchen, lurid lime-green chairs and a bright breezy atmosphere – as is the food (crepes, satay, waffles and pasta). Having said that, the homemade pasta is the highlight; make your selection at the counter and watch Frank or Piero go to work.

Nonna Marietta (☎ 080 495 94 28; Via Bari 18; meals €25-30; ☺ Tue-Sat, lunch Sun) Modelled on the home cooking of 'grandmother' Marietta, expect the full repertoire of homemade Pugliese classics focusing mainly on *la terra* (the earth). The speciality is the house antipasti – grilled smoked cheeses, squashy aubergines, vegetable torte and the like. Follow it up with roasted meat or game from the grill.

our pick **Pasha Cafe** (☎ 080 495 10 79; www.pasha conversano.it; Piazza Castello 5/7; meals €40; ☺ Wed-Mon) The most classy restaurant in Conversano is located on the 1st floor of an old *palazzo*. Top marks for décor; the burnt umber walls, leather sofas and wooden balcony create a romantic feel. The menu is as elegant as the surroundings: burrata cheese with chicory, saltcod and olive tart and pecorino fondue, followed by roasted rabbit rubbed with thyme.

Also recommended is **Pizzeria Terra Rossa** (☎ 080 495 72 08; Corso Domenico Morea 14/16; pizza €6-8; ☺ Wed-Mon), located in a barrel-vaulted room in the side of the castle.

Getting There & Away

Conversano is served by frequent Ferrovie Sud-Est trains direct from Bari (€1.80, 40 minutes), which then go on to serve Castellana Grotte (€1, 10 minutes), Alberobello (€2.30, 45 minutes) and Martina Franca (€2.90, one hour), from where you can connect with trains for Lecce (€9.10, three hours). To reach Polignano a Mare (€1.10, 30 minutes) on the coast it's best to take the bus, which departs from Viale dei Paolotti.

GROTTE DI CASTELLANA

Definitely worth the hassle of getting to, these spectacular limestone **caves** (☎ 800 21 39 76, 080 499 82 11; www.grottedicastellana.it; Piazzale Anelli; ☺ 8.30am-7pm 15 Mar-15 Oct, 9.30am-12.30pm 16 Oct-14 Mar), 40km southeast of Bari, are Italy's longest natural subterranean network. The interlinked galleries, first discovered in 1938 by Franco Anelli, contain incredible stalactite and stalagmite formations. The highlight is the Grotta Bianca (White Grotto), a cavern of eerie white alabaster hung with stiletto-thin stalactites.

There are two tours (in Italian): a 1km, 50-minute tour (every hour on the half hour, €8); and the full 3km, two-hour tour that includes the Grotta Bianca (every hour on the hour, €13). In high season tours are also available in English (short itinerary 1pm and 6.30pm, long 11am and 4pm) and German (short itinerary 9.30am and 2.30pm, long 11am and 4pm), but in low season they are only available for groups when reserved in advance.

The temperature inside the cave averages 15°C so take a light jacket. Visit, too, the **Museo Speleologico Franco Anelli** (admission free; ☺ 9am-noon & 3-6pm) or book a visit to the **osservatorio astronomico** (astronomical observatory; admission €2), which offers wonderful views of the surrounding countryside. Both are near the caves.

On 11 and 12 January the nearby town of Castellana Grotte holds the spectacular **Falò** festival. Over 50 big bonfires light up the night in celebration of the towns deliverance from the plague by the Madonna della Vetrana in 1691.

Sleeping & Eating

our pick **Serra Gambetta** (☎ 080 496 21 81; www.serra gambetta.it; Via Conversano 204; s €37-62, d €74-124; 🅿 ☯) Just 1.5km from the caves on the road to Conversano is the old farmhouse Serra Gambetta. It lacks the polish of some of the other 'hotel *masserie*' but what it lacks in pretension it makes up for in atmosphere. Guests are welcome to watch the goings on in the kitchen and take impromptu cookery or wine lessons. Domenico is a keen cyclist and is happy to offer advice and maps on itineraries around the area.

Getting There & Away

The grotto can be reached by rail from Bari (€2.60, one hour, hourly), Conversano (€1, 10 minutes) and Alberobello (€2.10, 35 minutes)

CARNIVALE DI PUTIGNANO

The Putignano Carnival, with its famous parade of papier-mâché floats, is both the longest and one of the oldest carnivals in the world. And there are records dating back to 1394 to prove it.

Unlike most carnivals, which may at best last a week or two, Putignano's merry-making goes on for two long months. It starts on 26 December when the relics of St Stefan Protomartyrs are transferred from Monopoli to Putignano. In the past this procession was celebrated by farmers with much dancing, singing and reciting of rhymes – hence the beginning of the carnival.

In the last 10 years, thanks to the enormous floats, the original satirical masks and the colourful masked groups, the parade has been the principal attraction of this extraordinary event. What is interesting is that the floats all carry stinging social or political messages that have a very 21st-century feel to them; this is certainly no medieval relic.

The figure that represents the carnival is the *Farinella*. Its costume is made of multicoloured patches with bells sewn on the three tips of the hat and on the shoes and collar. The name derives from *Farinella*, a chickpea and barley flour that is the staple food of country workers.

To find out more about the festival and what's going on when log on to www.carnevalediputignano.it. Processions, which usually start at 10.30am, take place on the three proceeding Sundays before Shrove Tuesday and on carnival day itself.

on the FSE train line. The train actually makes a stop near the car park of the caves. As there is no station here you need to buy a return ticket before you set off. The easiest way to reach the caves is by car on the SP240 from Conversano or the SP237 from Putignano. Parking costs €3/2 for campers/cars.

THE VALLE D'ITRIA

At the heart of the Murgia lies the idyllic Valle d'Itria, a place of rolling green hills criss-crossed by low-slung dry-stone walls *(parietoni)*, where vineyards, orchards and country lanes preserve a ridiculously rustic character. It is an extraordinary man-made landscape created by generations of farmers who built the strange *trulli* (curious 'hobbit' houses with distinctive conical roofs), and worked the fields around them. They can be found all over the Valle d'Itria from Noci to Ostuni, but they mass together in Alberobello and around Locorotondo.

Noci

pop 19,500

Located on the western edge of the Valle d'Itria, Noci is an unassuming agricultural town. It may not be as pretty as its neighbours but it prides itself on its cuisine and has a year-long calendar of far-fetched foodie events like the Festival of Chicory (July), the Rite of Ragù (September), the Mushroom Festival (September), the New Wine and Chestnut Festival (November) and the **Pettole nelle Gnostre e Cioccolato**, an extravagant chocolate festival held

in December. In the height of summer the town also holds the **Gustosamente Noci** festival, a weekend of food and wine tasting accompanied by music, art and theatre events. To keep up to date with the gastronomic goings-on log on to www.nocintavola.it. The weekly market is on Tuesday.

The oldest part of the village is clustered around the **Chiesa Madre**. There's not much to really see in Noci although in the evenings the *passeggiata* crowd around Piazza Plebiscito is full of local characters. Obviously the main activity in town is eating, and that you can do in style.

SLEEPING & EATING

our pick **Masseria Abate** (☎ 080 497 82 88; www.abatemasseria.it; Strada Provinciale per Massafra, km 0,300; s €52-79, d €80-124, trullo €120-198; P ☒ ☒) Situated amid green baize lawns as smooth as a billiard table, the whitewashed simplicity of Masseria Abate is the epitome of *trulli* chic. No olde-worlde rustic charm here, just minimal modern furnishings and the warm tones of natural materials.

Ristorante Vineria Barsento (☎ 080 497 96 57; www.cantinebarsento.it; Contrada da San Giacomo; meals €25-30, pizza €6-8; ☒ 7.30-11pm Wed-Mon & lunch Sun) Tour the cantina, buy the wine and then sit down to eat in the cantina's impressive restaurant. The cavernous dining hall with its long refectory tables serves up nouvelle cuisine–style meals and pizza.

L'Antica Locanda (☎ 080 497 24 60; Via Santo Spirito 49; meals €35; ☒ Wed-Mon) Mimmo Turi and Pasquale Fatalino, maestros of country cooking, run one of Noci's most reputable restaurants. You will have to try the local cheeses with various fruit compotes, and maybe the *brodo* (soup) with cheese, parsley and egg. For the main, the house speciality is undoubtedly the oven-roast lamb with artichokes and lampascioni onions.

Also recommended is **I Nusce** (☎ 080 497 90 99; Piazza Plebiscito 28; meals €25; ☺ Tue-Sun), where you can eat outside in summer.

Alberobello
pop 10,900
Alberobello is a victim of its own *trulli* fame. The town encompasses the extraordinary Zona dei Trulli, a dense mass of 1500 *trulli* that is now classified a Unesco World Heritage site. It is an extraordinary sight and as you wander around you can't help feeling as if you're in a Walt Disney film, and half expect a gnome to rush out of one of the wee houses. Its uniqueness means that Alberobello is absolutely top of Puglia's tourist sites (especially with families), and from Easter to October the town is saturated as coachloads of tourists pile into *trulli* homes, drink in *trulli* bars and shop in *trulli* shops.

ORIENTATION
Alberobello is divided into the old and new town. The new town is on a hilltop, while the Zona dei Trulli is on the opposite (south) slope. It consists of two adjacent neighbourhoods, the Rione Monti and the Rione Aia Piccola.

From the station, walk straight ahead along Via Mazzini, which becomes Via Garibaldi, to reach Piazza del Popolo in the heart of the new town.

INFORMATION
First Aid (☎ 118 or 080 432 11 12; Viale Margherita 26)
Internet Point (☎ 080 432 29 42; Corso Trieste e Trento 30; per 15min €1.50)
Money There is an ATM on Largo Trevisani and another on Via Vittorio del Fascismo.
Police (☎ 080 432 53 40; Piazza del Popolo) Right in the centre of the new town.
Post Office (☎ 080 432 03 11; Corso Trieste e Trento 104)
Tourist information office (☎ 080 432 28 22; Monte Nero 1; ☺ 9am-8pm summer) This is the most convenient information point in the Zona dei Trulli.
Tourist office (☎ 080 432 51 71; Piazza Ferdinando IV 4; ☺ 9.30am-12.30pm Mon-Fri) In the Casa d'Amore, just off the main square.

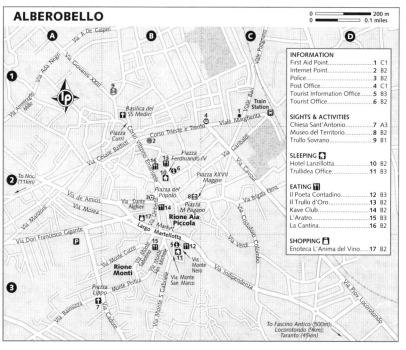

SIGHTS

Although there are a smattering of small museums in Alberobello, the real sight is the town itself and the main activity consists of wandering around its narrow lanes and poking your nose in people's houses or shops.

To the north the **Rione Monti** has around 1000 *trulli*, while to the east the **Rione Aia Piccola** is much less commercialised with only 400 *trulli*. Although it has a primitive look to it, the town has only existed since the 15th century, when farmers of the Acquaviva lands set up house here. Piazza XXVII Maggio and Piazza Mario Pagano used to be threshing squares, where farmers came to thresh their cereals under the watchful eye of the count's guards who ensured that nothing was stolen and the appropriate taxes were paid.

The farming history of the town is nicely explained in the **Museo del Territorio** (☎ 080 432 32 70; Piazza XXVII Maggio 22; admission €1.50; ☺ 9.30am-1pm & 2-8.30pm), a grand two-storey *trullo* built in 1780. The other museum worth a trip is the 18th-century **Trullo Sovrano** (☎ 080 432 60 30; Piazza Sacramento; admission €1.50; ☺ 10am-7pm Mon-Sat, 10am-1pm & 3-6pm Sun & holidays), which is located in the new part of town. It was built for the rich priest Cataldo Petra in 1785. Nowadays its rooms are all laid out with period furnishings to show you what life in a *trullo* was like. It is also the only *trullo* that has a second storey in the roof accessed by a staircase embedded in one of the massively thick walls.

One last bit of *trulli* madness is the **Chiesa Sant'Antonio** (Via Monte San Michele) a trullo-shaped church at the top of Rione Monti. It was built with donations from American émigrés and is topped by a *trullo* dome measuring 19.8m.

After battling the crowds in the *trulli* zone you may need a break in the relative sanity of the new town. The best time to come is the early evening when everyone is out for the lively *passeggiata*.

SLEEPING

Alberobello has dozens of hotels. You can also rent a *trullo* in the Rione Monti, but the best *trulli* are located out of town in quiet countryside settings (see the boxed text, opposite).

Camping dei Trulli (☎ 080 432 36 99; www.campingdeitrulli.com; Via Castellana Grotte, 1.5km; adult €5-7, caravan €5-7, car €2-3, tent €4-6, bungalows per person €20-30, trullo per person €30-40; P ☒) This huge, well-equipped camp site is just 1.5km out of town on the road to Castellana Grotte. It has every imaginable

facility including a restaurant, market, two swimming pools, tennis courts and bicycle hire. You can also hire bungalows or *trulli*.

ourpick Fascino Antico (☎ 080 432 50 89; www.fascinoantico.eu; SS172 per Locorotondo, km0.5; s €45-55, d €70-90; P ☒) Don't be put off by the poorly designed website, this is a lovely *trulli* complex just half a kilometre from Alberobello on the road to Locorotondo. Set in a pretty landscaped garden the rooms are light and comfortable with terracotta tiled floors and small kitchenettes. A number of rooms also have bunks and cater for families.

Hotel Lanzillotta (☎ 080 432 15 11; www.hotellanzillotta.it; Piazza Ferdinando IV 31; s €45, d €60-90; P) The Lanzillotta is really the best option in town. It's well located, the rooms are well appointed with period-style furnishings, and some of the bathrooms have baths. It is very popular so you'll need to book in advance. The three-course dinner for €13 is also excellent value.

You can rent your own *trullo* at **Trullidea** (☎ 080 432 38 60; www.trullidea.it; Via Monte Nero 15; d €86-102, tr €102). However, be aware that due to the compact nature of the Rione the *trulli* have few windows and can be quite dark.

EATING

Given the high tourist traffic in town, Alberobello has dozens of restaurants. Some of them are mediocre but there are a few notable options.

Kave Club (☎ 080 432 40 82; Piazza del Popolo 28/29; salads & plates €4-7) A modern café/bar right on the main piazza. The in-crowd comes here to watch the scene with a generous glass of wine and large plates of *aperitivi*. Service is terrible but that doesn't seem to deter anyone. There's a good selection of salads, cheese and meat plates.

ourpick La Cantina (☎ 080 432 34 73; Via Lippolis 9; meals €20; ☺ Wed-Mon Jul-Sep) In a town full of tourist traps this is a refreshingly good local restaurant serving fresh seasonal food. The service is slow but you can watch the chef preparing your meal in the open kitchen. Try the *involtini di vitello*, slow-cooked veal stuffed with strong cheese in a rich gravy.

Il Trullo d'Oro (☎ 080 432 18 20; Via Cavallotti 27; meals €35; ☺ Tue-Sun, closed Jan) Hidden behind the main drag in the new town is this cute *trullo* restaurant. Start with a dizzying array of *stuzzichini* (literally 'stimulants') – fried black olives and green peppers, eggplant, wild mushrooms and fried dough-balls – before ploughing through generous plates of pasta and on to thin salsiccie sausages or morsels of veal wrapped in pancetta.

Il Poeta Contadino (☎ 080 432 19 17; Via Independenza 21; meals €50; ☯ Tue-Sat, lunch Sun) Alberobello's fanciest restaurant has heavy red Liberty-style décor and an extensive menu which includes dishes like pumpkin cream with prawns and wild rice, and monkfish with a potato crust and cardoncelli mushrooms. This certainly isn't a place for t-shirts and trainers so dress the part and make a reservation.

Also recommended is **L'Aratro** (☎ 080 432 27 89; Via Monte San Michele 25; meals €30; ☯ Tue-Sun, closed Jan) in the Rione Monti.

SHOPPING

For excellent wines try central **Enoteca L'Anima del Vino** (☎ 080 432 13 88; Largo Marttellota 93; ☯ 9.30am-1pm & 3.30-9pm Tue-Sat, 9.30am-1pm Sun). There's also a very good fruit and vegetable market along the main drag of Largo Martellotta every Thursday.

TOP TRULLI

Bettina Marksteiner fell in love with Puglia's *trulli* in February 1998, when she saw their strange pointy roofs in a glossy travel brochure. A designer by trade, she now concentrates on renovating traditional Pugliese constructions – *trulli*, *lamia* and *masserie* – to the highest standards imaginable, giving them gorgeous modern makeovers within their traditional constraints. 'The style I've developed is very much about respecting the landscape. This isn't just about architecture. For me the most important thing is to integrate the house with its surroundings. You know, really integrate it, so you can see the house but not really see it, if you know what I mean?' She cites the Mediterranean climate, the continuum between exterior and interior spaces and the colours of the local materials as her inspiration. Looking around at the rocky land with its greying dry-stone walls you can see what she means; the *trulli* are really an organic part of the landscape.

'The construction is really specialised,' she explains. 'You must hire a *trullaro* for the work, and the good ones, who've learned the trade over generations, are hard to find.' Limestone is available everywhere and the *trulli*'s pointy roof and thick limestone walls make the interior cool in the summer and cosy in winter. The roof, in particular, is a curious construction. 'It's actually three roofs in one; the first roof, the interior dome, is known as the *candela* and is made of stone. This is covered with a layer of small stones, on top of which is placed the third roof, a spiral of flat limestone tiles known as *chianca*. The *chianca* are all laid by hand and need to lie at a particular inclination. This is the *trullaro*'s skill. You might need 200 to 300 *chianca* to make a single dome. It's extremely work intensive'.

When asked why Puglia and why the *trulli*, she pauses, then explains, 'I've never lived in one place for such a long time (nine years now), but these days it is difficult to find such a perfect combination of food, weather, and beautiful people in the heart of Europe. Elsewhere you are always missing something.' Stay in one of Bettina's beautifully converted *trulli* at some of the following rentals, you can't mistake her distinctive modern style.

Il Palmento (www.ilpalmento.com) A self-contained hamlet of 12 *trulli* suites that looks like a pixie village and provides excellent accommodation and facilities for families.

Truddhi (www.trulliresidence.it) A small cluster of self-catering *trulli* in the hamlet of Trito near Locorotondo. It's run by Mino and Carole, and being a lecturer in gastronomy Mino is happy to give cookery demonstrations.

Trulli Italian (www.trullitalian.com) A more modest three-bedroom *trullo*, at the end of a pretty country lane near Noci. Comes with bikes, PlayStation and a pool, which makes it perfect for families.

Trullo Mandorla (www.trullomandorla.com) Marries a 120-year-old *trullo* with contemporary, open-plan design to stunning effect. Situated on a terraced hill, it has views from the outdoor kitchen that stretch all the way to the coast.

Villa Antorea (www.villantorea.com) The home of interiors guru Bettina Marksteiner who is passionate about the restoration of traditional *trulli*. Expect uber-cool design, artworks and homeware in an idyllic location.

Villa Santoro (www.villapuglia.com) True *trullo* style, this sophisticated conversion looks like it just stepped out of the pages of *World of Interiors*.

GETTING THERE & AWAY

Alberobello is easily accessible from Bari (€4, 1½ hours, hourly) and Martina Franca (€1, 15 minutes) on the FSE Bari-Taranto train line. Services run from Monday to Saturday and there is a bus replacement service on Sunday leaving from Viale Bari near Albergo Astoria. If travelling on Sunday you need to buy your bus ticket the day before from the station **ticket office** (7am-1.30pm Mon-Sat).

There are car parking lots on Via Indipendenza or you can park in any of the blue bays. Parking costs €4.50 and you need to obtain a voucher from one of the bars or shops on Largo Mattelloti.

Locorotondo

pop 14,000

Locorotondo is a *borghi più belli d'Italia* (www.borghitalia.it), literally one of the most beautiful towns in Italy. It sits atop a small hill like a gleaming white constellation above the surrounding vineyards and it takes its name from the circular plan of the town.

There isn't really much to see in Locorotondo, but a morning spent meandering through the concentric circles of its streets is delightful. Your feet echo off the smooth ivory-coloured paving stones and once in a while you chance upon a sun-baked church like the baroque **Chiesa Matrice** or the gothic church of **Santa Maria della Greca**. Afterwards take a pew in the **Villa Comunale** from where you can enjoy panoramic views of the *trulli*-spotted valley. On Friday, things really liven up with the weekly **market**, which sells an odd assortment of clothes as well as fruit and veg.

You simply can't come to Locorotondo without sampling the local Spumante. You can do this at the local winery, **Cantina del Locorotondo** (080 431 16 44; www.locorotondodoc.com; Via Madonna della Catena 99), where you can also take a tour and do a spot of shopping. Ask for Oronzo Mastro for English-speaking tours.

The ladies of Locorotondo are also pretty handy when it comes to lacework and you can buy some beautiful pieces from **Il Tempo Ritrovato** (339 523 13 60; www.il-tempo-ritrovato.net; Piazza Vittorio Emanuele 20). The incredibly skilled work is reflected in the high prices.

St George is Locorotondo's patron saint and his feast is celebrated towards the end of April (22 to 24), when the townspeople make a symbolic gift to their protector. The town's other major festival is the **Festa di San Rocco** on 16 August, a big knees-up that sees the town decked out in fairy lights.

SLEEPING & EATING

Locorotondo is a romantic place to stay, with its bright white alleys in the historic centre adorned with trailing geraniums and full of the gentle murmur of chatting neighbours.

Sotto le Cummerse (080 431 32 98; www.sotto lecummerse.it; Via Vittoio Veneto 138; s €54-66, d €82-115, q €115-149) A collection of eight pretty apartments scattered through the old town centre. They consist of either one or two bedrooms and a kitchen, living and/or dining area, and some have spectacular views. Casa degli Angeli has a drop-dead gorgeous roof terrace.

our pick **La Braceria** (080 431 72 82; Via Cesare Battisti 28; meals €20; 7.30-11pm Tue-Sat) They don't just serve meat in this tiny subterranean restaurant, they worship it. Slices of flavourful prosciutto and salumi are followed by bowls of meatballs in a rich tomato sauce and then maybe steak, pork chops, horsemeat or veal. The house wine is rich and red and the glasses served are generous.

La Taverna del Duca (080 431 30 07; via Papadotero 3; meals €35) One of the best restaurants in the region, this tiny dining room has a devoted chef. The atmosphere is warm and welcoming and the menu depends entirely on what's available in the market. The antipasti is a real highlight as is the homemade pasta.

GETTING THERE & AWAY

Locorotondo is easily accessible from Bari (€3.60, one hour 40 minutes, hourly) on the FSE Bari–Taranto train line.

Cisternino

pop 12,050 / 394m

The further south you travel in Puglia the stronger the Greek influence becomes on its whitewashed towns. A case in point is the kasbah-like historic centre of Cisternino. Like all of Puglia's villages it has ancient roots, but the Roman town of Sturnium was razed by Hannibal during his Italian campaigns and was only resurrected again by Basilian monks who in the 8th century decided to found a Greek Orthodox abbey, which they called San Nicolo *cis-Sturninum*. Cisternino still attracts a spiritual crowd and is currently the centre of a hippy commune.

The 13th-century **Chiesa Madre** now rises where the abbey once stood, and the **Torre**

Civica acts as a doorway to the medieval town. If you take Via Basilioni next to the tower you can amble along past tiny courtyards and zig-zagging staircases, right to the central piazza, Vittorio Emanuele.

Cisternino has a grand tradition of *fornello pronto* (ready-to-go roast or grilled meat) and in numerous butchers shops you can select a cut of meat which is promptly roasted or grilled on the spot. You can mix it up with a pork chop, an escalop of veal with bread-crumb, parsley and Parmesan filling and a couple of sausages. You're walked up to the *arrosteria* where you take a seat on a hard bench at a bare table while your order sputters in the wood-burning oven.

Buy your meat at **Macelleria de Mola Vincenzo** (☎ 080 444 80 63; Via Giulio II 2; €15-20) and eat it up the road at **Arrosteria del Vicoletto** (Via Giulio II 6). Another place is **Al Vecchio Fornello** (☎ 080 444 64 31; Via Basilioni; €15-20; ⌚ Tue-Sun).

If you'd rather have a more conventional eating experience go to the friendly **Hosteria Bella Italia** (☎ 080 444 90 36; Via Duca d'Aosta 29; meals €20; ⌚ Thu-Tue). Another good restaurant and terrifically atmospheric *enoteca* (wine bar/shop) is **Il Cucco** (☎ 080 444 90 64; Corso Umberto I 137; meals €20; ⌚ Wed-Mon).

Cisternino is on the Bari–Brindisi line. From Bari (€5.10, two hours, three daily) you'll need to change at Martina Franca. By road you can reach the town along the SP134 from either Locorotondo or Ostuni.

Martina Franca
pop 49,000 / 431m

This graceful 18th-century town with its wrought-iron balconies and sculpted portals is the Valle d'Itria's crowning glory. Its genteel historic centre, one of the finest in Puglia, is characterised by meandering lanes sporting fine baroque and rococo buildings. It was founded in the 10th century by refugees flee-ing the Arab invasion of Taranto, although it only really started to flourish in the 14th cen-tury when Philip of Anjou granted it tax ex-emptions (*franchigie*, hence the name Franca). It was then held in fee by the Caracciolo family from 1506 to 1827, which explains its baroque makeover and air of modest sophistication. The modern-day town is as comfortable and content as its historic counterpart and is a prosperous wine-producing centre.

ORIENTATION
The FSE train station is downhill from the historic centre. Go right along Viale della Stazione, continuing along Via Alessandro Fighera to Corso Italia; continue to the left along Corso Italia to Piazza XX Settembre.

INFORMATION
Ambulance (☎ 080 480 17 17)
First Aid (☎ 080 483 52 27; Via San Francesco da Paola)
Internet Point (☎ 080 480 14 00; Via Mascagni 33; per hr €1.50; ⌚ 9am-1pm & 3.30-8pm Sep-Jun, 9am-1pm & 5-9pm Jul, 10am-1pm & 6-9pm Aug)
Municipal Police (☎ 080 483 62 21; Piazza Roma)
Post Office (☎ 080 480 54 13; Via Garibaldi 33)
Tourist Office (☎ 080 480 57 02; www.martinafranca tour.it; Piazza Roma 35; ⌚ 9am-1pm & 5-7pm Mon-Fri, 9am-1pm Sat) This helpful tourist offices occupies a couple of rooms within the Palazzo Ducale.

SIGHTS
The hub of the town is Piazza XX Settembre, flanked at one end by the communal gardens and at the other by the impressive baroque gate, the **Arco di Sant'Antonio**. It's nearly always full of groups of flat-capped men and small

---

MAVU

So you've seen a dozen churches, driven through fields of poppies and low-lying vines, eaten until you can eat no more, and now you're wondering where everyone goes for a night out?

In fact, one of Puglia's best clubs lies hidden in the midst of these green fields; the super-cool **Mavu** (☎ 393 021 38 50; www.mavu.it; Contrada Mavugliola 222; admission €20-30; ⌚ 11pm-5am). Housed in an old *masseria* with louche décor and a sexy candlelit patio, Mavu puts on class acts like Mario Biondo and Stefano Ghittoni almost every Friday and Saturday from April through to September.

To reach it take the road from Locorotondo to Cisternino (SP134). After about 2km you'll see a small sign on your left-hand side. Turn left and drive down to the crossroads and then turn right. After about 500m you'll see a large rust-red *masseria* on your left-hand side and signs for parking.

children running helter-skelter, and on festivals and feast days you'll find market stalls here.

Passing under the arch you emerge into Piazza Roma, an even more impressive public arena flanked by the 17th-century **Palazzo Ducale** (admission free; 9am-12.30pm & 4-7pm Mon-Fri, 10am-noon Sat & Sun) on the one side and the **Palazzo Martucci** opposite. Attributed to the architect Giovanni Carducci, the Palazzo Ducale stands on the site of the old Orsini castle, and was a lavish undertaking, originally conceived as having 300 rooms. Only a fraction of the palace was ever realised, but visit the royal apartments with Domenico Carella's frescoes and you'll get some idea of how ambitious the original design must have been.

From the piazza, follow Corso Vittorio Emanuele, lined with baroque townhouses, to reach Piazza Plebiscito. This is the heart of the historic centre and it is dominated by the exuberant baroque façade of the **Basilica di San Martino** (Piazza Plebiscito; 7.30am-12.30pm & 4.30-8pm), its centrepiece the good St Martin himself, swinging a sword and sharing his cloak with a beggar. Again it dates back to Martina's heyday in the 18th century and exhibits the same architectural and decorative exuberance as the Palazzo Ducale.

Piazza Plebiscito merges into Piazza Immacolata, the drawing room of Martina, ringed with restaurants and cafés beneath its shaded arcades. From here you can take any number of routes through the maze of streets, admiring tiny courtyards and geranium-clad balconies. To the right Via Principe Umberto will take you past the baroque church of **Chiesa di San Domenico** (7.30am-12.30pm & 4.30-8.30pm), completed in 1750 under the orders of Friar Cantalupi for the Domenican order next door. The façade, like that of the basilica, is a medley of nymphs and caryatids set amid curling leaves and volutes, but inside the rococo interior is altogether lighter and softer, made over in a pleasing lemon yellow with romantic paintings by Nicola Gliri and Domenico Carella. Head left down Via Cavour and then Via Micca and you'll find yourself in the **Lama**, the oldest quarter of the town, with tiny white houses with sloping roofs.

From here you can exit the historic centre and wander north to the **belvedere** on Via Pergolesi from where you get a great view of the valley.

FESTIVALS & EVENTS

Festival della Valle d'Itria (Valley d'Itria Festival; www.festivaldellavalleditria.it) is an annual feast for music-lovers as the town hosts international performances of opera, classical and jazz. For information, phone the **Centro Artistico Musicale Paolo Grassi** (080 480 51 00) in the Palazzo Ducale. It's held late July to early August.

SLEEPING

Most of the hotels in Martina are located outside the historic centre, a number of them on the road to Taranto.

B&B San Martino (080 48 56 01; http://xoomer.virgilio.it/bend-&-breakfast-sanmartino; Via Abate Fighera 32; 2-4-person apt per day €40-120, per week €250-620;) A nice B&B in a great location just off Piazza XX Settembre. The proto-rustic apartments have exposed stone walls, wrought-iron beds and small kitchenettes, and unbelievably there is a pool. Very good value.

Villaggio In (080 480 59 11; www.villaggioin.it; Via Arco Grassi 8; 2-person apt per day €75-125 & per week €355-720, 4-person apt per day €135-160 & per week €765-965) A tempting selection of apartments for rent in the old town. The buildings are historical treasures, with barrel vaulting and cool white interiors, but space is limited and stairs are steep. During the music festival these apartments get snapped up so book way in advance.

Villa San Martino (080 480 51 52; www.relaisvilla sanmartino.com; Via Taranto 59; s €180-240, d €220-310;) A pricy pink *masseria* set in a formal garden with a shimmering pool at the foot of the patio. Bedrooms are baroque in their décor – satin coverlets, swagged curtains and *pietra dura* lamps. There's also a wellness centre with a fully equipped hammam and an endless list of treatments.

At a more modest price point you could consider the **Hotel delle Erba** (080 430 10 55; Via Taranto 1; s €65-70, d €85-100;), part of the Rama hotel chain. Although it has a dated look the setting is lovely and the facilities good.

EATING

Martina's most famous product is its *capocollo*, a cured cut of pork taken from the muscle between the head ('capo') and the shoulder ('collo'), which is now listed by the Slow Food movement as a protected product. Other dishes you'll find in abundance are *arrosto misto* (mixed roast meats), cheeses like caccioricotta, and caciocavallo, mashed broad beans served with wild vegetables.

La Cantina del Toscana (☎ 080 430 28 27; Piazza Maria Immacolata; meals €20; ⏰ Thu-Tue) Set in one of the most romantic piazze in Puglia, the Tuscan cellar is unpretentious cooking at its best. The brochettes are part of an *arrosto misto* that includes sausage and baby kid chops. If you want to look like you belong, finish with raw vegetables and dip them in salt.

Trattoria La Tana (☎ 080 480 53 20; Via Mascagni 2-6; meals €35; ⏰ Wed-Mon) Despite its rather scruffy appearance, La Tana is a fine restaurant, serving a sophisticated menu. All the pastas and sweets are homemade and you can tempt your tastebuds with dishes like fillet of veal with mushrooms in a negroamaro glaze.

ourpick **Ciacco** (☎ 080 480 04 72; Via C Ugolino; meals about €35; ⏰ lunch Tue-Sun) Dive into Martina's historic centre to find Ciacco, a traditional restaurant with white-clad tables and a cosy fireplace, serving up Martinese classics. Stuffed peppers, fried meatballs, local cheeses and cured meats set the tone for a hearty meal. In summer you can sit out on the terrace.

Il Ritrovo degli Amici (☎ 080 483 92 49; Corso Messapia 8; meals €35; ⏰ Tue-Sat, lunch Sun) An elegant restaurant with heavy linen tablecloths and an after-dinner drinks trolley. The menu is upmarket rural classics including dishes like cream of chickpeas with cardoncelli mushrooms and slices of beef with grana cheese. The atmosphere is oiled by the region's fine Spumante wines.

Also recommended is the fiendishly popular **La Tavernetta** (☎ 080 430 63 23; Corso Vittorio Emanuele 30; meals €20; ⏰ Tue-Sun) on the main corso.

SHOPPING

As the centre of the Valle d'Itria, Martina is a good place to shop. The **weekly market** on Wednesday morning is the largest in the area and spreads out from Via Giulio Recupero to Piazza d'Angiò. There is also an all-day **antiques market** on the third Sunday of every month on Viale della Libertà.

Martina is well regarded for its cheese and oil production. You can pick up a nice selection of both, along with the famous *capocollo*, at **Pace** (☎ 080 430 61 06; Via Poerio 2). The produce here comes from Masseria Sant'Amen, and if you have a good-sized group they can arrange a visit to the *masseria* with lunch provided.

Martina also has a strong tradition of men's tailoring and you'll find many men's shops along the main shopping streets of Corso Messapia and Viale della Libertà and around Piazza XX Settembre. For handmade lace, go to **Pizzi e Merletti** (☎ 080 480 00 18; Piazza Roma 17).

GETTING THERE & AROUND

To get to Martina Franca, take the **FSE** (☎ 080 546 21 11) train from Bari (€4, two hours, hourly) or Taranto (€2.10, 40 minutes, hourly). Trains also connect Martina Franca with Alberobello (€1, 15 minutes) and Lecce (€6.30, two hours, seven daily). There are bus replacement services on Sunday.

Bus III and IV connect the FSE train station with Piazza XX Settembre.

Ostuni
pop 32,800 / 218m

The white beacon of Ostuni, draped across its three hills, marks the end of the Trulli district and the beginning of the hot, dry Penisola Salentina. Like Locorotondo, Ostuni has a commanding position, its maze of tightly packed streets twisting around a dramatic 15th-century cathedral encircled by medieval ramparts. It is the most popular Murgia town, mainly due to its proximity to the coast and the wealth of good farm accommodation surrounding it. In recent years it has become devilishly chic, and has the best after dark scene in the district.

ORIENTATION

From Piazza della Libertà, where the new town meets the old, take Via Cattedrale to the cathedral. The new town sprawls southwest of the historic centre rising up and over another hill. From Piazza della Libertà take Corso Cavour for the Villa Comunale (public gardens). The main north–south axis is Viale Pola, where all the main buses stop.

The train station is inconveniently located 3km north of the town centre.

INFORMATION

First Aid (☎ 0831 30 25 90)
Hospital (☎ 0831 30 91; Via Villafranca)
Municipal Police (☎ 080 33 74 11; Corso Vittorio Emanuele II 39)
Post Office (☎ 0831 30 57 41; Corso M Giuseppe 18)
Tourist office (☎ 0831 30 12 68; Corso Mazzini 8; ⏰ 8.30am-1.30pm & 5.30-8.30pm Mon-Fri, 8.30am-1.30pm & 6.30-8.30pm Sat, shorter hrs winter) Just off Piazza della Libertà.

TARANTO & THE MURGIA

TARANTO & THE MURGIA

SIGHTS

Despite its baroque and Renaissance flourishes, the historic centre of Ostuni, with its steep streets and blind walls, retains a huddled, defensive character. Throughout its history it passed from the Byzantines to the Normans, to the counts of Lecce and the princes of Taranto, then to the Sforzas and finally the dukes of Zevallo, a process that saw the town enriched with dozens of churches and ringed with monasteries like the huge **Chiesa Conventuale di San Francesco** and the **Chiesa del Carmine**.

Its central piazza, Piazza della Libertà, even boasts an ostentatious Neapolitan-style **guglia** (decorative spire) on which stands St Oronzo, the patron saint of the town. He overlooks the **Palazzo Municipale**, with its neoclassical façade, which previously housed another Franciscan convent.

From here Via Cattedrale winds its way up through the historic centre to the **cathedral** (Via Cattedrale; ⏰ 8am-noon & 4-6pm). You've probably seen it already as you drove along Via Panoramica, where you can see its distinctive ash-grey outline peeking above a crinoline of white houses. It was completed around 1495 and has an unusual Gothic-Romanesque façade with a frilly rose window and an inverted gable. As in Martina Franca, much of the town was made over in the 18th century and as a result the interior of the cathedral has a Spanish-inspired flavour with plenty of chapels, polychrome marbles and a painted ceiling. In the last chapel on the south side is Palma Giovane's *Madonna con il Bambino e Santi* (Madonna and Child with Saint).

Flanking the cathedral are the **Palazzo Vescovile** and the **Palazzo del Seminario**, which are joined by an elegant arched loggia. The Palazzo Vescovile houses what remains of the Norman castle, which was destroyed in 1559. Duck under the loggia and turn right down Vico Castello for breathtaking views towards the coast.

PUGLIA'S FORTIFIED FARMS

If the *trulli* are the hobbits of the housing world then the *masserie*, with their palatial accommodation, spas and pools, and hundreds of hectares of olive groves, are their aristocratic counterpart. Modelled on the classical Roman villa, these fortified farmhouses can be found all over Puglia although they concentrate in particular around Fasano and the central Murgia. The name 'masseria' derives from 'massaricius', meaning a farm equipped with buildings such as oil-mills, cellars, chapels, storehouses and farm accommodation, the intention being that they functioned as self-sufficient communities, able to shut their gates against attack and carry on with the business of stock-rearing and harvesting. Their solid square appearance, thick blind walls, embrasures, high boundary walls and in some cases towers has much to do with their defensive nature.

These days, the *masserie* still produce the bulk of Italy's olive oil, along with jam, meat and grain. The only difference is the farm accommodation is full of cashmere-clad tourists rather than peasant farmers.

ourpick Il Frantoio (☎ 0832 33 02 76; www.trecolline.it; SS16, km 874 Ostuni-Fasano Rd; s/d €103/206; P ✗) A fairytale farmhouse still very much in operation, producing high-quality organic olive oil. Rooms are gorgeously furnished with period beds, handmade embroideries and dozens of homely knick-knacks. An oasis of subtle style.

Masseria Marzalozza (☎ 080 441 37 80; Contrada Pezze Vicine 65; d €160-218; P ✗ 🖵) Many *masserie*, like Marzalozza, were owned by powerful monasteries, and were the ideal location for meditative monks. Now there's a pool in the lemon grove and the rooms have satellite TV.

Masseria Torre Coccaro (☎ 080 482 93 10; www.masseriatorrecoccaro.com; Contrada Coccaro 8, Savelletri di Fasano; d €333-466; P ✗ 🖵) More bohemian in flavour, Torre Coccaro has a subterranean Aveda spa carved out of caves once used for livestock, while the rooms are in converted haylofts.

Masseria Torre Maizza (☎ 080 482 78 38; www.masseriatorremaizza.com; Contrada Coccaro 8, Savelletri di Fasano; d €333-466; P ✗ 🖵) An ancient garrison with an austere square design. Guests sleep beneath cathedral-vaulted ceilings in cool tufa rooms.

Masseria San Domenico (☎ 080 482 77 69; www.masseriasandomenico; Strada Litoranea 379, Savelletri di Fasano; d €350-470; P ✗ 🖵) This imposing 15th-century building used to be the headquarters of the Knights of Malta and it is surrounded by a sea of manicured olive groves.

The only museum in Ostuni is the **Museo di Cività Preclassiche della Murgia** (☎ 0831 33 63 83; Via Cattedrale 15; admission €2; ☒ 9am-1pm & 3-6.30pm Tue-Sun), which is housed in the Convento delle Monacelle (currently closed for renovations). It houses the remarkable skeleton of a young pregnant woman dating back to the Upper Palaeolithic period (25,000 to 20,000 years ago). The other exhibits also come from the Palaeolithic burial ground, which is now the **Parco Archeologico e Naturale di Arignano** (☎ 0831 33 63 83; SS16, km878/11; adult/concession €3/1.50; ☒ by appointment only).

ACTIVITIES

Ostuni has an enviable location just 6km from the coast. And its pretty coastal fraction, **Villanova**, is a pleasant place to escape to in the evening for ice cream and sundowners. You'll find nice sandy beaches between Pilone and Torre Canne, one of the nicest and quietest being **Bosco Verde**.

In the opposite direction, about 16km south, is the scenic marine **Riserva di Torre Guaceto**, where you can indulge in any number of activities like biking, sailing, snorkelling and even yoga.

If you tire of the beaches you could always try horse-riding through the olive groves. Several *masserie* have their own horses or can arrange it for you. Otherwise contact **Parco di Mare** (☎ 335 721 87 82; www.parcodimare.com; Contrada Ottava, Montalbano), a well-equipped riding school offering lessons and excursions. Another popular activity is cycling and most *masserie* will provide their guests with bikes free of charge. Pick up the *Le Vie Verdi* leaflet from the tourist office; it describes eight different cycle routes within the Brindisi province.

If your idea of activity is lying on a sunlounger looking at a pool, then consider splashing out on one of the spa treatments at the luxurious **La Sommità Relais Culti** (☎ 0831 30 59 25; www.lasommita.it; Via Scipione Petrarolo 2; treatments around €80; ☒ ☒ ☒). It's part of the Milanese lifestyle brand Culti and is tucked away near the cathedral.

FESTIVALS

Ostuni's feast day, **La Calvalcata** (26 August), features processions of horsemen dressed in red-and-white uniforms. They follow the silver statue of St Oronzo in procession and symbolise the knights who once protected Christian pilgrims on their way to the sanctuary.

SLEEPING

Most people with a car prefer to stay outside Ostuni as the area is dotted with *masserie* (see the boxed text, opposite). There are a couple of good hotels in town for those who don't have a car.

Camping Villagio Il Pilone (☎ 0831 35 01 35; www.campingpilone.it; SS379 Bari-Brindisi, km14; camping 2-person €13-30, 4-person bungalows €300-1000; ☒ ☒ ☒) An enormous campsite with a write-home seafront location and every imaginable facility including a huge pool, tennis courts, football pitch, a sandy beach, restaurants, bars and a playground.

Nonna Isa (☎ 0831 33 25 15; www.nonnaisa.it; Via Vittorio Alfieri 9; s €28-36.50, d €18.50-36.50) A very comfortable B&B decorated with real verve. The three rooms are kitted out with African prints, Moroccan rugs and lace tablecloths, which give them a vibrant and inviting feel. It's in the newer part of the town.

Masseria Lamiola Piccola (☎ 0831 35 99 72; www.lamiolapiccola.com; Via Duca degli Abruzzi, Montalbano; d €80-100; ☒) A 17th-century farmhouse, now converted into a rural *agriturismo*. It still produces olive oil, jams, vegetables and liquors, which you can sample in the wood-beamed dining room. It's located around 10km from Ostuni on the SS16.

La Terra Hotel (☎ 0831 33 66 51; www.laterrahotel.it; Via G Petrarolo 20; s €80-105, d €130-170) A smart little hotel housed in a 13th-century *palazzo* on a narrow street in Ostuni's historic centre. It has 16 whitewashed rooms, furnished with cheerfully bright fabrics and Bassetta-tiled bathrooms. There are several terraces with views and a cosy cavelike bar.

EATING

Ostuni has a lively restaurant scene with most of the better restaurants located in the old town.

Taverna della Gelosia (☎ 0831 33 47 36; Via Andriola 26; meals €25; ☒ 7-11pm Oct-Mar) Located in the old town with a pretty terrace draped with roses, jasmine and vines and views all the way to the coast. Make sure you get a table in the dappled shade and order from the extensive list of red, green and black pastas.

Osteria Piazzetta Cattedrale (☎ 0831 33 50 26; Via Arcidiacono Trinchera 7; meals €30; ☒ Wed-Mon) A tiny hostelry opposite Ostuni's cathedral. The antipasti is exquisite and includes a melt-in-your-mouth courgette soufflé and the divine *burrata* cheese (a favourite of the Shah of Iran). It is small so be sure to make a reservation.

Osteria del Tempo Perso (☎ 0831 30 33 20; Gaetano Tanzarella Vitale 47; meals from €35; ☒ 7.30-11pm Mon-Sat, lunch Sun) Ostuni's most renowned restaurant, located in a rough-walled 16th-century bakery. The 15-dish antipasti is legendary, but the homemade pasta, like the mouthwatering *maccheroncini* with raw vegetables and salty ricotta is simplicity at its best.

Porta Nuova (☎ 0831 33 89 83; Via G Petrarolo 38; meals €40; ☒ Thu-Tue) Feast on rolling views from the terrace or nestle in the cosy interior lined with wine bottles and illuminated with the soft glow of candle light. This family-run restaurant specialises in fish; try the tasty seafood risotto.

our pick **Il Frantoio** (☎ 0832 33 02 76; SS16, km 874 Ostuni-Fasano Rd; meals €53; ☒ by reservation only) If you like excess, you'll love this storybook *masseria*, where the 10-course dinner makes it a must-stop for collectors of Eating Experiences. The degustation menu includes authoritative dishes like chickpea soup with fresh borage pasta and roast pork with an intensely sweet balsamic gravy. In summer the tables are set outside in the flower-filled patio.

If you have a car it's worth making the trip up the coast to Torre Canne where you'll find a string of seaside shacks serving barbequed fish and *ricci* (sea urchins) when they are in season (in spring). The best of the bunch is **La Rotonda da Rosa** (☎ 347 560 30 24). Take the SS379, exit for Torre Canne and head north to Savelletri. Just after Santos you'll see the shacks on your right-hand side.

DRINKING

In summer Ostuni's *passeggiata* goes on well past midnight and people arrive from the surrounding towns to hang out in its winding lanes and piazze.

Parisi Café (Via Cattedrale; ☒ 8-1am Apr-Oct, 7-5am Jul & Aug, 8am-6pm Thu-Tue Nov-Mar) A nice corner café full of fake gilt and red velvet with a few wicker chairs in the suntrap street outside. It has nice buns and cocktails and is next door to the Panificio al Forno.

Riccardo Caffè (☎ 0831 30 60 46; Via G Tanzarella Vitale 61/63; ☒ 6pm-4am Wed-Mon) High fashion meets history in Riccardo Semerano's super-cool American cocktail bar. Descend into the cave-like interior, with its glittering fairy lights, for cocktails amid the shadows.

SHOPPING

Ostuni is surrounded by olive groves so this is the place to pick up some of the region's DOC

'Collina di Brindisi' direct from producers such as **Oleificio Cooperativa Coltivatori** (☎ 0831 30 16 98; Corso Mazzini). A 750ml bottle costs €5.

Ostuni's weekly **market** (Via degli Emigranti; ☒ 8am-noon) is on Saturday. It is located to the south of the historic centre near the Chiesa di Madonna del Pozzo.

GETTING THERE & AROUND

STP buses run between Ostuni and Brindisi (€2.60, 50 minutes, six daily) about every two hours, arriving in Piazza Italia in the newer part of Ostuni. They also connect the town with Martina Franca (€1.70, 45 minutes, five daily). Trains run frequently to and from Brindisi (€2.60, 25 minutes) and Bari (€4.60, one hour 10 minutes). A half-hourly local bus covers the 2.5km between the station and town.

Between June and September, STP runs buses from Ostuni to Villanova and along the coast, and in July and August there is also a night bus. You can pick them up on Viale Pole.

You can rent a bicycle from **Alba Travel Agency** (☎ 339 866 43 66; Largo Bianchieri 2; per day/ week €13/35).

Around Ostuni

Although it is tempting to look seawards from Ostuni, there are lots of sights to see in the surrounding countryside. The crypts of San Biagio and San Giovanni at **San Vito Normanni**, for example, have faded 12th-century frescoes, while the mazelike historic centre of **Ceglie Messapica** is actually more authentic than that in Ostuni.

Ceglie also has a reputation for fine food so at the very least it's worth a lunch or dinner outing. The two standard-bearers of Ceglie's gastronomic reputation are **Cibus** (☎ 0831 38 89 80; Via Chianche di Scarano 7; meals €30; ☒ Wed-Mon), devoted to sourcing local produce, and **Al Fornello da Ricci** (☎ 0831 37 71 04; Contrada Montevicoli; meals €50; ☒ Wed-Mon lunch), which has a Michelin star.

ADRIATIC COAST

The Adriatic coast between Bari and Brindisi is a mixture of low-scale development and wild windswept coastline. Monopoli is the largest town, but despite being a thriving city the historic centre is sadly neglected. Not so for the tiny Polignano a Mare, one of the most photogenic seaside towns in all of Puglia. Beyond Monopoli the coast careers on south be-

ARTE POVERA

In the 1960s, '70s and early '80s Italian politics was in turmoil. The country had been devastated during WWII and its ill-advised love-affair with Fascism had left the country deeply divided. Known as the *anni di piombo* (years of lead), it was a period of social upheaval, characterised by conflict and acts of terrorism.

Hardly surprising then that young artists like Bari-born Pino Pascali (1936–68) were searching for new modes of expression; trying to break away from the weight of Italy's conservative artistic heritage and join the emerging contemporary art trends in Europe and America. Coming from the rural region of Puglia, Pascali grew up in a place where people were still very much in touch with their environment: close to the sea and soil, and subject to a terrible poverty that engendered a culture of make do and mend. His affiliation to the *arte povera* (poor art) movement was therefore not simply a matter of ideology but a clear expression of his southern roots.

Pascali studied in Naples and then moved to Rome where he soon became a star of the art world, producing works in many different styles and media. He used old cans, plastic brushes, fake fur, coloured water, hay and dirt, and even appeared in a film recording the 'planting' of loaves of bread on a beach. One of his most spectacular works is *Bridge* (1968), an 8m-long 'rope' bridge made of steel-wool scouring pads, which was strung across the Galleria Nazionale d'Arte Moderna in Rome. All these works ignore the boundaries between abstract and figurative art and revel in the playful transformation of materials.

Many of the techniques Pascali and his contemporaries pioneered – performance art, installation art, body art and assemblage – still have relevance for contemporary artists today.

tween stretches of beach and holiday hotspots like Savelletri and Torre Canne, until it peters out in Brindisi's ugly suburbs.

POLIGNANO A MARE
pop 17,550

Stacked like a cubist vision atop its rocky promontory, Polignano a Mare is the supermodel of the coastal scene. It is beautifully preserved, its chalk-white houses shining in the sun, its cobbled streets worn smooth through the centuries. It was originally built by the Greeks and it retains its Greek look and flavour. You can snap the perfect picture from the **Ponte Lama Monachile**, across the peacock-blue waters of Polignano's tiny cove, the **Cala Porto**. Then duck through the Arco Marchesale into the old town. Immediately on your left you'll find the Palazzo Pino Pascali, which houses contemporary exhibits in the **Museo d'Arte Contemporanea** (☎ 080 424 24 63; www .palazzopinopascali.it; ⏰ 6-9pm Wed-Sat during exhibitions). It is dedicated to Bari-born artist Pino Pascali, who died at the age of 32.

Wander down through the central Piazza Vittorio Emanuele and seek out the hidden belvederes dotted around town. In high summer it can be slow going through the crowds. Then make your way east, past the tiny **Capella di Santo Stefano** (the only church to survive in the historic centre) and exit the old town

through the café-lined Piazza San Benedetto. From here it's a short walk down Via Tritone to the **Grotta Palazzese**, an enormous sea cave located beneath the **Hotel Grotta Palazzese** (☎ 080 424 06 77; Via Narciso 59; s €50-60, d €100-150; 🖳). You need to ask the hotel if you want to see the cave, but from May to September they set up their restaurant here so why not book a table for lunch instead?

If you're in town on a Thursday it's fun to visit the **market** (⏰ 8am-noon) along Viale San Francesco d'Assisi. Hundreds of trucks come from all over the province to sell clothes, shoes, food and household items. Afterwards head for possibly the most famous ice-cream parlour in Puglia, **Il Super Mago del Gelo** (☎ 080 424 00 25; Piazza Garibaldi 22), and sample the sublime *caffè-nocciola* ice cream or a dark, slushy coffee granita.

For something more substantial **Osteria di Chichibio** (☎ 080 424 04 88; Largo Gelso 12; meals €40; ⏰ Tue-Sun) and **Ca Blu** (☎ 080 424 10 31; Via Porto 23; meals €25-30) are two good options.

Polignano is on the main train line and is served by dozens of trains from Bari (€2.10, 30 minutes) and Brindisi (€4.60, one hour). By road, take the SS16.

MONOPOLI
pop 49,700

By all rights Monopoli should be a seaside stunner like Polignano and Otranto. It has

PUGLIA BY BIKE

Cycling is one of the most popular activities in Puglia. The coast and the gently undulating countryside lends itself perfectly to free-wheeling around without too much strain. **Puglia in Bici** (www.pugliainbici.com) rents out absolutely top-of-the-range Carrraro bicycles with light aluminium frames, a 5-shift gear system, double water-bottle carriers, anti-theft locks and helmets. You'll find the main office at the **NRG Bike Shop** (☎ 080 413 64 29; Via Sabin 1-5) in Monopoli although you can arrange to have bikes delivered to any location in Puglia. Prices range from €15 per day to €90 per day, which includes delivery and pick-up. They also work in conjunction with Southern Visions to provide cycling itineraries and you even have your very own guide. Some circular routes worth considering are:

- Alberobello–Monopoli–Polignano a Mare–Castellana Grotte–Alberobello

- Ostuni–Marina di Ostuni–Torre Canne–Egnazia–Fasano–Locorotondo–Ostuni

- Ostuni–Locorotondo–Martina Franca–Ceglie Messapica–San Vito Normanni–Ostuni

- Martina Franca–Massafra–Mottola–Noci–Alberobello–Locorotondo–Martina Franca

all the right ingredients – a dense historical centre that looks like a Picasso painting and a crumbling medieval castle – but alas Monopoli's historic centre is sorely neglected and many of its prize sights, such as the **Palazzo Palmieri**, are in such a terrible state of repair that they're in danger of falling down.

Nevertheless, Monopoli is a big city that derives it livelihood from fishing and light industry. Its 18th-century **cathedral** (Piazzetta Cattedrale; 6.30-8pm Sat, 11am-12.30pm & 6.30-8pm Sun) is one of the largest in Brindisi province, remodelled in the 1700s according to the latest baroque fashions with an absolutely lavish interior of floor-to-ceiling polychrome marbles and notable artworks by Palma Giovani, and Francesco da Mura. The **Diocesan Museum** (☎ 080 74 80 02; Piazzetta Cattedrale; admission €2; 10am-12.30pm & 4.30-7.30pm) opposite contains more treasures, including a rare 11th-century reliquary from Constantinople and a miracle-working cross of Neapolitan workmanship.

From Largo Vescovado you can take Via San Cosmo down through the historic centre to Piazza Palmieri and its bone-white palace, where you'll likely encounter a game of football in the evenings, or you can pass under the shadow of the **Chiesa di San Domenico**, where Palma Giovani's *Miracle of Soriano* hangs, and head down Via Garibaldi to the **Porto Vecchio**. This is the most picturesque area of the old town, with the fishing boats still pulling up at the quay. From here you can see the pentagonal **castle** (Largo Castello; 10am-noon & 6-9pm Tue-Sun) on Punta Penna housing temporary exhibits.

Just off Piazza Garibaldi is the 12th-century **Chiesa di Santa Maria degli Almalfitani**

(Largo Amalfitana; 10am-noon & 6-8pm 15 Jun-Sep), built by sailors from Amalfi on top of an older Basilian cave-church which retains the faintest traces of frescoes.

You can stay in Monopoli, although on balance it probably isn't the best option. B&B **La Porta Vecchia** (☎ 080 80 26 90; www.laportavecchia.com; Via Peroscia 21; s/d €40/90) is a reasonable option in the old town. If you have deep pockets, then splash out on Monopoli's finest hotel, **Il Melograno** (☎ 080 6909030; www.melograno.com; Contrada Torricella 345; s €170-215, d €300-410; P ☒ ☒).

Monopoli's beach quarter, Capitolo, is the absolute centre of the summer disco scene, when hordes of partygoers converge on massive beachside clubs like **New Autodromo Club** (☎ 347 113 93 00; www.autodromoclub.it; Contrada Capitolo), **Il Trappeto** (☎ 080 690 91 11; www.iltrappeto.com; Contrada Cristo delle Zolle), **Masseria Garrappa** (☎ 080 528 95 58; www.masseriagarappa.com; Contrada Losciale) and **Barcollando** (☎ 339 220 10 42; www.barcollando beach.it; Lido Losciale). All these clubs have a full summer programme from June to September. Out-of-season events are usually confined to the weekends. They all charge an entry fee of around €15 to €25 and stay open until about 5am.

As with Polignano, Monopoli is on the main Bari–Brindisi train line and the SS16 coastal road.

EGNAZIA

About 18km south of Monopoli are the ruins of the Graeco-Messapian town of **Egnazia** (http://xoomer.alice.it/egnazia/; SS379 Fasano-Savelletri museum & park/park €3/2; 8.30am-7pm). It's easy to miss along the road as all that remains are

TARANTO & THE MURGIA

the foundation stones of houses and bākeries, roads and graves. It's one of those places that would probably be quite important elsewhere, but this is Italy, where ruins like these are found all over the place.

Egnazia dates from the 13th century BC. Yes, that's right, 13 centuries *before* Christ! But it only really flourished between the 5th century BC until end of the Roman era, when its position between Peucetia (Bari province) and Messapia (the Salento) made it a vital link along the Via Appia serving Rome. Originally the site occupied only 3 hectares of the small peninsula that juts out to sea; this later became the acropolis of the Roman town, as the city expanded to fill almost 40 hectares of land by the 3rd century BC. With the advent of the Via Traiana, Egnazia became Hellenised as ideas and influences crept up the coast from Brindisi until everyone was wearing Greek fashions and copying Greek designs and habits. You can still see a bit of the white limestone road today, and imagine Horace and his friends trundling along it on their way from Brindisi to Rome.

Signposts (in English and Italian) around the site explain everything clearly. Even if you're not an archaeology enthusiast it's a pretty site to walk around in full view of the sea. Then you can head to the **museum** (☎ 080 482 90 56; museum & park/museum €3/2; ⏲ 8.30am-7.30pm) and check out some of the fancy Messapian vases (known as Gnathian ware), mosaics and *objets d'art* that they found during the excavations.

TORRE GUACETO

About 15km northwest of Brindisi is the **Riserva di Torre Guaceto** (☎ 0831 98 98 85; www.riserva ditorreguaceto.it; SS379, exit Serranova), a protected coastal zone that attracts hosts of migrating birds and even turtles.

The inner part of the bay is a marshy lagoon filled with reeds, while the northern part of the reserve is given over to Mediterranean plants such as mastic, butcher's broom, myrtle and juniper. At either end of the marsh are sandy dunes rising to a height of 8m to 10m. The reserve is very well organised with walking and cycling trails and at the visitors centre you can also join one of the sailing or yoga courses.

TARANTO & THE MURGIA

Brindisi & the Salento

After Sicily and Sardinia, the Penisola Salentina (Salentine Peninsula) is considered by some to be the third island of Italy. It is hot, dry, cut off and remote, retaining a real flavour of its Greek past. Here the lush greenery of the Valle d'Itria gives way to ochre-coloured fields hazy with wildflowers and immense olive groves. And amid the cacti and the crickets you'll find Messapic, Greek and Roman relics popping up alongside much older menhirs and dolmens.

But it's not all dry sierras and sunny beaches; go inland and you'll find the beautiful city of Lecce, nicknamed the Florence of Puglia, for its heritage of highbrow scholarship and crazy carved churches. Its baroque elegance is echoed throughout the region, from big towns like Galatina and Gallipoli to tiny villages like Specchia.

Until quite recently the Salento was a poor and isolated region, as you can see in Eduardo Winspeare's film *Il Miracolo,* but with flash new neighbours in town like Lord MacAlpine and Helen Mirren, this southern outpost is enjoying a cultural renaissance as more and more people head south to savour its intriguing traditions and ancient history.

Add to this Italy's finest beaches (six of them blue-flag approved), almost endless sunshine and a general desire to party all night to musical styles as varied as *pizzica* and house, and you can see why the Italians have been keeping the Salento something of a secret.

HIGHLIGHTS

- Make new friends and learn to cook Pugliese at Lecce's **Awaiting Table** (p149) amid the town's legendary baroque extravagance

- Go crazy and dance like you've been bitten by a tarantula at Melpignano's **Notte della Taranta** (p153) or remember Otranto's 800 martyrs at the **Festa dei Martiri Idruntini** (p163)

- Dive the rock caves around **Santa Caterina** (p156) and eat fish so fresh it's actually raw in **Gallipoli** (p159)

- Party hard at **Gibò** (p160), near Santa Maria di Leuca, and sleep off the night's excesses on the white sandy beaches of **Marina di Pescoluse** (p160)

- Spend a lazy day sailing up the Adriatic coast visiting sea caves and sunbathing on the deck of one of the beautiful boats from **Smarè** (p160) in Santa Maria di Leuca

- Scuba dive in the grottoes of **Castro** (p161) or trek inland amid the *maquis*-covered hillsides of the Adriatic Coast

Lecce ★

Santa Caterina ★

Melpignano ★

Otranto ★

★ Gallipoli

Castro ★

Marina di Pescoluse ★

Santa Maria di Leuca ★

BRINDISI

pop 87,900

Brindisi is no stranger to fame. It has been southern Italy's busiest merchant and passenger port for centuries. It was the end of the ancient Roman road, Via Appia, down whose weary length trudged legionnaires and pilgrims, crusaders and traders, all heading to Greece and the Near East. Then it was the main terminus for the Indian Mail Route, a business that brought a steady stream of 19th-century society to the city's doorstep.

With a colourful past, Brindisi is searching for its soul in the 21st century. Sure it is southern Italy's busiest port – in summer about 1000 tourists transit through the city every day – but somehow that hasn't made it the focal point it should be and it continues to languish in Bari's shadow. Also, the city is struggling to discard a bad reputation – stories about thieves and touts have plagued Brindisi for years, but in reality the palm-planted *corso* is very pleasant, but there is simply very little to do.

HISTORY

There is a great scene in the film *Spartacus,* where Kirk Douglas enthusiastically exclaims to sidekick Tony Curtis that they are 'off to the Roman city of Brundisium!' And there, where the Appian Way meets the port, ships would lie waiting to take Spartacus and his great army of freed slaves off to Greece.

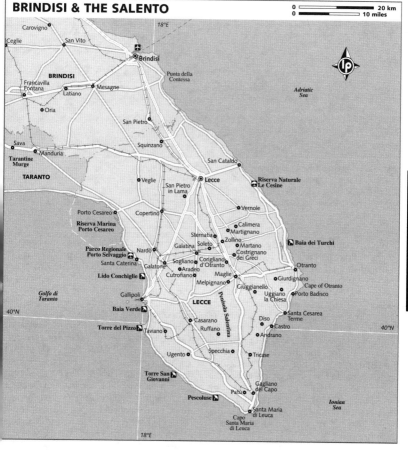

BRINDISI & THE SALENTO

0 — 20 km
0 — 10 miles

BRINDISI & THE SALENTO

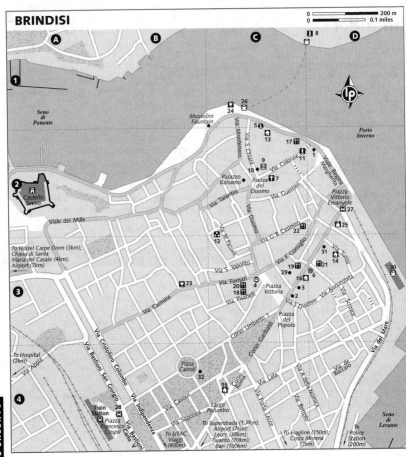

BRINDISI

Well, history (and Hollywood) have taught us that Spartacus got double-crossed in Brundisium: there were no ships waiting, and ultimately the end of the Appian Way was lined not with gold, but with crucified bodies. The city may predate that Roman heyday by several centuries, but it was the Romans who transformed it into a major centre of commerce and naval power. In subsequent centuries the city was destroyed by the Lombards (674), but such a fine natural harbour couldn't be left to go to waste so the city was soon rebuilt and later captured by the Normans (1070), who used it as the main embarkation point for their Crusades. Between 1096 and 1228 six Crusades departed from Brindisi.

But plague (1348 and 1456) and conquest were to take the edge off things following Frederick II's death in 1250, as Brindisi passed in quick succession from the Angevins to the Austrians and then the Bourbons. The city's fortunes were only resurrected in 1869 with the opening of the Suez Canal, when the Peninsular and Oriental Steam Navigation Company chose Brindisi as one of its termini for the Indian Mail Route. From 1871 to 1914, travellers once again journeyed the length of Europe to Brindisi where ships departed every Sunday for Port Said, Bombay and Calcutta.

Unfortunately, Brindisi's days on the mail route were numbered as war loomed, and in 1914 the mail company moved to Marseille, which was altogether safer. Given the bombings

INFORMATION	SLEEPING	DRINKING
Appia Travel..................... **1** D2	Grande Albergo	Big Ben.............................. **23** B3
Hellenic Mediterranean Lines......**2** C3	Internazionale..................**13** C2	Pub Aragonese...................**24** C1
Libreria...........................**3** C3	Hotel Altair..............................**14** D3	
Post Office.....................**4** C3	Hotel Colonna.....................**15** C4	SHOPPING
Tourist Office.........................**5** C1	Hotel Orientale.......................**16** C3	Supermarket.....................**25** D2
Webmaniacs............................. **6** D3		
	EATING	TRANSPORT
SIGHTS & ACTIVITIES	Betty's Bar..............................**17** C2	Boats to Monument of Italian
Cathedral........................**7** C2	Braceria Escosazio...................**18** C3	Sailors..................................**26** C1
Monument to Italian Sailors.......**8** D1	La Cantina ti L'Artisti...............**19** C3	Buses for Costa Morena...........**27** D2
Museo Archeològico...................**9** C2	Market...............................**20** C3	FSE & STP Bus Stops................**28** B4
Porta dei Cavalieri Templari......**10** C2	Trattoria da 'Vito'....................**21** D3	Marmara Lines.........................**29** C3
Roman Column.....................**11** C2	Trattoria	Old Ferry Terminal...................**30** D3
Tempio di San Giovanni al	Pantagruele.........................**22** C2	Skenderbeg Lines....................**31** D3
Sepolcro..............................**12** C2		STP Ticket Office....................**32** B4

Brindisi took in WWI it proved a good decision. Over 207 missions left its harbour during the war, earning the city the Military Cross of Honour. WWII brought more of the same, causing much damage to the historic centre until the city was finally occupied by Allied troops in September 1943 and Brindisi became the temporary capital of Italy for six months.

In the 1990s a new set of international organisations recognised the strategic benefits of Brindisi's port and the Office of the UN and the World Food Organisation set up camp in the disused sector of Brindisi's miliary airport. This time, however, they're sending emergency rations rather than warships.

ORIENTATION

Brindisi is built on a peninsula between two landlocked bays, the Seno di Ponente on the northwest and the Seno di Levante on the east.

From the train station Corso Roma and then Corso Garibaldi leads to Piazza Vittorio Emanuele, which faces the inner harbour and was once the location of the old port. To the east, in the bleak industrial wilderness of Costa Morena, is the new port (Stazione Marittima), while to the left the Viale Regina Margherita leads around the peninsula to the Castello Svevo.

INFORMATION
Bookshops

Libreria (☎ 0831 56 20 47; Corso Garibaldi 38a; 9am-1pm & 4.30-7.30pm Mon-Fri, 9am-1pm Sat) A small bookshop with a limited selection, but plenty of guidebooks.

Emergency

Police Station (☎ 0831 54 31 11; Via Bastioni S Giacomo)

Internet Access

Webmaniacs (☎ 0831 52 15 32; Vico Sacramento; per hr €3.50; 9.15am-8.15pm) New centre with fast computers.

Internet Resources

Brindisi Web (www.brindisiweb.com) A nonprofit website with everything you need to know about Brindisi.

Medical Services

First Aid (☎ 0831 52 14 10)
Hospital (☎ 0831 53 71 11; SS7 for Mesagne) Southwest of the centre.

Money

Corso Umberto I and Corso Garibaldi bristle with currency-exchange offices and banks. It's more reliable to change money at the banks.

Post

Post office (☎ 0831 47 11 11; Piazza Vittoria; 8am-6.30pm Mon-Fri, 8am-12.30pm Sat)

Tourist Information

Tourist office (☎ 0831 52 30 72; Viale Regina Margherita 44; 9am-1.30pm & 3.30-7.30pm Mon-Fri, 9.30am-1.30pm & 3.30-9pm Sat, plus 5-9pm Sun Jul & Aug) A sleepy tourist office, but helpful nonetheless.

Travel Agencies

Appia Travel (☎ 0831 52 16 84; Viale Regina Margherita 8/9; 9am-1pm & 4-8pm Mon-Fri, 9am-1pm Sat) A reputable agency in a convenient location. Here you can book ferries, trains and long-distance bus trips.
UTAC Viaggi (☎ 0831 52 49 21; Via Bastioni San Giacomo 70; 9am-1pm & 3-7pm Mon-Fri, 9am-1pm Sat) Another reliable agency. The website has good info on Greece.

DANGERS & ANNOYANCES

Since the break-up of Yugoslavia and the advent of war in Iraq, Italy's Adriatic ports have borne the brunt of illegal immigration. This has resulted in some disturbing reports of racism at key entry points like Brindisi. While this is not the norm it is something to be aware of while travelling this route.

In summer, theft can be a problem. Nothing of the remotest interest to a thief should be left unattended.

With regards to ticket scams, the safest strategy is to deal directly with a reputable ferry company; some are listed on p142. Some less scrupulous agents will assure you that your Eurail or Inter-Rail pass is invalid, or that the quota is full, in order to sell you a full-price ticket. Check with the ferry company.

SIGHTS

For the Romans, as for travellers today, Brindisi was the end of the line or, more specifically, of the Via Appia, which stretched cross-country from Rome to Brindisi. A second, faster branch, the Via Traiana, was added in 190 by the Emperor Trajan, linking Rome to Brindisi via Canosa di Puglia and Bari. For centuries, two great **columns** marked the end of the imperial highway. One was presented to the town of Lecce back in 1666 as thanks to Sant'Oronzo for having relieved Brindisi of the plague. The other is *in situ* and stands at the top of a sweeping set of sun-whitened stairs on Via Colonne. Legend has it that the Roman poet Virgil died in a house near here after returning from a voyage to Greece.

After the Romans, the next big event to hit Brindisi was the Crusades during the 12th and 13th centuries. The **Porta dei Cavalieri Templari**, an exotic-looking portico with pointy arches, is all that remains of the Knights Templar's main church. It stands beside the **cathedral** (Piazza del Duomo; [mark] 9am-noon & 6-8pm) in the heart of the small historic quarter. The cathedral, too, was constructed during the 12th century although it was remodelled following the earthquake of 1743. In its day it saw the comings and goings of the great and the good; Roger was crowned King of Sicily here in 1191 and in 1225 Frederick II married Jolanda of Brienne, Queen of Jerusalem.

With so many soldiers and pilgrims in town, the Teutonic Knights, Knights Templar and Knights of Malta built hospitals and residences to host them; the **Tempio di San Giovanni al Sepolcro** (Via San Giovanni) is one of the few that remain. It is modelled on the Holy Sepulchre in Jerusalem.

Abutting the north side of the cathedral is the small **Museo Archeológico** ([phone] 0831 22 14 01; Piazza del Duomo 8; admission free; [mark] 9.30am-1.30pm Tue-Sun, 3.30-6.30pm Tue, Thu & Sat) containing Brindisi's Punta del Serrone bronzes – a find of nearly 3000 bronze fragments and sculptures, including two complete statues, in Hellenistic Greek style.

A pleasant diversion is to take one of the regular boats (€1.20 return) on Viale Regina Margherita across the harbour to the **Monument to Italian Sailors**. It was erected by Mussolini in 1933 and commemorates the lives of 6000 fallen soldiers who lost their lives in WWI. It was designed by Luigi Brunati and Amerigo Bartoli and takes the form of a huge ship's rudder. It's situated on the bay, so you can enjoy a wonderful view of Brindisi's waterfront from its terrace.

Brindisi's main sight is the **Chiesa di Santa Maria del Casale**, 4km northwest of the centre. It has been a National Monument since 1875, and it's unfortunate indeed that they chose to build the airport right next door! It was commissioned by Prince Philip of Taranto in 1322, but its style is totally atypical, a curious melange of Puglian-Romanesque, Pisan-Romanesque, Gothic and Byzantine influences that make it look like no other church in Puglia. Still, the frescoes inside definitely take their cue from the rich Byzantine tradition and are incredibly well preserved. The most impressive is the *Last Judgement* on the entrance wall with its angels and apostles, river of fire, pig-faced devils and Leviathans spewing out mouthfuls of hapless sinners. It is the work of the talented Rinaldo di Taranto. Note also the elaborate *Tree of the Cross* and the unusual *Madonna with Knights*, a clear reference to Brindisi's crusading past.

To get there, follow Via Provinciale San Vito around the Seno di Ponente bay. Alternatively, take the airport bus.

FESTIVALS

Il Cavallo Parato (June) A ceremony recalling an incident in 1250, when St Louis, returning from the sixth Crusade, was shipwrecked off Brindisi and swam ashore with the Holy Sacrament. The re-enactment sees the Bishop atop a white steed, parading the Blessed Sacrament through the city.

La Processione a Mare dei Santi Protettori (September) A seaborne procession commemorating St Theodore and St Lawrence, the protectors of the city. It's held in the first 10 days of September.

SLEEPING

Brindisi has lots of uninspiring accommodation – hardly surprising, as most travellers stay here just one night before hopping on the ferry or the train.

Hostel Carpe Diem (☎ 0831 41 84 18, 338 323 55 45; www.hostelcarpediem.it; dm €13; **P** 🖳) Brindisi's youth hostel is terrifically inconvenient, situated midway between the airport and the city centre (3km). To reach it take bus 3 or 4, or give them a call and they'll come and pick you up in a free minivan.

Hotel Altair (☎ 0831 56 22 89; Via Giudea 4; s €20-40, d €30-50) Hidden away in a sidestreet off Corso Garibaldi, the Altair looks and feels like the oldest hotel in Brindisi. It must once have been a grand building as many of the rooms have vaulted ceilings, but these days creaky beds and low rates are its main selling point. Breakfast is an additional €2.50.

Hotel Colonna (☎ 0831 56 25 57; www.albergocolonna .it; Corso Roma 83; s €55-90, d €65-110; 🛱) A big bright modern hotel only 800m from the train station and right on the main drag. It's privately managed, which gives the place a more personal feel, and the rooms are comfortable and reasonably priced.

Hotel Orientale (☎ 0831 56 84 51; Corso Garibaldi 49; s/d €90/120; **P** 🛱) Brindisi's best modern hotel is right in the centre of the *corso*. The décor is unimaginative but the rooms are functionally comfortable, the breakfast buffet is generous and the reception is very efficient. It is very popular with the business crowd.

Grande Albergo Internazionale (☎ 0831 52 34 73; www.albergointernazionale.it; Viale Regina Margherita 23; s/d €160/250; **P** 🛱) The Hotel East Indies – one of the finest in the Med in its day – was inaugurated in 1870 amid much fanfare. It survives today as the fancy Albergo Internazionale and retains much of its ornate Liberty-style décor. It has great views over the harbour.

EATING

Great restaurants are a bit thin on the ground in Brindisi; instead fast-food joints and pizzerie dominate the *corso*.

Braceria Escosazio (☎ 0831 56 39 71; Piazza Mercato 15; meals €15-20; 🕑 Mon-Sat) This place is a carnivore's heaven – a butcher's counter filled with every barbecued meat possible and an enormous grill. The specialities are *bolpette* (meatballs), *gnummeriddu* (liver wrapped in goat's intestines) and sausages. Make your selection at the counter and watch them grill it for you.

ourpick La Cantina ti L'Artisti (☎ 0831 52 90 36; Via dè Terribile 11; meals €25; 🕑 Mon-Sat) An original restaurant, established by a family of artists right across from the cinema. The walls are lined with black-and-white photos and there's a great buzz in here when the place fills up with Brindisi's bohemian crowd, which comes for the occasional live music. The food is traditional, with local dishes like *taiedda di riso patate e cozze* (a dish of rice, potatoes and mussels).

Trattoria da 'Vito' (☎ 0831 56 42 14; Corso Garibaldi 72-76; meals €35; 🕑 Mon-Sat) This place is so obvious that you'll probably walk right past it, but that would be a huge mistake. Da 'Vito' serves up the freshest fish in Brindisi in a nice vaulted restaurant. Expect your fish antipasti to be served *crudo* (raw) and look out for the rare *schiuma di mare* (literally 'foam of the sea'), a mass of gelatinous baby fish served with lemon, olive oil and pepper.

Trattoria Pantagruele (☎ 0831 56 06 05; Via Salita di Ripalta 1; meals €35; 🕑 Thu-Tue, dinner only Nov-Mar) Named after the satirical character from Rabelais, this rather highbrow trattoria is well regarded. It serves up refined fish dishes, like shrimp with arugula, laganari with spiny lobster or simple grilled bream. In the summer, tables fill the little *piazza* outside.

For supplies for the boat trip, stock up at the colourful fresh-food **market** (Piazza Mercato; 🕑 mornings Mon-Sat), just behind the post office, or at the **supermarket** (Corso Garibaldi 106). Alternatively, hang out at **Betty's Bar** (☎ 0831 56 10 84; Viale Regina Margherita 6), one of the best ice-cream parlours in the city.

DRINKING & ENTERTAINMENT

There was a time when a city ordinance prohibited any pubs from opening in Brindisi, such was the illegal activity going on behind the bar, but then three years ago the ban was lifted and new pubs have started to pop up all over the place.

Big Ben (☎ 0831 58 42 06; Via Carmine 14; 🕑 8pm-2.30am) An English-style pub decked out in all the typical trappings, Big Ben is one of the most popular places in town to grab a beer. Local brews run to about €3, with brand names at €5 to €7.

Pub Aragonese (☎ 0831 41 20 88; Viale Regina Margherita 97; 🕑 8pm-4am) Another English-style pub with dark wood, dim lights, leather chairs and an 'outdoor lounge', which sits right on the water's edge. The location is inconvenient but the cheap drinks and waterside location are worth it.

GETTING THERE & AWAY
Air
From **Papola Casale** (BDS; ☎ 0831 411 72 08; www
.seap-puglia.it), Brindisi's small airport, there are
internal flights to and from Rome, Naples and
Milan. The airport is served mainly by Alitalia
and AirOne, although there are now direct
flights from London Stansted with Ryanair.

Major and local car-rental firms are represented at the airport and there are regular
buses to Lecce (€5, 40 minutes, six Monday to
Friday, one Saturday and Sunday).

Boat
Ferries, all of which take vehicles, leave
Brindisi for Greek destinations including
Corfu, Igoumenitsa, Patras and the Ionian
Islands (summer only). From Patras there is
a bus to Athens. Boats also service Albania
(daily) and Turkey (seasonal).

The tourist office has up-to-date schedules,
but between June and September it is advisable to book your passage well in advance.

Most ferry companies operate only in summer. All have offices at Costa Morena (the new
port), and the major ones also have offices in
town. There's a €10 port tax for each person
and car. Check in at least two hours before
departure or you risk losing your reservation
(a strong possibility in the high season).

Hellenic Mediterranean Lines (HML; ☎ 0831 52 85
31; www.hml.it; Corso Garibaldi 8) To Corfu, Igoumenitsa
and Patras (April to October), Cefalonia (June to September) and the Ionian Islands (July and August). The largest
and most reliable of the lines, Hellenic Mediterranean
accepts Eurail and Inter-Rail passes (€15 supplement is
payable in July and August). If you intend to use your pass,
it is best to reserve in advance in high summer.
Marmara Lines (☎ 0831 56 86 33; www.marmaralines
.com; Corso Garibaldi 19) Twice-weekly ferry to Cesme
(Turkey). Departs Saturday and Wednesday at 10.30pm
and 11.30pm respectively.
Skenderbeg Lines (☎ 0831 52 54 48; www
.skenderbeglines.com; Corso Garibaldi 88) Ferries most
days to and from Vlore (Valona; in Albania).
SNAV (☎ 0831 52 54 92; www.snav.it) Ferries to Corfu
and on to Paxos.

Bus
Buses operated by **STP** (☎ 0831549245; www.stpbrindisi
.it; Piazza Cairoli; ☷ 8am-8pm) connect Brindisi with
Ostuni (€2.60, 50 minutes, six daily), Cisternino (€3.40, 10 Monday to Saturday), Oria (€2,
11 Monday to Saturday) and Lecce (€2.30, 45

FERRY CROSSINGS FROM BRINDISI		
Destination	Return cost (€) high season for seat/bed in 4-person cabin/car	Duration (hr)
Cesme, Turkey	80/115/150	19
Corfu	127/177/100	12
Cephalonia, Greece	141/221/107	
Igoumenitsa, Greece	109/188/115	9-12
Patras, Greece	126/186/106	15-20
Vlore, Albania	88/118/90	8½

minutes, two daily), as well as towns throughout the Penisola Salentina. Most leave from Via
Bastioni Carlo V, in front of the train station.
FSE (☎ 099 477 46 27) buses serving local towns
also leave from here.

Marozzi (☎ 0831 52 16 84) runs to Rome's
Stazione Tiburtina (€35 to €38, nine hours,
four daily) and **Miccolis** (☎ 0831 56 06 78) runs
to Naples (€25.60, eight hours, four daily),
leaving from Viale Arno. **Appia Travel** (☎ 0831
52 16 84) sells tickets.

Car & Motorcycle
The Via Appia (now the SS7) still serves the
city well and remains the main route from
Brindisi to Taranto. The SS379 heads north up
the coast to Bari, although this route is slow
in summer, in which case take the alternative
route along the SS16 which takes you away
from the coast and through *trulli* country.
For Lecce take the SS613.

Train
Brindisi is on the main Trenitalia train line.
It has regular local services to Bari (€6.80,
Eurostar one hour, *regionale* one hour 40
minutes), Lecce (€2.30 to €5, 40 minutes)
and Taranto (€4, one hour 10 minutes). For
Rome (€31 to €48, six hours) you may have
to change in Bari.

GETTING AROUND
To get to the airport take the Cotrap bus (€5)
which leaves from Via Bastioni Carlo V (it also
has a stop along Viale Regina Margherita). It is
scheduled to coincide with the Alitalia flights
so it isn't always that convenient when trying
to hook up with other international airlines
such as Ryanair and Hapag-Lloyd.

There are plenty of taxis at the airport and a trip into town costs €16. All the major car-hire companies are also represented.

A free minibus operated by Portabagagli connects the train station and old ferry terminal with Costa Morena. It departs every 15 minutes from 6am until 8.30pm. You'll need to show a valid ferry ticket.

By car, follow the signs for Costa Morena from the *autostrada*. Allow plenty of time to board your ferry.

LECCE

pop 91,600

As you stare open-mouthed at Lecce's madcap baroque architecture, it's almost difficult not to laugh. So joyously extravagant is the stonework that it's either grotesquely ugly or splendidly beautiful; 18th-century traveller Thomas Ashe thought it was 'the most beautiful city in Italy', but the Marchese Grimaldi said the façade of Santa Croce made him think a lunatic was having a nightmare. The local stone, *pietra leccese,* actually encourages extravagance. The style to which it gave rise, generally known as *barocco Leccese,* flourished from the 16th to the 18th century, a period of great prosperity and cultural dynamism.

HISTORY

It's often touted that the Mycenean Greeks had a hand in influencing the early culture of the Salento, although the ancient population of Italy's 'heel' were probably not Greek at all but Dalmatian in origin. They lived a good pastoral life, based on farming and fishing, until the Romans conquered Brindisi and their influence spread south to Lupiae, as Lecce was then known.

As the Western Roman Empire began to disintegrate in the 6th century the Byzantines saw their chance and sacked the city in 549. The Byzantine period may not have been a time of great development but it was a time of cultural consolidation, as Eastern influences once again spread throughout the peninsula. This 'Easternisation' only increased during the 8th and 9th centuries when Orthodox monks, fleeing persecution from Leone III's iconoclastic policies (see p23), set up home here, establishing their religious centres and teaching the Salentines how to improve their techniques in olive-oil production.

Unlike Terra di Bari, the Salento was not such a feature of the Norman empire, but that's not to say it was neglected. Obsessed with defence, the Normans built a string of towers and fortress castles along the coastline, and during their stewardship the Benedictines arrived and established the beginnings of Lecce's long tradition of literature, philosophy and law. Between 1053 and 1463 Lecce and the Salentine were ruled as an independent county until Holy Roman Emperor Charles V (1500–58) conquered Puglia and incorporated Lecce into the Kingdom of Naples.

Despite Charles' unforgiving style of rule, Lecce became an important city in the Kingdom of Naples. Situated close to the commercial ports of Otranto and Gallipoli, Lecce was on the frontline of Charles' war with the Turks. While every other Italian city in the south declined, Lecce boomed and dozens of churches, cathedrals, palaces and *piazze* were built. By the early 17th century there were around 17 monasteries and eight convents in the city and the population swelled with nobles and the nouveaux riches. And yet, the Salentines were restive under autocratic Hapsburg rule and in 1647–48 Lecce was the scene of a broadly based revolt coinciding with the Masaniello revolt in Naples.

In 1734, the year of another popular uprising, Charles III conquered the Kingdom of Naples and heralded in the controversial Bourbon era. Many historians have painted the Bourbon era as one of exploitation and stagnation, yet Charles did many a good deed in Lecce curbing the immunities of the church, circumscribing their jurisdiction and confiscating the rich estates of the Jesuits, actions whose full benefit would not be felt for decades to come. But the local population was restive and further revolts ensued in the wake of the French Revolution and then again in 1848, until in 1861 Giuseppe Garibaldi swept the south up in his popular revolution and raised the flag for a unified and free Italy.

Despite their hard-won freedom, unjust economic treatment and strong prejudices against southerners marred the first decades of unification. Although a brief era of tobacco-growing kept Lecce's economy afloat during the early decades of the 20th century, Puglia had a huge peasant class unprepared for the modern market economy that was foisted

BRINDISI & THE SALENTO

upon them. As a result, Salentines began to emigrate to America and Europe. Conversely in the 1990s the Salento has seen an influx of immigrants from the Balkans, the Middle-East and Africa, making Lecce one of Puglia's most cosmopolitan cities.

ORIENTATION

The town centre's twin main squares are Piazza Sant'Oronzo and Piazza del Duomo, linked by the pedestrian Corso Vittorio Emanuele. The *corso* forms part of the main east–west artery that cuts across the historic centre from Porta Rudiae in the west to the castle in the east. The main north–south axis is Via G Palmieri, which merges into Via Paladini and then Via B Cairoli which exits the historic centre towards the train station in the southwest. The train station is about 1km from Piazza del Duomo.

INFORMATION
Bookshops

Librerrima (☎ 0832 24 26 26; www.librerrima.it; Corte dei Cicala 1; ☽ 10am-midnight Tue-Sat, 4.30pm-midnight Sun & Mon) A stylish bookshop focusing on highbrow literature. Also stocks DVDs and CDs.

Libreria Mondadori (☎ 0832 27 92 11; Piazza Sant'Oronzo 45/46; ☽ 9.30am-1.30pm & 5-9pm Mon-Sat, 10.30am-1.30pm & 5.30-10.30pm Sun) A well-stocked bookshop on the main *piazza* with plenty of maps and guides to the city.

Emergency

Police Station (☎ 0832 69 11 11; Viale Otranto 1)
Tourist Police (☎ 800 52 43 37)

Internet Access

All'Ombra dell'Barocco (Corte dei Cicala 10; per hr €3.50; ☽ 9.30am-9.30pm Mon-Sat, 3.30-9.30pm Sun) Handy, efficient café with wi-fi. English spoken.

Clioinformazione (Via Fazzi 11; per hr €4; ☽ 9am-1pm & 4-8pm Mon-Fri) Internet place popular with students.

Medical Services

Ambulance (☎ 0832 22 86 30)
Hospital (☎ 0832 66 11 11; Via San Cesario) About 2km south of the centre on the road to Gallipoli.

Money

You'll find several banks on and around Piazza Sant'Oronzo and on Via Augusto Imperatore.

Post

Post office (☎ 0832 24 35 36; Piazza Libertini)

Tourist Information

Tourist office (☎ 0832 24 80 92; Corso Vittorio Emanuele 24; ☽ 9am-1pm & 4.30-9pm Mon-Sat Jun-Sep, 9am-1pm Mon-Sat, 3-5pm Tue & Thu Oct-May) Full of information, but the staff seem half asleep.

Tourist office castle branch (Viale XXV Luglio; ☽ 9am-1pm & 4-8pm Mon-Fri, 9.30am-1pm & 4-8pm Sat & Sun)

Travel Agencies

CTS (☎ 0832 30 18 62; Via G Palmieri 89; ☽ 9am-1pm & 4-7.30pm Mon-Fri, 9am-noon Sat) Travel agency for youth bargain fares. You can also book long-distance bus journeys here.

SIGHTS

Lecce, with its baroque palazzi and stage-set *piazze*, is urban theatre on a grand scale, its exuberant decoration tamed by an innate sense of symmetry and visual harmony. There are more than 40 churches and at least as many palazzi, most of them built or renovated between the 16th century and the end of the 18th century to create one of the most unified urban landscapes in Italy.

Piazza Sant'Oronzo

Although it isn't really in the centre of town, Piazza Sant'Oronzo is the social and commercial hub of Lecce, surrounded by cafés, shops and offices and constantly full of people. In the past it did duty as the merchants square, when it was surrounded by shopping arcades and streets given over to shoemakers, booksellers and silversmiths. Behind much of this commercial activity was an influential community of Venetians. In fact, the little **Chiesa di San Marco**, was built for them in 1543, and clearly sports the Lion of St Mark in the decorated lunette above the door. It stands next to the **Sedile**, which was the seat of the Town Hall until 1851, the large glass windows a literal demonstration of governmental transparency.

Unfortunately, in the early 20th century much of the square, its arcades and the huge Governor's Palace were demolished to make way for a new Banca d'Italia. Workmen digging the foundations uncovered the remains of a 2nd-century **Roman amphitheatre**, the largest in Puglia, with a capacity for 15,000 rowdy Romans. Only the lower half of the grandstand survives.

Beside the sunken arena rises the **Colonna di Sant'Oronzo**, a copperplate statue of Lecce's patron saint perched precariously on the second

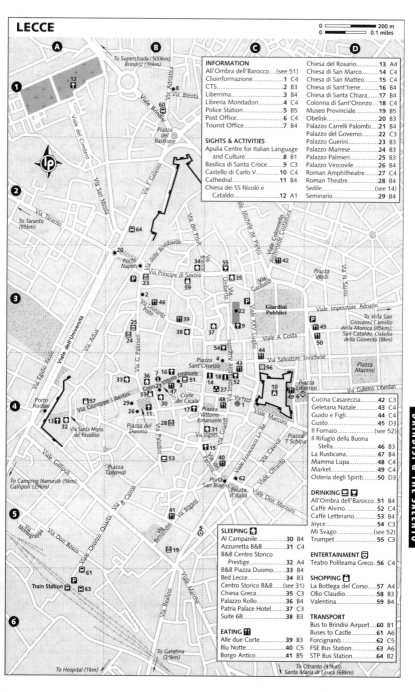

LECCE

0 — 200 m
0 — 0.1 miles

INFORMATION
All'Ombra del Barocco....(see 51)
Clioinformazione................1 C4
CTS.................................2 B3
Liberrima.........................3 B4
Libreria Mondadori............4 C4
Police Station....................5 B5
Post Office........................6 C4
Tourist Office....................7 B4

SIGHTS & ACTIVITIES
Apulia Centre for Italian Language
   and Culture...................8 B1
Basilica di Santa Croce........9 C3
Castello di Carlo V...........10 C4
Cathedral.......................11 C4
Chiesa dei SS Nicolò e
   Cataldo.......................12 A1

Chiesa del Rosario............13 A4
Chiesa di San Marco.........14 C4
Chiesa di San Matteo........15 C4
Chiesa di Sant'Irene.........16 B4
Chiesa di Santa Chiara......17 B4
Colonna di Sant'Oronzo....18 C4
Museo Provinciale.............19 B5
Obelisk............................20 B3
Palazzo Carrelli Palombi....21 B4
Palazzo del Governo.........22 C3
Palazzo Guerini................23 B3
Palazzo Marrese...............24 B3
Palazzo Palmieri...............25 B3
Palazzo Vescovile.............26 B4
Roman Amphitheatre.........27 C4
Roman Theatre.................28 B4
Sedile............................(see 14)
Seminario........................29 B4

SLEEPING
Al Campanile....................30 B4
Azzurretta B&B.................31 C4
B&B Centro Storico
   Prestige......................32 A4
B&B Piazza Duomo...........33 B4
Bed Lecce.......................34 B3
Centro Storico B&B......(see 31)
Chiesa Greca....................35 B4
Palazzo Rollo...................36 B4
Patria Palace Hotel...........37 C3
Suite 68...........................38 B3

EATING
Alle due Corte..................39 B3
Blu Notte........................40 C5
Borgo Antico...................41 B5

Cucina Casareccia.........42 C3
Geleteria Natale............43 C4
Guido e Figli.................44 C4
Gusto..........................45 D3
Il Fornaio..................(see 52)
Il Rifugio della Buona
   Stella.......................46 B3
La Rusticana................47 B4
Mamma Lupa...............48 C4
Market.........................49 C4
Osteria degli Spiriti.....50 D3

DRINKING
All'Ombra del Barocco...51 B4
Caffè Alvino..................52 B4
Caffè Letterario...........53 B4
Joyce............................54 C3
Mi Svago..................(see 52)
Trumpet.......................55 C3

ENTERTAINMENT
Teatro Politeama Greco...56 C4

SHOPPING
La Bottega del Corso....57 A4
Olio Claudio.................58 B4
Valentina......................59 B4

TRANSPORT
Bus to Brindisi Airport....60 B1
Buses to Castle.............61 A6
Forcignanò..................62 C5
FSE Bus Station.............63 A6
STP Bus Station.............64 B2

BRINDISI & THE SALENTO

pillar of the Appian Way. It was supposedly donated to the city of Lecce as a sign of thanks to Sant'Oronzo (Lecce's patron saint) for saving Brindisi from the plague in 1656.

A short walk south through Piazza Vittorio Emanuele will bring you to Lecce's second **Roman theatre** (☎ 0832 24 61 09; Via Ammirati; admission €2.60; ☺ 9.30am-1pm Mon-Sat) and amphitheatre, uncovered in the 1930s. It is a classic small theatre with a semi-circular auditorium, a marble-clad stage and the remains of an ornate *scaenae frons* (backdrop) which would have been decorated with columns and statuary (now missing). The museum here houses items from the excavation and well-preserved frescoes and mosaics, transferred from local sites.

Castello di Carlo V

Charles V considered Salento the frontline in his campaign against the Turks, whose devastating raids were wrecking havoc along the Adriatic coast. After the sack of Castro in 1534, Charles ordered Lecce's **castle** (Viale XXV Luglio; adult/concession €4/2; ☺ 9am-1pm & 4-8.30pm) to be restructured and fortified by Gian Giacomo dell'Acaja, the chief engineer for the Kingdom of Naples.

It consists of two concentric trapezoidal structures, with the outer fortification running to 1km in circumference, which makes it bigger even than Bari's castle. It is built around a Norman fortification, but General Acaja's renovations brought it right up to speed with military technology, with terreplains and sloped walls making it virtually impregnable. Inside you can wander around the echoing baronial halls, occasionally used for temporary art exhibits. There's usually an additional fee for any exhibition.

Basilica di Santa Croce

Little can prepare you for the opulence of the most celebrated example of Lecce's unique baroque style, the **Basilica di Santa Croce** (☎ 0832 24 19 57; Via Umberto I; ☺ 9am-1pm & 5-8pm). It took a team of Lecce's finest craftsmen – Gabriele Riccardi, Francesco Antonio Zimbalo, Cesare Penna and Giuseppe Zimbalo – over 100 years to create it and during that time layer after layer of decorative symbolism slowly built up to create the allegorical feast that you see today.

BAROCCO LECCESE

The distinctive character of many Salento towns comes from the unique southern style, known as *barocco Leccese*, which developed in Lecce between the latter half of the 16th century and the early 18th century. This unique adaptation of traditional baroque developed within the framework of the Counter-Reformation, when the church set about reasserting its authority through the establishment of magnificent religious orders like the Celestines and Jesuits.

The new style of architecture was an ostentatious display of the wealth and power of these religious orders, the stonework moulded into lavish decorative detail around porticoes, windows, balconies and loggias, which were crowded with human and zoomorphic figures as well as a riot of vegetal designs, gargoyles, corbels, columns and cornices. The local stone, a compact-grained limestone, was soft and easy to work – 'it can be carved with a penknife', said Cesare Brandi – encouraging local craftsmen to ever greater creativity and expression. It was then hardened using a fluid containing whole milk which reduced its porosity, making the surface harden and set. The leading exponents of the style were Gabriele Riccardi and Francesco Antonio Zimbalo, but it was Giuseppe Zimbalo (Lo Zingarello) who was its most exuberant disciple and the architect behind the extraordinary Basilica di Santa Croce.

From the late 1500s to the early 18th century this new architectural language marked the urban renewal of Lecce. By the end of the 15th century Lecce was already an important commercial centre of the Kingdom of Naples, attracting Venetian, Dalmatian, Greek and Lombard merchants. Later, when Charles V came to power in 1516, he appointed Lecce Puglia's regional capital and ordered extensive building and public works to renew its urban centre. Resident noblemen also contributed to the building boom, extending and renovating their *palazzi* in the new style.

Baroque art and its decorative criteria soon spread throughout the Salento peninsula. Today, every alley, every street, every square not only in Lecce but also in Nardò, Gallipoli, Martina Franca, Ostuni, Francavilla Fontana, Galatina, Galàtone and many others, testifies to the expressive feat of this uniquely southern style.

It was commissioned in the mid-16th century by one of the city's richest orders, the Order of the Celestines, a branch of the great Benedictine monastic order. They are remembered by the two enormous statues beside the rose window, St Benedict on the right and St Celestine on the left. The three-tiered façade is full of such symbolism, and it's well worth the €3 to pick up an audio tour from the small newsagent in front of the cathedral if you want to understand the iconography better.

Standing back you can see that the façade is divided into three distinct sections. The lower section is attributed to Gabriele Riccardo and is typically Renaissance in style, divided into sections by six classical columns that flank Zimbalo's imperial portal and support a richly carved entablature filled with lions and louche-looking, bare-breasted ladies. Above this frieze crouches a series of strange zoomorphic figures: griffons, caryatids, harpies and mermaids, who seem to groan beneath the weight of the stone balcony they support. Above the balcony rises the second course of the façade, and the rose window, the greatest piece of *barocco Leccese* carving that you're ever likely to see. It was executed by Francesco Zimbalo and Cesare Penna in 1646. Finally, right at the top is a tympanum depicting the Triumph of the Cross at its centre.

The interior is equally lavish. Although the structural plan is conventional Renaissance, the decorative effect certainly has that 'wow' factor. The nave has a gilded and coffered ceiling, the central altar is lavishly decorated with marble intarsia and down the aisles are a total of 14 chapels, each one more ornate than the last, although it's hard to beat Zimbalo's six-columned altar of San Francesco da Paola on the north side.

Giuseppe Zimbalo also left his mark on the adjoining Convento dei Celestini, nowadays the **Palazzo del Governo**, the seat of the local government. From here you can walk through the colonnaded courtyard to the **Giardini Pubblici**, a well-maintained formal garden on the opposite side.

Piazza del Duomo

The geographical heart of Lecce is the **Piazza del Duomo**, although it feels cut off from the city. It's a clever trick, intended by the architects who designed it; first they set it back down a small alley off the main *corso*, then they enclosed it with operatic buildings, leaving just one narrow access flanked by imposing entrance piers. In the past this could be closed by a huge oak door, although that is long gone. It is quite ingenious, and even now as you walk into the square you experience a feeling of wonder as the drama of the *piazza* reveals itself to you.

Directly in front of you is what appears to be the ornate façade of the **cathedral** (☎ 0832 30 85 57; Piazza del Duomo; 🕑 8.30am-12.30pm & 5-8pm), but this is another architectural conceit, a false façade created for dramatic effect. Modelled along the lines of a triumphal arch, it is a decorative exultation, accompanied by the highest campanile in Italy (68m). Inside the cathedral is a classic Latin plan, but there's nothing classic about the excess of decoration that adorns it. Stuccoed naves, ornate altars, marble *pavimenti* and polychrome altars all vie for your attention along with some of the most significant 16th- to 18th-century artworks of the Salento, by artists like Giuseppe da Brindisi and Giovanni Coppola.

Facing the cathedral is the 15th-century **Palazzo Vescovile** (Espiscopal Palace), with its arched arcade loggia. Adjoining this is the magnificent 18th-century **Seminario** (exhibitions only), constructed between 1694 and 1709 by Giuseppe Cino, one of Zimbalo's most promising pupils. The well in the courtyard is also a flight of fancy by Cino.

The Corso & Porta Rudiae

Piazza del Duomo is located at the main axis of town. From here Via Vittorio Emanuele II heads east to Piazza Sant'Oronzo past **Palazzo Carrelli Palombi** and the 17th-century **Chiesa di Sant'Irene** (closed for renovation at the time of research), which boasts a magnificent pair of mirror-image baroque altarpieces, squaring up to each other across the transept.

Head west and you'll pass another series of churches – Lecce has a lot of them! – the most interesting of which is the **Chiesa del Rosario** (Via G Libertini; 🕑 7.30am-12.30pm & 4.30-8pm), otherwise known as the Chiesa di San Giovanni Battista. It is Giuseppe Zimbalo's final work (completed in 1728) and the place where the great architect-craftsman is buried.

From here Via Libertini exits the historic centre through one of the city's three monumental gates, **Porta Rudiae**. It takes its name from the original Roman settlement of Rudiae (or Lupiae), which was located 3km southwest of Lecce.

Via Palmieri & Porta Napoli

North from Piazza del Duomo, Via Palmieri takes you past more stately *palazzi* from the 17th and 18th centuries, the most notable being **Palazzo Marrese** with its four female caryatids flanking the door. It is set back on Piazetta Ignazio Flaconieri and stands beside **Palazzo Palmieri**.

Further up the street is **Palazzo Guerini**. One of the best-preserved aristocratic residences in Lecce, it stands almost opposite the main city gate, **Porta Napoli**, which was erected in 1548 in anticipation of a state visit from Charles V. It's a typically militaristic effort by General Acaja (builder of the castle), who modelled it on a Roman triumphal arch and gave it a pointy pediment carved with toy weapons and an enormous Spanish coat of arms. Subtle it is not.

Just outside the gate a commemorative **obelisk** recalls another Spanish overlord, Ferdinand I, King of the Two Sicilies. It was carved by local sculptor Vito Carluccio in 1822–26, and depicts panels of mythological and historical symbolism relating to Lecce, Taranto, Brindisi and Gallipoli, the four districts of the Terra d'Otranto. From here it's a short walk to the Chiesa dei SS Nicolò e Cataldo.

Chiesa dei SS Nicolò e Cataldo

Sitting in the city cemetery, the **Chiesa dei SS Nicolò e Cataldo** (Via San Nicola; 🕑 9am-noon Sep-Apr, 5-7pm Jun-Aug) is surely one of the strangest looking churches in Lecce – a hybrid Byzantine-Romanesque church with a bizarre baroque facelift. The original church was founded in 1180 by Tancred, Count of Lecce, whose Sicilian roots obviously informed the exotic vegetal decoration of the portal and arabesque arches of the interior. Giuseppe Cino, who remodelled the church in 1716, had enough sense to leave the portal alone, but that didn't stop him going to town on the rest of the façade, which is now laden with an army of incongruous statues of Benedictine saints.

The interior, however, retains its simple integrity. The tall nave and narrow aisles produce an effect of soaring height, all the better to offset the 16th- and 17th-century frescoes that cover the walls and vaults.

To the right of the façade, a gate leads to the vast 16th-century cloister. It's a wide, plain space but at its centre is a gorgeous baroque canopy which once shaded the monastery's well. Built by Gabriele Riccardi (of Santa Croce fame), it has richly carved spiral columns topped by a small cupola.

South of Piazza Sant'Oronzo

South of Piazza Sant'Oronzo down the Via Augusto Imperatore, you move away from the more affluent end of Lecce into a popular and, in places, rundown residential district. Here you'll find fewer monuments, including the half-finished **Chiesa di Santa Chiara** (Piazza Vittorio Emanuele; 🕑 9.30-11.30am & 4.30-8.30pm), with its madly decorated altars, above which you can still see the grills where the nuns from the Poor Clares convent listened to mass, and the **Chiesa di San Matteo** (Via dei Perroni 29; 🕑 9am-12.30pm & 4-7.30pm). The latter is the most daring baroque construction in Lecce. Unlike the majority of other churches, which are essentially Renaissance in form and then overlaid with a layer of baroque decoration, San Matteo has an adventurous façade with a convex lower half and a concave second level. It is attributed to Giovanni'Andrea Larducci, who's thought to have based it on Borromini's San Carlo alle Quattro Fontane in Rome.

Carry on south and the road will bring you out at **Porta San Biagio**, Lecce's third city gate, which opens out onto another park on the other side of Piazza Italia.

Museo Provinciale

Named after local patriot and culture-vulture Duke Sigismondo Castromediano Lecce's **Museo Provinciale** (☎ 0832 24 70 25; Viale Gallipoli 28; admission free; 🕑 9am-1.30pm & 2.30-7.30pm Mon-Sat, 9.30am-1.30pm Sun) has an impressive archaeological collection garnered from throughout Puglia. Its patron, Duke Sigismondo, was passionate about preserving Puglia's cultural heritage and as the president of the Commission of Art and Antiquities he was instrumental in creating what was Puglia's very first museum.

As this was Puglia's only museum for years the Museo Provinciale amassed a sizable collection from towns as far afield as Taranto, Bari, Egnazia and even Canosa di Puglia. Ascending its corkscrew ramp you can browse through 10,000 years of Puglian history from Palaeolithic and Neolithic bits and bobs, to Egnazia's Gnathian ware and a handsome display of Greek and Roman coins, jewels, black-and-red Attic vases, weaponry and ornaments, all neatly displayed in chronological order. The stars of the show are the

Messapians, who were making jaunty jugs and bowls centuries before the Greeks arrived to give them pottery lessons – just have a look at those elegant *trozzelle* (vases characterised by a pair of small 'wheels', *trozze*, at the base of their slender handles) with their modern monochrome designs. Also interesting are the *tintinnabula*, terracotta children's toys in the shapes of animals which once contained a little jingling bell.

The museum also houses statues, reliefs and sculptures from Lecce's Roman theatre and the amphitheatre; and there's a small section dedicated to medieval and baroque art, which contains a very fine late-Gothic polyptych (altarpiece) from the church of Santa Caterina in Galatina alongside paintings in the Neapolitan school by the likes of Oronzo Tiso.

ACTIVITIES

Lecce's main beaches lie 8km east of the city at the seaside resort of San Cataldo. It's a bit of a breeze-block settlement, but on a nice strip of sea. In the summer it throbs with activity and, if you have your own transport, there are dozens of appealing coastside bars – mainly huts in scenic spots – that dot the coast from here to San Foca.

TOURS

You don't need a guide to enjoy Lecce, but to the untutored eye one baroque church can look very much like another. So if you're serious about architecture it's well worth considering a local guide. **Simona Melchiorre** (☎ 0832 30 25 37, 347 015 40 03) is a fluent English-speaking guide and the current president of the **AGTRP** (Associazione Guide Turistiche Regione Puglia; www .assoguidepuglia.it). If you want to get in touch with skilled guides speaking a variety of languages visit the site. An average three-hour tour costs around €85, although it does depend on the number of people and the itinerary.

COURSES

Just like Florence, Lecce is a popular destination for language courses. **Apulia Centre for Italian Language and Culture** (☎ 0832 39 03 12; www .apuliadomus.com; Via Adriatica 10) is a well-established school with an international reputation. It offers both group and individual courses and also runs lots of activities.

Those with a culinary bent should consider one of the cookery courses at **Awaiting Table** (www.awaitingtable.com), run by the multifarious Silvestro – photographer, writer, raconteur and king of the kitchen. The weekly course costs €1795 per person (double occupancy) and classes are restricted to a total of six people. Prices include all lessons, meals and accommodation in their own stylish *palazzo*. Advance booking is essential.

FESTIVALS & EVENTS

Lecce has a pretty full calendar of festivals and events, which goes into overdrive between April and September.

Holy Week (Easter) A typically flamboyant weekend of festivities followed on Tuesday by Lu Riu, a popular folk festival with performances and exhibitions of craftwork.

Notte Bianca (April) In 2007 Lecce celebrated its first Notte Bianca (White Night), where for a single night the whole city, its museums and monuments, stay open until dawn. Events, exhibits and concerts also take place all around the town.

Festival of European Cinema (www .europecinefestival.com; April) A popular festival of cinema that sees the town booked out. Films screen at the Santa Lucia Multiplex.

Cortili Aperti (Open Courtyards; May) A good opportunity to have a snoop around some of Lecce's lovely private courtyards while listening to a classic concert or two.

Rally del Salento (www.rallydelsalento.com; 15-17 June) Organised by the Automobil Club Lecce, this is a classic rally and one of the oldest races in Italy.

Mediterranea Estate (June to September) A summer-long series of free events including classical concerts, comedy, theatre, dance and all manner of musical performances.

Fiera di SS Oronzo (24-26 August) Lecce's patron saint day starts off with a sombre procession and ends with a costumed cavalcade and a big party which sees the city decked out in a spectacular light display.

Fiera di Santa Lucia (13-24 December) A week-long Christmas fair commencing on St Lucy's day, where you can buy *cartapesta* (papier-mâché) and terracotta crib figures. There's also a Nativity Scene set up in the amphitheatre.

SLEEPING

With more than 600 B&Bs in its historic centre, Lecce has some of the best and most varied accommodation in Puglia, from elegant small hotels to good value-for-money apartments and B&Bs.

Budget

There is no youth hostel in Lecce itself. The nearest one is in San Cataldo on the coast.

Camping Namasté (☎ 0832 32 96 47; www.camping -lecce.it; Via Novoli; person/tent/car €5/8/8) Just over

4km out of town is the 35,000-sq-m camp site Camping Namasté. It forms part of an organic farm and runs yoga classes on site. To get to Namasté take bus No 26 from the train station.

Ostello della Gioventú (☎ 0832 650890; Via Amergigo Vespucci 45; s/d/q €30/40/60, 3/4-person tent €10/16) Located 8km east of Lecce on the coast road, in San Cataldo. Take bus no 32 from Lecce. It's dead out of season, but between June and September it is totally packed.

Azzurretta B&B (☎ 0832 24 22 11; www.bblecce.it; Via Vignes 2; s/d €30-38/55-70; P 🐾) Run by the same family as the Centro Storico, the Azzurretta is a long-standing Lecce B&B. Its cheaper price point is reflected in the more dowdy rooms. Still, it's one of the cheapest places in town and it is in a nice palazzo.

Centro Storico B&B (☎ 0832 24 27 27, 338 588 12 65; www.bedandbreakfast.lecce.it; Via Vignes 2b; d €35-60, ste €70-100; 🐾) Despite its fancy website this is a modest bed-and-breakfast in the renovated Palazzo Astore. Rooms are bright and cheerful and each has a private balcony. However, years of guidebook coverage has not done much for the service.

B&B Piazza Duomo (☎ 392 651 23 71; www.bbpiazzaduomo.it; Via Euippa 4; d/tr/q €60/90/120) Right on the cusp of the midrange category, this B&B is in a big ancient house right near the Duomo and has two lovely self-contained rooms decorated with antiques and original tiled floors. Ideal for a family.

Midrange

B&B Centro Storico Prestige (☎ 0832 30 88 81; www.bbprestige-lecce.it; Via Santa Maria del Paradiso 4; s €60-70, d €70-80; 🖳) Run by the irrepressible Renata, the Prestige is a home away from home. Rooms are light and airy and beautifully finished, Renata is great company and there is a pretty communal terrace with views over the church of San Giovanni Battista.

our pick Bed Lecce (☎ 0832 24 61 19; www.bedlecce.com; Via di Brienne; s €40-80, d €50-80; 🐾) Splendid apartments in the historic centre that make you feel like you've stepped into the pages of *Elle Decoration*. They're gorgeously decorated in white with flashes of colour provided by ethnic rugs and chic retro furniture, such as Smeg fridges.

Al Campanile (☎ 0832 30 88 64; Via Arcivescovo Petronelli 6; s/d €85/95) A real B&B in Lucia De Secly's well-located apartment. Sleep in quilt-laden beds amid a lifetime's clutter of antiques and

pictures, and in the evening enjoy the view of the Duomo's belltower. Ms De Secly is a retired librarian so if you're thinking late nights and partying this isn't the place for you.

Suite 68 (☎ 0832 30 35 06; www.kalekora.it; Via Leonardo Prato 7; s €51-102, d €60-120; 🐾) A super-stylish residence with six rooms decked out in strong colours and abstract canvases that give them a contemporary feel. The 17th-century palazzo has been renovated to the highest standard and rooms come with gimmicks like LCD TVs as well as flower-decked terraces and balconies.

Palazzo Rollo (☎ 0832 307 152; www.palazzorollo.it; via Vittorio Emanuelle II 14; B&B d Oct-Mar €90 & Aug €120, 4-person studios €100) A step from Piazza del Duomo, you can stay in palatial rooms in a 17th-century palace – the family has lived here for over 200 years. The three suites have high curved ceilings and chandeliers. Downstairs three more stylish studios open onto an ivy-hung courtyard.

Also recommended is **Chiesa Greca** (☎ 0832 30 23 30; www.chiesagreca.it; s €32-45, d €64-90; 🐾), parts of which were once incorporated in the old Greek church next door.

Top End

Rather surprisingly, Lecce does not have a great selection of top-end hotels; in fact there's only one really good hotel in the historic centre.

Patria Palace Hotel (☎ 0832 24 51 11; www.patriapalacelecce.com; Piazzetta Riccardi; s €145-195, d €190-250; 🐾 🖳) Right in the middle of barmy baroque territory, this top-end option has all the requisite comforts and elegant Liberty décor. The deluxe rooms boast views of the Basilica Santa Croce as does the flower-clad roof terrace. Rates are lower at the weekends.

EATING

Despite its urban sophistication, Lecce's restaurant scene has few really outstanding eating experiences. However, there's a good selection of unpretentious midrange eateries to while away the afternoons.

Budget

Pick up your own ingredients at Lecce's fresh-produce **market** (Piazza Libertini; 🕑 8am-noon Mon-Sat). For freshly baked bread, all manner of foccaccia, pizza and *pasticciotto* (custard-filled pastry) take a ticket and line up in **Il Fornaio** (☎ 0832 30 00 64; Piazza Sant'Oronzo 23).

Another fiendishly popular place for takeaway is **La Rusticana** (☎ 0832 30 05 44; Corso Vittorio Emanuele II 31), where you can fill up on *rustica*, a confection of puff pastry, mozzarella cheese and tomato.

ourpick Gelateria Natale (☎ 0832 25 60 60; Via Trinchese 7a; ice creams €1.50; 🕑 8am-1am) The best ice cream in Lecce – you might have to queue but this will give you time to make up your mind. It's also a fabulous confectioner with counters full of sugared treats, truffles, pannacotta and chocolate cakes that pool like oil slicks on golden plates.

Alle due Corti (☎ 0832 24 22 23; www.alleduecorti .com; Corte dei Giugni 1; meals €15-20) For a taste of the sunny Salento, this laid-back restaurant stands out. The menu is classical Pugliese with plenty of fresh vegetables and homemade pasta.

Mamma Lupa (Via degli Acaja 12; meals €15-20; 🕑 Tue-Sun) Not only rustic-looking but rustic-tasting too. Opt for one of the bruschetta boards (small toasts with different toppings) and follow it up with a piece of juicy chargrilled meat. Or try something seasonal like baked potatoes and artichokes. Portions are huge.

Il Rifugio della Buona Stella (☎ 0832 30 42 97; Via Leonardo Prato 28; meals €15-20; 🕑 lunch & dinner Mon-Sat, lunch Sun) A self-consciously rustic restaurant, decked out in gingham. It's friendly and popular and the simple local cooking is tasty, with dishes such as mushroom lasagne and lemon and pine nut pastries.

Guido e Figli (☎ 0832 30 58 68; Via XXV Luglio 14; meals €15-20; 🕑 Mon-Sat) A big cavernous restaurant with well priced food and few pretensions. The self-service buffet with its large choice of antipasti is what everyone comes for although you can order off the menu or have pizza.

Midrange

ourpick Cucina Casareccia (☎ 0832 24 51 78; Viale Colonnello Archimede Costadura 19; meals €20; 🕑 lunch Tue-Sun) Reserve a table at this unique restaurant, actually the downstairs rooms of a house, and put yourself in the capable hands of Carmela Perrone. She'll whisk you through a dazzling array of Salentine dishes from the true *cucina povera* (literally 'cooking of the poor').

ourpick Osteria degli Spiriti (☎ 0832 24 62 74; Via Battisti 4; €25; 🕑 dinner Mon-Sat) Possibly the best restaurant in Lecce with the Slow Food badge of approval and an intimate vaulted dining room. The menu is also more varied than usual with some Sicilian-inspired dishes such as *caponata* and *arancini*. Otherwise, the *orec-*

chiette with chickpeas and clams and the lamb stand out.

Blu Notte (☎ 0832 30 42 86; Via Brancaccio 3; meals €30; 🕑 Tue-Sun) This place has a great reputation for seafood, including dishes like fish soup *alla gallipolina* and grilled bream. In summer you can dine out at the foot of the city wall. Afterwards it's a short walk to Via Augusto Imperatore which is lined with bars.

Also recommended is **Gusto** (☎ 0832 24 19 70; Via Cesare Battisti 1; meals €30; 🕑 lunch & dinner Wed-Mon, lunch Tue), with its views over the Villa Comunale.

Top End

Borgo Antico (☎ 0832 24 15 69; Via Bernardini 14; meals €40; 🕑 Tue-Sun) Probably the most pricey place in Lecce, Borgo Antico is a tiny restaurant, again specialising in fish. Dine in refined rusticity on Gallipoli-inspired dishes such as *maccheroncino* with prawns and clams or potato gnocchi with shrimps.

DRINKING

Lecce is a university town so as you'd expect there's more than enough pubs and winebars to keep you occupied.

Cafés

Caffè Alvino (☎ 0832 24 74 36; Piazza Sant'Oronzo 30) At the time of research this Lecce institution was closed – sold to the jewellers next door. But we've been reliably informed that it will reopen as a café some time in the near future. In the meantime its local clientele have decamped to modern **Mi Svago** (Piazza Sant'Oronzo 22; cocktails €5) next door, which is more of a bar than a café. Try the *espressino freddo*, a delicious variation on espresso which is served cold with *fiore di latte* (literally 'flower of the milk', fresh mozzarella).

All'Ombra dell'Barocco (☎ 0832 24 26 26; Corte dei Cicala; 🕑 8am-1am) Browse for books and then sit down for a quiet read in the bookshops outdoor café. Tables fill the square and give you a frontline view of the *corso* – an ideal place to watch the world go by. Service is slow enough for you to get through a good book.

ourpick Caffè Letterario (☎ 0832 24 23 51; www .caffeletterario.org in Italian; Via Paladini 48; 🕑 8am-1.30am) A literary café stuffed with books, comics and magazines; it hosts an interesting programme of lectures, book signings and concerts. All you have to do to become a member is donate a book.

Bars

Although most of Lecce's bars are on the south side of Piazza Sant'Oronzo along Via Augusto Imperature, there are a couple of gems tucked away north of the *corso*.

Joyce (☎ 0832 27 94 43; Via Matteo da Lecce 5; ⏱ 3pm-midnight) A winebar-cum-Irish pub which serves up Guinness, Kilkenny and Harp. In winter it is a great cosy place to drink, and it's a firm favourite on the student circuit.

Trumpet (Via Principi di Savoia; meals €12; ⏱ 8pm-2am Tue-Sun) Another good drinking den popular with the football crowd because of its enormous wide-screen TV. It starts to fill up with regulars around 10.30pm. Aside from the huge glasses of wine (€2.50), you can get an excellent meal here. The grilled steak, potatoes and salad is more than enough for two people.

ENTERTAINMENT

Teatro Politeama Greco (☎ 0832 24 14 68; Via XXV Luglio 30) Lecce's only real theatre and the most important in the Salentine, the Teatro Greco hosts an interesting programme of theatre exploring Pugliese and Salentine issues and traditions. It also stages opera and classical concerts.

SHOPPING

Lecce's streets are lined with pretty boutiques, well-stocked bookshops and inviting delicatessens. The city is most famous for its tradition of papier-mâché and *pietra Leccese* (sculpture using the local Leccese stone), both of which you can find in small studios all over town. A whole variety of *cartapesta* (papier-mâché) studios fill the streets leading to the Duomo and along Corso Vittorio Emanuele II.

La Bottega del Corso (☎ 0832 24 98 66; Via Libertini 52) A well-stocked deli full of typical produce and freshly baked breads.

Olio Claudio (☎ 0832 82 29 04; www.olioclaudio.com; Via Principi di Savoia 43) This small oil-packed shop is where to head for some classy olive oil. A litre costs from €3.50.

Valentina (☎ 0832 30 05 49; Via Petronelli 3) The most famous deli in Lecce. You can get almost anything here from typical Salentine pastas to artichokes pickled in chilli and buttermilk curd and cheese.

GETTING THERE & AWAY

Bus

It is easier and more convenient to travel by train to towns in the vicinity of Lecce. For long-distance travel the bus is a better op-tion as they're faster and don't involve any changes.

STP (☎ 0832 22 84 41; www.stplecce.it in Italian) runs buses connecting Lecce with towns throughout the Salentine Peninsula, including Santa Maria di Leuca (€2, two hours), Galatina (€1.50, one hour 15 minutes) and Brindisi (€2, 45 minutes, two daily), departing from Via Adua. You can buy tickets from the newsagent outside the main station or at Via Adua 18.

FSE (☎ 0832 66 81 11) runs buses to towns including Gallipoli (€2.30, one hour, four daily), Otranto (€2.60, one hour, two daily) and Taranto (€6.80, two hours, three Monday to Saturday) leaving from Via Torre del Parco.

Car & Motorcycle

The *autostrada* only really extends as far as Bari (either the A14 from Bologna or the A2/A16 from Rome). From Bari you'll need to take the SS16 to Lecce via Monopoli and Brindisi. From Taranto take the SS7.

From Lecce, the fastest route south to Santa Maria di Leuca is the SS16, although the coast road south of Otranto is very scenic and lightly trafficked out of season.

Train

Two lines operate out of Lecce, **Trenitalia** (www.trenitalia.com) and the very old **Ferrovie Sud-Est** (www.fseonline.it), which services towns to the south. You can buy tickets for the main Trenitalia services (Brindisi, Bari, Rome etc) in the main station. The ticket office for the FSE line is on platform 1.

Frequent Intercity and Eurostar trains head to Brindisi (€2.30 to €5, 40 minutes), Bari (€8.60 to €12, 2¼ hours) and even Rome (€45 to €48, five to seven hours). For Naples (€30 to €48, six hours), change in Caserta, Benevento or Foggia.

FSE trains depart for Otranto (€2.30, one hour), Galatina (€1.80, 30 minutes), Gallipoli (€3.40, one hour) and Martina Franca (€6.30, two hours). There are no services on Sunday when a bus replacement service operates. Buy tickets in the FSE office the day before or in the newsagent outside the station.

Between 16 June and 9 September there is a special schedule of trains and buses, **Salento in Treno e Bus** (www.salentointrenoebus.it), connecting Lecce with the smaller towns and beaches in the province. This way you can reach places like Porto Cesareo, which are impossible to reach without a car in the low season.

GETTING AROUND

The historic centre of Lecce is best seen on foot. However, if you are staying for an extended period of time you may want to hire a bike.

To/From the Airport

The nearest airport to Lecce is Brindisi, 40km to the northwest. There is an airport shuttle but it is only scheduled to link up with Alitalia flights so if you're flying with another carrier you may find yourself hanging around for hours. The airport bus costs €5 and departs from Viale Porta d'Europa.

Bicycle

Forcignanò (☎ 0832 30 60 62; Piazza d'Italia 2/3) at Porta San Biagio hires out bikes for €1.50/10 per hour/day.

Bus

Among others, buses 1, 2 and 4 run from the train station to Viale Marconi.

Car & Motorcycle

The whole of the historic centre is now subject to traffic control, which means that you can't drive or park within the city walls unless you have a permit. Most B&Bs will provide you with one if you want to park close to your accommodation. Be sure to ask before you arrive.

Out of season it's worth considering car hire for a day or two if you want to visit some of the surrounding towns and beaches. **Rent a Smart** (www.rentasmart.it) has some good deals and the cars are ideal for parking.

THE GREEK SALENTINE

The Greek Salentine is a historical oddity, left over from a time when the Byzantine Empire controlled southern Italy and Greek culture was the order of the day. It is a cluster of nine towns – Calimera, Castrignano dei Greci, Corigliano d'Otranto, Martano, Martignano, Melpignano, Soleto, Sternatia and Zollino – in the heart of Terra d'Otranto.

Why this pocket of Puglia has retained its Greek heritage is not altogether clear. The Salento, like much of Southern Italy, was heavily colonised by Ancient Greeks and Basilian monks fleeing the iconoclastic policies of Emperor Leon III (717–41). They arrived in the region establishing their Orthodox churches and monasteries, the largest of which was Sant'Nicola di Casole in Otranto. Greek became the language of learning and the Greek Orthodox rite was practised throughout the Salento. Although Bari, the last Byzantine outpost, fell to the Normans in 1071, the Normans took a fairly laissez-faire attitude to the Latinisation of Puglia. Greek continued to be spoken and the Orthodox rite celebrated. With the fall of Constantinople in 1453 more Greeks and Albanians arrived in Puglia, bolstering the local populations and revitalising the flagging Greek communities, and so *griko* survived although the Orthodox rite was only abandoned in the 17th century.

Even today local traditions, folklore and the remnants of the *griko* dialect are preserved. If you're in the region at the end of March (25 March to 1 April), you'll be able to catch the **Canti di Passione** (Chants of Passion; www.cantidipassione .it), an international music festival linked to the Easter rites, where artists and confraternities from all over the Mediterranean celebrate the Passion of Christ.

However, the biggest event, and possibly the biggest festival in the entire Salentine Peninsula, occurs from 11 to 26 August in tiny **Melpignano**. The **Notte della Taranta** (Night of the Taranta; www.lanottedellataranta.it) is a massive celebration of traditional *pizzica* music, once used as a form of faith healing to cure women apparently poisoned by the local tarantulas (see the boxed text, p154). All-night concerts are held in each of the different towns, culminating in the mother of all parties in Melpignano in front of the backlit **Convento degli Agostiniani**.

Melpignano acts as something of a hub so for further information on the Greek towns call in at the **Municipio** (☎ 0836 33 21 61; www .comune.melpignano.le.it; Via Garibaldi 2). Between June and September there is an information point next to the Convento degli Agostiniani where you can pick up free bikes.

GALATINA

pop 27,700

Nowhere is the Salentine's Greek past so evident than in the town of Galatina, 18km south of Lecce. It is almost the only place where the ritual of tarantism is still remembered. The *taranta* folk dance evolved from it, and each year on the feast day of SS Peter and Paul the ritual is performed at the (now deconsecrated) church dedicated to the saints.

SPIDER MUSIC

Tarantism is a very peculiar aspect of Pugliese culture. It was believed that field workers who were bitten by one of the region's tarantulas would then be held in thrall by the spider's song, its *cantum tempore*.

The different responses that people had to the spider's bite – nausea, headaches, livid complexion, paroxysms of laughter or tears, paranoia or a state of listless abjection – were commonly believed to reflect the different characteristics of the offending spider. To purge the venom, musicians attempted to evoke cadences that matched the music of the spider. The lively *panno rosso*, the wistful *panno verde* and the slow and staggering *spallata* were some of the melodies that were performed.

Although a public experiment carried out in 1693 by Bernardo Clarizio illustrated that the tarantula's bite was, in fact, far from fatal, it wasn't until the 1740s, when Francesco Serao published his *Della Tarantola,* that the medical community began to seriously question the belief. But such scientific questioning was a long way from popular belief and during the same period the chapel of St Paul in Galatina, where the waters were meant to have been blessed by Paul (himself miraculously immune to venomous bites), was growing in fame as the spiritual refuge for the *tarantati*.

When the religious historian Ernesto De Martino came to Galatina in July of 1959, he was highly critical of the way scholarship had blithely turned tarantism into a 'hysterical malady'. Over the course of three weeks, De Martino observed and interviewed more than 30 of the *tarantati* who attended the chapel. What he believed he found was not a magical cure for a poisonous bite but some serious psychological disorders.

The young girl, Maria di Nardó, for example, had lost her father at 13 and been raised by her aunt and uncle. She was first 'bitten' at 18, when, because of her poor social standing, the family of her fiancé opposed marriage. Finding herself cast out and condemned to a life of hopeless poverty, she became a bride of St Paul, taking mystic succour from her yearly abandonment at the feast of SS Peter and Paul in Galatina. The *taranta* was never the real story: the spider, the bite and St Paul were, for De Martino, simply symbols in a psychic drama that allowed individuals to express their pent-up desires, hopes and unresolved grief.

Galatina is the location of one of the Salento's most beautiful artistic treasures, the frescoed interior of the Basilica di Santa Caterina, which is certainly worth the trip in itself.

Orientation & Information

From the train station head directly south down Corso Re d'Italia, past the museum, to arrive at the central Piazza Dante Alighieri. The south side of the square merges with Piazza San Pietro, the main *piazza* of the historic centre, which is lined with cafés and has metered parking.

From here walk southeast down Corso Vittorio Emanuele II for the **Tourist Office** (☎ 0836 56 99 84 Via Vittorio Emanuele II, 35; ⏲ 9.30am-12.30pm & 3.30-6.30pm), where you can pick up a free bike for the day, and then south again down Via Umberto for St Catherine's Basilica.

Sights

Galatina is a regal town, with a refined and faded atmosphere. Hardly surprising given

that it was held in fee by Raimondello Orsini del Balzo, the most powerful lord in the Salentine. A man of apparently passionate beliefs, he journeyed to Sinai to pay his respects to the remains of St Catherine. Before departing he bent to kiss her hand and rather impiously bit off one of her fingers, which he neatly pocketed and took home to Galatina. On his arrival, in 1383, he ordered the construction of one of the Salento's most remarkable churches, the **Basilica di Santa Caterina d'Alessandria** (⏲ 8am-12.30pm & 4.30-6.45pm Apr-Sep, 8am-12.30pm & 3.45-5.45pm Oct-Mar), to house his purloined relic.

It's a good tale but the real story behind the church is much more mundane. In the 14th century the Salentines were still practising Orthodox rituals and Pope Boniface IX was not impressed, so he sent forth his Franciscans to 'Latinise' the wayward south. The basilica and convent were built to house the Franciscan order in Galatina. Although started by Raimondello, the real treasures of the church, its glorious frescoes, were commissioned by his wife, Marie d'Enghien de Brienne.

No one knows who Marie's artists were; they could have been itinerant painters down from Le Marche and Emilia, or southerners who had been sent north to absorb the latest Renaissance innovations (the Giotto influence is clear to see). Whoever they were, they covered the interior of the basilica with a unique series of frescoes depicting stories from the Old and New Testament. It's articulated into three distinct bays with huge wide drop arches, and each bay tells a different set of biblical stories. The counter façade and the first span depict scenes from the Apocalypse; the second, stories from Genesis, with a pot-bellied Adam and Eve disobeying God and taking that fateful bite of the fruit; and the third bay is a transcendent series of images from the life of Christ, culminating in a cross-vault crowded with golden angels. Also of interest, for their lifelike detail, are the series of images from Mary's life in the south aisle and the cycle of 17 frescoes devoted to the life of St Catherine in the presbytery.

The basilica is a hard act to follow for any museum, and it has to be said the **Museo Civico d'Arte Pietro Cavoti** (☎ 0836 56 15 68; www.museocavoti .it; Piazza Dante Alighieri 51; admission free; ☺ 9.30am-1pm Mon-Fri, 4.30-8pm Tue, Thu & Sat) pales in comparison. The museum was founded in the name of Pietro Cavoti (1819–90), a contemporary of Sigismondo Castromediano (of Lecce museum fame), and one of a bunch of Galatina scholars. It showcases his collection of notebooks, prints and watercolours alongside the earthy sculpture of Gaetano Martinez (1892–1951) and work by other Galatina notables.

Festivals

Now a solemn religious occasion, the **Festa di SS Pietro e Paolo** (28 to 30 June) was once one of the most bizarre events in the Puglian calendar. *Tarantati* (victims of a tarantula bite) travelled to Galatina every year to dance themselves into a cathartic trance. The next day they would go to be blessed in the church of SS Peter and Paul (see the boxed text, opposite).

Sleeping

There is limited accommodation in Galatina although there is the very good **Hotel Palazzo Baldi** (☎ 0836 56 83 45; www.hotelpalazzobaldi.com in Italian; Via Corte Baldi 2; s €50-125, d €80-200; ⓟ ⚙). It is perhaps slightly over-romantic, the air heavy

with floral air-freshener, and rooms are kitted out with come-hither beds and heavy swagged curtains. Still, it's located right in the centre of town in a nicely restored *palazzo*. Parking costs an additional €11.

Shopping

Galatina now makes its living from winemaking, and there are a couple of big producers like **Santi Dimitri** (☎ 0836 56 58 66; www.santidimitri.it; ☺ 8am-1pm & 4-7pm Mon-Fri, 8am-1pm Sat) where you can purchase wine and olive oil.

Another shop worth visiting in the centre of Galatina is Luigi Salvatore's **Latticini** (Via Vittorio Emanuele II, 16), a cheese cooperative that sells the cheese of local producers.

Getting There & Away

FSE runs regular trains between Galatina and Lecce (€1.30, 30 minutes, hourly) from Monday to Saturday. On Sunday there is a bus replacement service.

THE IONIAN COAST

Apart from the endless sunshine, fabulous food and easy-going southern charm, why do Italians love the Salento? Drive along the Ionian coast south of Lecce and you'll see – miles and miles of soft, sandy beaches that make this stretch of coastline the best beach resort in the whole country.

PORTO CESAREO

During the 1970s Porto Cesareo was a tiny, wind-whipped beach with a motley collection of fishermen's houses. But the booming tourism industry coupled with local corruption have since done their best to destroy what was a pretty nice piece of coastline, as row upon row of illegal holiday homes now threaten to choke the life out of this place. In summer, when the population more than quadruples in size and the days and nights merge into one long beach party, its easy to overlook the aesthetic scars, but come out of season and you'll be greeted by the depressing sight of shuttered breeze-block houses with tumbleweed blowing in between.

Rather miraculously, the centre of Porto Cesareo manages to retain some vestiges of charm, with colourful fishing boats bobbing in the small bay. In summer (June to September) you can take the yellow boat taxi out to the Isola dei Conchigli, or hire a pedalo and muck around the bay. Given its view over the bay, the lemon-yellow **Hotel Falli** (☎ 0833 56 90 82; www.hotelfalli.com; Riviera di Ponente 16; s €50-75, d €70-160; P ✖) is one of the nicest places to be.

If you're looking for something more beachy, try the **Conchiglia Azzurra** (☎ 0833 56 63 11; www.conchigliaazzurra.com; Via dei Bacini 1; s €61-116, d €90-200; ✖ ▯), a big boxy hotel with its own private lido. **L'Angolo di Beppe** (☎ 0833 56 53 31; www.angolodibeppe.it; Via Zanella 24; meals €35; ✦ Tue-Sun) is a good place for creative seafood.

The wide, curved bay is family-friendly and it's a good place to scuba dive as it's been a protected marine reserve since 1997. There are several dive outlets in town, including **Centro Subacqueo Sasà Sub** (☎ 338 822 80 56; www .sasasubdivingcenter.com; Piazza Nazario Sauro 32) along the main *lungomare* near all the fish shops. The small **tourist office** (☎ 0833 56 90 86; Piazzale A de Gasperi 36; ✦ 10am-noon & 7-9pm) is also on the seafront.

PARCO REGIONALE PORTO SELVAGGIO

Drive south along the SP286 out of holiday hell, and you'll quickly leave the hotel residences behind for some bosky Mediterranean coastline. There's a quieter beach at Torre Isidoro but the real belle of the coastline is the **Parco Regionale Porto Selvaggio** (www.portoselvaggio .net in Italian), a protected area of rocky coastline covered with umbrella pines, eucalyptus trees and olives. There are walking trails amid the trees and you can print off a fairly decent map from the website. Right in the middle of the park is the elegant **Santa Caterina**, a quiet seaside centre.

The rocky shore around Santa Caterina is full of grottoes and is another great place for diving. Between May and October, **Costa del**

Sud Diving Centre (☎ 335 527 38 23; www.costadelsud .it; Via Lungomare 6) runs courses and hires out gear. Between February and May the strong currents around here also make this a popular kite-surfing spot.

If you're here between October and May you'll need you own car to see any of this. The coastal bus service, **Salento in Treno e Bus** (www.salentotrenoebus.it), only runs between June and September.

GALLIPOLI

pop 20,900

Kallipolis, the 'beautiful city' of the Greeks, may be a faded beauty now, but it still retains its island charm. The Salentines see it as a kind of southern Portofino, and its weathered white *borgo* has a kind of grungy chic: part fishing village, part fashion model.

In the 16th and 17th centuries Gallipoli was one of the richest towns in the Salento, exporting its famous olive oil to Naples, Paris and London, where it was used to illuminate the streets of nearly every major European capital. That explains the rather elegant air of the old town, which is divided into two distinct halves: the patrician quarter which housed the wealthy merchant class to the north of Via Antonietta de Pace and the popular quarter with its rabbit-warren of streets to the south.

Orientation & Information

Gallipoli's old town is on an island connected to the mainland by a causeway so all roads eventually converge on Corso Roma, the central artery of the new town. Corso Roma heads west and then bottlenecks over a narrow bridge onto the island where a one-way system operates right-to-left around the old town.

THE GOOD LIFE

In 2003, having spent years working in Milan, Amedeo and Giuseppe took the scary decision to pack up, move south and run a sustainable, organic olive farm. They bought 14 hectares of olives just outside Cutrofiano and spent the next four years setting up the farm **Piccapane** (☎ 0836 54 91 96; www.piccapane.it; Contrada Spadafore, Cutrofiano), where they now produce grains, pastas and two varieties of olive oil: the robust Cellina and the slightly fruity-tasting Leccino.

Piccapane is currently joining the **World Wide Organisation of Organic Farming** (www.wwoof .org) so you may have the chance to go and pick its olives all by yourself. Alternatively, you could just pop along to one of the farmers markets that take place on the last Sunday of every month. Phone ahead to ask about where and when the next one takes place.

To reach Piccapane take the road from Cutrafiano to Aradeo and turn off to Sogliano. You'll then find the driveway on your left-hand side.

The **tourist office** (☎ 0833 26 25 29; Piazza Imbriani 9; 🕑 9am-1pm Mon-Fri, 3-6pm Tue & Thu, longer hr in summer) is just over the bridge although it keeps very erratic hours. If it's closed try the **Pro Loco** (☎ 0833 26 30 07; www.prolocogallipoli.it; Via Kennedy; 🕑 8.30am-1.30pm & 3.30-8.30pm). You'll find plenty of banks along Corso Roma and the **post office** (☎ 0833 26 17 76) on Via Genova.

A useful internet resource is www.salentosummer.com, which has all the most up-to-date info on the beaches and summer activities.

Sights

Originally Gallipoli was an island, which explains the landward-facing position of its squat Angevin **castle**. Opposite the castle, just below the bridge, is the town's **fish market** (🕑 6am-9am), still an important business for the city today and well worth getting up to see at least once during your stay.

Also worth seeing is the **Frantoio Ipogeo** (☎ 0833 26 42 42; Via Antonietta de Pace; 🕑 10am-noon & 4-6pm), only one of some 35 olive presses buried in the tufa rock below the town. It's here that they pressed Gallipoli's olive oil, which was then stored in one of the 2000 cisterns carved out beneath the old town.

With all the spare cash floating around and a fairly pretentious merchant class, Gallipoli could afford to splash out on some nice civic design and on the island there are no less than 14 churches, including the baroque **Basilica di Sant'Agata** (☎ 0833 26 19 87; Via Antonietta de Pace; 🕑 services only) and numerous smaller churches devoted to different saints. The best of these are the **Chiesa della Purità** (Riviera N Sauro; 🕑 closed for renovation) with its stuccoed interior and 18th-century majolica-tiled floor, and the **Chiesa di San Francesco** (Riviera N Sauro; 🕑 services only), the oldest church in the historic centre, famous for Vespasiano Genuino's wooden carving of the *Two Thieves*.

Gallipoli also has a small **Museo Civico** (☎ 0833 26 42 24; Via Antonietta de Pace 51; admission €1; 🕑 10am-1pm & 3.30-6.30pm Mon-Fri, 10am-1pm Sat, 4-7pm Sun) with a jumbled collection of antiquities and ethnographic curiosities – no labels, no fuss.

Activities

Gallipoli's beaches stretch in great curves both north and south of town. To the north is the **Lido Conchiglie** and the disco quarter, but it's south you want to go, to the long sandy stretch of **Baia Verde**. Between September and May the lidos (managed sections of beach with umbrellas and beds) are closed so you can enjoy the beach pretty much all to yourself for free.

In May things start to crank up, the beach is raked to perfection and the lidos are renovated and repainted ready for the hectic summer months. Gallipoli's best lidos are **Punta della Suina** (www.puntadellasuina.it) and, further south, the super-pretty **Lido Pizzo** (www.lidopizzo.it), backed by whispering pine trees. A day at the beach with umbrella and beds will usually cost around €20 to €25. There's also the tiny **La Purita** beach on Gallipoli island.

For boat trips up and down the coast you'll find a mobile info point just by the bridge to the old town. **Salento in Barco** (☎ 347 371 05 72; www.salentoinbarcagallipoli.com) run trips up and down the coast to Porto Cesareo and Santa Maria di Leuca. Boats depart around 11am and return at 7pm.

Festivals

Gallipoli's **Holy Week** (Easter) processions are on a par with those of Taranto. Hooded penitents carry statues of the Madonna and Christ through the narrow streets dressed in blood-red robes, wearing crowns of thorns.

Sleeping

Gallipoli has a good selection of hotels and rental apartments. It gets extremely busy in summer so you'd be well advised to book in advance.

ourpick **Baia di Gallipoli** (☎ 0833 27 32 10; www.baiadigallipoli.com; Litoranea per Santa Maria di Leuca; tents €5-14.50, car €2-4, camper €7-17, 2-person bungalow €45-80; 🕑 May-Sep; ℗ 🏊) A luxury camp site if ever there was one, with a pool, tennis courts, regular shuttles to the beach, bicycle hire, a disco, supermarket and a laundrette. The site is in a shady spot set back from the road 8km south of Gallipoli near all the best beaches.

ourpick **La Casa del Mare** (☎ 0833 26 13 68; www.lacasadelmare.com; Piazza de Amicis 14; s €30-50, d €60-100; 🌐 🖳) A 16th-century merchant's palace that has been lovingly restored. It's run by Frederico, a demon host, who has even been known to load his guests into his car and party all night with them at the Notte della Taranta. The three rooms on the 1st floor, with their huge comfy beds and traditional furnishings, are the ones to go for.

B&B La Riviera (☎ 0833 26 10 96; www.bedandbreakfastlariviera.com; d €60-120; 🌐) Overlooking the sea wall, La Riviera is the kind of place you could

BRINDISI & THE SALENTO

GALLIPOLI

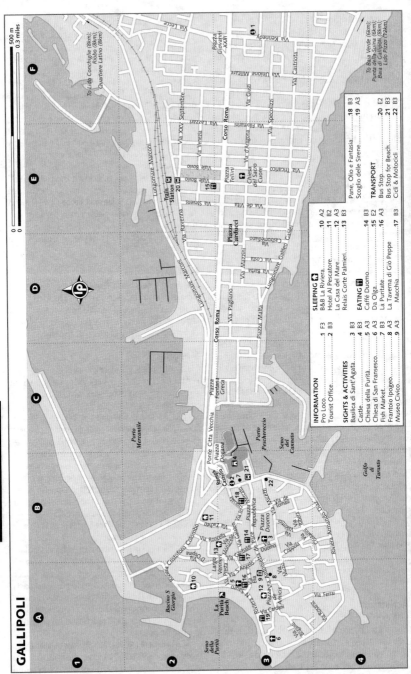

INFORMATION	
Pro Loco	1 F3
Tourist Office	2 B3

SIGHTS & ACTIVITIES	
Basilica di Sant'Agata	3 B3
Castle	4 B3
Chiesa della Purità	5 A3
Chiesa di San Fransesco	6 A3
Fish Market	7 B3
Frantoio Ipogeo	8 A3
Museo Civico	9 A3

SLEEPING	
B&B La Riviera	10 A2
Hotel Al Pescatore	11 B2
La Casa del Mare	12 A3
Relais Corte Palmieri	13 B3

EATING	
Caffè Duomo	14 B3
Da Olga	15 E2
La Puritate	16 A3
La Taverna di Gio Peppe	17 B3
Macchia	18 B3
Pane, Olio e Fantasia	18 B3
Scoglio delle Sirene	19 A3

TRANSPORT	
Bus Stop	20 E2
Bus Stop for Beach	21 B3
Cicli & Motocicli	22 B3

imagine an elegant and impecunious maiden aunt visiting for a spot of sea air. The rooms are decorated with romantic murals and furnished with faux antiques, and have great sea views.

Hotel Al Pescatore (☎ /fax 0833 26 36 56; Riviera Colombo 39; s €60-90, d €100-180; 🅿) A tired hotel in a handsome old *palazzo*. Rooms are no-frills but some of them have great sea views, and they're all cool and comfortable in summer. In winter they're just bare and cold. Half-board is compulsory during August and September (€90 per person). There's a decent restaurant downstairs (meals €25).

Relais Corte Palmieri (☎ /fax 0833 26 25 63; www .relaiscortepalmieri.it; Corte Palmieri 3; s €90-170, d €120-200; 🅿 🖳) White-on-white décor with strong splashes of colour give the Corte Palmieri a slightly Greek-island feel. It's run by the Palazzo del Corso chain so you can expect professional service. The best feature is the roof terrace that overlooks the old town.

Eating

Fish, fish, fish – that's what Gallipoli is all about, and people travel from far and wide to eat here, although they also complain about Portofino-style prices.

Da Olga (☎ 0833 26 19 82; Viale Bovio; meals €25) A big rowdy restaurant near the train station, well known for its good prices, large portions and tasty *frittura* (mixed fried fish). It's a no-fuss dining room with an open kitchen and in summer there is outdoor seating.

Scoglio delle Sirene (☎ 0833 26 10 91; Riviera N Sauro 83; meals €25; 🕒 Wed-Mon) With tables out on the ramparts overlooking Purita beach, this restaurant couldn't get much closer to the sea if it tried. The kitchen is devoted to all things marine: mussels with gorgonzola, macaroni with prawns and mint, and great big lobsters that you have to do battle with. The word is, if you can't afford La Puritate, come here instead.

ourpick La Taverna di Giò Peppe Macchia (☎ 0833 26 17 56; Via Garibaldi 7; meals €30; 🕒 Thu-Tue) Of all the restaurants in the historic centre, Peppe Macchia stands out for its style and originality. Traditional favourites like the seafood antipasti are combined with original recipes mixing fish and vegetables. Try the signature dish, the tagliolini with swordfish and *rucola* pesto.

ourpick La Puritate (☎ 0833 26 42 05; Via S Elia 18; meals €45; 🕒 Thu-Tue) By general consensus the

finest restaurant in Gallipoli. Situated next to the church of the Puritate, this elegant dining room is all high-backed chairs and linen tablecloths. The menu is accomplished and includes some more unusual offerings like *scapece gallipolino* (sardines or anchovies marinated in vinegar and saffron and tossed in breadcrumbs).

If you're all fished out try the very good **Pane, Olio e Fantasia** (☎ 0833 26 17 79; Piazza della Repubblica; meals €20; 🕒 8-11pm Fri & Sat, lunch Sun & hols). It can look very empty but that's no reflection on the food, it just shows how fish-mad this town is. For good Gallipoli *spumone*, go to **Caffè Duomo** (Via A de Pace 72), where you can also get good ice cream.

Entertainment

Outside the summer season the bigger discos are only open on Friday and Saturday and sometimes one night during the week if they have a special gig. Admission costs around €20, which usually includes one drink.

Gallipoli's most stylish venue is **Riobo** (www .riobodiscoteca.it; Strada Provinciale, Lido Conchiglie; 🕒 Wed, Fri & Sat), a huge club set around a turquoise blue pool. Another tried and tested favourite is Gallipoli's oldest disco, **Quartiere Latino** (☎ 0833 20 94 27; www.quartierelatino.com; Pineta del Lido Conchiglie; 🕒 Thu-Sat). Things don't get going until 11pm and it stays open until the early morning.

Getting There & Around

FSE trains link Gallipoli to Lecce (€3.40, one hour) and Galatina (€1.80, 40 minutes). If you want head to Otranto you'll need to take a train to either Zollino or Maglie and change there. Train services only run from Monday to Saturday with a bus replacement service on Sunday. For Porto Cesareo you need to take a train to Nardò and change there. Between June and September the **Salento in Treno e Bus** (www.salentointrenoebus.it) service puts on additional services.

Buses for the beach make the round of the island and take about 15 minutes to reach the beach. Between June and September metered parking operates at the beach between 9am and 1pm and 3pm and 7pm. An hour's parking costs €1.50 or €6 per day. The historic centre is also a car-free zone between 10 June and 10 September.

You can hire bikes and scooters from **Cicli & Motocicli** (☎ 347 685 67 26; Riviera A Diaz 119). They cost €4 and €25 per day respectively.

WORTH A TRIP

our pick **A Casa Tu Martinu** (☎ 0833 91 36 52; www.acasatumartinu.com; Via Corsica 95; meals €25-30, s €45, d €80-95; ☺ Tue-Sun) A classic hostelry in the tiny village of Taviano. The 18th-century house, with its flagstone floors and cool vaulted ceilings, is a picture of rustic chic, the tables laid with checked tablecloths, the walls hung with old pots and pans. Between June and September you'll be lucky to get a table here, such is its reputation. If you do get a table be prepared to spend a long time savouring the delectable antipasti (tiny rondels of aubergine loaded with bright red pomodorini), the homemade pastas (cavatelli with veal, pepperoni and tomatoes) and succulent cuts of meat. On summer evenings opt for a table in the candlelit patio under the heady scent of trailing jasmine. Well-appointed rooms are also available and provide a good alternative to the more expensive places on the coast.

SOUTH OF GALLIPOLI

Sandy beaches and seaside resorts strung between dozens of medieval watchtowers meander all the way south of Gallipoli to Santa Maria di Leuca. It's a great scenic trip and between February and May this sunny road is a biker's heaven. The absolute best beach along the coast is right down south at the **Marina di Pescoluse**, known more fondly to the locals as Le Maldives.

Inland, tiny villages sit amid the olive groves and vineyards, some of which are worth a detour. In **Casarano**, for example, you can take a peak at the oldest Christian mosaics in Puglia in the **Chiesa di Santa Maria della Croce** (Via IV Novembre), and in **Patù** you'll find one of the most sophisticated megalithic monuments, the **Centropietre** opposite the church of San Giovanni. Further inland, **Specchia**, with its buttery buildings and well-kept *piazza*, is one of the prettiest villages in the Salento, well worth an amble with an ice cream.

There are more good beaches at **Ugento Marina**, and you can stay nearby in the stylish **Masseria Don Cirillo** (☎ 0832 30 35 06; www.kalekora.it; Torre San Giovanni, Ugento; s €95-150, d €140-250; ☺ Apr-Sep; Ⓟ ✖ ☎).

SANTA MARIA DI LEUCA

When you reach the resort town of Santa Maria di Leuca, you've hit the bottom of the heel of Italy and the dividing line between the Adriatic and Ionian Seas. The Romans called this *finibus terrae*, the end of the earth, and the spot is marked by the **Chiesa di Santa Maria di Leuca**, an important place of pilgrimage built over an older Roman temple dedicated to Minerva.

Santa Maria, with its Gothic- and Liberty-style villas, is a holiday resort pure and simple. In summer it throngs with people parading along the waterfront and clicking pictures at the sanctuary. Many people come here to take one of the boat trips to visit the sea grottoes like the **Grotta del Diavolo**, the **Grotta della Stalla** and the **Grotta Grande di Ciolo**. Trips depart from the little *porto* between June and September. **Piccola Nautica** (☎ 0833 75 81 84; www.piccolonautica.it; Porto Vecchio di Leuca) runs trips and hires boats.

If you're more serious about sailing then consider spending a week with the sailing school, **Smarè** (☎ 0833 75 81 10; www.centronauticosmare.it; Via Doppia Croce). It runs courses for both children and adults. A five-day course, with four hours sailing a day costs around €130 for under-15s and €160-180 for adults. Great day charters on beautiful sail boats are also offered, where you can spend all day drifting up the coast. If you're interested in diving in the grottoes contact **Diving & Service** (☎ 0833 71 14 39, 335 584 60 92; www.divingservice.it; Lungomare C Colombo).

Eating, Sleeping & Entertainment

Villa Ramirez (☎ 0833 75 35 98; villaramirez@libero.it; Lungomare Cristoforo Colombo; s €40-160, d €60-160; Ⓟ ✖ 🖵) is a sweet B&B right on the seafront. It has five sunny rooms, kitted out with Sky and wi-fi, and there are even PlayStations for the kids. The higher prices only apply to two weeks in mid-August, otherwise it's very reasonable.

Alternatively, head inland to the charming **Agriturismo Alcorico** (☎ 0833 54 73 91; www.agriturismoalcorico.com; d €70-150; ☺ May-Sep; Ⓟ ✖ ☎). It's situated high above the coast amid unspoilt farmland and offers comfortable accommodation in its low-lying stone farmhouse. It's also a popular place for Sunday lunch (meals €30). You'll find the signpost 2 to 3km north from Santa Maria on the SS173.

In case anyone's thinking that Puglia's just all farms and fishing villages, spend an evening at swanky **Gibò** (☎ 0833 54 89 79; www

.gibo.it; Località Ponte Ciolo; admission €25-30). It attracts a beautiful crowd to its smart restaurant and live gigs, and you can understand why when you see the spectacular sea views from the terrace. From mid-July to 20 August it's open every night; and in June, early July and September it's open at the weekends. In July and August it is best to book ahead to be sure of getting in. You'll find it 6km north of Santa Maria on the SS173.

ADRIATIC COAST

Where the Ionian coast is spattered with reasonable beaches, the Adriatic side rears up in rocky cliffs covered with maquis, and precariously positioned coastal towns. It's a beautiful coastline, as yet almost totally unspoilt by development, the local stone houses sitting pretty against a background of Mediterranean greenery.

CASTRO & AROUND

Almost midway between Santa Maria and Otranto is the town of **Castro** and its marina. It's another boating and diving hub as the rocky coastline around it is riddled with seacaves. Most famous of all is the **Grotta Zinzulusa** (☎ 0836 94 38 12; Castro Marina; admission €3.50; ☼ 10am-4.30pm Oct-May, 9.30am-7pm Jun-Aug), filled with stalactites that hang like sharp daggers from the ceiling. It can only be visited on a guided tour and in summer it gets very, very busy (nearly 150,000 tourists come through here every year!).

Nearby is the more famous but inaccessible **Grotta Romanelli**, with its priceless prehistoric graffiti, paintings and engravings of animals like the wild ox that date back some 11,000 years. There are plenty of other grottoes to visit in the vicinity and from July to September boat trips run from Castro Marina up and down the coast. **Nautica Red Coral** (☎ 340 830 11 72; www.nauticaredcoral.it; Porto Vecchio) hires out boats ranging from €70 to €90 for half a day and €160 to €180 for a whole day. Out of season it's still possible to book a trip or rent a boat but you need to book in advance. Divers should contact Salvatore at **DWD Diving** (☎ 0836 92 12 76, 339 254 90 04, www.divingdwddiso.it; Via Pastorizza 20, Castro Marina). A single dive costs €30 (€50 for two people) and an Open Water divers course costs €300. If you just want to rent some gear it costs €25.

Barely 10km up the coast from Castro is the thermal spa of **Santa Maria Cesarea Terme**. Like Santa Maria di Leuca it boasts a number of large Liberty-style villas, reminiscent of the days when spa-going was all the rage. There are still some huge hotels that cater to the summer crowds of Italians who come to bathe in the thermal spas. But don't have visions of stylish hammams and soothing massages; here spa-going is a serious medical business and the **Terme di Santa Cesarea** is a fusty old hospital with a lingering smell of sulphur about it.

The main town of Castro is set back from the coast and is a nice little town with a Romanesque cathedral and a big medieval castle. You'll find www.castro.it a useful web resource. The main bus connection from Castro is to Maglie.

Sleeping & Entertainment

ourpick **Macchia di Pele** (☎ 328 356 74 60; www .macchiadipele.it; Litoranea Castro-Santa Cesareo; d with shared bathroom 45-60, d with bathroom €58-85; **P**), Amedeo's and Nancy's friendly B&B, is one of the best value accommodation options on the coast. Set high above the sea, the traditional stone built house commands fabulous views, a view shared by three of five rooms. As this is their home you can expect great personal service and they're full of ideas for excursions as Amedeo keeps in touch with local trekking and cycling groups like **Cea** (☎ 0836 92 60 41, 328 725 32 22; www.ceadian drano.org) and **Avanguardia** (www.avanguardie.net). If you don't have a car get the train to Poggiardo and they'll come and pick you up.

Castro has its own summer club scene, with August nights just one long party. The best disco is **Blue Bay** (☎ 0836 58 92 68; www.bluebaydisco teca.it; Via S Antonio; admission €20; ☼ 11pm-5.30am Fri & Sat Jul-Sep). Further up the coast near Santa Maria Cesarea is the Salento's trendiest disco, **Guendalina** (www.guenda.dj; Litoranea per Castro; admission €30; ☼ Fri & Sat Jun-Jul, daily Aug)

OTRANTO
pop 5500
Hydruntum was Italy's main port to the Orient for a thousand years and as a result has suffered a brutal history. There are fanciful tales that King Minos was here and St Peter is supposed to have celebrated the first Western Mass at the top of the hill. It was Rome's leading port and under the Byzantines and Normans it played a pivotal role between Venice, the Balkans and the Levant.

A regional powerhouse, Otranto was a target of jealous neighbours and opportunist Turks who, in league with Venice against the Kingdom of Naples, attacked the city in 1480, brutally murdering 800 of Otranto's faithful Idruntini who refused to convert to Islam on pain of death. They were executed on the nearby hill of Minerva, a quiet and eerie place presided over by the Chiesa dei Martiri.

Today the blood and gore are a thing of the past and the only fright you'll get is the number of people on Otranto's scenic beaches during the summer months.

Orientation & Information

The historic centre perches on a small hill overlooking the bay with the new town sprawling north and west around its huge fortifications. The town straddles the dry River Idro from which the town took its name.

The train station is in the new town to the northwest about 1km from the historic centre. From there head southeast down Via Vecchia Stazione to the *lungomare* in front of the small beach. Here you'll find a cluster of hotels, banks and cafés. You'll find an internet connection at **Bar Ai Giardini** (Via V Emanuele II 12; per hr €3.50) on the *lungomare*. A useful web resource is www.otrantoinforma.com.

The **tourist office** (☎ 0836 80 14 36; Piazza Castello; 9am-2pm & 3.30-6.30pm Mon-Sat, later in summer) is in the historic centre opposite the castle.

Sights

Otranto's premier attraction is the audacious mosaic in the Romanesque **cathedral** (Piazza Duomo; 8am-noon & 3-7pm Jun-Sep, 8am-noon & 3-5pm Oct-May). Built by the Normans in the 11th century and subsequently subjected to a facelift or two, the magnificent cathedral is a forest of slender pillars and carved capitals. Underfoot is a vast 12th-century floor mosaic occupying the whole of the nave. It is a technicolour vision of heaven and hell, a bizarre syncretism of the classics, religion and plain superstition. What's even more striking is the naive rendering of the subjects, who look almost cartoon-like with their large, white eyes, flat feet and creative proportions.

The mosaic was executed by a young monk called Pantaleone. The scheme is based on three great trees, whose sinuous branches support a medley of scriptural scenes, monsters, animals, mythological figures and the Labours of the Months. It's good fun trying to spot

things that you recognise like the Tower of Babel, Noah and his ark, Diana the Huntress, King Arthur and even Alexander the Great. The further up the tree you go the more esoteric the images. In the choir, for example are a whole series of medallions, some with Latin and Arabic inscriptions, that are impossible to decipher although some theories hypothesise that it's a medieval cosmogenesis.

It is amazing that it has survived at all, as the Turks stabled their horses here when they beheaded the martyrs of Otranto on a stone now preserved in the altar of the side chapel to the right of the main altar. You can inspect their skulls in the glass cases that line the walls.

Just opposite the cathedral is the small **diocesan museum** (admission €1; 10am-noon & 4-8pm Jun-Sep, 10am-noon & 3-6pm Oct-May) where you can see segments of a 4th-century Roman mosaic that was recently discovered under the cathedral floor.

As a point of contrast it is interesting to see the tiny **Chiesa di San Pietro** (Via San Pietro; 10am-12.30pm & 3-6pm Apr-Sep, 10am-noon & 3-6pm Oct-Mar), thought to be the original cathedral of Otranto. It is built in the form of a Greek cross with a cylindrical cupola supported by four squat columns. The interior retains its worn Byzantine frescoes, which are so different in their cool stylisation to the exuberance of Pantaleone's characters.

Although Alfonso of Aragon recaptured Otranto from the Turks in 1481, the sack of the city left an indelible sense of fear and Alfonso ordered a whole series of renovations to the **castle** (Piazza Castello; adult/concession €2/1; 10am-noon & 4-7pm Mon-Sat) and fortifications of the city. The fortified walls still enclose the historic centre and give a real sense of what an original walled town would have felt like.

Activities

The clear waters and rocky coast around here are good for diving, and **Scuba Diving Otranto** (☎ 0836 80 27 40; www.scubadiving.it; Via San Francesco di Paola 43) offers day or night dives as well as introductory dives and courses.

The countryside around Otranto is wild and unspoilt, especially if you head south towards the **Cape of Otranto** and **Porto Badisco**. The local cooperative **Navera** (☎ 329 677 85 10; www.navera.it) can organise a whole range of excursions from horse-riding around the cape and trekking up the Valle d'Idro to guided tours of Otranto. For an English-speaking contact call **Andrea Merico** (☎ 340 641 30 30).

Every Wednesday from 7.30am to noon the local **market** sets up in the Villa Comunale.

Festivals

Otranto's biggest festival, the **Festa dei Martiri Idruntini** (11 to 14 August) commemorates those 800 faithful martyrs who fell at the hands of the Turks. The real party begins on the 12th when a crowd makes the walk to the **Chiesa di Martiri** for a commemorative speech. The next day, after a solemn church service and procession, there's a huge fireworks display.

Courses

The **Italian Language School** (☎ 0836 80 15 52; www .ilsonline.it; Traversa Sforza 18) offers a whole range of courses from one to 12 weeks, starting at €135 per week. It provides accommodation and runs a whole range of excursions, which include anything from horse-riding to visiting the local market or nearby towns.

Sleeping

Otranto is a superpopular summer resort with some big hotels and residences. Most of these are located to the north of town, leaving only a few modest places in the town centre overlooking the waterfront.

Balconcino d'Oriente (☎ 0836 80 15 29; www.balcon cinodoriente.com; Via San Francesco di Paola 71; s €35-60, d €50-100; ⚙) A friendly B&B in a great location near the castle. The Eastern theme is taken seriously here as you can see from the colourful bed linens, Oriental pictures, Moroccan lamps and orange colour washes. The best room has a small terrace overlooking the castle ramparts.

Hotel Albania (☎ /fax 0836 80 11 83; www.hotel albania.com; Via San Francesco di Paola 10; s €50-85, d €80-145; P ⚙) A no-fuss, modern hotel in the new part of town, set a block back from the waterfront. There are views from the rooms, which are all cool and modern, and the top-floor restaurant has a scenic outdoor terrace.

our pick **Palazzo de Mori** (☎ /fax 0836 80 10 88; www .palazzodemori.it; Bastione dei Pelasgi; s €80-100, d €100-150; ☽ Jan-Oct; ⚙) Finally, an intimate hotel of real character in Otranto's historic centre. Enjoy a breakfast of fruits and yogurt on the sun terrace overlooking the port and in the afternoon retire for a siesta in one of the soothing white-on-white rooms.

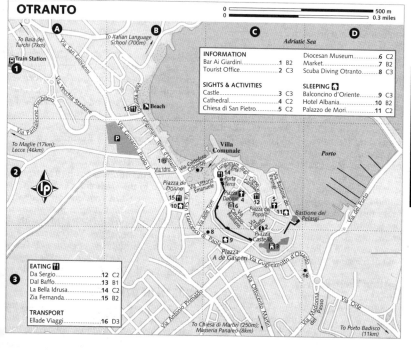

OTRANTO

0   500 m
0   0.3 miles

INFORMATION		
Bar Ai Giardini.................1	B2	
Tourist Office..................2	C3	

SIGHTS & ACTIVITIES		
Castle.............................3	C3	
Cathedral.......................4	C2	
Chiesa di San Pietro.........5	C2	

Diocesan Museum...........6	C2
Market..........................7	B2
Scuba Diving Otranto......8	C3

SLEEPING 🛏		
Balconcino d'Oriente........9	C3	
Hotel Albania................10	B2	
Palazzo de Mori.............11	C2	

EATING 🍴		
Da Sergio......................12	C2	
Dal Baffo......................13	B1	
La Bella Idrusa...............14	C2	
Zia Fernanda.................15	B2	

TRANSPORT		
Ellade Viaggi.................16	D3	

BRINDISI & THE SALENTO

Masseria Panareo (☎ 0836 81 29 99; www.masseria panareo.com; Litoranea Otranto-Santa Cesarea; d €80-120, with sea view €90-130; P ⬛ ⬛ ⬛) Masseria Panarea is more like a small village set in a superlative position in the Porto Badisco park with far-reaching views over the coastal plains to the sea. The modern-rustic rooms with their private patios are elegant and airy and are arranged around the grand vaulted dining room.

Eating

Otranto is awash with trattorie and restaurants, many of them terribly mediocre. Restaurants in the old town tend to be more touristy and expensive. Many restaurants stay open all week in July and September.

our pick La Bella Idrusa (☎ 0836 80 14 75; Via Lungomare Eroi 1; meals €20) In a prime position right by the huge Porta Terra, this may seem like an obvious tourist trap. But go inside and you'll see it's one of Otranto's most popular pizzerie serving enormous pizza *Napolitana*. It is also the one place that will be full outside high season when many restaurants are pitifully empty.

Dal Baffo (☎ 0836 80 16 36; Lungomare Terra d'Otranto; meals €30; Tue-Sun) A busy trattoria on the seafront with sea-themed décor and a menu devoted to fish including a delicious salted seafood risotto. It gets mixed reviews from the locals as it is quite expensive, but in a mixed restaurant scene it's an OK choice.

Zia Fernanda (☎ 0836 801884; Via XXV Aprile; meals €30; Tue-Sun) Tucked up a side street just off the *lungomare*, Zia Fernanda is another formal-feeling restaurant with a heavy leather-bound menu and an extensive wine list. Again the emphasis is on fish with favourites like the seafood risotto, fish soup and octopus filling the menu.

Da Sergio (☎ 0836 80 14 08; Corso Garibaldi 9; meals €35; Thu-Tue Mar-Dec) One of Otranto's longest standing restaurants with a formidable reputation for fresh seafood. It's an elegant place in the historic centre with a canopied terrace beneath which you can sample mussels *au gratin*, marinated prawns, linguine with lobster or just plain grilled fish. Shame the service isn't of the same standard as the food.

Getting There & Away

Otranto can be reached from Lecce by FSE train (€2.30, one hour, seven Monday to Saturday), or by bus (€3.10, 50 minutes). For any other destination you'll probably have to change in Maglie (€1.80, 20 minutes, 11 Monday to Saturday).

Marozzi buses run daily to and from Rome (€43, 10½ hours, four daily). They stop at Lecce (€2.60, one hour, three daily), Brindisi (€6.50, 1½ hours) and Bari (€13.50, 4½ hours, three daily) en route. They depart from the port.

Buy tickets at **Ellade Viaggi** (☎ 0836 80 15 78; www.elladeviaggi.it in Italian; Via Guglielmotto d'Otr 33; 9am-8pm Mon-Fri, 9am-1pm & 4-8pm Sat) at the port. It also handles bookings and reservations for ferries and trains.

SOUTH OF OTRANTO

Otranto is popular with good reason, and much of that reason has to do with the coastline immediately north and south of the city.

To the south the coast is high and rocky, covered with cactuses and macchia, tumble-down towers and yellow gorse bushes. Keep to the coast road and you'll soon spot the **Cape of Otranto**, the easternmost point in Italy, marked by the **Torre di Serpe** (Tower of the Serpent), before you dip down into picturesque **Porto Badisco**. Near Porto Badisco is another grotto, the **Grotta dei Cervi**, full of Neolithic hunting scenes and magic symbols which are now off limits although there is talk of opening a small antiquarium to display pictures of the caves' extraordinary artwork.

Inland you can skirt through Uggiano la Chiesa and hunt down its rough-rock dolmen, the **Dolmen di Scusi**, the best-preserved example of dozens of dolmens and menhirs that are scattered around villages like **Giurdignano**. One of the menhirs in Giurdignano, a strange thin, standing stone, stands above the **Cripta di San Paolo**, a Byzantine crypt that retains some traces of frescoes, as does the **Cripta di San Salvatore**.

If you're in Giurdignano on 19 March, you should go to the **Tavole di San Giuseppe** (Table of St Joseph), when you can scoff your way around 46 houses that open their doors to the public and prepare tables laden with all sorts of local specialities. You can then walk it off in the pleasant botanic gardens, **La Cutura** (☎ 0836 35 41 64; www.lacutura.it; SS Maglie-Poggiardo km5; 10am-1pm & 3.30-7pm), in Giuggianello.

NORTH OF OTRANTO

If the southern coast is wild and rocky, the coast north of Otranto couldn't be more different. This is what all those holidaying Italians come for: the long stretches of sandy beach at **Baia dei Turchi** with its translucent blue water.

By day the lidos are packed with sun-worshippers methodically roasting themselves to a perfect pitch of bronze. Parking, beds and umbrellas are all available for a fee, and will set you back around €18 to €25 per day. There are areas of beach where you don't have to pay, but the best spots are taken up with paying punters. One of the best is the blue-flag beach **Atlantis** (☎ 0836 80 40 80; Via Porto Craulo; admission €20), which turns into another clubbing venue at night, with Ibiza mixes and guest DJs like Claude Challe, creator of the Buddha Bar phenomenon.

Most of the lidos are only open between June and September, when a shuttle bus operates from Otranto to the beaches. Outside those months you'll have the beach almost all to yourself for free but you will need a car to get here.

Northern Basilicata

Basilicata's isolated yet strategic location on routes linking ancient Rome to the eastern Byzantine empire has seen it successively invaded, pillaged, plundered and neglected. Its tragic and violent history produced a wary people suspicious of strangers and resigned to a life of hardship and suppression. As recently as 60 years ago, Carlo Levi, author of the superb book *Christ Stopped at Eboli*, exposed the harsh life of the average Basilicatan peasant. His treatise, that Christ stopped at Eboli (256km south of Rome), alluded to Basilicata's wild and unloved nature; it was a place beyond the hand of God, where outlaw bandits roamed the forests and pagan magic still existed and thrived.

However, it is exactly Basilicata's isolation and 'lost' reputation that is attracting the attention of travellers. In the last few decades roads have slowly opened up the once-secluded land of ancient Lucania, an exposure accompanied by a strong self-awakening in its people. This and a strengthening economy – the revival of the Fiat works at Melfi, the discovery of Western Europe's largest oil field near Potenza in the 1980s and the emerging tourist market – has seen them wear their turbulent past with pride and the ever-increasing trickle of travellers is now warmly welcomed.

The only towns of any size in Basilicata are the provincial capitals, Potenza and Matera, both found in the north. The landscape is a fertile zone of gentle hills and deep valleys once covered in thick forests, now cleared and cultivated with wheat, olives and grapes. Frederick II loved this land, leaving a legacy of castles in his wake. Towards Matera in the east the rocky limestone bedrock is harsher and drier, the famous *sassi* of the cave city presiding over a rugged landscape of ravines and caves inhabited since Palaeolithic times.

HIGHLIGHTS

- Sleep in Matera's stylishly converted **medieval caves** (p176)
- Hike the rocky **Matera Gravina** (p176)
- Explore the **sassi** (p170) of Matera during the day; return for an eerie night walk through the cave city
- Visit beautiful **Venosa** (p179), birthplace of the Latin poet Horace
- Cycle through the timeless landscape of the Murgia plateau to the medieval hilltop town of **Montescaglioso** (p175)

MATERA & THE MURGIA PLATEAU

Matera is ancient; a difficult-to-reach, isolated town heavily influenced by its earthy roots and the succession of passing races and cultures.

History lies in thick layers on the surface of the land – Neolithic settlements, ancient Greek and Roman artefacts and abandoned limestone caves in the Murgia bedrock – but the most impressive layer of history is the city itself. In Matera, the ash-grey *sassi* – the famous cave-and-stone houses inhabited since the Palaeolithic Age – sprawl below the rim of a yawning ravine like a giant nativity scene, its 21st-century makeover highlighting its austere beauty.

It was these same caves that in the 8th to 9th centuries attracted Byzantine monks seeking refuge from persecution (p23). Painting coloured frescoes on the walls, they transformed the dank, dark cells into places of worship. These *chiese rupestri* (rock churches)

are scattered throughout the *sassi* and the scrubby rock-strewn countryside of the Murgia plateau. Once past the ravine the landscape changes markedly, the Matera Murgia smoothing into undulating wheatfields and olive groves that sweep around the pretty medieval hilltop town of Montescaglioso and into nearby Puglia, while only 60km to the south are the long sandy beaches of the Ionian Coast.

Matera has some of Basilicata's best hotels and is a good starting place from which to explore the region, but be warned that public transport is severely limited and a car is highly recommended.

MATERA
pop 59,144 / elev 405m

Matera is unique. In no other city do you come face to face with such powerful images of Italy's lost peasant culture. Its famous *sassi* tell of a poverty now difficult to imagine in a developed European country, a clichéd image of rudimentary human civilisation that made it Mel Gibson's location of choice for the film *The Passion of the Christ*.

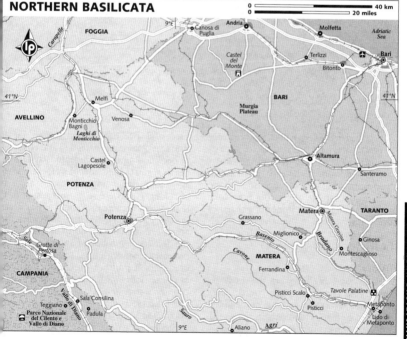

NORTHERN BASILICATA

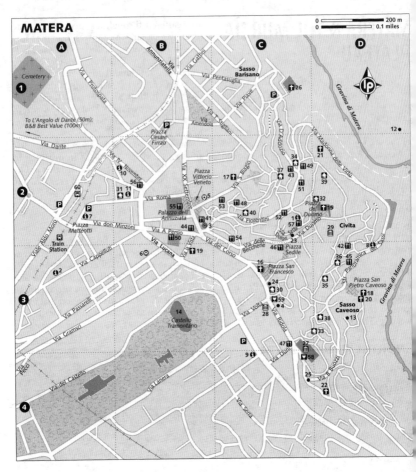

Disguised in the deep ravine on whose edge the new town is set, Matera's dramatic appearance is hidden until you round the corner of Via d'Addozio. In the early evening this all-encompassing view of the Sasso Barisano is magical, a jumble of glowing tufa-stone houses hugging the limestone hill which they cover entirely; from its pinnacle rises the elegant campanile of the cathedral. It is a view that fills you with anticipation.

History

Matera's cave dwellings are the most extensive and complete troglodyte complex in the Mediterranean, and one of the oldest inhabited human settlements in the world. Until the 20th century the *sassi* were pretty successful dwellings – what started out as simple grottoes were extended and enlarged to become homes. An ingenious system of canals regulated the flow of water and sewage, and small hanging gardens lent a splash of colour. They were so prosperous, in fact, that Matera became the capital of Basilicata in 1663, a position it held until 1806 when the accolade moved further north to Potenza. In the decades that followed an unsustainable increase in population led to the habitation of unsuitable grottoes – originally intended as animal stalls – which lacked both light and running water.

By the 1950s more than half of Matera's population lived in the *sassi*, a typical cave sheltering an average of six children despite

INFORMATION			
Ente Parco	1 C2	Chiesa di Santa Lucia alle	
Ferula Viaggi	2 A3	Malve	19 B3
Internet Point	3 B2	Chiesa di Santa Maria d'Idris	20 D3
Libreria dell'Arco	4 C3	Chiesa Madonna delle Virtù	21 D2
Mediateca	(see 55)	Convincio di San Antonio	22 D4
Police Station	5 B2	Entrance to Sasso Barisano	23 C2
Post Office	6 B3	Entrance to Sasso Caveoso	24 C3
Tourist Information Kiosk	7 A2	Entrance to Sasso Caveoso	25 C4
Tourist Information Kiosk	8 D3	Monasterio di Sant'Agostino	26 C1
Tourist Information Kiosk	9 C4	Museo di Arte Medievale e	
Tourist Office	10 B2	Moderna	27 C4
Tourist Office	11 B2	Museo Nazionale Ridola	28 C3
		Musma	29 D2

SIGHTS & ACTIVITIES			
Belvedere	12 D1	**SLEEPING**	
Casa-Grotta di Vico Solitario	13 D3	Albergo Italia	30 D3
Castello Tramontano	14 B3	Albergo Roma	31 B2
Cathedral	15 D2	B&B Capriotti	32 D2
Centro Carlo Levi	(see 27)	B&B Il Vicinato	33 D3
Chiesa di San Francesco d'Assisi	16 C3	Casa d'Imperio	34 C2
Chiesa di San Giovanni Battista	17 C2	Caveoso Hotel	35 D3
Chiesa di San Giovanni in		Hotel Sant'Angelo	36 D3
Monterrone	(see 20)	Hotel Sassi	37 C3
Chiesa di San Nicola dei Greci	(see 21)	La Casa di Lucio	38 D3
Chiesa di San Pietro Caveoso	18 D3	Le Monacelle	39 D2
		Locanda di San Martino	40 C2

EATING			
19a Buca Winery?	41 B2
Baccanti	42 D3
Caffè del Cavaliere	43 C2
Caffè Tripoli	44 B2
Il Convivio	45 D3
L'Arturo Enogastronomia	46 C3
La Latteria	47 C3
La Stalla	48 C2
Le Botteghe	49 C2
Market	50 B2
Oi Mari	51 C2
Osteria "Al Vicinato"	52 C2
Ristorante Don Matteo	53 C2
Ristorante Il Cantuccio	54 C2
Terrazza dell'Annunziata	
Caffè	55 B2
Trattoria Lucana	56 B2
Vecchia Matera	57 C2

DRINKING	
Morgan Pub	58 C4
Shibuya	59 C3

TRANSPORT	
Bus Station	60 A2

an infant mortality rate of 50%. Carlo Levi's impassioned writings about the town told of how the wretched inhabitants would beg passers-by not for money but for quinine to stave off the deadly malaria. Such publicity finally galvanised the authorities into action, and in the late 1950s about 15,000 inhabitants of the *sassi* were forcibly relocated to new government housing schemes.

In 1993 Matera's *sassi* were declared a Unesco World Heritage Site. Ironically, the town's history of outrageous misery has now made it Basilicata's leading tourist attraction and the *sassi* are now undergoing systematic and stylish renovation.

Orientation

A short walk down Via Roma from the train and bus stations off Piazza Matteotti brings you to Piazza Vittorio Veneto, the pedestrianised heart of town. The two *sassi* districts open up to its east and southeast. From the *piazza*, Via delle Becchiere feeds into Via Duomo as it climbs a spur to the cathedral, the highest point in town, in the area known as the *civita*.

Information

BOOKSHOPS

Libreria dell'Arco (☎ 0835 31 11 11; Via Ridola 37) This well-stocked bookshop (with some English titles) also sells maps of the *sassi*, *Matera: Percorsi Turistici*, (€1.30) with four walking itineraries in English.

EMERGENCY

Ambulance (☎ 118)
Police (☎ 113; Piazza Vittorio Veneto)

INTERNET ACCESS

Mediateca (☎ 0835 33 06 71; Piazza Vittorio Veneto; per hr €2; ⏰ 8.30am-6.30pm Mon-Thu, 8.30am-1.30pm Fri & Sat)

MEDICAL SERVICES

Guardia Medica (☎ 0835 26 22 60)
Hospital (☎ 0835 24 32 12; Via Montescaglioso) About 1km southeast of the centre.

MONEY

All the main banks can be found around Piazza Vittorio Veneto and along Via del Corso to Piazza San Francesco.

POST

Post Office (☎ 0835 26 87 11; Via Passarelli 13b; ⏰ 8am-6.30pm Mon-Fri, 8am-12.30pm Sat)

TOURIST INFORMATION

Tourist office Via De Viti De Marco (☎ 0835 33 19 83; www.materaturismo.it; Via De Viti De Marco 9; ⏰ 9am-1pm Mon-Sat, 4-6.30pm Mon & Thu); Via Spine Bianche (☎ 0835 33 18 17; www.aptbasilicata.it; Via Spine Bianche 22; ⏰ 9am-1pm & 3.30-7pm Mon-Sat)
Tourist information kiosk (☎ 0835 24 12 60; Via Madonna delle Virtù; ⏰ 9.30am-12.30pm & 4-7pm summer) This kiosk is handy if you're in the *sassi*. There are other kiosks at Piazza Matteotti and Via Lucana; they're all run by the Comune di Matera.

NORTHERN BASILICATA

TRAVEL AGENCY

Ferula Viaggi (☎ 0835 33 65 72; www.ferulaviaggi.it; Via Cappelluti 34; ☑ 9am-1.30pm & 3.30-7pm Mon-Fri, 9am-1.30pm Sat) A tourist cooperative dedicated to promoting Basilicata. It operates as a travel agency, has English-speaking guides, and runs good cultural, walking, wine-tasting and gastronomic tours.

Internet Point (☎ 0835 34 61 12; Piazza Vittorio Veneto 49; per hr €5; ☑ 8am-1pm & 5-8.30pm Tue-Sat)

Sights

Nothing quite prepares you for the sprawling tufa city built into the slopes of the Matera Gravina. The *sassi* are unquestionably the main attraction but the new town with its elegant churches and *palazzi* is a lively spot and worth exploring.

For a great photograph of the *sassi* take the Taranto–Laterza road and follow signs for the *chiese rupestri*. This road takes you to the **Belvedere**, the location of the crucifixion in *The Passion of the Christ*, which has fantastic views of the plunging ravine and Matera.

The two *sassi* districts are the northwest-facing Sasso Barisano and the more impoverished, northeast-facing Sasso Caveoso. The *sassi* are extraordinary; riddled with serpentine alleyways and staircases, dotted with over 150 *chiese rupestri* and some 3000 habitable caves where façades are often adorned with baroque and classical motifs.

The *sassi* are accessible from several points around the centre of Matera. There is an entrance just off Piazza Vittorio Veneto. Alternatively, take Via delle Becchiere to Piazza del Duomo and follow the tourist itinerary signs to enter either Barisano or Caveoso. Sasso Caveoso is also accessible from Via Ridola by the stairs next to Albergo Italia.

Armed with a map you can easily navigate the *sassi* on your own, but wandering aimlessly through the warren of stairways, narrow alleyways and abandoned caves can lead to unexpected discoveries and pleasant surprises. Qualified guides can take you straight to the most interesting sites and offer a great deal of background. They also hold the keys to many of the more interesting cave churches. For some reliable guided itineraries, see p172.

SASSI BARISANO

This is the larger of the two *sassi* districts, and many of the cave dwellings have been restored and converted into houses, shops and restaurants. For interesting souvenirs, traditional whistles *(cuccu)* and ceramics visit the craft shops on **Via Fiorentini**. Continue to Via Madonna delle Virtù for a panoramic view of the ravine and the caves on the opposite hillside.

Chiesa Madonna delle Virtù

One of the most important monuments in Matera, the monastic complex of **Madonna delle Virtù** and **San Nicola dei Greci** (Via Madonna delle Virtù; ☑ 10am-7pm Sat & Sun) is composed of dozens of caves spread over two floors. The church of the Madonna delle Virtù was built in the 10th or 11th century and restored in the 17th century. Above it, the simple church of San Nicola dei Greci is rich in frescoes. The complex was used in 1213 by Benedictine monks of Palestinian origin. From late June to October a modern art exhibition is showcased in Madonna delle Virtù.

Monasterio di Sant'Agostino

The monumental church and monastic complex of **Sant'Agostino** (Via D'Addozio; ☑ 7am-1pm & 4-8pm), built in the 16th century, served time as a military barracks and a home for the elderly. The church was built above the underground church of St William and is impressively situated on the edge of the Gravina.

SASSI CAVEOSO

Considered to be the older and wilder quarter which grew around Piazza San Pietro Caveoso, Sasso Caveoso is more evocative of what life must have been like in a cave city.

All the cave churches are open from 9am to 1pm and 3pm to 7pm in summer (June to September). In winter they open from 9.30am to 1.30pm and from 2.30pm to 4.30pm.

Chiesa di San Pietro Caveoso

Located in the Piazza San Pietro Caveoso, this is the only church in the sassi not dug into the tufa. It was originally built in 1300 but the façade is a 17th-century Romanesque-Baroque makeover. Note the 16th-century tufa sculpture of the *Madonna col Bambino* (Madonna with child) in the right aisle and the wood polyptych *Madonna col Bambino e i santi Pietro e Paolo* (Madonna with child and St Peter and St Paul) on the main altar.

Chiesa di Santa Maria d'Idris

Dug into Mount Errone (also known as the Idris rock), the rock church of **Chiesa di Santa Maria de Idris** (adult/concession €2.50/1 or per 4 people €6) has an unprepossessing façade but the narrow corridor communicating with the recessed church of **San Giovanni in Monterrone** is richly decorated with frescoes dating from the 12th to the 17th centuries. San Giovanni in Monterrone was originally used as a baptistery, later as a crypt, and until a few years ago contained human bones clothed in rotting rags.

Chiesa di Santa Lucia alle Malve
Built in the 8th century to house a Benedictine convent, the **Chiesa di Santa Lucia alle Malve** (Rione Malve; Via del Corso) has an ornate entrance door and a number of frescoes dating to the 12th century, including one of the *Madonna del Latte* (showing the Virgin Mary breastfeeding the infant Jesus).

Convincio di San Antonio
Built around the 12th or 13th century, the **Convincio di San Antonio** (Rione Casalnuovo) is a complex of four rock churches grouped around a central courtyard. There are many frescoes in the churches but look for the wine spouts in the altars that tell of their 18th-century conversion into cellars.

Casa-Grotte di Vico Solitario
A refurbished cave dwelling, **Casa-Grotte di Vico Solitario** (☎ 0835 31 01 18; off Via Bruno Buozzi; admission €1.50; 9am-1pm & 4-8pm) has an engaging multilingual audio explanation describing the typical living conditions in the *sassi*. There's a bed in the kitchen, a room for manure, and a section for a pig and a donkey!

MUSMA
The **Museo della Scultura Contemporanea** (Musma; ☎ 0835 33 64 39; www.musma.it; Via San Giacomo; adult/concession €5/3.50; 10am-2pm Tue-Sun Nov-Mar, 10am-2pm & 4-8pm Tue-Sun Apr-Oct) located in the 17th-century Palazzo Pomarici is not to be missed. Exhibits are artfully displayed in atmospherically lit caves where rock-hewn silos and wine palmettos blend easily with contemporary representations of space, thought-provoking interpretations of Adam and Eve, and a sumo-wrestling St Francis. Upstairs the collection tells the story of sculpture from 1880 to the present day using a variety of media: bronze, marble, stone, terracotta, plaster, papier-mâché and wood. A current project involves restoring and converting the former home of *sassi*-loving Spanish artist Jose Ortega into a museum. The **Casa di Ortega** will open in late 2007.

THE NEW TOWN
Piazza Vittorio Veneto is the centre of town and the great *passeggiata* meeting point. Stairs lead down from the square into a series of excavated caves and impressive ancient cisterns. Around town, elegant churches and noble buildings boast of Matera's great wealth during the 16th and 17th centuries.

Cathedral
Apart from the impressive rose window above the door, the relatively sedate exterior of the 13th-century Puglian-Romanesque **cathedral** (Piazza del Duomo) ill-prepares you for the neobaroque excess within: ornate carved capitals, sumptuously decorated chapels and tons of gilding everywhere. In the left aisle an altar dedicated to the *Madonna della Bruna,* Matera's patron saint, has a 13th-century Byzantine fresco of the Virgin Mary with Child. With its 54m belltower and its position on the highest hill in town, the cathedral dominates the skyline. It was closed for restoration at the time of research.

Chiesa di San Francesco d'Assisi
This church in Piazza San Francesco has an impressive 17th-century baroque façade. It was originally built in the 13th century above two rock churches, which can be accessed through the third chapel on the left. The church is currently closed for restoration.

Museo Nazionale Ridola
The national **museum** (☎ 0835 31 12 39; Via Ridola 24; adult/concession €2.50/1.25; 9am-8pm Tue-Sun, 2-8pm Mon) in the 17th-century convent of Santa Chiara has an extensive selection of prehistoric finds and classical artefacts including Bronze Age weapons and Magna Graeca pottery. The exhibits in the museum are well displayed and one room is dedicated to doctor and archaeologist Domenico Ridola, whose private collection started the museum.

Museo di Arte Medievale e Moderna
A little south, in Palazzo Lanfranchi, the Museum of Modern Art houses the **Centro Carlo Levi** (☎ 0835 31 01 37; adult/concession €2/1; 9am-1pm & 3.30-7pm Tue-Sun). Not only was Carlo Levi (see the boxed text, p172) a writer, he was also an accomplished artist, his paintings maturing from earlier stylistic works to bold, broad-stroked primal images including the enormous mural *Lucania '61*, which depicts

peasant life in Matera in biblical technicolour. The small bookshop sells maps of the *sassi*. Piazza Pascoli in front of the museum has breathtaking views of Sasso Caveoso.

Chiesa di San Giovanni Battista

This 13th-century church on Via San Biagio is an interesting example of Romanesque architecture. Entry is through the side door as the original entrance and façade were incorporated into adjacent buildings during the 17th-century baroque additions and alterations. In 1926 the church was restored to its Romanesque simplicity. It was closed for restoration at the time of research.

Castello Tramontano

Situated on a hill near the town centre, the 15th-century castle was left unfinished after the unpopular Count Tramontano was killed by Matera's townsmen after leaving the cathedral. Didn't he realise bedding every new bride on her wedding night was not going to endear him to the peasants? Four small tiles on Via Riscatto to the left of the cathedral paint a tale of the count's violent death. The castle is currently closed for restoration.

Tours

There are plenty of official guides to the *sassi* – the tourist office has details. **Ferula Viaggi** (☎ 0835 33 65 72; www.ferulaviaggi.it; Via Cappelluti 34; ☼ 9am-1.30pm & 3.30-7pm Mon-Fri, 9am-1.30pm Sat) offers guided trekking and mountain-biking trips (with English-speaking guides), a range of tours in the *sassi* and the Murgia, as well as cultural, cooking and archaeological tours around Basilicata. It also rents bikes and is an excellent source of information on self-guided trips.

Festivals

In the **Sagra della Madonna della Bruna** (2 July) a colourful procession transports the Madonna from the cathedral on an ornately decorated papier-mâché float. When the procession is finished (and once the statue has been removed), it is time for the *assalto al carro*, when the crowd descends on the cart and tears it to pieces in order to take away the precious relics.

Sleeping

There's plenty of choice in Matera, from pleasant B&Bs to atmospheric cave hotels in the *sassi*, but in August booking accommodation ahead of time is vital. If you want to bed down in a cave be aware that sweating rocks can make them damp.

BUDGET

B&B Best Value (☎ 333 2310789; losino@hotmail.com; Via Fratelli Grimm 5; s/d €30/45) Although this basic B&B (curtains replace bathroom doors) is 300m from the *sassi*, the congenial owner is multilingual and offers a free pick-up from the train station and impromptu trips to nearby sights.

Albergo Roma (☎ 0835 33 39 12; Via Roma 62; s/d €42/60; ❄) Another option if you don't want to stay in the *sassi* is this basic hotel not far from the train station. It won't win any rave reviews but it's quiet and clean and within walking distance of the *sassi*.

B&B Il Vicinato (☎ 0835 31 26 72; www.ilvicinato.com; Piazzata San Pietro Caveoso 7; s/d €45/70) This cute little spot in a restored 17th-century *palazzotto* in the heart of Sassi Caveoso has a room with a balcony and a small apartment, both with private entrances.

CARLO LEVI & LA VERGOGNA NAZIONALE

Carlo Levi (1902–75) may have been interred at Aliano but his greatest impact was felt in Matera. A true Renaissance man – artist, writer, doctor and philosopher – he was born in Turin, studied medicine and founded an anti-fascist movement. In 1935 he was arrested and exiled as a political activist to the wild *mezzogiorno* (the poor south, 'land of the midday sun'). Shocked at the bleak living conditions of Basilicata's peasant culture he wrote a book, *Christ Stopped at Eboli*, an impassioned account of the daily hardships he witnessed during his seven month internment. About Matera, he quoted his sister's shocking description of the *sassi* as a Dante's *Inferno* where men, women, children and beasts, often sharing the same small cramped cave, lived in miserable squalor. Matera became known as *la vergogna nazionale* (Italy's shame). Levi's powerful writing awakened national sympathy – in 1952 Matera's inhabitants were evacuated to newly built modern housing developments and in 1993 (after years of abandonment) the *sassi* were designated a Unesco World Heritage site. Ironically, Italy's shame is now Matera's fame.

MIDRANGE

B&B Capriotti (☎ 0835 33 39 97; www.capriotti-bed
-breakfast.it; Piazza del Duomo; s/d €50/70) This is a
quaint B&B beside the cathedral with fantastic views of Sassi Barisano and the Murge.
The apartments are tiny but have individual
entrances and it's a short stroll to Piazza Vittorio Veneto and the evening *passeggiata*.

Le Monacelle (☎ 0835 34 40 97; www.lemonacelle
.it; Via Riscatto 9-10; s/d/tr/q/ste €55/86/105/135/120;
🖥) Once a convent and spiritual retreat;
the grills on the windows kept the cloistered
nuns pious. Rooms verge on austere but the
fabulous terrace provides near-religious views
of the *sassi* and the ravine. In summer, cultural
performances and concerts are held in the
central courtyard. Also has two bunk-style
hostel rooms (€16 a night).

Hotel Sassi (☎ 0835 33 10 09; www.hotelsassi.it; Via San
Giovanni Vecchio 89; s/d/ste €65/90/120; 🖥 🅃) The first
hotel in the *sassi* district is looking a little tired,
and the furniture is a mish-mash of styles, but
the rooms – carved out of tufa – retain their
original charm. It's a long walk from the nearest car park but the views are outstanding.
Also has bunk-style hostel accommodation
(beds €16 a night without breakfast).

Locanda di San Martino (☎ 0835 25 66 00; www
.locandadisanmartino.it; Via Fiorentini 17; s €68-88, d €99-129,
ste €120-200; 🅃 🖥 🅟) A swish warren of cave
dwellings connected by a series of balconies,
external stairways and an elevator in the rock.
Elegantly furnished and conveniently located
in the heart of the *sassi*, the Locanda is a good
choice for views and value.

Albergo Italia (☎ 0835 33 35 61; www.albergoitalia
.com; Via Ridola 5; s/d/tr/ste €75/98/120/130; 🅃 🖥) Mel
Gibson chose this old-world hotel overlooking
the *sassi* as his base while filming *The Passion
of the Christ*. Rumour has it he received com-
munion in his room each morning.

TOP END

[ourpick] Hotel Sant'Angelo (☎ 0835 31 40 10; www
.hotelsantangelosassi.it; Piazza San Pietro Caveoso; s/d/ste
€90/120/160; 🅃 🖥) A class act that makes sleeping in a cave a luxury you can't afford to miss.
The 16 renovated cave dwellings vary in size
and shape; the rooms are spacious and stylish
with a panoramic view of the pretty Chiesa
di San Pietro Caveoso, the Idris rock and the
wild ravine behind. Romantic – even without
the mood lighting and welcoming red rose.

Caveoso Hotel (☎ 0835 31 09 31; www.caveosohotel
.com; Piazza San Pietro Caveoso; s/d/ste €90/120/150; 🅃 🖥)

In this recently opened hotel in the *sassi* each
of the rooms has a separate entrance and full
frontal views of the Chiesa di San Pietro Caveoso and the Idris rock opposite. One suite
is built into a grotto, the rest are modern,
comfortable and pristinely white.

La Casa di Lucio (☎ 0835 31 27 98; www.lacasadilucio
.it; Via San Pietro Caveoso 66; s/d/ste €100/135/200; 🅃 🖥)
This converted 17th-century house nestled
in the Sassi Caveoso district is a residence
rather than a hotel. The two suites and twelve
bohemian apartments are decorated with an
eclectic mix of modern furnishings, bold paint
finishes and unexpected prints.

Eating

THE SASSI

L'Arturo Enogastronomia (☎ 0835 33 06 78; Piazza
Sedile 15; panini €2.50; h8.30am-3.30pm & 5.30-9.30pm) At
the entrance of the *sassi*, this small deli, built
from recycled materials, is a cool hang-out
for students from the nearby Conservatorium
of Music. A rustic wooden table fills the tiny
back room; a great place to crowd around a
bottle of wine.

Oi Marì (☎ 0835 34 61 21; Via Fiorentini 66; pizza from
€4, meals €20; 🕑 8-11pm Wed-Mon, lunch Sat & Sun) This
place sells itself as a stylish Neapolitan pizzeria –
and with some justification as the setting is
original, the pizzas well prepared and the
prices reasonable. Explode your tastebuds
with a *pizza vesuvio*.

Osteria "Al Vicinato" (☎ 0835 34 41 80; Via Fiorentini
58; pasta €5) A basic no-frills *osteria* with minimal seating, blaring TV and a limited menu.
Good for a quick bite but if you're after leisurely or intimate, go elsewhere.

Vecchia Matera (☎ 0835 33 69 10; Via Sette Dolori
62; meals €20-25; 🕑 lunch & dinner Thu-Tue, lunch Wed)
Split levels and candlelight make dining in
this large cave cosy and atmospheric. An interesting pizza menu as well as traditional
Lucanian dishes.

La Stalla (☎ 0835 24 04 55; Via Rosaria 73; meals €25) A
family-run *osteria* in a converted stable with
rustic artefacts, farming pieces and a feeding
trough carved in the rock. The menu is limited
but the homemade pasta *dell'osteria* is recommended. Intimate indoors, the *osteria* opens
onto an impressive outdoor terrace.

Il Convivio (☎ 0835 31 00 55; Via Madonna delle Virtù;
meals €25; 🕑 lunch & dinner Wed-Mon May-Sep, dinner only
Oct-Apr) This rambling series of barrel-shaped
rooms burrowed into the hillside serves up
smashing local specialities, including great

NORTHERN BASILICATA

antipasti of salamis and cheese. There's only one menu in the entire restaurant and service can mean that meals here take some time.

Baccanti (☎ 0835 33 37 04; Via Sant'Angelo 58-61; meals €30; ☺ lunch Tue-Sun, dinner Tue-Sat) Minimalist but stylish décor reflects the simple but elegantly presented meals. In summer, dine alfresco on the huge terrace a stone's throw from Hotel Sant'Angelo.

Le Botteghe (☎ 0835 34 40 72; Piazza San Pietro Barisano; meals €40; ☺ lunch daily, dinner Mon-Sat) In Sassi Barisano, this is an excellent, classy but informal restaurant in gloriously high arched whitewashed rooms. Try the mixed antipasti and follow with delicious local specialities such as *strascinate salsiccia e funghi* (pasta with sausage and mushrooms).

THE NEW TOWN

La Latteria (☎ 0835 31 20 58; Via Duni 2; panini/pasta €2/4; ☺ 8.30am-8.30pm) A popular lunch spot and well-stocked deli where you can sample typical Lucanian cuisine but where cheese reigns supreme. Try the *provolone in grotta* – cheese matured in a cave – or the cheese platter (€10 to €12).

L'Angolo di Dante (☎ 0835 33 15 54; Via Dante 72; pizza €4; ☺ Thu-Tue) According to the newspaper clippings on the wall this unpretentious *trattoria*/pizzeria boasts the reigning 'world champion of quality pizza'. What better reason do you need?

Terrazza dell'Annunziata Caffè (☎ 0835 33 65 25; Piazza Vittorio Veneto; sandwiches/salads €4-5) An amazingly quiet place right on the main *piazza*. This café is actually the roof terrace of the old convent Palazzo dell'Annunziata (now converted into a cinema and public library and the Mediateca where you'll find internet access). Enjoy a cocktail (€5) with panoramic views over Matera.

Trattoria Lucana (☎ 0835 33 61 17; Via Lucana 47; meals €20-25; ☺ Mon-Sat) The favourite dish in the most popular restaurant in town is *fettucine alla Mel Gibson*, an interesting combination of pureed fava, mushrooms, rucola and tomato. The menu is as diverse as the clientele with a mouth-watering selection of homemade pastas and local meat dishes. Reservations are recommended.

our pick **Ristorante Il Cantuccio** (☎ 0835 33 20 90; Via delle Beccherie 33; meals €20-25; ☺ Tue-Sun) This quaint, homey *trattoria* near Piazza Vittorio Veneto is as welcoming as its chef and proprietor, Michael Lella. The menu is written

in pencil and changes often. A recommended and interesting choice is the *strascinate al peperone crusco e condite con crema di fagioli sarconi* – tastes as poetic as it sounds.

19a Buca Winery? (☎ 0835 33 35 92; www.dician novesimabuca.com; Via Lombardi 3; meals €30; ☺ 11am-midnight Tue-Sun) The question mark says it all. Thirteen metres below Piazza Vittorio Veneto the past takes a futuristic twist. Suffering an identity crisis, this ultra-chic wine bar/restaurant/café/lounge has white space-pod chairs sprawling across a suspended wooden floor and a 19-hole indoor golf course surrounding an ancient cistern. Innovative lighting, clever use of glass and metal, an impressive wine cellar and degustation menu makes a visit to this grotto a uniquely surreal experience – even if you don't play golf.

Drinking

Shibuya (☎ 0835 33 74 09; Vico Purgatorio 12; ☺ 8am-3am Tue-Sun) This cool little café and CD shop is also a bar and has regular DJs. Make a beeline for the few outside tables at the top of an ancient alley.

Morgan Pub (☎ 0835 31 22 33; Via Bruno Buozzi 2; ☺ Wed-Mon) In Sasso Caveoso, Morgan is a hip, cavernous cellar pub that's something of a surprise on the quiet street. In summer the few small outside tables get busy.

Getting There & Away

Hiring a car will save considerable time, as train travel to Matera is a problem. There is no direct connection with Potenza, and trains from Bari are slow as they involve a change at Altamura.

BUS

The bus station is just north of Piazza Matteotti, near the train station. **SITA** (☎ 0835 38 50 07) buses connect Matera with Taranto (€4.60, 1½ hours, five daily) and Metaponto (€2.70, one hour, up to six daily), as well as many small towns in the province. **Grassani** (☎ 0835 52 71 80) has buses to Potenza (€5.35, four daily).

Marozzi (in Rome ☎ 06 225 21 47; www.marozzi .it) runs three buses every day from Rome to Matera. A joint SITA and Marozzi service leaves at 10.35pm daily for the northern cities of Siena, Florence and Pisa, via Potenza. Advance booking is essential.

Buy your ticket for all services except Grassani (pay on the bus) at the newsagent stands in Piazza Matteotti.

CAR & MOTORCYCLE

From Bari follow the SS96 to Altamura then the SS99 to Matera. From Potenza follow the SS407 taking the SS7 exit to Matera.

From Naples follow the A1 to Salerno then the A3 to Sicignano and from here take the SS407 towards Potenza. If you are driving from Rome you can skirt around Naples by taking the A30 to Salerno.

TRAIN

Ferrovie Appulo-Lucane (FAL; ☎ 0835 33 28 61; www .fal-srl.it) runs regular trains (€4, 1½ hours, frequent) and buses (€4, six daily) to and from Bari. For Potenza, take a FAL bus to Ferrandina (€2, five daily) and connect with a Trenitalia train, or head to Altamura (€1.70) to link up with FAL's Bari–Potenza run.

Getting Around

Matera is a compact town and most areas of interest are within easy walking distance of each other. Since September 2006 the *sassi* district has been trialling a Restricted Traffic Zone. At the time of research nothing definite had been finalised but assume you won't be permitted to park your car here.

The best parking spots are near Piazza Vittorio Veneto and in Piazza Matteotti (€0.70 per hour). Alternatively, you can use one of the local garages on Via Lucana, Via Casalnuovo and Piazza Cesare Firrao (€9 per day).

A brightly painted minibus (€0.80) leaves Piazza Matteotti and Piazza Vittorio Veneto every half-hour for a 10-minute trip to Piazza San Pietro Caveoso.

AROUND MATERA

Il Parco delle Chiese Rupestri & Around

Il Parco delle Chiese Rupestri (Park of the Rock Churches) was established in 1978 to protect over 150 rupestrian churches and neolithic settlements found in the area immediately around Matera. Of particular interest is the **Cripta del Peccato Originale** (the Crypt of Original Sin) with its well-preserved 9th-century frescoes. The Crypt is 14km from Matera and bookings are essential; book through Musma (p171) or the **Foundazione Zetema** (☎ 0835 33 05 82; www.zetema.org).

In 1990 the protected area was extended to 66 sq km and renamed the **Parco Archeologico Storico Naturale della Murgia e delle Chiese Rupestri del Materano** (Murgia and Matera Rock Churches Natural History and Archaeological Park); it's a dramatic craggy landscape of calcareous rocks and deep ravines.

For information on the park and walking itineraries see **Ente Parco** (☎ 0835 33 61 66; www .parcomurgia.it; Via Sette Dolori 10; 🕙 9am-2pm daily; 4-7pm Tue & Thu) in Matera. As many of the rock churches can be difficult to access a guided tour is recommended. For a more interesting alternative take a long hike through the park. **Ferula Viaggi** (☎ 0835 33 65 72; www.ferulaviaggi .it) in Matera offers half-day (€10) to two-day (€162) hikes.

For more ravine gazing head to **Gravina di Puglia**, where there are two excellent museums with exhibits of grave goods and a fully reconstructed cave church. Altamura (p82) also has a good museum, but more to the point you can compare their famous bread with that of Matera. After all, the Materese maintain that it was their recipe all along.

Miglionico

pop 2592 / elev 461m

Miglionico is perched on a hilltop in the fertile valley between the Basento and Bradano Rivers. The impressive 11th-century castle (closed for restoration at the time of research) goes by the curious name of **Castello del Malconsiglio** (Castle of Bad Advice). In 1481 a band of rebellious barons gathered here to plot against Ferdinand I of Aragon – the so-called 'Baron's Conspiracy' – but the plot failed and the conspirators were murdered instead.

The **Chiesa Madre di Santa Maria Maggiore** (Piazza del Popolo) in the centre of the village has an 18-panel polyptych (1499) by Cima de Conegliano depicting a number of saints. According to local rumours the rather graphic crucified Christ on the crucifix inspired Mel Gibson during filming of *The Passion of the Christ*.

Miglionico is 20km from Matera. SITA buses run frequently (30 minutes, €1.55).

MONTESCAGLIOSO

pop 10,112 / elev 336m

The origins of this picturesque hilltop town date back to the 4th century BC. Conquered by the Greeks and later the Romans, Montescaglioso didn't acquire much importance until it came under Norman rule, a time when monastic communities were granted land and privileges and enjoyed a period of expansion throughout the country. It was during the Norman era that the monumental Abbey of

NORTHERN BASILICATA

TREKKING THE GRAVINA

In the picturesque landscape of the Murgia plateau the Matera Gravina cuts a rough gouge in the earth, a 200m-deep canyon pockmarked with abandoned caves and villages. You can hike from the *sassi* into the ravine and then up to the Belvedere in one to two hours, but a hike along the canyon rim gives you a better appreciation of the termite-like network of caves that gave birth to the *sassi*.

The vegetation along the top of the Gravina is scrubby and sparse but the rare orchids and wild herbs of the Mediterranean maquis (thyme, oregano, wild mint and sage) soften the rocky landscape. Birds of prey including red kites, buzzards and kestrels nest in the rocks, and in the ravine the Torrente Gravina winds its way into the Bradano River and eventually the Ionian Sea, 50km to the south.

A guided trek takes you to abandoned Neolithic villages and shepherd's retreats and to a number of rock churches including **Cristo La Selva**, with its Romanesque façade and medieval frescoes. But it is the rugged landscape of the canyon that sets the scene and the mood: walking in a silence broken only by the distant sound of rushing water in the ravine evokes images of those Basilian monks who, fleeing persecution in the East, founded the cliff-face rock churches and monastic cells.

San Michele Arcangelo was built. The views from the town are stupendous, overlooking the Matera Gravina and the richly cultivated fields of the Bradano Valley.

Information

The **tourist information office** (☎ 0835 20 06 20; Piazza San Giovanni Battista 15; ✆ 10am-1pm & 4-7pm) is in a square just off the main street, Corso della Repubblica. If you happen to be here on Good Friday don't miss the evocative **Procession of the Mysteries**.

Sights

The 16th-century **Chiesa di San Rocco** in Piazza Roma has a 19th-century belltower and a statue of the patron saint on the façade. From here walk up the hill on Corso della Repubblica with its many churches and elegant 17th-century buildings.

Along the Corso and down a short side-street is the 15th-century baroque **Chiesa Maggiore** (Via Chiesa Maggiore), which was reconstructed after the 1827 earthquake. Inside are four paintings by famous Napoli painter Matteo Preti, and a statue of the Addolarata in the right nave. Back on the Corso is the 17th-century baroque **Chiesa di SS Concezione** and the Romanesque **Chiesa di Santa Maria in Platea**. Turning right into Via Gramsci you reach the vast complex of the **Abbazia di San Michele Arcangelo** with the **Chiesa di Sant'Angelo** annexed to it. The church has a Renaissance-style dome. The abbey (closed for restoration at the time of research) has 365 rooms and Gothic-style cloisters, and is decorated with 16th- to 17th-century frescoes of sacred images and pagan divinities.

Sleeping & Eating

B&B da Pacifica (☎ 0835 20 02 21; www.dapacifica.it; Via Matteotti 26; s/d €30/50) The room upstairs has a private rooftop terrace with fantastic views over the town while the mini-apartment has a large, comfortable bed, a decent kitchen and loads of space. It's only a 15-minute drive to Matera.

Osteria dei Nanni (☎ 338 7036055; Piazza Mianulli; ✆ Thu-Tue; sandwiches €1.50, pasta €10) All he needs is a pointed hat and a beard and the congenial, multilingual host could pass for one of the *nanni* (dwarves) on the counter. Sit at the homemade wine-barrel tables outside to watch the evening *passeggiata* and down a few sangrias at the regular summer weekend 'anti-stress' party.

Getting There & Around

There are frequent daily bus services (€1.19) from Matera.

POTENZA & AROUND

The fault line running the length of the Apennines from Sicily to Genoa has resulted in some massive earthquakes in Basilicata, with Potenza somehow attracting more than its fair share of seismic chaos. With a history of earthquakes, invasions and brigands, instability seems to be a key word in Basilicata but one enduring constant has been the fertile agricultural land around Potenza, particularly north towards the extinct volcano of Monte Vulture.

The landscape is enchanting, with its wide valleys and pockets of thickly wooded forest. Gently undulating hills capped with castles and medieval towns, cultivated cereal farms, vineyards and olive groves become more and more frequent the further north you drive. This is the land of delicious olive oil and the famous Aglianico del Vulture wines.

POTENZA

pop 68,839 / elev 819m

The architecturally innovative supports (in place of traditional pylons) beneath the Basento River bridge may be an indication of Potenza's attempt to look to the future. Considering the number of earthquakes that have regularly rocked the city and destroyed most of its medieval buildings and historical sites it might sound like a good idea. But the attempt has resulted in some of the most brutal housing blocks you're ever likely to see and some

of the most bizarre architecture in Basilicata (including the visually uninspiring 1km escalator system presently under construction that will link the old town with the western commercial and residential districts).

As the highest capital in Italy, Potenza is cloyingly hot in summer and bitterly cold in winter. But the city is an important industrial and transport hub and despite first impressions the old town (with commanding views of the Basento Valley) does retain some of its former charm, especially during the evening *passeggiata*.

Orientation

The centre of town straggles east to west across a high ridge. To the south lie the main Trenitalia and Ferrovie Appulo-Lucane train stations, connected to the centre by buses 6, 10 and 11.

Potenza's sights, such as they are, are in the old centre of town, which is at the very top of the hill; to get there take the elevators from Piazza Vittorio Emanuele II. Piazza Mario Pagano and Via Pretoria are pedestrianised and the main *passeggiata* areas.

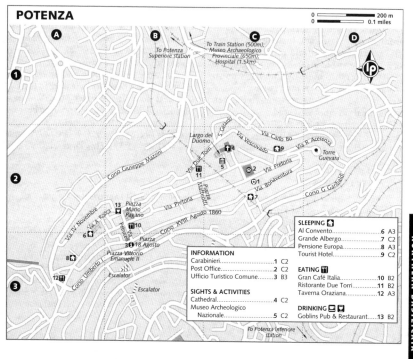

POTENZA

0   200 m
0   0.1 miles

To Potenza Superiore station

To Train Station (500m); Museo Archaeologico Provinciale (650m); Hospital (1.5km)

Largo del Duomo

Via Carlo Bo

Via Vescovado

Via R. Acerenza

Torre Guevara

Via Pretoria

Via Due Torri

Corso Giuseppe Mazzini

Piazza Matteotti

Via Bonaventura

Corso G. Garibaldi

Via Pretoria

Piazza Mario Pagano

Via IV Novembre

Via A. Rosica

Pretoria

Via Pretoria

Corso XVIII Agosto 1860

Piazza 18 Agosto

Piazza Vittorio Emanuele II

Corso Umberto I

Escalator

Escalator

To Potenza Inferiore station

INFORMATION
Carabinieri..........................1 C2
Post Office..........................2 C2
Ufficio Turistico Comune......3 B3

SIGHTS & ACTIVITIES
Cathedral..........................4 C2
Museo Archeologico
Nazionale..........................5 C2

SLEEPING 🛌
Al Convento..........................6 A3
Grande Albergo.....................7 C2
Pensione Europa...................8 A3
Tourist Hotel.......................9 C2

EATING 🍽
Gran Café Italia...................10 B2
Ristorante Due Torri.............11 B2
Taverna Oraziana................12 A3

DRINKING 🍷
Goblins Pub & Restaurant.....13 B2

NORTHERN BASILICATA

Information

There are a number of banks and ATMs along Via Pretoria.

Carabinieri (☎ 112; Via Pretoria 300) A law-enforcement body similar to the police and conveniently located along Via Pretoria in the old centre of town.

Guardia Medica (☎ 0971 45 66 13)

Hospital (☎ 0971 61 11 11; Via Potito Petrone)

Medical Emergency (☎ 118)

Police (☎ 0971 41 57 54; Via Di Giura)

Post Office (☎ 0971 32 64 22; Via Pretoria 253-259; ☯ 8am-6.30pm Mon-Fri, 8am-12.30pm Sat)

Tourist office (☎ 0971 50 76 22; www.aptbasilicata .it; Via del Gallitello 89; ☯ 9am-1pm & 4-7pm Mon-Fri, 9am-1pm Sat) The main tourist office is in an inconvenient location.

Ufficio Turistico Comune (☎ 0971 41 51 50; ☯ 9am-1pm & 4-7pm Mon-Fri, 9am-1pm Sat) In a much better location on Piazza Agosto (take the elevator at the end of Via Petrucelli off the main square, Piazza Mario Pagano).

Sights

From the moment you see the contemporary Trojan horse in the central courtyard of the stately 17th-century Palazzo Loffredo you know the **Museo Archeologico Nazionale** (☎ 0971 2 17 19; Via Andrea Serrao; adult/concession €2.50/1.25; ☯ 9am-8pm Tue-Sun, 2-8pm Mon) won't disappoint. Opened in 2004, the museum showcases finds from all over Basilicata, including jewellery and artefacts from the 2nd-century BC tomb of a seven-year-old princess from Vaglio; the skeleton of a 6th-century BC Enotrian woman from Alianello; and an impressive priestess' headpiece adorned with cavorting young men and animals in embossed gold.

Close by, the **cathedral** (☎ 0971 2 24 88; Largo del Duomo; ☯ 7.30am-1pm & 5-8pm) is the ecclesiastical highlight. Originally erected in the 12th century but rebuilt in the 18th, the cathedral houses the remains of St Gerard, Potenza's patron saint.

North of the town centre is the **Museo Archeologico Provinciale** (☎ 0971 44 4833; Via Ciccotti; admission free; ☯ 9am-1pm & 4-7pm) with a collection of local and regional finds from prehistoric to Roman times. It's not as interesting or well presented as the National Museum but does have a beautiful alabaster statuette of the goddess Persephone dating from the 5th to the 6th century BC.

Sleeping

Although it's the capital city of Basilicata, Potenza has limited sleeping options.

Pensione Europa (☎ 0971 3 40 14; Via Albini 3; s/d €20/40) This unprepossessing *pensione* in the centre of the old town has three rooms, a shared bathroom and no extra frills like breakfast but it's clean and close to bars and cafes.

Al Convento (☎ 0971 2 55 91; www.alconvento.eu; Largo San Michele Arcangelo 21; s/d €50/80; ☒) In central Potenza, this is a charming choice, an early 19th-century building (funnily enough, once a convent), with some modern features, set on a medieval square opposite a church. Inside is a mix of polished antiques and design classics, with wood-beamed ceilings and tiled floors.

Tourist Hotel (☎ 0971 214 37; www.touristhotelpo tenza.com; Via Vescovado 4; s/d €57/82; ☐ ☒ ☐) A no-surprise 80-room business hotel – except for the owner, Antonio Romano, an extremely talented artist whose works feature in the gallery next door. His abstract Mona Lisa is a sensual, kaleidoscopic interpretation bearing no resemblance to the original.

Grande Albergo (☎ 0971 41 02 20; Corso XVIII Agosto 46; s/d €73/100; ☒ ☐) This large, flashy hotel

---

CASTEL LAGOPESOLE

A solitary bastion dominating the landscape, the monolithic **Castel Lagopesole** (admission €1.55; ☯ 9.30am-1pm & 4-7pm Mar-Sep, 9.30am-1pm & 3-5pm Oct-Feb) was one of Frederick II of Hohenstaufen's favourite haunts. Indulging a passion for falconry (he wrote a book on the arts and secrets of falconry) Frederick and his cronies hunted in the forest below the castle. Now a small nature reserve is all that remains of his former playground.

The castle's most impressive attributes are its sheer size and commanding hill-top position. The stark, barrack-like structure has a rectangular plan with two courtyards and a central donjon. Oxidation of iron salts in the stonework has turned the walls red. Legend says it was built by a Byzantine commander in the 8th-century but first mention of it was made in 1137. Frederick made renovations to the castle in the years before his death in 1250 leaving it as his final monumental legacy to Basilicata.

The castle is 25km north of Potenza on the SS93.

NORTHERN BASILICATA

with its marble floors, wood-panelled walls and black leather couches has all the creature comforts and fantastic views of the Basento Valley but lacks warmth and atmosphere.

Eating

Gran Café Italia (☎ 0971 2 28 24; Via Pretoria 102; sandwiches/gelati €2/1.50; 7am-midnight) A great breakfast, coffee or *gelati* break in front of Piazza Mario Pagnano, this café in the heart of town is also a cool hang-out in the summer evenings.

ourpick **Ristorante Due Torri** (☎ 0971 41 16 61; Via Due Torri 6/8; meals €18-22; Tue-Sun) Inside an old stone tower Donato Bochicchio makes magic – transforming his passion for food into a sub-lime palette of flavours, textures and gustatory delights. Using the freshest local ingredients he makes simple dishes like *crema di zucca e funghi* (pumpkin and mushroom soup) unforgettable. Highly recommended.

Taverna Oraziana (☎ 0971 27 32 33; Via Orazio Flacco 2; meals €25; Mon-Sat) In a 19th-century *palazzo*, this restaurant lacks the intimacy and warmth suggested by the central fireplace. The home-made pasta dishes live up to expectations but the service can be over-attentive or politely cool.

Drinking

Goblins Pub & Restaurant (☎ 0971 2 10 01; Via A Rosica 82; 7.30am-4pm & 6pm-1am Mon-Sat, 7pm-1am Sun) Near the main square, this popular English-style pub serves good cheap eats and is packed on weekend nights.

Getting There & Away

BUS

The main bus station is in the central square on Via Zara. **Grassani** (☎ 0835 72 14 43) has buses to Matera (€5.35, one hour, four daily). **SITA** (☎ 0971 50 68 11) has daily services to Melfi (1½ hours) and Maratea (€7.39, three hours). **Liscio** (☎ 0971 5 46 73) serves destinations including Venosa (€6, 1½ hours, one daily), Rome (€20, 4½ hours, three daily) and Naples (€7.50, two hours, three daily) via Salerno (€5.40, 1½ hours, two daily).

CAR & MOTORCYCLE

Potenza is connected to Salerno in the west by the A3. Metaponto lies southeast along the SS407, the Basentana. For Matera, take the SS407 and then turn north onto the SS7 at Ferrandina.

TRAIN

There are regular train services from **Potenza Inferiore** (☎ 0971 20 21) to Taranto (€8.20, two hours), Salerno (€6, 1¾ hours) and Foggia (€6, two hours). To get to Matera (€5.32, one hour, frequent), change to an **FAL** (☎ 0971 41 15 61) bus at Ferrandina on the Metaponto line (although it is far more convenient to catch a bus).

For Bari (€8.60, three hours, three daily), use the **Ferrovie Appulo-Lucane** (☎ 0971 41 15 61) at Potenza Superiore station.

Getting Around

The main sights are within walking distance of each other. Local buses run from town to Via Zara and Potenza Inferiore (€0.50).

VENOSA

pop 12,147 / 415m

Venosa, home town of the Latin poet, Horace (65–8 BC), retains the elegance and charm of its Roman past. Named Venusia after the goddess Venus, the town seems to have taken her divine attributes of beauty, love and art to heart, producing not only a poet but a musical prince, Carlo Gesualdo. A 16th-century composer of the *madrigali* (musical word-painting), Gesualdo's experimental genius was surpassed only by the passion with which he murdered his wife ('viciously stabbed in the parts which it is best for a woman to keep modest') and her lover. During Gesualdo's reign Venosa enjoyed a period of intense cultural and artistic activity, a reputation it continues to promote. *Carpe diem,* as Horace would say.

History

Legend has it that when the child Horace became lost in the woods, doves covered him with a blanket of leaves to keep him safe from bears and snakes. What else would you expect of a Venusian poet? Venosa's history is slightly less romantic. Conquered by the Romans in 281 BC, the town prospered from its strategic position on the Via Appia (the route that linked Rome with the eastern provinces) but when the Emperor Trajan moved the Via Appia further north, Venosa suffered a slow, crippling decline. Matters weren't improved by the Barbarian invasions and things didn't begin to brighten up until the Norman conquests in the 11th century and Frederick II's reign.

Orientation & Information

All incoming roads lead to the central square, Piazza Umberto I, in front of the massive castle. Corso Vittorio Emanuele II, facing the castle entrance, leads to the archaeological park out of town. To the right as you enter this street you will find a helpful, English-speaking tourist guide in **Minutiello Viaggi** (☎ 0972 3 25 69; ⏰ 9am-1pm & 5-8pm Mon-Sat). Also along here are cafés, shops, a bank, the cathedral and a statue of the town's favourite, Horace. The **post office** (☎ 0972 3 18 61; Via Battaglini 10) is north of the castle while the **police station** (☎ 0972 3 11 43; Via General Pennella 20) is to the west.

Sights

The **castle** was built in 1470 by the duke Pirro del Balzo on the site of the town's cathedral (but to appease the God-fearing townsfolk he built a brand new cathedral just down the road). Inside the present-day **cathedral** (Corso Vittorio Emanuele II) is a 13th-century painting of the *Madonna dell'Idria* and the tomb of the duke's wife, Maria Donata Orsini.

The castle is surrounded by a deep moat and contains the small **National Archaeological Museum** (☎ 0972 36095; Piazza Umberto I; adult/concession €2.50/1.25; ⏰ 9am-8pm Wed-Mon, 2-8pm Tue). The collection houses the finds from the nearby excavations of Roman Venusia.

The **Parco Archeologico** (admission free; ⏰ 9am-1hr before sunset) is at the northeastern end of town. Here lie the ruins of a Roman settlement including an amphitheatre, a spa and a 2nd-century BC house. Next to the ruins is the intriguing **Abbazia della Santissima Trinita** (admission free; ⏰ 9am-noon & 4-8pm), the largest monastic complex in Basilicata. It was erected above a Roman temple in 1046 by the Benedictines and predates the Norman invasions. Within the complex are an 11th-century abbey, an unfinished 12th-century church, and the Holy Trinity Church (begun in the 5th century and restored after successive earthquakes) which contains the tomb of the mighty Norman crusader Robert Guiscard (d 1085), his wife Aberada, and his much-feared brothers. Inside the church are some beautiful frescoes and mosaics and the so-called 'column of friendship' – according to local legend linking hands while circling the column will make a friendship eternal.

About 3km further on are **Jewish catacombs** dating back to the 4th to 9th centuries (closed for restoration at the time of research).

Back in town you can pay a visit to the **Casa di Orazio** (☎ 339 480 74 31; admission free; ⏰ by appointment), supposedly the house of the poet Horace. In fact it is a private bath complex from the 1st century AD. There's not much to see in the way of Horace or baths.

As you wander through the town centre look closely at the elegant buildings and *palazzi* and you will see parts of capitals, oddly positioned statues and stone blocks inscribed with ancient writing. The Roman ruins were put to good use in constructing and restoring Venosa over the past millennia.

Sleeping

L'Oranziano (☎ 0972 3 23 33; Vittorio Emanuele III 131; s/d €28/50) In a historic building on the narrow main drag that wends its medieval way through the walled city, this is a central B&B, peach, pink and full of elderly furniture, close to the cathedral.

Hotel Orazio (☎ 0972 3 11 35; Vittorio Emanuele II 142; s/d €41/50; ✕ ♿) Once home to the Knights of Malta, this 17th-century palace, complete with antique majolica tiles and marble floors, is now a family-run hotel presided over by a pair of grandmotherly ladies. The terrace has beautiful views of the valley.

Agriturismo La Maddalena (☎ 0972 3 27 35; www.argrilamaddalena.it; Contrada La Maddalena; s/d €35/70; ⏰ Mar-Nov; ✕ P ♿) This delightful *agriturismo* is only 500m from the archaeological park. Each of its seven rooms is named after a fruit (except for *hippos* the horse), and furnished in a style to suit. Be warned, the grape-room, *uva*, takes purple to extremes. The restaurant is in a converted stable. It has a swimming pool and offers horse-riding.

Hotel Il Guiscardo (☎ 0972 3 23 62; www.hotelilguiscardo.it; Via Accademia dei Rinascenti 106; s/d/tr/q €45/60/75/90; ♿ P ✕) In this large, modern hotel the rooms are spacious and adequate but the walls are depressingly devoid of artwork. Tucked away behind reception is a surprisingly cosy restaurant where you can eat good Lucanian cuisine. Another pleasant surprise is the wood-fired pizza oven on a sprawling 2nd-floor terrace with views over Venosa.

Eating

Il Grifo (☎ 0972 3 51 88; Via delle Fornaci 21; meals €18-20; ⏰ Wed-Mon) Highly recommended by the locals this restaurant/pizzeria is tucked away behind the museum. A buffet of local vegetable dishes complements a menu of meats cooked in the traditional Lucanian style.

Ristorante Ducale (☎ 0972 3 71 00; Piazza Municipio 2; meals €25-30; ☺ lunch) To get to this cosy restaurant in a converted cantina walk through the bar and down the stairs. The *agnello alla paesana* (a hearty lamb stew) suits the grotto surrounds. The upstairs bar is open from 3.30am and serves delicious cakes and pastries.

Al Frantoio (☎ /fax 0972 3 69 25; Via Roma 21; meals €40; ☺ Tue-Sun) For a blowout meal in Venosa, head to this elegant, very well-regarded restaurant occupying several graceful rooms in a building backed by olive groves. It specialises in spectacular takes on local dishes, especially spicy Italian sausages. Try the *salsicce con rape.*

Getting Around
The museum, cathedral and local sights are all within easy walking distance of each other. A city bus sweeps along Via Melfi every 20 minutes for the archaeological park (€0.30; buy tickets on the bus).

Getting There & Away
Train travel to Venosa is not recommended; from Rome a number of changes are required, and from Potenza the train stops at Rionero in Vulture and Melfi but connections are unreliable. Instead, **Liscio** (☎ 0971 5 46 73) runs a daily bus from Potenza (1½ hours, €6), but not on Sunday. **SITA** (☎ 0971 27 30 84) buses from Foggia also operate six times a week (1½ hours, €8).

By car, drive north on the SS658 from Potenza, exiting at Barile onto the SS93. From Rome and Naples take the A16, exiting at Candela, or the Cerignola exit if you are travelling north along the A16 from Bari.

MELFI
pop 17,138 / elev 530m
Melfi has an impressive history, even if the modern town is unprepossessing. It was a favourite residence of Frederick II, who loved to hunt the nearby wooded slopes of Monte Vulture, shacking up in his huge Melfi castle. It was here in 1231 that he issued the *Constitutiones Augustales,* the first written laws of the Middle Ages – a constitution quite remarkable for the times. Before Frederick, the castle was already famous. The Norman knight Robert Guiscard was crowned Duke of Apulia and Calabria here, and Pope Urban II declared the First Crusade within its walls in 1089.

BANDITS & BRIGANDS
One of northern Basilicata's infamous sons was the outlaw bandit Carmine Crocco, a leader of the 19th-century peasant revolts during the unification of Italy. Like an Italian Robin Hood, he and his merry bandits fought against poverty and suppression, hiding out in the woods around Monte Vulture, living off the land and handouts from local peasant supporters. Hiking trails around the Monticchio Lakes and Monte Vulture follow some of the pathways of these daring brigands.

Orientation & Information
The main road from the train station climbs up the hill and winds inside the Norman walls to the impressive castle dominating the skyline. The **tourist office** (☎ 0972 23 97 51; ☺ 9am-1pm & 4-7pm) in central Piazza Umberto isn't always open.

Sights
The formidable 12th-century castle has a moat, a bridge and eight towers. It houses the **Museo Archeologico del Melfese** (☎ 0972 23 87 26; adult/concession €2.50/1.25; ☺ 9am-8pm Tue-Sun, 2-8pm Mon), which has an excellent collection of regional artefacts dating from the 8th-century BC. Pick of the exhibits is the *sarcofago di Rapolla,* an intricately carved marble sarcophagus from the 2nd century.

The **cathedral** (☎ 0972 23 81 80; Piazza Duomo; ☺ 9am-1pm & 4-8pm), originally constructed in 1056, was rebuilt in baroque style following the 1694 earthquake. Inside is a fine gilded wooden ceiling and a 13th-century fresco of Madonna with Child and Angels. In a chapel towards the right is the Madonna dell'Assunta, protector of the city. The original belltower (note the two griffins – symbols of the Norman dynasty) has somehow miraculously survived the succession of devastating earthquakes.

Sleeping & Eating
The charming and graceful town of nearby Venosa is a better choice for a stopover, or if you prefer a night in the country stay in an *agriturismo* in the Monticchio Lakes area.

For lunch, **Delle Rose** (☎ 0972 2 16 82; Via Vittorio Emanuele 29; pizza €4-5; ☺ Fri-Wed) is a decent restaurant/pizzeria.

NORTHERN BASILICATA

Getting There & Away

Melfi is 53km north of Potenza on the SS658. **SITA** (☎ 0971 50 68 11) has frequent daily bus services from Potenza (1½ hours). **Liscio** (☎ 0971 54 67 34) has one service (70 minutes). Trains run five times a day from Potenza (€2.89, 1½ hours).

AROUND MELFI

The rich volcanic soil of the Vulture area around Mt Vulture and Melfi is intensely cultivated with vineyards, olives and wheatfields. In this beautiful landscape the large industrial Fiat factory to the north is a visual eyesore but an economic drawcard.

Laghi di Monticchio

The Monticchio Lakes (652m) southwest of Melfi are a perfect example of how to spoil a beautiful natural environment. The two volcanic lakes are surrounded by a stately wooded forest, but in summer the narrow isthmus separating Lago Piccolo and Lago Grande is a noisy strip of kitschy souvenir stalls, loud bars and some dodgy-looking eateries. The imposing white hulk of the 18th-century **Benedictine Abbey of San Michele** stands high above the lakes, its blind façade staring blankly down on the pedal-powered boats and *gelati*-eating crowds that have replaced the devout pilgrims of another time.

ACTIVITIES

To get in touch with nature hike up to the abbey or along marked trails through the forest where outlaw bandits once roamed. Or hire a pedal-boat from **Noleggio barche e pedalo da Antonio** (☎ 338 676 00 84; per person per 30 min €2; ☒ Mar-Nov), which also runs 15-minute motor boat cruises of Lago Piccolo (adult/child €2.50/2).

Horse-riding around the lakes and the Vulture region can be organized through **Agriturismo La Valle dei Cavalli** (☎ 0972 71 62 40; www.lavalledeicavalli.it; Locanda Piano di Carda). A half-day ride with a guide is €40.

SLEEPING & EATING

There's a campground near the lakes, **Parco Naturale Europa** (☎ 0972 73 10 08; www.campingeuropa .net; Via Lago Grande 28) but the site is unappealing and the facilities rudimentary. Instead, enjoy the tranquil and beautiful Vulture countryside in an *agriturismo*.

Il Casale dell'Acqua Rossa (☎ /fax 0972 73 10 72; www.ilcasaledellacquarossa.3000.it; Monticchio Bagni; s/d/tr/q €35/50/60/75; ☒ Apr-Nov) This lovely pink villa 2km from the lakes has simple, comfortable rooms with private bathroom and TV, and a restaurant with an enviable reputation.

Cantuccio del Vulture (☎ 0972 73 13 14; www.cantucciodelvulture.it; Monticchio Sgarroni; s/d €26/52) Dominating an 80-hectare wheat field, this reconverted farmhouse has large modern bedrooms with comfortable wrought iron beds and great views of the surrounding countryside. At night the stars do their thing in blissful silence. The guest lounge has a cosy fireplace.

GETTING THERE & AWAY

At Rionero in Vulture leave the SS658 from Potenza and follow the signs to the Laghi di Monticchio.

Trains from Potenza stop at Rionero in Vulture (€2.69, one hour, five daily). From here catch a local bus to the lakes.

Southern Basilicata

Southern Basilicata is Italy's last true wilderness, a chaotic landscape of tremendous mountain ranges, dark forested valleys and villages so melded to the rock face that sometimes you don't know they are there at all. The purple-hued mountains of the interior are impossibly grand, a wonderful destination for naturalists; particularly grand are the soaring peaks of the Lucanian Apennines and the Parco Nazionale del Pollino where wild boars and wolves still roam. The mountains divide Basilicata's two vastly different coastlines: in the southeast lie the flat plains of the semi-arid Ionian coast; in the southwest are the dramatic plunging cliffs of the Tyrrhenian coast. While winter snows cover the mountain peaks the coastal beaches enjoy a Mediterranean climate of mild, wet winters and hot, dry summers.

The Ionian coast was once a prosperous colony of Magna Graecia, but centuries of conflict, maritime raids, feudal wars, malaria and mass emigration saw it increasingly isolated, forgotten and poverty-stricken. Even though large funds have been injected into massive irrigation and agricultural schemes, Basilicata remains one of the poorest regions in Italy.

Southern Basilicata's rugged terrain and infertile soil may be difficult to tame, but the beauty and diversity of its landscape is also the main attraction for its burgeoning tourist industry. Nowhere is this more evident than on the majestic Tyrrhenian coast, where Maratea is fast making a name for itself as one of Italy's most chic seaside resorts.

HIGHLIGHTS

- Roam the snow-streaked peaks in search of the rare *pino loricato* in the **Parco Nazionale del Pollino** (p192)
- Spend an eerie night in the vertiginous cliff-hugging village of **Pietrapertosa** (p186)
- Tuck into a fresh seafood platter as the sun sets over **Maratea** (p186) and the dramatic Tyrrhenian coast
- For a hauntingly unforgettable experience visit the ghost town of **Craco** (boxed text, p200)
- Have a bizarre day – drive through the lunar landscape of the *calanchi* in the **Appennino Lucano** (p184) then hike through the incredibly green and beautiful **Parco Naturale Gallipoli Cognato** (boxed text, p186)
- After a day lazing on the sandy beaches of the Ionian coast, head inland for a poetic night in **Tursi** (p200)

SOUTHERN BASILICATA

APPENNINO LUCANO

The Appenino Lucano (Lucanian Apennines) rear up sharply just south of Potenza. They cut Basilicata in half, protecting the lush Tyrrhenian coast and leaving the Ionian shores of Basilicata and Calabria gasping in the semi-arid heat. The landscape is surreal. Tiny mountain villages curl between great fangs of perforated rock in the soaring sandstone peaks and spires of the Lucanian Dolomites (so named because they resemble their dolomitic cousins in the Alps). Further south the land morphs into the equally spectacular *calanchi* – sharp ridges and eroded furrows of sun-baked clay. The lunar landscape of the *calanchi* is surprisingly dynamic as the unstable craggy outcrops are continuously subjected to eroding rains and winds.

ALIANO

pop 1244 / elev 497m

A remote village in Basilicata's isolated interior, Aliano would still languish unknown had not writer, painter and political activist Carlo Levi been exiled here during the Fascist regime. In his classic book *Christ Stopped at Eboli* Levi graphically describes the aching hardship of peasant life in 'Gagliano' (in reality, Aliano) where 'there is no definite boundary between the world of human beings and that of animals and even monsters.'

An earthquake in 1980 saw most inhabitants leave the old village crumbling on its hilltop spur. Aliano is a sleepy town that only seems to come alive late in the afternoon when old men congregate on the park benches in the pleasant tree-lined Via Roma, and black-shrouded women exchange news and gossip on the streets. But as a tribute to Levi and the tourism he has generated, life is gradually seeping back into the old town – the house where Levi lived has been preserved as a museum and other old buildings are currently undergoing restoration with grand plans of alfresco bars and souvenir shops.

Orientation & Information

The **tourist office** (☎ 0835 56 80 74; Via Roma 5; ☒ 10am-12.30pm & 4-7.30pm Wed-Mon Jun-Sep) is on the main street and is run by the parish priest, Don Pierino. If it's closed, ask at the Bar Capr-

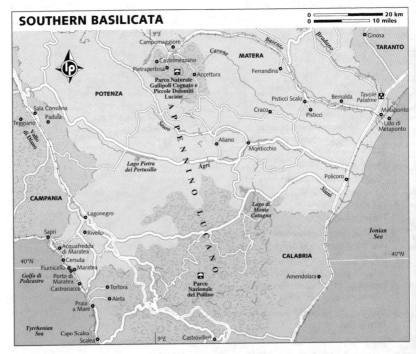

SOUTHERN BASILICATA

iccio (a couple of doors down) and someone is likely to go and find him. To see all the Carlo Levi sights follow Via Roma towards the old town.

Sights & Activities

Carlo Levi is Aliano's cultural claim to fame and in 2000 a Literary Park was formed (one of 17 in southern Italy; the aim is to educate and encourage interest in famous writers) under the umbrella heading of **Parco Letterario Carlo Levi** (☎ 0835 56 85 20; Via Martiri d'Ungheria 1; ☽ 9am-12.30pm & 4-7.30pm Thu-Tue).

The **Pinacoteca Carlo Levi** (☎ 0835 56 83 15; Piazza Garibaldi; admission incl guided tour of Levi's house €3; ☽ 10am-1pm & 4-7.30pm summer, 10am-12.30pm & 3.30-6.30pm winter) in what was originally the post office also houses the **Museo Storico di Carlo Levi**. Here you will find papers, documents and paintings of the writer, including seven lithographs he bequeathed to the museum only months before he died.

La Casa di Confino di Carlo Levi (Via Collina), where Levi spent the seven months of his confinement in 1935 to 1936, has a multimedia display. The **Museo della Civiltà Contadina** is directly under the house in an old *frantoio* (olive-oil mill). You'll find tools and equipment used by the peasants for agriculture, husbandry and handcrafts.

To round off the Levi experience head to the cemetery, the highest point in town. His **gravesite** has a simple tombstone with outstanding views of the *calanchi* and the distant Pollino mountains.

Sleeping & Eating

Taverna 'La Contadina Sisina' (☎ 0835 56 82 39; www .lacontadinasisina.com; Via Roma 13; s/d €25/50; meals from €15) About your only choice in this little town, the taverna is conveniently located in the main street. There's no menu – you'll be served whatever delicious *piatti contadini* (traditional peasant dishes) Sisina decides to cook. With its wooden ceiling, fireplace and old photographs on the wall it's a cosy place, but it can get quite noisy – a problem if you want to retire early. The three upstairs bedrooms share a common bathroom while the three-bedroom apartment close by has a miniscule bathroom – but greater privacy.

Getting There & Away

Unless you have a car, reaching this small town will be an ordeal.

BUS

A **SITA** (☎ 0971 50 68 11; www.sitabus.it) bus from Potenza (€5.32) requires a changeover at Sant'Arcangelo. Grassani runs a bus from Matera (€4) which also involves a changeover at Stigliano.

CAR & MOTORCYCLE

From Potenza take the SS407 towards Matera. Exit for Campomaggiore and follow the signs for Accettura. From the Ionian Coast drive south along the SS106 from Metaponto, turn onto the SS598, exiting at Monticchio.

CASTELMEZZANO

pop 946 / elev 750m

One of the highest villages in Basilicata, Castelmezzano looks like something out of a fairytale. The houses huddle along an impossibly narrow ledge that falls away in vertigo-inducing gorges to the Caperrino River. Spotlights pick out the towering needle spires above the village and when the mist swirls in (as it often does) the effect is otherworldly. It's not surprising to discover a sorcerer once lived in this hilltop eyrie – a plaque on an abandoned stone house in the main street identifies his home (look for the plaque *Il Mago di Lucana*).

Hiking tracks weave through the sandstone spires and across the slopes above the village, and others wind along the cliffs and down into the river gorge. A hike to Pietrapertosa will take about one hour. For an adrenaline rush, fly across the gorge at 120km/h on **Il Volo dell'Angelo** (www.volodellangelo.com). The 1550m-long Tyrolean traverse is due to open in June 2007. See the **tourist office** (☎ 0971 98 60 20; Piazza Rivelli 3; ☽ 9am-1pm & 3-8pm Jun-Sep) for details.

Al Becco della Civetta (☎ 0971 98 62 49; Vico I Maglietta 7; meals €25-30; ☽ lunch & dinner Wed-Mon) has a basic menu of mountain fare – homemade pastas and roasted meats. Mushrooms feature prominently when in season. There's a 24-room B&B attached, **La Locanda di Castromediano** (s/d/tr/q €45/75/95/115; 🖩), with panoramic views over the gorge.

A cheaper option is the very basic **Hotel Dolomiti** (☎ 0971 98 60 89; Via Michele Volini; s/d €35/50). It only has five rooms so book ahead.

From Potenza take the SS407 towards Matera, exiting at Campomaggiore. SITA runs four buses each day from Potenza (€2.50,1½ hours).

PIETRAPERTOSA
pop 1252 / elev 1088m

As the highest town in Basilicata, Pietrapertosa is possibly even more dramatic than Castelmezzano. The 10th-century Saracen fortress at its pinnacle is difficult to spot because it is actually carved out of the mountain.

Pietrapertosa literally translates as 'perforated stone' and, indeed, the village sits in the midst of bizarrely shaped rocky towers with imaginative names like golden eagle, big mother, the anvil and the little owl.

A **tourist information kiosk** (Via della Stazione; 9am-noon & 4-7pm Jun-Sep) is located in the car park at the entrance to Pietrapertosa.

our pick **La Casa di Penelope e Cirene** (☎ 0971 98 30 13; Via Garibaldi 32; s/d €25/50; Apr-Nov) Highly recommended, this three-bedroom B&B is run by the very mod and cool Teresa Colucci whose eclectic tastes are reflected in carefully selected antique furnishings, music and artwork. She is also a mine of information on Pietrapertosa's history and Basilicata in general.

Another good choice soon to open is the **Borgo Albergo 'Sulla Riva dei Cielo', Una Locanda sul Mare delle Stelle** (☎ 0971 98 30 35; www.borghidi basilicata.eu; Via della Stazione 1). Twelve recently renovated houses have been turned into comfortable one- to six-bed apartments. Each one is named after a constellation – hence its poetic name, In the River of the Sky. The reception is in Orso Minore, opposite the tourist information kiosk. Prices were not finalised at time of writing.

By car, take the SS407 from Potenza, exiting at Campomaggiore. **Autolinee Renna** (☎ 0971 98 30 94) has bus services from Potenza (€2.50, one hour, five daily).

TYRRHENIAN COAST

Basilicata's small share of the Tyrrhenian coast is short (only about 30km) but very sweet. Squeezed between Calabria and Campania's Cilento peninsula, it shares the same beguiling characteristics: hidden coves and grey sandy beaches backed by majestic coastal cliffs. The SS18 threads a spectacular route along the mountains to the coast's number one attraction, the charming seaside town of Maratea.

MARATEA
pop 5287 / elev 300m

Situated high on a hilltop overlooking the sparkling Golfo di Policastro, Maratea is indeed Italy's well-kept secret. Boasting its turquoise seas and plunging cliffs it is often referred to as a mini-Amalfi. Sophisticated Italians escape here to enjoy the charming town, its elegant hotels and its clean, unpolluted and relatively uncrowded beaches. For once, responsible town planning has checked the worst excesses of coastal development, leaving this tiny little enclave as one of the most picturesque spots on the Tyrrhenian coast.

PARCO NATURALE GALLIPOLI COGNATO E PICCOLE DOLOMITI LUCANE

The Gallipoli Cognato and Lucanian Dolomites Regional Park covers a total of 270 sq km in the heart of Basilicata. Piercing sandstone peaks and deep ravines contrast with the leafy unspoilt beauty of the Gallipoli Cognato forest and the Montepiano wood. The Gallipoli Cognato forest (41.6 sq km) is a hiker's paradise: a network of well-signposted trails weaving through a forest of towering Turkey oaks, hornbeam, maple, beech and holly trees. It is home to foxes, deer, hares, wild cats and birds of prey. In spring the forest floor is carpeted in anemones, cyclamens and rare orchids, while in autumn the foliage blazes with fiery reds and yellows.

The five towns in the park include the spectacular mountain villages of Pietrapertosa and Castelmezzano, which perch dramatically on steep cliff faces. Accettura is famous for a bizarre yearly ritual called Il Maggio, originally a pagan fertility rite to improve seeding and planting. In May, a Turkey oak is felled and dragged by oxen into the town square where a holly tree is grafted to its top. The 'married' trees are then hoisted upright and the town's fit young men compete to see who can climb the highest.

La Mappa dei Sentieri is a useful map with detailed descriptions (in Italian) of over 30 cycling, horse-riding and hiking trails in the park. It's available from the **park office** (☎ 0835 67 50 15; www .parcogallipolicognato.it; Localita Palazzo; 10am-1pm & 3-6pm summer, 10am-2pm winter) in the heart of the park, 12km north of Accettura, or from the tourist offices in Castelmezzano and Pietrapertosa.

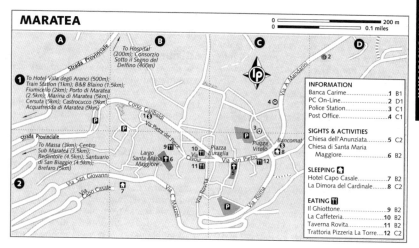

MARATEA

INFORMATION	
Banca Carime	1 B1
PC On-Line	2 D1
Police Station	3 C1
Post Office	4 C1

SIGHTS & ACTIVITIES	
Chiesa dell'Anunziata	5 C2
Chiesa di Santa Maria	
Maggiore	6 B2

SLEEPING	
Hotel Capo Casale	7 B2
La Dimora del Cardinale	8 C2

EATING	
Il Ghiottone	9 B2
La Caffeteria	10 B2
Taverna Rovita	11 B2
Trattoria Pizzeria La Torre	12 C2

Orientation

Maratea is actually a jumbled collection of small hamlets scattered along the coastal cliffs and it can be quite confusing to orientate yourself when you first arrive. Maratea Inferiore (simply referred to as Maratea) is the main hub and lies on the lower slopes of Monte San Biagio. Further up the mountain towards the gleaming white 22m Redentore are the ruins of Maratea Superiore, all that remains of the original 8th-century BC Greek colony.

The harbour of Porto di Maratea is on the coast directly below Maratea. About 3km south of the Porto on the SS18 is Marina di Maratea and a further 6km is Castrocucco, the southern end of Basilicata's west coast.

Taking the SS18 coast road north towards Sapri from Maratea are the characteristic hamlets of Fiumicello (2km), Cersuta (5km) and Acquafredda di Maratea (9km).

Information

EMERGENCY
Ambulance (☎ 118)
Police Station (☎ 113; Piazza Vitolo, Maratea)

INTERNET
La Bottega del Porto (☎ 0973 87 64 28; Via Porto Arenile, Porto di Maratea; ☼ 8.15am-1pm & 4.30-8pm Mon-Sat, 8.30am-1pm Sun; per 15 min €1)
PC On-Line (☎ 0973 87 77 94; Via A Mandarini 52, Maratea; per 15 min €1; ☼ 9am-1pm Mon-Sat year-round, 4.30-8.30pm May-Jun & Sep, 5-9pm Jul & Aug, 4-8pm Oct-Apr)

MEDICAL
Guardia Medica (☎ 0973 87 62 62)
Hospital (☎ 0973 87 51 11; Via San Nicola, Maratea)

MONEY
Banca Carime (☎ 0973 87 69 33; Via Pietra del Sole 5, Maratea)
Banco Popolare di Bari (☎ 0973 87 64 12; Via Garibaldi 1, Maratea)
San Paolo Banca di Napoli (☎ 0973 87 78 09; Via Santa Venere 61, Fiumicello)

POST OFFICE
Post Office Acquafredda di Maratea (☎ 0973 87 81 47; Via Stazione; ☼ 8.30am-1.30pm); Maratea (☎ 0973 87 60 50; Via A Mandarini; ☼ 8.30am-1.30pm); Porto di Maratea (☎ 0973 87 68 59; Via Bunchino Porto 29; ☼ 8.30am-1.30pm)

TOURIST INFORMATION
APT Tourist Office (☎ 0973 87 69 08; Piazza del Gesu 40, Fiumicello; ☼ 8am-8pm Jun-Sep, 8am-2pm Mon-Sat & 3-8pm Mon & Thu Oct-May)
Consorzio Sotto il Segno del Delfino (☎ 0973 87 64 99; Via San Nicola 43, Maratea; ☼ 10am-1pm & 4-7.30pm Mon-Sat) A consortium with an informative and helpful English-speaking guide.

Sights

Maratea is a pretty village of bar-studded piazze, wriggling alleys and interlocking houses, and a ramble through its streets is a pleasant way to fill a couple of hours. Starting from the modern mermaid fountain in Piazza Vitolo, wander down Via San Pietro to Piazza

Buraglia and its assortment of souvenir and craft shops. This is the hub of town and gets quite lively on summer evenings. The tables and chairs of La Caffeteria (p190) spill into the piazza, the perfect spot for a delicious *bocconotto* (sweet pastry) and coffee.

For a small town, Maratea packs a lot of churches (44 in total). The main church is the 15th-century **Chiesa di Santa Maria Maggiore** (☎ 0973 87 62 24; Largo Santa Maria Maggiore; ☼ by appointment) which has a baroque interior. Look for the **obelisk of San Biagio** in front of the **Chiesa dell'Annunziata** (Via San Pietro); the marble column was apparently salvaged from the sea.

The **Redentore** is an omniscient presence in Maratea, an enormous marble Christ dominating the peak of Monte San Biagio (624m). It was built in 1965 by Bruno Innocenti and, in case you're wondering, it isn't as tall as the 30m Christ in Rio de Janeiro – but with its outstretched arms it is no less impressive. Drive up the winding 5km road from Maratea for a closer look at the statue which, curiously, has its back turned to one of the finest views of the Golfo di Policastro on the entire coastline. Instead it faces the **Santuario di San Biagio** (☎ 0973 87 82 11; ☼ 9.30am-12.30pm & 4.30-7.30pm Apr-Oct, 5-6pm winter), originally built in the 6th to 7th century on the site of a pagan temple dedicated to Minerva. The remains of San Biagio, Maratea's patron saint, are preserved in a white marble urn inside.

As you drive along the coast road look for the six Spanish **towers** built in the 16th century as defence against pirates and invaders. The **Torre Apprezzami L'Asino** ('Value my donkey' tower) between Fiumicello and Cersuta is said to derive its name from an encounter between two travellers on a narrow cliff-side path. Coming from different directions and unable to pass each other they decided to throw the donkey of lesser value off the cliff.

The coastline is also dotted with numerous grottoes or sea caves, some of which can only be reached by boat. One that is accessible by car is **La Grotta delle Meraviglia** (☎ 0973 87 63 93; SS18km236, Marina di Maratea; ☼ 9.30am-12.30pm & 4-7pm Jul 1-Sep 15, other times by appointment). Spotlights highlight the spectacular stalactite and stalagmite formations in this large chamber 100m underground.

To round off a day of Mediterranean sun-worship head to the Porto, where you can eye up the sleek yachts and bright-blue fishing boats bobbing in the water. The swish restaurants and lively bars are the place for the chic-elite to see and be seen.

Activities

Maratea's chief attraction is its dramatic rocky coastline and stunning blue sea, so outdoor action – such as it is – focuses on the beach. Don't expect long white sandy beaches; the sand here is coarse – even gravelly – and often greyish-black in colour. **Fiumicello** is a popular spot and has a decent stretch of sand, as has **Acquafredda**, while **Castrocucco** boasts the longest beach on the coast. All three beaches can be reached by car. Local favourites Spiaggia Nero and Macarro near **Marina di Maratea** are black sand beaches set in idyllic little bays and involve a short hike from the nearest car park.

All the beaches are dotted with *lidi* (beach-bars and kiosks) where you can hire watersport equipment (kayaks, windsurfers and pedal boats) as well as umbrellas and chairs. **Centro Sub Maratea** (☎ 0973 87 00 13; www.csmaratea.it; Località Santa Caterina, Maratea) offers diving courses for all levels, motorboat excursions and hire. **Gita in Barca a Vela** (☎ 339 751 36 48) offers a full day trip on board a sailing boat with lunch, a cave visit and a swim for €60. **Velieri North Star e Samp** (☎ 348 385 56 74; www.costadimaratea.com/northstar) organizes yacht charters and tours.

For a spot of ocean fishing, the Sapri-based **Pescaturismo con Sara** (☎ 0973 38 11 51; jerry2001@libero.it; min 7-8 people €30) can organise a pick-up at Porto di Maratea.

To fully appreciate the rugged headlands, cliffs and mountains of Maratea, take a hike – literally. *I Sentieri di Maratea* (published by Amici di Maratea Associazone) has detailed descriptions of ten hiking trails in both English and Italian. The hikes range from one to five hours in length and take you through the typical scrubby bushland of the Mediterranean *maquis*. Pick up a free copy from either of the tourist offices.

Cyclists will find *Bicycle Tourism in Basilicata* published by APT Basilicata, a useful publication. It details eight cycling itineraries in Basilicata and is also available from the tourist office. Bring your own bike as there is no bike hire in town.

Festivals & Events

The **Festival of San Biagio** (Maratea's patron saint) takes place on the second Saturday in May. The silver bust of San Biagio from the

Santuario di San Biagio is covered with a red cloth and ceremoniously carried down the long winding road to Maratea's main piazza. The weeklong celebrations begin when the bust is uncovered.

During the summer months Maratea is a hive of cultural activity with jazz concerts, music shows, artistic performances and exhibitions.

Sleeping

Maratea is one of the most stylish resorts in the south, with accommodation to match. Fiumicello and the town of Maratea have a greater range of accommodation options and both make a good central base from which to explore the coast. During Easter and the summer holiday season advance booking is essential.

BUDGET

our pick B&B Nefer (☎ 0973 87 18 28; www.bbnefer.it; Via Cersuta; s/d €50/60; P) A B&B set in the small hamlet of Cersuta, 5km from Maratea, with two attractive rooms opening onto a small garden that overlooks the sea. The morning *cornetti* (croissants) are particularly good. From here you can walk along narrow seaside paths to a dramatic small, black-sanded beach.

Hotel Ristorante Fiorella (☎ 0973 87 69 21; Via Santa Venere 21, Fiumicello; d €60-70) This old 36-room hotel close to the train station is open year-round. Accommodation is basic, the lobby gloomy and the rooms spartan. If you arrive in the high season when nearly everything is booked you could get lucky here.

MID RANGE

Hotel Villa degli Aranci (☎ 0973 87 63 44; Via Profiti 7, Fiumicello; s €40-90, d €80-130; P) Its name means House of Oranges, and with a garden of sweetly scented orange and lemon trees, the hotel resembles a country villa. The furniture is starting to look a little worn, but the rooms are bright and airy, the blue-and-white colour theme reflecting the aqua sea views from the balcony. Tiles painted with local water scenes are a cute touch. The hotel is close to the train station and a bus stops out the front.

our pick B&B Laino (☎ 0973 87 65 06; www.beblaino .it; Via Rasi 4c, Fiumicello; s €40-70, d €50-160, 4-bed apt weekly €350-1400; ⊠ 🖳 P 🐾) This recently opened B&B is beautifully finished with stone, wood and wrought-iron fittings and

has large modern bathrooms. It's 800m to the port and to the bay of Fiumicello, but it might be hard to drag yourself away from the fabulous ocean views from your private sun-bed by the pool.

La Dimora del Cardinale (☎ 0973 87 77 12; www .lamoradelcardinale.com; Via Cersuta, Maratea; s €55-90, d €70-125, ste €100-170; ⊠) In the centre of old Maratea, this was home to a 19th-century cardinal. The 16 rooms have inoffensive peachy décor – it's worth staying here to nab the room with a fabulous terrace overlooking the town and mountains.

Hotel Capo Casale (☎ 0973 87 13 08; www.capocasale .it; Via Capo Casale 10, Maratea; s €60-85, d €80-130; 🌙 Apr-Oct; ⊠) If it feels as though you're in a little village rather than a hotel, that's because you are. Thirty individual houses on the slope behind Maratea have been restored and reconverted into a *borgo*-style hotel. Narrow alleys and stairways connect rooms decorated with terra cotta tiles and rustic wooden furniture. Have breakfast on the terrace overlooking town.

Hotel Settebello (☎ 0973 87 62 77; Via Fiumicello 52, Fiumicello; s €60-90, d €75-125, tr €103-150, ste €150-280; Apr-Oct; P ⊠) Basing yourself slap-bang on the beachfront at Fiumicello's most popular beach may or may not be a good idea. The rooms are fairly nondescript – basic, but adequate – and you won't need to change when you leave the sand. In the height of summer you won't escape the noise or the crowds.

TOP END

Hotel Gabbiano (☎ 0973 87 80 11; www.hotelgabbiano maratea.it; Acquafredda; s €60-105, d €120-210; 🌙 Easter-Oct; ⊠ P 🐾) With its arches, whitewashed façade and garden terrace, the hotel vaguely resembles a hacienda. The room décor is slightly kitschy, but the dramatic views more than compensate. Sitting on the beachfront, Acquafredda's sandy bay spreads from its doorstep to a headland of rocky cliffs. The seafood restaurant (meals €25 to €30, open for lunch and dinner) overlooking the bay serves freshly caught fish.

Hotel Villa delle Meraviglie (☎ 0973 87 13 19; www .hotelvilladellemeraviglie.it; Contrada Oligastro, Fiumicello; s €66-112.50, d €94-200; ⊠ P 🐾) Not quite on the beach, this pretty hotel is nestled in private bushland above the blue waters of the Golfo di Policastro. A pleasant five-minute walk down a steep path leads to a secluded rocky headland. The woods keep it private and the 16 double rooms keep it nice and intimate.

our pick **Romantik Hotel & Restaurant Cheta Elite** (☎ 0973 87 81 34; www.villacheta.it; Acquafredda; s €90-125, d €180-250, with sea view add per person €15; ☺ Apr-Oct; **P** ✗ □) Once owned by nobility, this enchanting 140-year-old villa has an air of aristocratic elegance. The rooms are gracefully decorated with antiques, lace and art nouveau glass. The broad terrace has spectacular views of the Golfo di Policastro, perfect for long summer lunches or romantic candlelit dinners. Steps across the road lead down to a small beach.

Eating

The coast is a short 30km long, but the waters of the Golfo di Policastro abound with fish including tuna, swordfish, perch, octopus and squid.

BUDGET

La Caffeteria (☎ 0973 87 18 02; Piazza Buraglia, Maratea; pastries €1-1.50, sandwiches €2.50; ☺ 7.30am-midnight) A delightful café in Maratea's central piazza with outdoor seating for dedicated people-watching. The cakes and pastries on display deserve serious attention. Try a local favourite, the almond-filled *mandola*. Also a great spot for evening drinks when the piazza is alive with music.

Il Faro Rosso (☎ 0973 87 62 13; Via Porto Arenile, Porto di Maratea; sandwiches €3, ice creams €4.50; ☺ 7am-midnight) The liveliest café and bar at the port has an extensive menu of teas, hot chocolates, cocktails, wine and beer. The tables and chairs in the piazza are a great place for pre- or post-dinner drinks or even to while away an entire evening.

La Bussola Pizzeria (☎ 0973 87 68 63; Via Santa Venere 43, Fiumicello; pizza €5-8; ☺ 7.30pm-midnight) A welcoming pizzeria in Fiumicello recommended by the locals. It's small, it's packed and the pizzas are hot and smoky. It's open year-round, but only at night.

Il Ghiottone (☎ 0973 87 75 96; Via Pietra del Pesce 11, Maratea; meals €15; ☺ 11am-midnight Apr-Oct) In this small hole-in-the wall bar you can have a glass of wine and a sandwich for €4. The bizarre mural on the wall takes some working out. Is it the Redentore meets the Hells Angels? Look again, it's a beer-swilling Neptune. What it means is anybody's guess.

MID RANGE

Trattoria Pizzeria La Torre (☎ 0973 87 62 27; Piazza Vitolo, Maratea; pizza €5-9, meals €20-25; ☺ noon-4pm &

6.30pm-midnight) La Torre, a family-run *trattoria* opposite the mermaid fountain in the centre of Maratea, serves local Lucanian fare and freshly caught fish at reasonable prices. It can get noisy and crowded. The family operates the hotel La Dimora del Cardinale, just a few steps away.

Da Peppe (☎ 0973 87 80 00; Via Luppa 1, Acquafredda di Maratea; meals €25; ☺ lunch & dinner) There aren't too many options in Acquafredda, but you can't go wrong in this breezy restaurant and pizzeria. Tuck into the house specialty, *antipasto alla peppe*, while drinking in the sea views from the garden terrace.

Ristorante La Fenice (☎ 0973 87 68 00; Via Fiumicello 13, Fiumicello; meals €30; ☺ lunch & dinner) This unpretentious restaurant makes up for its lack of sea views with its simple and delicious fresh seafood dishes. *Calamarata con pesce spada* (pasta with swordfish and vegetable ragu) is an interesting choice, but if you haven't yet tried *calamari ripieno* (stuffed squid) now is the time to do it. In August the restaurant stays open all day.

White Horse (☎ 0973 87 90 09; SS18km238, Marina di Maratea; meals €30; ☺ lunch & dinner daily Jun-Sep, Thu-Tue Oct-May) One of the few restaurants in the Marina district, the White Horse has an excellent view of the Golfo di Policastro. A huge bougainvillea shades the outdoor terrace where you can dine on fresh seafood (what else?) or Neapolitan wood-fired pizza.

TOP END

1999 (☎ 0973 87 66 77; Via Racia, Porto di Maratea; meals €30-40; ☺ lunch & dinner Tue-Sun, closed Jan) The blue cane lounges and nautical décor might give it away but there are no prizes for guessing what's on the menu in this snazzy restaurant overlooking the port. The seafood, straight off the boat, doesn't come any fresher. The *antipasto misto* is a recommended choice.

Taverna Rovita (☎ 0973 87 65 88; Via Rovita 13, Maratea; meals €40; ☺ lunch & dinner Wed-Mon Mar-Dec) Right in the historic centre of Maratea, this tavern is just off the main piazza. Rovita is cosy and intimate and specialises in local seafood but also puts the rich ricotta, aubergines and meat of the surrounding woodlands to good use.

our pick **Ristorante Lanterna Rossa** (☎ 0973 87 63 52; Via Porto Arenile, Porto di Maratea; meals €50; ☺ lunch & dinner daily summer, Thu-Tue autumn & spring, Sat & Sun winter) With scenic views of the port, Lanterna Rossa is a pricey seafood restaurant with a well-deserved reputation. *Linguine alla Lanterna* (fresh pasta with clams and red chicory) is a signature dish, but if lobster or crayfish take your fancy, place your request when booking. The graceful raku sculptures of African heads and dancing figurines are the work of the talented proprietor.

Getting There & Away
BUS
SITA (☎ 0971 50 68 11) buses have a daily service from Potenza (€7.39, three hours) with a change in Lagonegro.

CAR & MOTORCYCLE
From Rome head along the A3, exiting onto the SS585 at Lagonegro Nord. After 20km you reach the exit for Maratea.

From Bari and Potenza drive west along the SS407 to meet up with the A3 at Sicignano. (You can take a short-cut by exiting the SS407 at Tito, 16km west of Potenza. Follow the SS95 south through Brienza and turn west onto the SS598 to reach the A3 at Atena Lucana. Follow the signs south for Reggio-Calabria, exiting onto the SS585 at Lagonegro Nord. After 20km you reach the exit for Maratea.

From Calabria take the A3 north exiting at Lauria Sud or Lauria Nord where there are signs for Maratea.

TRAIN
Trains connect Maratea with Rome (€32, 4½ hours, five daily) and Naples (€16.50, three hours, four daily). The station is 3km from the centre of Maratea, and a five-minute bus ride into Fiumicello.

Getting Around
Every two hours in summer local buses run along the coastal road. A one-way ride from Maratea to Acquafredda di Maratea costs €1.50. Frequent services operate between Maratea and Fiumicello (€0.50).

For a taxi, call **Cab-Mar** (☎ 0973 87 02 75; Localita S Catarina, Maratea) or **'Eurotravel' Trasporti & Turismo** (☎ 0973 87 60 77; Piazza Vitolo, Maratea).

RIVELLO
pop 2950 / elev 479m
Coiling around its hilltop perch, Rivello is not just another picture-pretty medieval village. The entire town is a national monument and has a curious history. Due to its strategic position overlooking the Noce Valley and the Sirino mountain range it was fought over for centuries by the Lombards and the Byzantines. Neither power managed to gain the upper hand so they reached an unlikely compromise – the Lombards settled in the lower part of town, the Byzantines in the upper. This resulted in two separate centres with two diverse cultures developing in the one town, a division which lasted until the 17th century when the Greek rite was abolished.

Rivello's charm lies in its narrow alleys and stairways, and houses decorated with balconies and architectural motifs. The monumental flight of stairs of the main church in the upper part of town engulfs the original Byzantine church of **San Nicola dei Greci** (☎ 0973 4 61 90; Via San Nicola; ☾ 5-8pm Jul & Aug). Other traces of Byzantine influence can be seen in the tiny tiled cupolas and frescoes of the churches of **San Michele dei Greci** and **Santa Barbara** (☎ 0973 4 61 90; Via Roma; ☾ by appointment).

Rivello still bears the scars of a 1998 earthquake that has left a number of buildings (particularly in the lower part of town) in a damaged or semi-restored state. The Lombards' nucleus in the lower part of town was the church of **Santa Maria Maggiore** (closed for restoration). Also in the lower part of town is the former **Convento di Sant'Antonio** (☎ 0973 4 61 90; Viale Monastero; ☾ 5-8pm Jul & Aug). The entrance porch is painted with 17th-century frescoes by Pietrafesa and has an impressive 16th-century wooden door flanked by two stone lions. The church has a baroque interior and an interesting 17th-century wooden choir carved by Ilario Montalbano (a Benedictine monk) with images of daily life and religious themes. Upstairs there is a small but not terribly interesting **civic museum** (admission free; ☾ 10am-1pm & 4-8pm Jul & Aug) displaying archaeological finds.

Trattoria Pizzeria del Pellegrino (☎ 0973 46617; Corso Vittorio Emanuele II 2; meals €15; ☾ 12.30-3.30pm & 8.30pm-midnight Fri-Wed) is in an ideal position on the main piazza. It is close to the church of San Nicola dei Greci, has outstanding views of the valley, and serves up homemade ravioli and fusilli with locally made ricotta.

SITA (☎ 0971 50 68 11) has a daily bus service from Maratea (€1.55, 35 minutes). By car take the SS585 towards Lagonegro. From Rome or Potenza head south along the A3, exiting onto the SS585 at Lagonegro Nord. From Rotonda head north along the A3, exiting at Lauria to reach the SS585.

PARCO NAZIONALE DEL POLLINO

The **Pollino National Park** (www.parcopollino.it) is Italy's largest national park, a 1960 sq km wilderness divided equally between Basilicata and Calabria. It is a landscape of extremes, from soaring snow-capped mountains and deep ravines to centuries-old forests and wind-blown karstic plateaus.

The highest peaks in the park are found in the Pollino Massif – Monte Pollino (2248m) in Basilicata and Serra Dolcedorme (2267m) in Calabria. Forests of oak, alder, maple, beech, pine and fir trees cover the sheer mountainsides, while in spring the meadows blaze with yellow gentians, dog-roses, peonies, aromatic wild herbs and rare orchids. The air is as intoxicating as the god-like views from the summit of Monte Pollino. On a clear day when you can see both the Tyrrhenian and Ionian coasts it's easy to believe the mountain might be named after the Greek god Apollo.

Over 20 small villages can be found in Basilicata's section of the park. For centuries they have fiercely maintained their traditions and independence and nowhere is this more evident than in the Albanian villages of San Paolo Albanese and San Costantino Albanese. The park also protects a number of rare species like the Apennine wolf (at last count there were 54), the roe deer, wild cat, birds of prey and the *Lutrus lutrus* otter. But the most unique living specimen in the park (also the park emblem) is the *pino loricato*. Only found here and in the Balkans, these ancient pine trees, reaching to 40m in height, form weird arboreal sculptures on the windswept, rocky summits.

ORIENTATION

The lack of a decent road network across the mountain chain running north–south in the centre of the park has effectively cut the park into eastern and western regions. Bear this in mind when planning a visit. Base yourself in the western region to cover areas around Rotonda, San Severino Lucano and Viggianello, or go east for Terranova di Pollino and the Albanian villages. The park continues across Basilicata's southern border and into Calabria.

The main centre of the park is Rotonda in the southwest close to the Calabrian border.

Here you will find the official park office. Terranova di Pollino is the main hub in the eastern region.

Maps

Carta Excursionistica del Pollino Lucano (1:50000) is a useful driving map that also has marked hiking trails. It's available from tourist offices in Rotonda, Matera and Maratea as well as at Asklepios. The *Parco Nazionale del Pollino* map shows the main routes through the park, its flora and fauna, and notable sights.

INFORMATION

Ambulance (☎ 118)

Asklepios (☎ 347 263 14 62; www.viaggarenelpollino .com; Contrada Barone 9) Giuseppe Cosenza, at this *agriturismo*, is one of the few English-speaking guides in the park and the most reliable source of information.

Associazione Guide Ufficiali del Parco Nazionale del Pollino (☎ 0981 339 98; guidepollino@libero.it) Contact this association for a list of the official guides of the Pollino National Park.

Ente Parco Nazionale del Pollino (☎ 0973 66 93 11; Via delle Frecce Tricolori 6, Rotonda; 🕙 9am-2pm Mon-Fri, to 5pm Mon & Wed)

Police Station (☎ 113)

Post Office Rotonda (☎ 0973 66 18 63; Via Roma 3; 🕙 8am-1.30pm Mon-Fri, 8am-12.30pm Sat); Terranova di Pollino (☎ 0973 935560; Via Dante 1; 🕙 8am-1.30pm Mon-Fri, 8am-12.30pm Sat)

Tourist Office (☎ 0973 93489; Via Castellano, Terranova di Pollino) A volunteer organisation with no set hours.

DANGERS & ANNOYANCES

As in all mountainous areas the weather is often unpredictable. Landslides and rockfalls can follow heavy rains and the narrow, winding and pot-holed roads can prove treacherous. Snow can fall any time of the year, so check conditions before you visit.

When hiking, make sure you use common sense – take an extra layer, snacks and plenty of water.

SIGHTS & ACTIVITIES

The Pollino is a vast outdoor playground and the best way to experience the incredible mountain scenery is to get out there among it. Signposts at trail heads give useful information on short day hikes but if seeing a *pino loricato* is your goal, he,ad for Belvedere del Malvento near the Rifugio di Gasperi. Independent hikers should be aware that the maps available have a scale of 1:50000 and may not be reliable for extended hiking in unfamiliar terrain. For information on maps and hiking trails contact the park office or an official hiking guide.

If you plan to mountain bike in the park, bring your own bike and maintenance equipment as services are few and far between. A useful publication available at official tourist offices is *Bicycle Tourism in Basilicata*, published by APT Basilicata. It details eight cycling itineraries in Basilicata including one in the Parco Nazionale del Pollino.

For horse-riding tours out of San Severino Lucano contact **Club Ippico 'Residenza delle Rose'** (☎ 340 575 80 52; Via Timpona). They can tailor group rides, panoramic trips by the river or full-day excursions to the Serra dei Crispi. Prices start from €60 per person for half-day rides. In San Costantino Albanese contact **Giuseppe Fuccella** (☎ 347 9402063; Contrada Cerasia 5).

Head south of the border for white-water thrills. **LAOsrl Rafting** (☎ 0981 856 44; www.laosrl.it; Via Corso Umberto 1; 1hr raft trip €15, half-day €40; ☼ 9am-1pm & 2-6pm Mar-Oct) in Laino Borgo offers white-

water rafting from gentle Grade I-II rapids to more adventurous Grade III-IV action. Giuseppe Cosenza at Asklepios (see opposite) can also organise rafting trips.

In winter, the snow-covered mountains are perfect for snow-shoeing and cross-country skiing.

Most hotels and *agriturismi* will help you organize outdoor activities during your stay.

Pollino Towns

The wild terrain and lack of roads isolated the towns of the Pollino for centuries. This, and the mountain folks' close relationship with nature, has given rise to some unusual and interesting rites and rituals. In the southwest of the park, Rotonda is the Pollino's main hub and a convenient base. See p194 and p195 or places to sleep and eat in the towns listed below.

ROTONDA
pop 3814 / elev 626m

There's not much to see in town except for the **Museo Naturalistico e Paleontologico del Pollino** (☎ 0973 66 73 21; Piazza Giuseppe Falcone; adult/child

PARCO NAZIONALE DEL POLLINO

0 — 10 km
0 — 6.0 miles

Moliterno
San Chirico Raparo
Roccanova
To Metaponto (46km)
Castelsaraceno
Valsinni
SS653
Carbone
Senise
Chiaromonte
To Maratea (40km)
Fardella
San Giorgio Lucano
Latronico
Episcopia
Francavilla in Sinni
Lauria
SS653
La Taverna del Brigante
San Costantino Albanese
Oriolo
Lauria Nord
San Severino Lucano
Parco Nazionale del Pollino
San Paolo Albanese
Lauria Sud
Castelluccio Inferiore
Il Ristoro del Carbonaio
Locanda il Salice
BioAgriturismo La Garavina
A3
Laino Borgo
Viggianello
Terranova di Pollino
Alessandria del Carretto
Rotonda
Agriturismo Civarra
Basilicata
Agriturismo Il Calivino
Belvedere del Malvento
Serra del Prete (2181m)
Albidona
Rifugio di Gasperi
Monte Pollino (2248m)
San Lorenzo Bellizzi
Mormanno
Serra Dolcedorme (2267m)
Plataci
A3
Calabria
Cerchiara di Calabria

€2/1; ⊙ 9am-1pm & 4.30-7pm winter, 9am-1pm & 5-8pm summer). Despite its bare and unsophisticated appearance the museum houses a fascinating find – the remains of a prehistoric elephant found only 2km from Rotonda. Dating to the Pleistocene era (400 to 700 million years ago), it was an impressive 4m high and 6m long. Also in the museum is an entire hippopotamus skeleton discovered in the same place in 2006.

The **Festa dell'Abete** (8 to 13 June) is a ritualistic 'marriage of the trees' (a pagan ceremony similar to that held in Accettura). Following a midnight procession to Piano Pedarreto, a beech tree is chopped down, stripped bare and drawn into town by ten pairs of oxen. A silver fir is grafted onto the top of the beech and the 'married' trees are erected in the main piazza.

VIGGIANELLO
pop 3396 / elev 500m
Legend says the town's name came from a Barbarian queen who lost her wedding ring in the waters of the nearby Mercure stream. Upon finding the ring, a servant shouted, 'Vidi agnello' ('I see the ring').

A 15th-century Norman castle (now a hotel, opposite) sits on a rocky spur overlooking the small village. Of interest is the **Cappella SS Trinità**, a 16th-century Byzantine chapel with a characteristic basilian dome.

SAN SEVERINO LUCANO
pop 1855 / elev 877m
Founded in the 15th century, this village is one of the prettiest in the Pollino. It lies in the Frido River valley close to the heavily wooded Bosco Magnano. Ruined timber mills can be found along the streams surrounding San Severino Lucano. If you're lucky you might spot one of the rare *Lutrus lutrus* otters frolicking in the water.

In the 16th-century **Chiesa di Santa Maria degli Angeli** is the Byzantine-style statue of the *Madonna del Pollino*, the star of a yearly rite in July when she is hauled up to the Sanctuary of the Madonna of the Pollino. The sanctuary has outstanding views of the Frido Valley. It was built in the 18th century in a cave where, apparently, the statue of the Madonna was found. Pilgrims play harmonicas and *zampognes* (a type of bagpipe made from goat skin) and dance the *taranta* during the three-day festival.

TERRANOVA DI POLLINO
pop 1612 / elev 926m
At the foot of Monte Calvario, Terranova di Pollino is a lovely village surrounded with beech and chestnut trees. As the main town in the eastern region of the park it is an excellent base for hiking trips to the Serra Dolcedorme and Monte Pollino. Get maps and information on hiking trails from your hotel or the tourist office.

Most travellers come for the woods but if you have time take a look at the 18th-century florentine-style painting of the Madonna in the **Chiesa della Madonna delle Grazie** then treat yourself to lunch at Luna Rossa (p196).

SAN PAOLO ALBANESE & SAN COSTANTINO ALBANESE
The towns of San Paolo Albanese (population 378, elevation 800m) and San Costantino Albanese (population 886, elevation 650m) were settled by Albanian refugees fleeing the Turkish invasions of the 16th century. A mountain people fiercely proud of their customs and culture, they have managed to keep their language, dress and traditions intact. The communities were so isolated that the language they speak today is a unique derivation of the Arbereshe spoken five centuries ago. As you wander through the streets you're likely to see women dressed in brightly coloured traditional Albanian costumes. This is a great place to purchase lace and handwoven fabrics.

Lying at the foot of Monte Carnara, San Paolo Albanese, with less than 400 inhabitants, is the smallest (and one of the most enchanting) towns in Basilicata. For a further peek into Albanian culture and traditions visit the **Museo della Cultura Arbereshe** (☎ 0973 944 69; Via Regina Margherita; adult/child €2.50/1.50; ⊙ 9am-1.30pm & 3-7pm Mon-Fri, 10am-1.30pm Sat & Sun) in Palazzo Smilari.

SLEEPING
To fully appreciate the fresh air and natural beauty of the Pollino stay in an *agriturismo* – there are plenty to choose from. The restaurants are open to all, with traditional homemade meals of whatever the cook decides on the day.

Budget
Locanda il Salice (☎ 0973 57 00 05; www.ebasilicata.net; Località Mezzana Salice; s/d €15/30; ⊙ Mar-Dec) A simple

hostel in a lovely little village near the Frido River, Ostello il Salice has a quaint restaurant serving dishes made with home-grown produce. There's also an apartment complex in the old schoolmaster's house – five comfortable family rooms sharing a central lounge (€15 per person).

Rifugio di Gasperi (☎ 0973 66 60 04; www.rifugio digaspari.it; Piano Ruggio; r per person €20) This bare and rustic mountain refuge on Piano Ruggio (1550m) sleeps 30 and is a good base for cross-country skiing or high-altitude hiking. It's in the heart of the Pollino and a short hike to the Belvedere del Malvento and the rare *pino loricato*. The restaurant menu is what you'd expect – mountain meats and wild boar.

Asklepios (☎ 347 263 14 62; www.viaggarenelpollino .com; Contrada Barone 9; per person €25) Serious hikers might want to bunk in this basic *agriturismo* near Rotonda run by Giuseppe Cosenza, one of the most experienced guides in the Pollino. He also stocks tourist information on Basilicata and can tailor itineraries to suit individuals or groups. The three rooms share one bathroom and advance booking is essential.

Midrange

OURPICK Agriturismo Civarra (☎ 0973 66 91 52; www .viaggiarenelpollino.com; Contrada Valli 5; s/d €20/50, half board per person €45) Vivacious hostess Maria Teresa is as warm and friendly as this beautifully decorated *agriturismo* overlooking Rotonda. The six-hectare farm grows olives, fruit, vegetables and cereals. The welcoming fireplace, homey restaurant and sprawling outdoor terrace will make you want to linger longer.

BioAgriturismo La Garavina (☎ 0973 933 95; www .lagaravina.it; Contrada Casa del Conte; s/d €25/44) Only 6km south of Terranova di Pollino, the only certified organic farm in the park will have you eating healthy greens and free-range meats. The fabulous views, rustic décor and country-style bedrooms are faultless. It's run by a hiking guide, and you can hike to trails directly from your door.

Agriturismo Il Calivino (☎ 0973 661688; www .aziendacalivino.it; Contrada San Lorenzo; s/d €28/56) Near Rotonda, this *agriturismo* has a small vineyard and olive grove. The outside bar, with its wooden tables and benches, is the perfect spot to sample the regional and international wines on the menu. The restaurant serves 20 different antipasti every day. It only has four rooms; pick the one with the bathtub! Pets welcome.

B&B Al Vecchio Camino (☎ 0973 66 79 13; www .alvecchiocamino.it; Via Vittorio Emanuele 47; s/d €40/60) If you want to stay in town, this B&B on the edge of Rotonda is a good choice. The five large rooms are each named after a flower. Settle in front of the fire and try the homemade salami and cheese.

La Locanda di San Francesco (☎ 0973 66 43 84; www.locandapollino.it; Via San Francesco 4; s/d €44/68) This elegant 18th-century *palazzo* in Viggianello has enormous rooms in pleasing pastel shades, with wood-beamed ceilings and great mountain views. The restaurant is a highlight; the menu changes daily but the focus remains firmly fixed on traditional Lucanian dishes.

Hotel Picchio Nero (☎ 0973 931 70; www.picchionero .com; Via Mulino 1; s/d €55/67) A gem in the village of Terranova di Pollino, this chalet-style hotel has wood-panelled rooms, a small garden overlooking the valley and a recommended restaurant. The perfect base for hikers in the eastern region of the park, the hotel is owned by the congenial, multilingual Pino Golia, who will happily give advice on hiking trails or organize hiking guides.

Top End

Il Castello dei Principe (☎ 0973 66 40 42; Via Ponte Castello; s/d/ste €50/100/130) If you fancy a priceless royal experience spend a night in this Norman castle overlooking Viggianello. It's large and cold but the views are stupendous and the stately rooms include a honeymoon suite with a four-poster bed and a king-size bathroom. There's an underground chamber and a secret tunnel.

EATING
Budget

Pizzeria A'Carmata (☎ 0973 66 13 14; Via Roma; pizza €5; ⏲ 8pm-midnight Tue-Sun) The agricultural theme in the Pollino is everywhere and you won't escape it in this quaint pizzeria in the main street of Rotonda. There's a horse-shoe wine rack, and decorative farming tools on the counter. A recommended choice is the *pizza a'carmata*.

Trattoria Il Nascondiglio (☎ 0973 66 15 51; Corso Garibaldi 17; meals €15; ⏲ lunch & dinner Fri-Wed) This tiny hide-out in Rotonda serves quick cheap eats. There's not much on the menu but it's seasonal and satisfying. Try the local take on the ubiquitous Lucanian *salsiccia* (grilled pork sausage) while contemplating the four silhouettes on the wall: are they Arabian nomads, French Legionnaires or just shifty characters?

Midrange

Il Ristoro del Carbonaio (☎ 349 351 43 32; Locandà Croce Pantana; sandwiches €2.50, meals €20; ☽ lunch Tue-Sun) A popular lunch stop between Viggianello and San Severino Lucano serving up wild meats, hearty stews and a delicious pecorino cheese made from a blend of local goat and sheep milk. There's no official campground but you can pitch a tent then hire a mountain bike from the owner and ride through the rolling green hills below Monte Pollino.

La Taverna del Brigante (☎ 0973 64 09 76; Contrada Taverna Magnano; meals €20) Close to San Severino Lucano, the taverna is a good (actually, the only) choice after a hike in the Bosco Magnano. The restaurant crowds into three small rooms and serves Lucanian dishes. Recently renovated and furnished (country-style, of course), it also operates a B&B (€25 per night).

La Bella Rotonda (☎ 0973 66 12 52; Via Roma 7a; meals €30; ☽ Wed-Mon) The atmosphere might not be cosy in this large, brightly lit restaurant but if you fancy fish from Maratea while you're deep in the woods follow local advice and try this place in Rotonda. Also serves a buffet and specialises in local meats.

Top End

Ristorante De Pepe (☎ 0973 66 12 51; Corso Garibaldi 13; meals €25; ☽ Tue-Sat) Highly recommended around town, this classic restaurant near Rotonda's main piazza has a warm and intimate feel. The menu is seasonal and serves such delicacies as *antipasta alla Rotondese* (featuring the unique red eggplant of Rotonda) and *agnello con patate e peperoni* (a typical lamb dish).

our pick **Ristorante Tipico Luna Rossa** (☎ 0973 93254; www.federicovalicenti.it; Via Marconi 8, Terranova del Pollino; meals €30-35; ☽ lunch & dinner Thu-Tue) Federico Valicenti draws inspiration from Basilicata's colourful history, transforming ancient recipes into exquisite masterpieces. If he's not too busy, Federico delivers each dish with an entertaining anecdote. The restaurant has breathtaking views and is a gustatory highlight.

GETTING THERE & AWAY

It is virtually impossible to navigate the park without your own vehicle. There are no trains, and bus services are severely limited (and virtually nonexistent outside high summer).

Bus

There are no direct services from Potenza or Matera to the Pollino. It's impractical to visit the park without a car but if you're determined to do so then take a **SITA** (☎ 0835 38 50 07) bus from Metaponto to Policoro (1½ hours, four daily). Change buses here for the once-daily service to Terranova di Pollino (€3.10, one hour). It stops at San Paolo Albanese and San Costantino Albanese on the way.

Car & Motorcycle

To reach Rotonda from Rome or Naples take the A3, exiting at Lauria Sud for Rotonda. If you are travelling north on the A3 from Calabria take the SS19 from Campo Tenese. If you are on the SS106 from Matera and Metaponto, take the SS653, exiting for Terranova di Pollino after 24km. To reach Rotondo continue on the SS653 to Lauria Nord, turn south onto the A3 and exit at Lauria Sud for Rotonda. You can reach Rotonda by exiting the SS653 at Francavilla in Sinni, but the road is narrow and winding so you should add on more time.

IONIAN COAST

Unlike the tremendous Tyrrhenian coast, the Ionian coast is a listless affair of flat, unaggressive seashore and large tourist resorts. However, the Greek ruins at Metaponto and Policoro give a picture of the enormous influence of Magna Graecia in southern Italy before continual river floods turned the land swampy and malarial (p28).

Drainage and irrigation works begun in the 1950s have cleared the swamps and beaches that kept the coast disease-ridden and underpopulated. In place of ancient Greek colonies, new developments have sprung up along the coastline providing beach facilities for their sister inland towns. This, and the now intensively cultivated fields of citrus fruits, apricots, peaches, strawberries, grapes and kiwis, has seen a surge in the Ionian coast's economic importance.

Although the beach resorts are overcrowded focal points in summer, by exploring side roads and coastal tracks off the SS106 you can find secluded stretches of beach along the 40km coastline.

METAPONTO

pop 1560 / elev 2m

The ancient Greek town of Metapontum was founded in the 8th century BC in a strategic

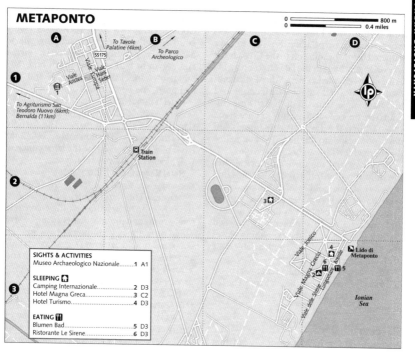

METAPONTO

SIGHTS & ACTIVITIES
Museo Archeologico Nazionale........1 A1

SLEEPING
Camping Internazionale....................2 D3
Hotel Magna Greca.........................3 C2
Hotel Turismo...............................4 D3

EATING
Blumen Bad..................................5 D3
Ristorante Le Sirene.......................6 D3

position between the Bradano and Basento Rivers. During its heyday, mathematician, philosopher and alchemist Pythagoras founded a school in Metaponto in 510 BC after being banished from Crotone (in what is now Calabria), and the town flourished as an important trading and agricultural area (important enough that its coins were stamped with an ear of wheat).

But its low-lying position left it prey to malaria and for centuries the town was plagued by devastating malarial epidemics, which were only finally eradicated in the 1950s. Since then Metaponto has reinvented itself as an agricultural zone and in recent years has been actively promoting itself as a beachside tourist resort.

These days Metaponto is a straggling and rather unattractive township in the Gulf of Taranto. Hollywood actor Nicolas Cage probably thinks otherwise – rumours abound he's set to build an experimental centre for visual and musical arts here. For now, the only real attraction is its sandy beach, Lido di Metaponto, which is completely swamped in summer.

Orientation & Information

From the train station, go straight for 500m to a roundabout. About 1.5km to your right (east) is the Parco Archeologico and to your left is the Museo Archeologico Nazionale.

Metaponto's beach is at Lido di Metaponto, 3km east of the train station.

Sights & Activities

The **Museo Archeologico Nazionale** (☎ 0835 74 53 27; Via Aristea 21; adult/concession €2.50/1.25; ☼ 9am-8pm) houses finds from excavations at the archaeological park and from around Metaponto. Iron Age pieces through to the ancient Greek and Roman periods include ceramics, statues and jewellery. The Medusa heads are of particular interest.

Crossing the SS175, follow the lane to the **Parco Archeologico** (admission free), the site of ancient Metapontum. In the park you can see the remains of the 6th-century BC **Temple of Apollo Licius** (which had 32 columns, 6m high) and outlines and fragments of temples dedicated to Hera, Athena and Aphrodite. The **Greek theatre** dating to the same period is undergoing reconstruction.

The best-preserved and most impressive ruin is the **Tavole Palatine** (Palatine Tables) where knights, or paladins, are said to have gathered before heading off to the Crusades. It was originally built in the late 6th century BC as a temple dedicated to Hera. After Pythagoras died, his house and school were incorporated into the temple. Only 15 of its 32 Doric columns remain, enough to picture its once grand state. To find the Tavole Palatine head 3km north of Metaponto on the SS175 and follow the sliproad for Taranto onto the SS106.

After covering the town's historical sites the only thing on offer is the beach. Long stretches of pale gold sand and limpid blue seas should spell summer paradise but the carnival-like atmosphere of the lido is tacky and unattractive. In summer it is crowded and noisy while in winter everything closes and the tourist strip droops with an abject air of abandonment.

To while away a few hours rent pedal boats and kayaks from the *lidi* (beach bars). The sea is shallow; wade out 30m or more to reach deep water.

Sleeping

Accommodation in Metaponto is not that great. There are lots of bog-standard seaside hotels but prices are high and in summer everything is booked up, while in winter nothing is open. Better alternatives are camping villages or nearby *agriturismi*.

Camping Internazionale (☎ 0835 74 19 16; www .villageinternazionale.com; Viale delle Nereidi; person/tent/car high season €9/10/6, 4-bed bungalow low season per week €380, high season per week €730; 🖥 🅿 🛁 🔥) Only 20m from the beach this camping village has it all – a restaurant, bar, pizzeria, cinema and a gym to buff up your beach bod. The bungalows are clean, comfortable and well equipped, and pets are welcome.

Hotel Turismo (☎ 0835 74 19 17; Viale delle Ninfe 5; s €45-68, d €60-68; 🛁) It's clean, it's basic and it's slap-bang on the main piazza. The friendly staff aim to please. The downstairs restaurant has a nice terrace – shame the large concrete wall blocks off any view of the sea.

Hotel Magna Grecia (☎ 0835 74 56 61; www.magna greciavillage.com; Viale del Lido 1; s €53-127, d €106-252; 🕑 May-Sep) This large hotel/village resort, recently opened, resembles a huge concrete monstrosity and proudly boasts an impressive range of facilities including two swimming pools, an amphitheatre for stage shows, tennis and volleyball courts, a football field, gym and aerobic classes, and a shuttle bus to its own private beach. Sleeps 500 close friends.

our pick **Agriturismo San Teodoro Nuovo** (☎ 0835 47 00 42; www.santeodoronuovo.com; Contrada da San Teodoro Nuovo; s/d €70/120; 🛁 🛁 🅿) By far one of Basilicata's best-kept secrets, this gorgeous *agriturismo* makes a great base not only for exploring the Ionian coast, but also for day trips to Matera and the Lucanian Apennines. The converted farmhouse, set on 150 hectares of citrus and olive trees, was once the home of a duke. The 10 apartments are furnished with family heirlooms and antiques and retain the charm of an aristocratic residence. Depending

---

THE GREEK MYSTIC OF METAPONTUM

Best remembered for the Pythagorean Theorem, Pythagoras was much more than a brilliant mathematician. Born on the Greek island of Samos around 580 BC, Pythagoras travelled and studied esoteric philosophies in Egypt, Babylon, Persia and India before settling on the Ionian coast. In Metapontum he opened a school of wisdom, coined the term philosophy and devoted his life to studying the laws of nature. His inner circle of students, the *mathematikoi*, were in some ways a cult: both men and women lived at the school, renounced personal possessions, grew their hair and followed a strict discipline of exercise, philosophical study and vegetarianism. The outer school, the *akousmatikoi*, were taught laws of morality and behaviour, but weren't privy to the inner school's secret teachings, which included the concepts of reincarnation and the transmigration of the soul.

Pythagoras believed that reality was mathematical in nature, and he discovered the mathematical basis of music. He was the first to propose the 'harmony of the spheres' – believing the planets moved through the universe according to mathematical equations that could be translated into a harmonious symphony.

Although none of his writings survive, his philosophy has influenced scientists, philosophers, musicians and mystics through the ages including the current New Age movement.

PINO LORICATO

The scaly bark of the *pino loricato* (the Bosnian pine) looks like a *lorica*, a centurion's cuirass, but that's where the likeness ends. Growing at altitudes between 900m and 2200m, this hardy pine is tormented relentlessly by savage, icy winds, twisting a little this way, bending a little that way – a contorted, knotted but ever-enduring giant. Some of the oldest Bosnian pines in the Pollino are 40m high and over 1000 years old.

Before the last Ice Age the trees were widespread throughout Europe, but now they exist only in the Balkans and the rocky, impervious peaks of the Pollino (including the high slopes of Monte Alpi, Monte Pollino, Serra Dolcedorme, Serra di Crispo and Serra del Prete).

Its bark sheds with age, revealing a sturdy white-skinned trunk and the origin of its vaguely vulgar scientific name *Pinus leucodermis*.

when you visit you can prune grapes, pick oranges, bottle marmalade, make ricotta cheese or simply relax in this lovely country estate. Horse-riding and bike hire can be arranged and dogs are welcome.

Eating

There are plenty of beach bars for quick bites, and restaurants in the hotels and camping-villages, but not as many beachfront restaurants as you might expect for a seaside resort.

Blumen Bad (☎ 333 6029755; Lungomare Arenile; gelati €1.50, sandwiches €2.50; 🕑 6am-midnight) If you want to be in the heart of the action, hang out at this beach bar on the promenade near the main piazza. You can lounge on a sunbed or play with the pedal boats. Bonus – the owner is president of the tourist association and speaks some English.

Ristorante Le Sirene (☎ 0835 74 18 91; Vialle delle Sirene; meals €20; 🕑 lunch & dinner May-Sep) Set one street back from the beach, this seafood restaurant recommends its *antipasto di mare* (a plate of squid, salmon, octopus and mussels) and tempting range of pizzas.

Getting There & Away

The Taranto to Reggio Calabria train line parallels the coast and the SS106. All coastal towns are connected by bus and rail.

BUS

SITA (☎ 0835 38 50 07) buses connect with Matera (€2.70, one hour, six daily) and Taranto (€2.70, 75 minutes, two daily).

CAR & MOTORCYCLE

From Matera take the SS7 to join the SS407 south, the Basentana, from Potenza. Metaponto is on the SS106 southwest of Taranto.

TRAIN

As well as Taranto (€2.60 to €5.60, 45 minutes, six daily), trains connect with Potenza (€10.50, 1½ hours, five daily). The station is 3km west of Lido di Metaponto and regular SITA buses pass by on the way to the beach (€0.70).

BERNALDA

pop 12,056 / elev 130m

Only 15km from the sea, Bernalda clings to a hilltop above the Basento valley. Its historic centre dates from the 15th century, with a privately owned two-tower **castle** opposite the 16th-century Byzantine-domed **San Bernardino** church. Bernalda is the first town on the river Basento and modern times have seen its development sprawl towards the coast. In August, a costumed procession of knights carries the statue of San Bernardino around town in a painted wooden cart. Francis Ford Coppola is this town's favourite son (his grandparents emigrated to the United States in the early 19th century), and he re-created the festival in *The Godfather III*. Coppola is currently converting the 19th-century Palazzo Margherita into a small boutique hotel – it should be very luxurious, judging by his other hotel ventures.

The ambience is intimate, the setting rustic, and the owners (four women from the same family) delightful at **Trattoria La Locandiera** (☎ 0835 54 32 41; www.lalocandiera.biz; Corso Umberto I,194; meals €20; 🕑 noon-4pm & 7.30-midnight Wed-Mon). Foodies come from far away just to dine on La Locandiera's famous horsemeat dishes such as *pasta fresca con carne di cavallo* (homemade pasta with horsemeat ragu) and *bracioline di cavallino* (rolled horsemeat simmered in tomatoes).

From Matera drive southeast on the SS7 to reach the SS407 (the Basentana) and turn

SOUTHERN BASILICATA

THE GHOST TOWN OF CRACO

The hilltop town of Craco looms into the sky like some wicked Grimm brothers fairytale, its medieval castle tower guarding a crumbling skeleton of collapsed and abandoned buildings. In the 12th century it was known as Graculum (a name fit for a Grimm brothers story), but it only assumed its ghost-town status in 1974 after a continual succession of landslides forced the population to re-settle in the valley. The retaining wall built after the 1961 landslide seemed like a good idea at the time, but it possibly hastened matters by retaining water in the underground clay layer, further increasing ground instability.

At dusk the lifeless town is a haunting silhouette above the beautiful Salandrella valley. Approaching the town in full daylight the effect is no less surreal. A broken flight of steps leads up to the ruins where rubble and rubbish obstruct narrow alleys, steep stairways and disappearing lanes. Ornate stonework, damaged wood panelling and faded frescoes can be glimpsed through the broken windows and the half-collapsed ceilings and balconies of once-elegant *palazzi*. The castle tower and the old baroque church of San Nicolà (where 20 brigands were shot in 1862) are still standing, but it is unsafe (and not permitted) to wander through the ruins.

Around the back of the hill is a rather drab government housing division built for those Craco residents who did not relocate to the valley.

Craco is an eerie day's outing, 15km west of Pisticci. There's no public transport, so you'll need a car.

---

towards Metaponto, or take the SS380 off the SS7 and follow signs to Bernalda. From Metaponto, Bernalda is 15km northwest along the SS407.

SITA (☎ 0835 38 50 07) operates a daily service from Matera (50 minutes) and Metaponto (15 minutes).

POLICORO

pop 15,422 / elev 28m

Originally the Greek settlement of Heraclea (named for Hercules) where in 280 BC Pyrrhus and his war elephants crushed the Roman army, modern-day Policoro has little of interest apart from the **Museo Archeologico Nazionale della Sirtide** (☎ 0835 97 21 54; Via Colombo 8; adult/concession €2.50/1.25; ☉ 9am-8pm Wed-Mon, 2-8pm Tue). The museum has a fabulous display of artefacts excavated in the area, where you can work your way from 7000 BC through the jewellery, ornament and dress of the Lucanians to the mirrors and vases of the Greeks and then to the spears and javelins of the Romans who put paid to them all. There are also two complete tombs with skeletons surrounded by the objects and jewellery with which they were buried.

In the **archaeological park** (admission free) behind the museum you can see the town plan of ancient Heraclea. The 13th-century **castle** (closed for restoration) is on a hill northeast of town and until 1900 it was the only building in Policoro.

Policoro's beach is at the **Lido di Policoro** where the ubiquitous bars and cheesy market stalls spoil an otherwise beautiful stretch of golden sand. Just off the gravel car park along the beachfront is a short concrete pathway complete with streetlights where well-dressed Italians take their daily *passeggiata* oblivious to the long broad expanse of seashore literally at their feet.

Policoro is 21km south of Metaponto on the SS106. SITA buses run down the coast from Metaponto (20 minutes) but are frequent only in summer. A better option is the train (€1.76, 20 minutes, five daily).

TURSI

pop 5390 / elev 243m

> To reach Rabatana/you climb a flinty road/that looks just like a ladder laid/against a crumbling wall of clay.
>
> *Albino Pierro, 1916–95*

Tursi's Arab or Rabatana quarter, the oldest part of the village, was built in the 10th century during the Saracen invasions. From its cliff-top perch a maze of crumbling buildings, narrow alleys, steep stepped pathways and semi-restored houses cascade down the steep slopes to the main town below.

Tursi's favourite son, one of the 20th century's most distinguished composers of dialect poetry, Albino Pierro, wrote almost excluively about his hometown and childhood – in the archaic Tursi dialect. The poet's house, the **Casa di Albino Pierro** (☎ 0835 53 38 62; Via Umberto I 4; admission free; 10.30am-1.30pm & 4.30-7.30pm Mon-Sat, 10am-12.30pm & 4.30-7.30pm Sun), displays photographs of the man, his library and the studio where he wrote his great works. It's a steep walk uphill from the cathedral in the main piazza and there's not much to recommend unless you're a die-hard Pierro fan. For a better idea of what inspired this Nobel Prize nominee take an even steeper walk up to the Rabatana (or a long drive along the winding road around the back of the hill).

Little remains of the castle that once dominated the town, but legend says an underground passage used to connect it to the **Chiesa di Santa Maria Maggiore** (10am-noon & 4-6pm), a lovely pastel-pink church in the heart of the Rabatana. The interior of the church has a 14th-century triptych of the *Madonna dell'Icona*. In the crypt down the steps are 16th-century frescoes, a charmingly naive 15th-century stone nativity scene and a 16th-century marble sarcophagus.

ourpick **Palazzo dei Poeti** (☎ 0835 53 36 06; Via Manzone; s/d €50/70; Dec-Oct) is the brainchild of architect-cum-poet Paolo Popia; he has designed a 'ristorarte' hotel to encourage creativity and art appreciation. The rooms are restored Rabatana houses named after famous literary figures, each individually decorated with hand-picked antiques and curios of poets and writers, and none are inconvenienced with anti-creative distractions like TV. The restaurant (meals €25, open noon to 4pm and 7pm to late Tuesday to Sunday) is a romantic warren of rooms, the menu a *poesia in gastronomia*, the dishes delivered with poetic renditions.

When leaving Tursi stop to admire the **Santuario di Santa Maria d'Anglona** (☎ 0835 81 40 02; 9am-1pm & 4.30-7pm Sun or by appointment), 12km out of town on the road to Policoro. This isolated church set amidst pine and eu-

calypt trees was built in the 12th century on the site of the ancient Greek Pandosia and was declared a national monument in 1931. Inside the sanctuary, frescoes from the 12th to 14th centuries include scenes from Genesis (in the right nave) while the apse exterior is adorned with arches, pilaster strips and sculpted panels.

Tursi is 24km from Policoro. From Metaponto head south along the SS106, exiting at Policoro.

PISTICCI

pop 17,855 / elev 364m

Pisticci's characteristic single-storey *casedde* (white houses with red pointed roofs) were built after a landslide in the 17th century. Viewed from the piazza in front of the cathedral on top of the hill the *casedde* resemble a stack of dominoes falling towards the valley below. It's a steep climb up the hill from Piazza San Rocco, but the panoramic view is worth the climb. Cultivated cereal farms and citrus groves reach towards the coast while olive groves and barren clay *calanchi* spread inland.

After all that effort reward yourself with a hearty lunch at **Ristorante Borgo Antico** (☎ 0835 58 31 93; Via Minghetti 17; meals €25; lunch & dinner Tue-Sun), an intimate stone and wood-beamed restaurant in the style of a rustic tavern. The typical Mediterranean cuisine focuses on seafood and has mouth-watering dishes like *ravioli all'aragosta* (ravioli with lobster and shrimp sauce).

Marina di Pisticci, 30km from Pisticci, has a lovely long stretch of pale sand minus the souvenir and market-stall frenzy of Metaponto and Policoro's beaches, and is an idyllic spot for a summer picnic. On the way to the beach look out for a recently built piazza lined with pizzerie and funky bars; it's a happening aprés-beach scene.

SITA has daily buses from Matera (45 minutes) and Potenza (1½ hours) to Pisticci.

Directory

CONTENTS

BOOK ACCOMMODATION ONLINE

For more accommodation reviews and recommendations by Lonely Planet authors, check out the online booking service at www.lonelyplanet.com. You'll find the true, insider lowdown on the best places to stay. Reviews are thorough and independent. Best of all, you can book online.

ACCOMMODATION

Accommodation in Puglia and Basilicata is ever improving. There's a growing number of characterful B&Bs and *agriturismi* everywhere, and more and more luxurious options: Puglia's most gorgeous and glamorous are clustered around Ostuni and Fasano, while those in Basilicata are in Matera and Maratea.

The Gargano coast is lined by well-appointed camp sites (see p94), and there are some lovely sites between Otranto and Santa Maria on the Salentine Peninsula.

In this book we list price ranges for accommodation: from the low-season minimum price to the high-season maximum. Puglia is more expensive than Basilicata, so there are two separate price ranges for the two regions. However, Maratea, on the Basilicata coast, is more expensive, so falls in the same budget range as Puglia.

The high season is July and August, though prices peak again around Easter and Christmas. It's essential to book in advance during these periods. Prices rise around 5% to 10% annually and drop between 30% and 50% in low season.

In the winter months (November to Easter) many places, particularly on the coast, completely shut down. In the cities and larger towns accommodation tends to remain open all year. The relative lack of visitors in these down periods means you should have little trouble getting a room in those places that do stay open.

Agriturismo & B&Bs

An *agriturismo* is accommodation on a working farm, where you'll usually be able to sample the produce. Traditionally families rented out rooms in their farmhouses; it's still possible to find this type of lodging, although many *agriturismi* have now evolved into sophisticated accommodation. There are several Italian guidebook directories devoted solely to *agriturismi*, or try www.agriturismo.it or www.agriturismo.net (also good for self-catering apartments and villas).

Another increasingly popular option (especially in Lecce and Matera) is the B&B – try the excellent website www.bed-and-breakfast.it – though, confusingly, breakfast is not necessarily provided.

On average *agriturismi* and B&Bs cost €25 to €50 per person per night.

Masserie

Masserie are unique to southern Italy – large farms or estates, usually built around a fortified watchtower, with plenty of surrounding accommodation to house workers and live-stock. Many have been converted into luxuri-ous hotels, *agriturismi*, or holiday apartments. A *masseria* isn't necessarily old: sometimes new buildings built around similar principles are called *masserie*.

Recommended places are listed throughout this book.

Camping

Italians go camping with gusto and most camping facilities in Puglia (less so in Basili-cata, where camping options are few and far between) are major complexes with swimming pools, restaurants and supermarkets, usually offering camping space and bungalows and/or apartments. With hotel prices shooting up in July and August, camping grounds can be a splendid option, especially given that quite a few have enviable seaside locations.

In July and August, prices range from around €8 to €15 per adult. Tent space can cost from €8 to €30, and there are usually extra charges for parking, showers and electricity. A two-person bungalow generally works out between €50 and €100 per night. You'll need to book well ahead in high season.

Most camping grounds operate only in sea-son, roughly April to October (in many cases June to September only).

Independent camping is not permitted. However, outside the summer season, inde-pendent campers who are inconspicuous and don't light fires should be OK. Always get permission from the landowner if you want to camp on private property.

Lists of campsites are available from local tourist offices, or check www.touringclub.it, the website of Touring Club Italiano. Mem-bership costs €25 per year.

TCI also publishes an annual book listing all Italian campsites, *Campeggi in Italia*, and the Istituto Geografico de Agostini publishes the annual *Guida ai Campeggi in Europa*, sold together with *Guida ai Campeggi in Italia*. Otherwise check www.camping.it.

Hostels

Youth hostels *(ostelli per la gioventù)* – only found in Brindisi, Lecce, Taranto, and Matera – are run by the **Associazione Italiana Alberghi per la Gioventù** (AIG; www.ostellionline.org), affiliated to **Hostelling International** (HI; www.hihostels.com). You need to have an HI card. Nightly rates are around €15 to €20.

Hotels & Guesthouses

There's often no difference between a *pensione* (guesthouse) and an *albergo* (hotel). However, a pensione will generally be of one- to three-star standard, while an *albergo* can be awarded up to five stars.

A one-star *pensione* will tend to be basic and will usually have shared bathrooms. Standards at two-star places are often only slightly better, but rooms will generally have a private bathroom. Three stars will assure you of comfort, and four- and five-star hotels

---

PRACTICALITIES

- Italy uses the metric system for weights and measures.

- Plugs have two round pins; the current is 230V, 50Hz.

- Regional papers include: Taranto-based *Corriere del Giorno; Il Grecale*, which covers Foggia, the Gargano, northern Puglia and the Murgia; Brindisi's *il Quotidiano;* and *La Gazzetta del Mez-zogiorno*, which covers Puglia and Basilicata. Italy's leading dailies, the *Corriere della Sera* and *La Republica* are also available. In large towns, you can buy the *International Herald Tribune*, which has a daily four-page supplement, *Italy Daily*.

- There are tonnes of poppy local radio stations: try Bari-based Canale100 (94.9) and Brindisi-based CiccioRiccio (frequency varies). Otherwise tune into RAI-1 (1332AM or 89.7 FM), RAI-2 (846AM or 91.7 FM) and RAI-3 (93.7 FM), combining music with news broadcasts and discus-sion programmes; the BBC World Service is on medium wave at 648kHz, short wave 6195kHz, 9410kHz, 12095kHz and 15575 kHz, and on long wave at 198kHz.

- Somewhat cheesy local TV stations include Telenorba, Tele Citta Bianca (from Ostuni) and Antenna Sud (covering Puglia and Basilicata). You can also watch Italy's commercial stations Canale 5, Italia 1, Rete 4 and La7, as well as state-run RAI-1, RAI-2 and RAI-3.

offer facilities such as room service, laundry, parking and internet.

Tourist offices have booklets listing all local accommodation, including prices.

ACTIVITIES

From cycling and climbing to trekking, diving and sailing, Puglia and Basilicata offer a cornucopia of outdoor fun.

Cycling

Cycling is hugely popular in Puglia (and, to a lesser extent, Basilicata), and one of the nicest ways to see the region – the best time weatherwise – and busiest – is spring or autumn. Almost every *masseria* and many B&Bs will offer bikes free to guests. It's difficult to obtain good cycling maps, but on the plus side, the country roads are lightly trafficked and easy to navigate.

Good places to cycle are the Murgia around Ostuni, Locorotondo, Alberobello, Martina Franca, Ceglie Messapica and along the coast between Riserva Marina Torre Guaceta, all the way up to Polignano. For more information see p134. Porto Cesareo–Gallipoli is another popular route.

There are marked cycle routes in the Salento between the villages of Castro, Marettima di Diso, Spongano, Andrano, Tricase, Specchia and Alessano.

The Via Verde is a signposted cycle route around Ostuni; the map (available from tourist offices) is easy to follow – and helpful as the signposts are not always reliable.

Organisations like **CEA** (www.ceadiandrano.org) based in Andrano also organise cycling and trekking itineraries. **Puglia in Bici** (www.pugliainbici .com) in Monopoli (Murge) is a professional cycling outfit that hires bikes and can work out itineraries.

In the Laterza ravine (Italy's longest ravine) you can do some serious mountain biking with the **Centro Visite** (☎ 339 331 19 47; Via Selva San Vito).

Mountain bikers will thrill around Basilicata's winding mountain tracks. Try **Bike Basilicata** (www.bikebasilicata.it) for more information and details of tours.

Basilicata Tourist Information offices also supply a free booklet on cycling: *Bicycle Tourism in Basilicata*, with eight detailed itineraries.

Horse Riding

A number of *masserie*, such as Il Frantoio (p132) near Ostuni, offer riding. Otherwise there are numerous stables in the Murgia and you can go trekking around Otranto. You can also go riding in the Gargano (Puglia) and Pollino (Basilicata).

Walking

Walkers will find thrilling routes around Basilicata's Pollino and Puglia's Murgia Plateau, near Castro in the Salento, and at Torre Guaceta and the Massafra, Mottola, Laterza and Castellaneta ravines. There are also some stunning walks around the Gargano Promontory.

Water Sports

There's good diving around the Salentine Peninsula (Otranto and Gallipoli) and also the Gargano and in the translucent waters around Isole Tremiti, as well as Porto Cesareo, Parco Regionale Porto Selvaggio, Santa Maria di Leuca and Castro, and Maratea in Basilicata. For more information try www .diveitaly.com.

There's a sailing school in Santa Maria di Leuca (see p160), and boat trips are possible around Gallipoli, Otranto, Castro, the Isole Tremiti and Maratea.

Windsurfing is not big here as the coast is either too rocky (Adriatic coast) or not windy enough (Ionian coast), but there is kite-surfing in Santa Caterina (p156) in Parco Porto Selvaggio, from February to April.

White-water rafting is a way to get thrills in the Pollino, with several operators offering trips. You can also ski in the mountains in the winter months.

BUSINESS HOURS

Generally shops open 9am to 1pm and 4pm to 8pm (or 5pm to 9pm) Monday to Saturday. In summer, in the more touristy areas, shops tend to open until at least 11pm and sometimes as late as 1am. The midday break, starting at 1pm, can last three to five hours.

Some supermarkets (usually the larger ones on the edge of towns) have continuous opening from 9am to 8.30pm Monday to Saturday. A few open on Sunday.

Banks tend to open from 8.30am to 1.30pm and 3pm to 4.30pm Monday to Friday. They close at weekends, when in most places you will have difficulty changing money. Most banks have ATMs that accept foreign credit/ debit cards.

Major post offices open from 8.15am to 5pm or 6pm Monday to Friday, and also from

8.30am to noon or 1pm on Saturday. Smaller post offices generally open from 8.15am to 1.15pm Monday to Friday, and 8.30am to noon on Saturday. All post offices close at least two hours earlier than normal on the last business day of each month (not including Saturday).

Farmacie (pharmacies) open 9am to 12.30pm and 3.30pm to 7.30pm. Most close on Saturday afternoon and Sunday. In any given area there'll be at least one pharmacy open extra hours, usually until 10pm. When closed, pharmacies are required to display information on the nearest open pharmacies.

Bars (in the Italian sense; that is, coffee-pastry-sandwich-beer places) and cafés generally open from 7am to 8pm, though some open as early as 4.30am. Those with a nocturnal vocation open until about 1am during the week but as late as 3am on Fridays and Saturdays. Clubs and discos might open from around 10pm to 5am (sometimes later), but often there'll be nobody there until after midnight.

Restaurants open from about noon to 3pm and 7.30pm to 11pm. Many restaurants shut for several months in the low season, and some take their holidays in August. Those that stay open all year usually close one day a week, often Monday (although most open daily from June to September).

The opening hours of museums, galleries and archaeological sites vary enormously. As a rule, museums close on Monday, but from June to September many sights open daily. Outside the high season, hours reduce drastically and out-of-the-way sights close altogether.

CHILDREN

Children will be fêted wherever you go, welcomed and catered for with enthusiasm. The flip side of this is that there are few special amenities for children – child menus, changing facilities, child-geared entertainments and so on.

Practicalities

Discounts are available for children (usually aged under 12) on public transport. Museums and sites are usually free to under 18s. Although trains are seldom busy it's always advisable to book in advance. You should also book car seats in advance if hiring a car.

If you're travelling with young children, it's much easier to stay in a villa, an apartment or somewhere with self-catering facilities. There are dozens of hotel-residences (hotels with self-catering) available in summer and many B&Bs have kitchen facilities. Some upmarket or resort hotels offer babysitting.

You can buy baby formula in powder or liquid form, as well as sterilising solutions such as Milton, at *farmacie*. Disposable nappies (diapers) are widely available at supermarkets and *farmacie* (where they are also costlier). Fresh cow's milk is sold in cartons in some bars and in supermarkets.

For more information, see Lonely Planet's *Travel with Children* or check out www.travelwithyourkids.com and www.familytravelnetwork.com.

Sights & Activities

Successful travel with children requires some special effort, but there's tonnes for them to enjoy in these regions, particularly if they like the seaside. Don't overdo things, factor in time to play and plan activities that include the kids – older children could help you plan these. An *agriturismo* with animals on the farm, or one that offers horse-riding excursions, is a good idea. Alternatively, coastal resorts with balmy beaches – with lots of sandcastle and ice-cream potential – and boating trips will all be hits.

Seaside towns such as Otranto (p161), Vieste (p88), Peschici (p92) and Maratea (p186) are good places to start. Beaches on the Ionian coast (mainly between Gallipoli and Santa Maria di Leuca; p160) are fabulously family friendly (sandy, shallow, and served by lots of lidos), as are those around the Gargano Promontory.

Children will also find the cave architecture of Matera (p170) bewitching and Alberobello (p123), with its stubby, cute houses, could have been built with children in mind. The Grotte di Castellana (p121) are spectacular underground caves, while near Castro you can take boat trips to seacaves such as the watery wonder of Grotta Zinzulusa (p161). **Zoosafari** (www.zoosafari.it), a big wildlife park, is close to Fasano.

CLIMATE CHARTS

Southern Italy is famous for its *solleone* (lion sun), the baking heat in the middle of a summer's day.

Puglia has a Mediterranean climate, defined by hot dry summers followed by mild winters

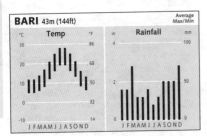

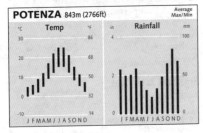

with light rainfall. The finest weather is usually found around the coast.

Basilicata, with its extremes of altitude, presents a different story. The inland mountains have a continental climate, the coastline a much milder, Mediterranean one. On the highest mountains there is substantial snowfall in winter. Rain falls mainly in spring and autumn, with much more rainfall in the southwest.

See p13 for information on the best times to visit Puglia and Basilicata.

CUSTOMS

Duty-free sales within the EU no longer exist. Under the rules of the single market, goods bought in and exported within the EU incur no additional taxes, provided that duty has been paid somewhere within the EU and the goods are only intended for personal consumption.

Travellers entering Italy from outside the EU are allowed to import, duty free: 200 cigarettes, 1L of spirits, 2L of wine, 60ml of perfume, 250ml of eau de toilette and other goods up to a total value of €175. Anything over this limit must be declared on arrival and the appropriate duty paid (carry all your receipts with you).

Bear in mind when entering or leaving Italy by air that there are restrictions on the amount of liquids that you are allowed to carry in your hand luggage.

DANGERS & ANNOYANCES

Petty crime can be a problem in larger towns, but common-sense precautions should limit the risk.

Racism

Apart from Lecce, which has a more mixed population, many of these regions' towns are largely homogenous and racism and closed-mindedness can be a issue.

Theft

Theft is not a big problem in Puglia and Basilicata. Still, use your common sense. Wear a money belt under your clothing and keep important items, such as money, passport and tickets, there at all times. If you are carrying a bag, wear the strap across your body and have the bag on the side away from the road. Don't leave valuables laying around your hotel room.

Never leave valuables in your car – try not to leave anything in the car, especially not overnight.

On the beach, keep an eye on your valuables or, better still, avoid taking them in the first place so you can relax while swimming.

In case of theft or loss, always report the incident at the municipal police station (*questura*) within 24 hours and ask for a statement, otherwise your travel insurance company won't pay out. Emergency numbers are listed on this inside front cover of this book.

Traffic

In July and August, traffic on Puglia and Basilicata's many minor roads can be a pain, not to mention parking.

Out of season, roads are often near empty and driving is not as intimidating as in Italy's large cities. However, in Basilicata's mountains roads are narrow and winding and can be dangerous in bad weather.

Road signs can be confusing and unclear.

DISCOUNT CARDS
Senior Cards

Admission to most museums and sites is reduced for those 65 (sometimes 60) and over.

Senior citizens' organisations and travel agencies in your own country will be able to tell you more about travel packages and discounts for senior travellers.

Student & Youth Cards

Discounts (usually half-price) are available to EU-citizens aged between 18 and 25 (you may need to produce proof of your age) at many of Puglia and Basilicata's sights. An ISIC (International Student Identity Card) is usually sufficient proof of age. If you're under 26 but not a student you can apply for a **Euro<26** (www.euro26.org). Similar cards are available to teachers (ITIC). For nonstudent under 25s, there's the **International Youth Travel Card** (IYTC; www.istc.org), which offers the same benefits.

Student cards are issued by student unions, hostelling organisations and some youth travel agencies. **Centro Turistico Studentesco e Giovanile** (CTS; ☎ 06 44 11 11; www.cts.it) a youth and travel organisation has 11 branches in Puglia and two in Basilicata and can issue ISIC, ITIC and Euro<26 cards. You have to join first, however, which costs €28.

EMBASSIES & CONSULATES

It's important to realise what your own embassy – the embassy of the country of which you are a citizen – can do to help you if you get into trouble. Generally speaking, it won't be much help in emergencies if the trouble you're in is remotely your own fault. Your embassy will not be sympathetic if you end up in jail after committing a crime locally, even if such actions are legal in your own country.

In genuine emergencies you might get some assistance, but only if other channels have been exhausted. For example, if you need to get home urgently, a free ticket is unlikely – the embassy would expect you to have insurance. If you have all your money and documents stolen, it might assist with getting a new passport, but a loan for onward travel is out of the question.

Italian Embassies & Consulates

The following is a selection of Italian diplomatic missions abroad. As a rule, you should approach the consulate rather than the embassy (where both are present) on visa matters. All offices here are embassies unless otherwise stated.

Australia Canberra (☎ 02-6273 3333; www.ambcanberra.esteri.it; 12 Grey St, Deakin, ACT 2600); Melbourne consulate (☎ 03-9867 5744; consolatogenerale.melbourne@esteri.it; 509 St Kilda Rd, VIC 3004); Sydney consulate (☎ 02-9392 7900; info.sydney@esteri.it; Level 43, The Gateway, 1 Macquarie Pl, NSW 2000)

Austria (☎ 01-712 5121; ambitalviepress@via.at; Metternichgasse 13, Vienna 1030)
Canada Ottawa (☎ 613-232 2401; www.ambottawa.esteri.it; 21st fl, 275 Slater St, Ontario K1P 5H9); Montreal consulate (☎ 514-849 8351; www.consmontreal.esteri.it/Consolato_Montreal; 3489 Drummond St, Montreal, Quebec H3G 1X6); Toronto consulate (☎ 416-977 1566; www.constoronto.esteri.it; 136 Beverley St, Toronto, Ontario M5T 1Y5)
France (☎ 01 49 54 03 00; www.ambparigi.esteri.it; 47 Rue de Varenne, 75007)
Germany Berlin (☎ 030-25 44 00; www.ambberlino.esteri.it; Hiroshimastr 1, 10785 Berlin); Frankfurt (☎ 069-753 10; www.consfrancoforte.esteri.it; Kettenhofweg, 1, 60325 Frankfurt-am-Main)
Ireland (☎ 01-660 1744; www.ambdublino.esteri.it; 63-65 Northumberland Rd, Dublin 4)
Netherlands (☎ 070-302 1030; italemb@worldonline.nl; Alexanderstraat12, The Hague 2514 JL)
New Zealand (☎ 04-473 53 39; www.italy-embassy.org.nz; 34 Grant Rd, Thorndon, Wellington)
Spain Madrid (☎ 91 423 3300; segreamb@ambitaliamadrid.org; Calle de Lagasca 98, Madrid 28006); Barcelona (☎ 93 467 7305; www.italconsulbcn.org; Calle Majorca 270, Barcelona 08037)
UK Embassy (☎ 020-7312 2200; www.embitaly.org.uk; 14 Three Kings Yard, London, W1K 4EH); Consulate (☎ 020-7235 9371; www.conslondra.esteri.it; 38 Eaton Pl, London SW1X 8AN)
USA New York (☎ 212-737 9100; www.consnewyork.esteri.it; 690 Park Ave, New York, NY 10021-5044); Washington, DC (☎ 202-612 4400; www.ambwashingtondc.esteri.it; 3000 Whitehaven St, NW Washington, DC 20008)

Embassies & Consulates in Italy

Most countries have an embassy in Rome, where passport enquiries should be addressed. Most embassies and consulates open between around 8.30am and 5pm Monday to Friday. However, the immigration section is usually only open from around 8.30am to 11.30am All offices following are in Rome unless otherwise stated.

Australia (☎ 06 852 721; www.italy.embassy.gov.au; Via Antonio Bosio 5, 00161)
Canada (☎ 06 854441; www.international.gc.ca/canada-europa/italy; Villa Grazioli, via Salaria 243, 00199)
France (☎ 06 68 60 11; www.france-italia.it in French & Italian; Piazza Farnese 67, 00186)
Germany (☎ 06 49 21 31; Via San Martino della Battaglia 4, 00185)
Ireland (☎ 06 697 91 21; Piazza Campitelli 3, 00186)
Netherlands Bari (☎ 080 5569222; Via Ennio, 2-I, 70124); Rome (☎ 06 32286 001; www.olanda.it in Dutch & Italian; Via Michele Mercati, 8, 00197)

New Zealand (☎ 06 441 71 71; www.nzembassy.com; Via Zara 28, 00198)
Spain (☎ 06 684 04 01; www.mae.es/Embajadas/Roma/es/home in Spanish; Palazzo Borghese, Largo Fontanella Borghese 19, 00186);
UK (☎ 06 4220 00 01; www.fco.gov.uk; Via XX Settembre 80a, 00187)
USA (☎ 06 4 67 41; www.usembassy.it; Via Vittorio Veneto 119a-121, 00187)

FESTIVALS & EVENTS

The Italian south is famed for its festivals. Traditional celebrations mark the coming and going of the seasons or religious events. The most important pre-date Christianity and are linked to the farming calendar

Although some traditions have disappeared, many festivals are observed with great enthusiasm. Since the 1970s there has been a revival of interest in local traditions and many events are more vibrant than ever.

January

Falò (11–12 January) More than 50 large bonfires light up the night in Castellana Grotte, celebrating the deliverance from the plague in 1691.
Sant'Antonio Abate (16 January) A huge bonfire dwarfs Novoli, celebrating the hermit saint.

February

Carnevale (Carnival) During the period running up to Ash Wednesday, many towns stage carnivals. The finest is in Putignano – Italy's longest carnival, it starts on 26 December and ends on Shrove Tuesday. Other big Shrove Tuesday bashes are at Gallipoli, Massafra, Manfredonia and Molfetta.
San Valentino (14 February) The saint of love (and citrus fruit) is celebrated in Vico del Gargano, with a procession of his statue, adorned with oranges and orange blossom.
Disfida di Barletta (22 & 23 July) A re-enactment of when Italian and French duelled in 1503.

March/April

San Giuseppe (19 March) More huge bonfires celebrate St Joseph, in Altamura, Bitetto, Faeto, Ginosa, Pulsano, Mottola, S Giorgio Jonico, Bolvino, Deliceto, Troia and Turi.
Pasqua (Easter) Holy Week is a big deal. On Maundy Thursday, Ruvo di Puglia sees the Processione degli Ottosanti (procession of eight saints), and Ginosa has a beautiful mystery play, staged in its canyon. The Processione dei Misteri take place on Good Friday in many towns – including Bari, Barletta, Bitonto, Andria, Molfetta, Ruvo di Puglia, Francavilla Fontana, Fasano, Gallipoli, Taranto, Lecce, Troia, Vico del Gargano, and Trani in Puglia, and Montescaglioso in Basilicata. In San Marco in Lamis there is a long parade of

carts bearing burning torches. Easter Sunday is big in Ruvo di Puglia, with the Processione del Cristo Risorto (procession of resurrected Christ), as well as in Troia, which stages the Processione del Bacio (procession of the kiss).
San Leone (6 April) This Bitonto country fair is one of Italy's oldest, mentioned by Boccaccio in the *Decameron*.
San Giorgio (23 April) Manfredonia re-enacts the story of the city's birth in honour of St George.
Festa dell'Incoronata (last Saturday of April) The Cavalcata degli Angeli (Angels' Cavalcade) takes place in Foggia, with children dressed as angels, saints and Madonnas.

May

San Nicola (Festival of St Nicholas; 7–8 May) Bari's greatest shindig: parades, sea processions, fireworks and music.
San Cataldo (8–10 May) In Taranto, there is a sea procession, fireworks, and a medieval-style boat race.
Pellegrinaggio di San Michele (8 May) Pilgrims congregate at Monte Sant'Angelo.
San Biagio (second Sunday of May) Week-long celebrations celebrating Maratea's patron saint, starting with a long procession from Santuario di San Biagio.
San Bernardino (20 May) Procession parading Bernalda's patron saint around town, on the anniversary of his death.
Il Maggio (May) Accettura, in Appennino Lucano, is famous for this annual marriage of trees, followed by tree-climbing competitions.
Cortili aperti (end May) Countless noble Lecce *palazzi* throw open their gardens.

June

San Antonio (8–13 June) In Rotonda, this religious feast is accompanied by a tree marriage similar to that in Accettura.
Processione del Cavallo Parato (Corpus Christi Sunday) A celebration dating from the 16th century, in Brindisi, when the archbishop carries the Monstrance on a white horse.
San Pietro e Paolo (29 June) Galatina pays tribute to Saints Peter and Paul with a *taranta* festival.
Mediterranea Estate (June–September) Lecce's summer-long series of free events including concerts, comedy, theatre, and dance.

July

Disfida di Barletta (22 & 23 July) A repeated re-enactment (the first was in February) of when Italian and French duelled in 1503.
Madonna della Bruna (2 July) In Matera, a colourful procession followed by the *assalto al carro*, when the crowd tears the main cart to pieces in order to take away the precious relics.
Madonna del Carmine (16 July) Trani celebrates the protector of fishermen, laying floral crowns in the sea.

Festival della Valle d'Itria (22 July–10 August) Martina Franca holds its renowned international music festival, featuring opera, classical and jazz.

San Nicola Pellegrino (last weekend of July) Three days of revelries in honour of Trani's patron saint.

August

Corto Storico di Federico II (2nd weekend of August) Medieval procession in Oria, with a tournament between the town's four quarters.

Festa dei Martiri idruntini (11–14 August) Otranto commemorates the martyrs of 1480.

Notte della Taranta (16 August) A mammoth *taranta* concert swamps the small town of Melpignano.

San Rocco (16 August) Spectacular fireworks in Locorotondo.

Sant'Oronzo (24–26 August) Lecce's saintly celebrations are busy and spectacular, with processions, fireworks, music and lots of shows.

La Cavalcata (26 August) Ostuni celebrates with processions of horsemen dressed in glittering red-and-white uniforms.

San Bernardino (31 August) Bernalda's patron saint saved the town from the plague – a procession celebrates.

September

San Theodore (1–10 September) Historic regatta, boat race and water fireworks in Brindisi.

Talos Festival (1–10 September) Ruvo di Puglia has five days of jazz concerts in the name of a Cretan hero depicted at the museum.

Fiera del Levante (2nd Sunday of September) Biggest country fair in the south of Italy takes place in special grounds in Bari.

Pellegrinaggio di San Michele (29 September) Pilgrims congregate at Monte Sant'Angelo.

October

Intorciata (3rd Sunday of October) Bitonto sees a candle-lit procession honouring doctor SS Cosmas and Damian.

December

Fiera di Santa Lucia (13–24 December) A week-long Christmas fair commencing on St Lucy's day, where you can buy *cartapesta* and terracotta crib figures.

Natale (Christmas) There are many processions and religious events in the run up to Christmas. Many churches set up elaborate *presepi* (nativity scenes). Live nativity scenes (using real people) take place in Fasano and Rignano Garganico and many other towns, most spectacularly in Crispiano, which uses artificial snow.

FOOD

In this book we have used the term budget to describe places where you can get a meal for under €15. For a full, midrange restaurant meal you should reckon on €15 to €35 per person. A top-end meal will set you back around €35 upwards per person. These prices include primo, secondo, dolce and house wine.

Within each section, restaurants are listed in order of budget.

For more on eating and drinking in Puglia and Basilicata, see p42.

Where to Eat & Drink

A *trattoria* is a cheaper version of a *ristorante* (restaurant) with less-aloof service and simpler dishes. A *ristorante* generally has a wider selection of dishes, printed menus, a higher standard of service and higher prices. However, distinctions are blurred: *ristoranti* call themselves *trattorie*, and vice versa, usually to capture the spirit of the other establishment – sophisticated elegance or rustic charm, respectively. It's best to check the menu for prices. Don't judge the quality of a *ristorante* or *trattoria* by its appearance. You are likely to eat your most memorable meal at a place with plastic tablecloths in a backstreet, a dingy piazza or on a back road in the country. And don't panic if you find yourself in a *trattoria* that has no printed menu: they often offer the best and most authentic food.

A pizzeria will, of course, serve pizza but usually also has a *trattoria*-style menu. An *osteria* is likely to be either a wine bar offering a small selection of dishes with a verbal menu, or a small trattoria.

Bars are popular hang-outs, serving coffee, soft drinks and alcohol. They often sell *cornetti* (croissants), *panini* (bread rolls with simple fillings) and *spuntini* (snacks). You can round off a meal with a *gelato* (ice cream) from a *gelateria* – a crowd outside is always a good sign.

Most eating establishments have a cover charge (*coperto;* usually around €1 to €2) and a *servizio* (service charge) of 10% to 15%.

QUICK EATS

Pizza al taglio (by the slice) is available in larger towns. Look out for delicious tomato and oregano-topped *focaccia* in local bakeries and *alimentari* (grocery stores), which will also sometimes make a *panino* with the filling of your choice.

A Lecce speciality is a *rustica,* a delicious pastry puff filled with a kind of creamy bechamel set against a tang of tomato.

If you're after meat-to-go, look no further than Cisternino, with its tradition of *fornello pronto* (ready-to-go roast or grilled meat).

Drinks

COFFEE

Coffee in Italy isn't like anywhere else in the world: it's better.

An espresso, simply called *un caffè*, is a small, strong, black-coffee shot. You can ask for a *caffè doppio* (a double shot), *caffè lungo* (literally 'long coffee') or *caffè Americano*, although the last two will usually be an espresso with water run through the grinds and may taste bitter.

A *caffè corretto* ('corrected') is an espresso with a dash of grappa or some other spirit, and a *macchiato* ('stained' coffee) is an espresso with a dash of milk. You can ask for a *macchiato caldo* (with a drop of hot, foamed milk) or *freddo* (with cold milk). *Latte macchiato* is warmed milk stained with a drop of coffee. *Caffè freddo* is a long glass of cold, black, sweetened coffee. If you want it without sugar, ask for *caffè freddo amaro*.

Then, of course, there's the *cappuccino* (coffee with frothy milk). If you want it without froth, ask for a *cappuccino senza schiuma*. Italians tend to drink *cappuccini* only with breakfast and during the morning, never after meals. You will also find it difficult to convince bartenders to make your cappuccino hot rather than *tiepido* (lukewarm) – overheating the milk destroys its natural sweetness. If you must, ask for your cappuccino *ben caldo* (hot), *molto caldo* (very hot) or *bollente* (boiling) and wait for the same 'tut-tut' response that you'll attract if you order one after dinner.

Variations on the milky coffee menu include a *caffè latte,* a milkier version of the cappuccino with less froth. In summer the *cappuccino freddo,* a sweet, iced coffee, is a good choice. You will also find *caffè granita,* sweet and strong, traditionally served with a dollop of whipped cream.

A height-of-summer speciality worth asking for in Lecce and around is *caffè in ghiaccio,* an espresso poured over ice cubes, served in a chilled glass.

WATER

Tap water is drinkable, but many Italians prefer to drink bottled *acqua minerale* (mineral water), either *frizzante* (sparkling) or *naturale* (still) – you'll be asked in restaurants and bars which type you would prefer. If you just want a glass of tap water, you should ask for *acqua dal rubinetto* or *acqua naturale.*

Vegetarians & Vegans

Vegetable-based dishes are abundant in Puglia and Basilicata – meat was a treat here for a long time, so the local cuisine is mainly based around vegetables, pasta and pulses. However, vegetarians should be aware of misleading names and remember that many Italians don't think that eating a bit of prosciutto is actually eating meat. Look for the word *magro* (thin or lean) on menus, which usually means that the dish is meatless. Vegans are in for a much tougher time. You'll have to specify '*senza formaggio*' (without cheese) as a matter of course. Also remember that *pasta fresca* (fresh pasta), which may also turn up in soups, is sometimes made with eggs (though *orecchiette* is traditionally made without).

Eating with Kids

You'll be hard-pressed to find a children's menu in most Italian restaurants. Not because kids are not welcome but rather because they are. Local children are treated very much as adults and are taken out to dinner from a young age. You'll often see families order a *mezzo piatto* (half-plate) off the menu for their smaller members. Most restaurants are perfectly comfortable tailoring a dish to meet your kid's tastes.

High chairs are available in some restaurants, but don't tend to be the norm.

For more information on travelling with your little ones, see p205.

GAY & LESBIAN TRAVELLERS

There's practically no open gay scene in Puglia and Basilicata, though homosexuality is legal and the age of consent is 16. The culture of the south is conservative and macho and overt displays of affection by homosexual couples could attract consternation and unpleasant responses. This makes all the more amazing the election of the gay communist governor of Puglia, Nicky Vendola in 2005.

Gay-friendly bars, clubs and saunas can be tracked down through the useful site www.gay.it/guida/ (in Italian). There's also a dedicated website for **Gay Puglia** (www.gaypuglia .it in Italian). **Venture Out** (www.venture-out.com) offers tours for gay and lesbian travellers, including a trip to Puglia.

You may also find information through the national Italian organisations **ARCI-GAY & ARCI-Lesbica** (☎ 051 649 30 55; www.arcigay.it; Via Don Minzoni 18, 40121 Bologna).

HOLIDAYS

Most Italians take their annual holiday en masse in July/August. What this means for Puglia (and to a lesser extent, Basilicata) is that a good deal of Italy's populace heads south. It's the liveliest (and most expensive and crowded) time to be here, but a few businesses and shops close in midsummer, particularly during the week around Ferragosto (Feast of the Assumption) on 15 August. The crowds tend to dissipate after Ferragosto. Settimana Santa (Easter Week) is another busy holiday period for Italians.

Individual towns have public holidays to celebrate the feasts of their patron saints (see p208). National public holidays in Puglia and Basilicata include the following:

New Year's Day (Anno Nuovo) Celebrations take place on New Year's Eve (Capodanno)
Epiphany (Befana) 6 January
Good Friday (Venerdì Santo) March/April
Easter Monday (Pasquetta/Giorno dopo Pasqua) March/April
Liberation Day (Giorno della Liberazione) 25 April (marks the Allied victory in Italy)
Labour Day (Giorno del Lavoro) 1 May
Republic Day (Giorno del Repubblica) 2 June
Feast of the Assumption (Ferragosto) 15 August
All Saints' Day (Ognissanti) 1 November
Feast of the Immaculate Conception (Concezione Immaculata) 8 December
Christmas Day (Natale) 25 December
Feast of Santo Stefano (Boxing Day; Festa di Santo Stefano) 26 December

INSURANCE

A travel insurance policy to cover theft, loss and medical problems is a good idea. It may also cover you for cancellation of, and delays in, your travel arrangements. Paying for your ticket with a credit card can often provide limited travel accident insurance and you may be able to reclaim the payment if the operator doesn't deliver.

Some policies specifically exclude 'dangerous activities', which can include scuba diving, climbing, even trekking.

Usually you have to pay on the spot and claim later. If you do, ensure you keep all documentation. Some policies ask you to call back (reverse charges) to a centre in your home country where an immediate assessment of your problem is made. Check that the policy covers ambulances or an emergency flight home.

For details of car insurance see p224.

INTERNET ACCESS

If you plan to carry your laptop or palmtop computer with you, remember that the power supply voltage in Italy may vary from that at home, risking damage to your equipment. The best investment is a universal AC adapter for your appliance, which will enable you to plug it in anywhere.

Also, your PC-card modem may not work once you leave your home country. The safest option is to buy a reputable 'global' modem before you leave or buy a local PC-card modem if you're spending an extended time in Italy. Keep in mind that the local telephone socket may differ from the ones at home so ensure that you have at least a US RJ-11 telephone adapter that works with your modem. You can almost always find an adapter that will convert from RJ-11 to the local variety.

Major internet service providers have dial-in nodes throughout Europe; it's best to download a list of the dial-in numbers before you leave home. If you access your internet account at home through a smaller ISP or your office or school network, your best option is either to open an account with a global ISP or to rely on internet cafés to collect your mail. For more information on internet roaming, see www.kropla.com.

If you do intend to rely on internet cafés, you'll need to carry three pieces of information with you to enable you to access your internet mail account: your incoming (POP or IMAP) mail server name, your account name and your password. Your ISP or network supervisor will be able to give you these. You also will have to register at the café, so will have to show your passport or ID card the first time you use it (even if it will also be the last time).

You'll find internet cafés in most of Puglia and Basilicata's towns (but not in smaller towns and villages) and some of them are listed throughout this book. Some upmarket hotels and cafes have wi-fi. It's also expensive, frequently costing €4 to €5 an hour.

LEGAL MATTERS

Puglia and Basilicata are orderly places and the average tourist will probably only have a brush with the law if robbed.

Drink & Drugs

In 2005 Italy's drugs laws were tightened in a zero-tolerance policy that abolished the

DIRECTORY

distinction between hard and soft drugs and made possession, as well as dealing, a criminal offence. Under these laws, anyone found in possession of as little as two cannabis joints could, in theory, be prosecuted as a dealer – it's up to the police to decide.

The legal blood-alcohol limit is 0.05% and random breath tests do occur.

Police

If you run into trouble, you're likely to end up dealing with the *polizia statale* (state police) or the *carabinieri* (military police). The former are a civil force and take their orders from the Ministry of the Interior, while the *carabinieri* fall under the Ministry of Defence. There's a considerable duplication of their roles, despite a 1981 reform of the police forces. Both forces are responsible for public order and security, which means that you can visit either in the event of a robbery or attack.

The *carabinieri* wear a black uniform with a red stripe and drive dark-blue cars with a red stripe. They are well trained and usually helpful. Their police station is called a *caserma* (barracks), a reflection of their military status.

The *polizia* wear powder-blue trousers with a fuchsia stripe and a navy-blue jacket, and drive light-blue cars with a white stripe. People wanting a residence permit will have to deal with them. Their headquarters is called the *questura*.

Vigili urbani are the local traffic police. You will have to deal with them if you get a parking ticket or your car is towed away.

Your Rights

Italy has anti-terrorism laws that could make life difficult if you are detained by the police. A suspected terrorist can be held for 48 hours without a magistrate being informed and can be interrogated without the presence of a lawyer. It is difficult to obtain bail and you can be held legally for up to three years without being brought to trial.

MAPS

Detailed maps are available in Puglia and Basilicata in town bookshops (the best places being Lecce and Bari). The best large-scale maps are produced by Litografia Artistica Cartografica (LAC), with maps including Il Gargano (1:80,000), and Il Provincia di Foggia (1:160,000), with regional maps at 1:250,000. Otherwise Belletti Editore pro-

duces maps at a scale of 1:300,000. The Carta Excursionistica del Pollino Lucano (scale 1:50000), produced by the Basilicata tourist board, is a useful driving map. You can also buy the Parco Nazionale del Pollino settore centro-settentrionale map (1:55.000; €6) from http://ecommerce.escursionista.it.

MONEY

Italy's unit of currency is the euro (€), divided into 100 cents. Coin denominations are one, two, five, 10, 20 and 50 cents, €1 and €2. The notes are €5, €10, €20, €50, €100, €200 and €500. All euro notes of each denomination are identical on both sides in all EU countries, and the coins are identical on the side showing their value, but there are also 12 different obverses, each representing one of the 12 euro-zone countries. For more information on the euro check out the website www.europa.eu.int/euro.

See Quick Reference on the inside front cover for a handy table to help you calculate the exchange rate or log on to www.oanda .com. See p14 for information on costs.

Money can be exchanged in banks, post offices and exchange offices. Banks generally offer the best rates, but shop around as rates fluctuate.

ATMs

Credit cards can be used in ATMs *(bancomat)* displaying the appropriate sign or (if you have no PIN) to obtain cash advances over the counter in many banks – Visa and MasterCard are among the most widely recognised. Check what charges you will incur with your bank.

You'll find ATMs in towns throughout Puglia and Basilicata and this is undoubtedly the simplest (and safest) way to handle your money while travelling. However, there is a limit of €250 on withdrawals.

Cash

There is little advantage in bringing foreign cash to Puglia and Basilicata. True, exchange commissions are often lower than for travellers cheques, but the danger of losing the lot far outweighs such petty gains.

However, you will need cash for many day-to-day transactions as credit cards are not accepted in many hotels and restaurants.

Credit/Debit Cards

Carrying plastic is the simplest way to organise your holiday funds. You don't have large amounts of cash to lose, you can get money after hours and the exchange rate is often better.

Major cards, such as Visa, MasterCard, Eurocard, Cirrus and Eurocheque, are accepted in Puglia and Basilicata, though not usually at small hotels, B&Bs and restaurants. Check charges with your bank but, as a rule, there's no charge for purchases on major cards.

You should check the procedure on what to do if you experience problems or if your card is stolen. Most card suppliers will give you an emergency number you can call free of charge for help and advice.

Tipping

You are not expected to tip on top of restaurant service charges, but it is common to leave a small amount, perhaps €1 per person. If there is no service charge, the customer might consider leaving a 10% tip, but this is by no means obligatory. In bars, Italians often leave small change as a tip. Tipping taxi drivers is not common practice, but you should tip the porter at top-end hotels.

Travellers Cheques

Travellers cheques can be cashed at most banks and exchange offices. Amex, Thomas Cook and Visa are the most widely accepted brands.

It may be preferable to buy travellers cheques in euros rather than another currency, as they are less likely to incur commission on exchange. Get most of the cheques in largish denominations to save on per-cheque exchange rates.

It's vital to keep your initial receipt, a record of your cheque numbers and the ones you have used, separate from the cheques themselves. If your travellers cheques get stolen, you'll need these documents to get them replaced. You must take your passport with you when cashing cheques.

POST

Italy's postal system is notoriously slow and unreliable.

Stamps (*francobolli*) are available at post offices and authorised tobacconists' (look for the official *tabacchi* sign, a big 'T', usually white on black).

Postcards and letters up to 20g sent airmail (*via aerea*) cost €0.62 to Australia, Japan, New Zealand, the USA, Africa and Asia, and €0.45 within Europe. It can take up to two weeks for mail to arrive in the UK or USA, while a letter to Australia will take between two and three weeks. Postcards take even longer.

You can also send letters express, using *posta prioritaria*, which guarantees to deliver letters within Europe in three days and to the rest of the world within four to eight days. For more important items, use registered mail (*raccomandato*), or insured mail (*assicurato*), the cost of which depends on the value of the object being sent.

Information about postal services and rates can be obtained at www.poste.it.

Receiving Mail

Poste restante (general delivery) is known as *fermo posta* in Italy. Letters marked thus will be held at the counter of the same name in the main post office in the relevant town.

You'll need to pick up your letters in person and you must present your passport as ID.

SOLO TRAVELLERS

Travelling alone can work out more costly. In many places you will find yourself paying around two-thirds the double room rate and in high summer single rooms are impossible to find – you'll probably have to pay as much as for two. If you are on a budget you should seek out hostels, B&Bs and *agriturismi* where the rates are much more reasonable; many places charge per person, rather than per room, although again in high summer this can be a problem in smaller places.

Italians don't tend to travel alone, so be prepared to be regarded as something of an oddity or possibly to feel a bit lonely.

As in any place, women will find it more difficult to travel alone than men, as they might receive a bit of macho hassle or increased curiosity. If you are travelling alone or with female friends, you are likely to receive quite a lot of amorous attention, but it's generally harmless – at most annoying. Travelling as a lone woman even has its advantages, as people will go out of their way to help you, be friendly, and treat you well (both men and women).

TELEPHONE
Mobile Phones

Italy uses GSM 900/1800, compatible with the rest of Europe and Australia but not with North American GSM 1900 or the totally different system in Japan (although some North

American GSM 1900/900 phones do work here). If you have a GSM phone, check with your service provider about using it in Italy and beware of calls being routed internationally (very expensive for a 'local' call).

The cheapest way to use your phone abroad is to use a local SIM card. You can buy SIM cards in Italy for your own national mobile phone (provided you own a GSM, dual- or tri-band cellular phone) and buy prepaid time. This only works if your national phone hasn't been blocked, something you might want to find out before leaving home. If you buy a SIM card and find your phone *is* blocked you won't be able to take it back.

Both TIM (Telecom Italia Mobile) and Vodaphone-Omnitel offer prepaid *(prepagato)* accounts for GSM phones (frequency 900 mHz). The card can cost around €30 to €60 and includes some prepaid phone time; you can then top up in their shops or by buying cards in outlets like tobacconists and newsstands. You need your passport to open any kind of mobile phone account, prepaid or otherwise.

TIM and Vodaphone-Omnitel retail outlets operate in most cities. Call rates vary according to an infinite variety of call plans.

Payphones & Phonecards

The partly privatised Telecom Italia is Italy's largest phone company and its orange public pay phones are liberally scattered all over Puglia and Basilicata. The most common accept only telephone cards *(carte/schede telefoniche),* although you will still find some that accept both cards and coins. Some card phones now also accept special Telecom credit cards and even commercial credit cards.

You can buy phonecards (usually €5 or €10) at post offices, tobacconists and newsstands. For directory enquiries within Italy, dial ☎ 12.

Phone Codes

The international country code for Italy is ☎ 39. Direct international calls can easily be made from public telephones using a phonecard. Dial ☎ 00 to get out of Italy, then the relevant country and area codes, followed by a telephone number of anything from four to eight digits. If you're calling Italy from abroad, you do not knock off the '0' at the beginning of the number, so you would call Bari thus: ☎ +39 080…

Area codes are an integral part of all telephone numbers in Italy, even if you are calling within a single zone. If you are in Bari and are calling another fixed line in Bari the first three digits of the phone number will be ☎ 080. Mobile phone numbers begin with a three-digit prefix such as ☎ 330, 335, 347, 368 etc. Free-phone or toll-free numbers are known as *numeri verdi* and start with ☎ 800. The national-rate phone numbers start with ☎ 848 and ☎ 199.

TIME

Italy operates on a 24-hour clock. It's one hour ahead of GMT/UTC. Daylight-saving time starts on the last Sunday in March, when clocks are put forward one hour. Clocks are put back an hour on the last Sunday in October.

There's a time-zone world map at the back of this book.

TOURIST INFORMATION

The quality of tourist offices in Puglia and Basilicata varies dramatically. One office might have enthusiastic staff, another might be indifferent. Most offices can offer you a plethora of brochures, maps and leaflets, even if they're uninterested in helping in any other way. It's fairly unusual for the staff to speak English.

Puglia's regional **tourist office** (☎ 080 524 23 29; www.regione.puglia.it) has its headquarters in Bari. You can also find information on the website of the **Italian State Tourist Office** (ENIT; www.enit.it).

Throughout the island, three tiers of tourist office exist: regional, provincial and local. They have different names (see below) but roughly offer the same services, with the exception of the regional offices, which are concerned with promotion, planning and budgeting. Throughout this book, offices are referred to as 'tourist office' rather than by their elaborate and confusing titles. Most offices will respond to written and telephone requests for information.

Azienda Autonoma di Soggiorno e Turismo (AAST) Otherwise known as Informazioni e Assistenza ai Turisti, is the local tourist office. These local offices have town-specific information and should also know about bus routes and museum opening times.

Azienda di Promozione Turistica (APT) The provincial – read main – tourist office should have information on the town you are in and the surrounding province.

Pro Loco This is the local office in small towns and villages and is similar to the AAST office.

TRAVELLERS WITH DISABILITIES

Puglia and Basilicata have little infrastructure to help ease the way for disabled travellers. Few museums have wheelchair access, and only a few upmarket hotels have adapted accommodation. Streets tend to be cobbled, and though Puglia is mostly flat, Basilicata is all hills.

The Italian railways have a reception service for disabled people at certain stations, to be booked 24 hours in advance. First-class special wagons have fully accessible facilities on some trains.

The Italian State Tourist Office in your country may be able to provide further advice.

Organisations

Accessible Italy (☎ 378- 0549- 941111; www .accessibleitaly.com) Specialises in holiday services for the disabled, ranging from tours to the hiring of adapted transport.

Disabili.com (☎ 049 8763875; www.disabili.com in Italian) Padua-based organisation, with an excellent website that includes a forum and some useful travel-related links. It lists the museums in each region that have disabled access (shamefully few).

Good Italy (http://gooditaly.net/accessodisabili/ italia/puglia) Lists disabled accessible accommodation (26 places) in Puglia.

Holiday Care Service (☎ 0845 124 9971; www .holidaycare.org.uk) Produces an Italy information pack for the disabled. The website also has lots of useful resources.

Royal Association for Disability & Rehabilitation (Radar; ☎ 020-7250 3222, www.radar.org.uk) A UK-based charity with some useful links from its website.

VISAS & PERMITS

Italy is one of 15 countries that have signed the Schengen Convention, an agreement whereby all EU member countries (except the UK and Ireland) plus Iceland and Norway have abolished checks at common borders. EU, Norwegian and Icelandic nationals do not need a visa, regardless of the length or purpose of their visit. Citizens of the UK and Ireland are also exempt from visa requirements. In addition, nationals of some other countries, including Australia, Canada, Japan, New Zealand, Switzerland and the USA do not require visas for tourist visits of up to 90 days to any Schengen country.

All non-EU nationals entering Italy for any reason other than tourism (such as study or work) should contact an Italian consulate as they may need a specific visa. They should also insist on having their passport stamped on entry as, without a stamp, they could encounter problems when trying to obtain a *permesso di soggiorno* (resident permit; see below). If you are a citizen of a country not mentioned in this section, you should check with an Italian consulate whether or not you need a visa.

The standard tourist visa issued by Italian consulates is the Schengen visa, valid for up to 90 days. However, individual Schengen countries may impose additional restrictions on certain nationalities. It's therefore well worth checking visa regulations with the consulate of each Schengen country you intend on visiting.

It's mandatory that you apply for a visa in your country of residence. You can apply for no more than two Schengen visas in any 12-month period and they are not renewable inside Italy. It's a good idea to apply early for your visa, especially in the busy summer months.

Study Visas

Non-EU citizens who want to study at a university or language school must have a study visa. These visas can be obtained from your nearest Italian embassy or consulate. You will normally require confirmation of enrolment, proof of payment of fees and adequate funds to support yourself before a visa is issued. The visa will then cover only the period of the enrolment. This type of visa is renewable.

Permits

EU citizens do not require permits to live, work or start a business in Puglia or Basilicata. They are, however, advised to register with a police station *(questura)* if they take up residence. Failure to do so carries no consequences, although some landlords may be unwilling to rent out a flat to you without proof of registration. Those considering long-term residence will eventually want to consider getting a work permit, a necessary first step to acquiring a *carta d'identità* (ID card). While you're at it, you'll need a *codice fiscale* (tax-file number) if you wish to be paid in Puglia or Basilicata.

WORK PERMITS

Non-EU citizens wishing to work in Puglia or Basilicata need to obtain a *permesso di lavoro* (work permit). If you intend to work for an Italian company, the company must organise the *permesso* and forward it to the Italian consulate in your country – only then will you be issued an appropriate visa. In other cases, you must organise the permit through the Italian consulate in your country of residence.

RESIDENCE PERMITS

Visitors are technically obliged to report to the *questura* (police headquarters) and receive a *permesso di soggiorno* (permit allowing them to remain in the country) if they plan to stay at the same address for more than one week. Tourists staying in hotels and the like need not bother, as hotel owners register guests with the police.

A *permesso di soggiorno* only becomes a necessity if you plan to study, work (legally) or live in Puglia or Basilicata. Obtaining one is almost always a hassle, although for EU citizens it is usually fairly straightforward and success is all but guaranteed. For details of what you will need, approach the nearest police station.

Transport

CONTENTS

THINGS CHANGE...

The information in this chapter is particularly vulnerable to change. Check directly with the airline or a travel agent to make sure you understand how a fare (and ticket you may buy) works and be aware of the security requirements for international travel. Shop carefully. The details given in this chapter should be regarded as pointers and are not a substitute for your own careful, up-to-date research.

GETTING THERE & AWAY

Barely five years ago Puglia and Basilicata were well beyond the radar of the average traveller, but in 2005 Bari unveiled a new, expanded airport, low-cost airlines started to run routes to both Brindisi and Bari and the Alitalia monopoly was broken. Since then tourism figures have shown a startling rise for inbound arrivals as holidaymakers start to discover the joys of two of Italy's most unspoilt provinces.

Direct flights now run to both Bari and Brindisi (the preferred airport if you're visiting the Salento). There are no major entry points in Basilicata but Eurostar trains run through the province stopping at the major transport hubs of Potenza and Foggia. Another alternative is to arrive in Bari or Brindisi by ferry from Greece.

ENTERING THE COUNTRY

Direct flights from the UK, France, the Netherlands, Germany, Albania and even Brussels serve Puglia's airports. Bari boasts the largest airport and airport procedures are pretty painless. The same goes for Brindisi, although the airport here is much smaller and currently undergoing renovations, which is causing some short term inconvenience.

Boarding a ferry to Puglia is almost as easy as getting on a bus, although you'll probably want to consider prebooking your passage if you are travelling during the high season. EU nationals with a valid passport can stay in Italy for as long as they like. Citizens of the USA, Canada, Australia and New Zealand need only a valid passport to stay for up to three months. Nationals of other countries will need to check visa requirements with the Italian embassy in their home country prior to their departure.

AIR

High season in Italy is June to September and prices are at their highest during this period. The months of April, May and October are the shoulder season, while low season is November to March. Holidays such as Christmas and Easter also see a huge jump in prices. If you are travelling to Puglia or Basilicata from outside Europe you may have to change at either Rome, Naples or Milan, where you will transfer to a local carrier.

Airports & Airlines

Puglia's two main airports are **Palese airport** (BRI; ☎ 080 583 52 00; www.seap-puglia.it) in Bari and **Papola Casale** (BDS; ☎ 0831 411 72 08; www.seap-puglia .it) in Brindisi.

The region is not served by intercontinental flights although a recent deal with the Star Alliance group (which controls airlines such as Lufthansa, SAS, Air Canada, US Airways, TAP and Austrian Airlines) should enable intercontinental services to connect more efficiently with internal flights. Otherwise a number of European carriers offer direct routes to Bari. The busiest of these are from London Stanstead with Ryanair and German flights through Frankfurt, Munich, Cologne and Stuttgart with TUIfly and Lufthansa. You can also fly to Bari from Brussels, Paris and Moscow with Brussels Airlines, My Air and Alpi Eagles.

New routes, such as Romania and Albania, are served by My Air, Albanian Airlines and Belle Air.

Brindisi is served by fewer routes although regional authorities have ambitions to expand the airport and apply for new services. Currently, though, Ryanair offers a service from London Stanstead and Helvetic from Zürich. Otherwise, you'll need to make a connection in either Rome or Milan.

INTERNATIONAL & NATIONAL AIRLINES

Air Berlin (AB; ☎ 848 39 00 54; www.airberlin.com; hub Düsseldorf International Airport)

Air One (AP; call centre Italy ☎ 199 20 70 80, 064 888 00 69; www.flyairone.it)

Albanian Airlines (LV; call centre Italy ☎ 080 522 76 22, call centre Albania 04 23 51 62; www.albanianairlines .com.al; hub Tirana Rinas Airport, Albania)

Alitalia (AZ; ☎ 06 22 22; www.alitalia.com; hub Leonardo da Vinci Airport, Rome)

Alpi Eagles (E8; ☎ 899 50 00 58; www.alpieagles.com; hub Marco Polo International Airport, Venice)

Belle Air (LZ; call centre Italy ☎ 02 610 14 48, call centre Albania 04 24 01 75; www.belleair.it; hub Tirana International Airport Nënë Teresa, Albania)

Brussels Airlines (SN; ☎ 0902 516 00; www.brussels airlines.it; hub Brussels Airport)

Helvetic (2L; call centre Italy ☎ 026 968 26 84; www .helvetic.com; hub Zürich Airport)

Lufthansa (LH; ☎ 199 40 00 44; www.lufthansa.com; hub Frankfurt Airport, Frankfurt)

My Air (8I; call centre Italy ☎ 899 50 00 60; www.myair .com; hub Orio al Serio International Airport, Bergamo)

Ryanair (FR; ☎ 899 67 89 10; www.ryanair.com, hub Prestwick Airport, Glasgow)

TUIfly (X3; ☎ 199 19 26 92; www.tuifly.com; hub Köln Bonn Airport, Cologne)

Volare (VE; call centre Italy ☎ 199 41 45 00, 070 460 33 97; www.volareweb.com; hub Leonardo da Vinci Airport, Rome)

Tickets

The cheapest tickets are found on the internet, but you'll need to book well in advance to secure the best deals, especially in high season.

Many of the major travel websites can offer competitive fares, such as:

Booking Buddy (www.bookingbuddy.com)
Cheap Flights (www.cheapflights.com)
Discount-Tickets.com (www.discount-tickets.com)
Ebookers.com (www.ebookers.com)
Expedia (www.expedia.com)
Kayak (www.kayak.com)
Last Minute (www.lastminute.com)
Orbitz (www.orbitz.com)
Priceline (www.priceline.com)
Travelocity (www.travelocity.com)

Full-time students and people aged under 26 (under 30 in some countries) can get discounted fares. You need a document proving your date of birth or an International Student Identity Card (ISIC) when buying your ticket. Other cheap deals are the discounted tickets released to some travel agents and specialist discount agencies.

Australia

There are no direct flights between Australia and southern Italy so you'll need to change planes at some point in Italy. Cheap flights from Australia to Europe generally go via Southeast Asian capitals. Qantas and Alitalia have occasional direct flights or more regular trips that make one stop. Also try Malaysia Airlines and the Star Alliance carriers (www .staralliance.com), such as Thai Air, Singapore Airlines or Austrian Air. Flights from Perth are generally a few hundred dollars cheaper.

Canada

As with Australia and the USA, there are no direct flights to southern Italy and you will have to connect through Rome or Milan. Alitalia flies direct to Milan from Toronto, with connections to Rome. Air Transat flies nonstop from Montreal to Rome in summer.

Air Canada flies daily from Toronto to Rome, direct and via Montreal and Frankfurt. British Airways, Air France, KLM and Lufthansa all fly to Italy via their home countries.

Continental Europe

All national European carriers offer services to Italy. The largest – Air France, Lufthansa and KLM – have offices in all major European cities. Italy's national carrier, Alitalia, has a huge range of offers on all European destinations and can then connect you with one of its internal flights to Puglia.

The local Italian airlines Air One, Alpi Eagles and My Air offer routes from Bari to a few European destinations, like Bucharest, Moscow and Paris, but even these flights will require a change in Rome or Milan. Otherwise, low-cost airlines like TUIfly (formerly Hapag-Lloyd), Brussels Airlines, Helvetic, Albanian Airlines and Belle Air offer flights from Germany, the Netherlands, Switzerland and Albania.

New Zealand
Singapore Airlines flies from Auckland via Singapore to Rome Fiumicino – sometimes with more than one stop. Otherwise, Qantas or Alitalia flights from Australia are the most direct way to get to Italy and then Basilicata or Puglia.

UK & Ireland
Ryanair now operates direct routes to both Bari and Brindisi, by far the most convenient way to arrive. There are also dozens of Alitalia and British Airways flights between London and Milan or Rome, where you can transfer onto another plane or continue your journey by rail. Italian **Air One** (www.flyairone.it) also operates flights between London City Airport and Bari and Brindisi.

There are no direct scheduled flights to southern Italy from Ireland, so you will need to pick up a connection in Milan or Rome. It is worth comparing the cost of flying to Italy directly from Dublin with the cost of flying to London first and then on to Italy.

Both Alitalia and **Aer Lingus** (☎ 0818 365 000; www.aerlingus.com) have regular daily flights to Rome from Dublin.

USA
Delta Airlines (www.delta.com) and Alitalia have nonstop daily flights from New York's JFK airport to Rome Fiumicino and Milan Malpensa, while **Continental Airlines** (www.continental.com) flies nonstop to both from Newark. **American Airlines** (www.aa.com) flies from Chicago and JFK to Rome.

Discount travel agencies in the USA are known as consolidators, and San Francisco is the ticket consolidator capital of America, although some good deals can be found in other big cities. The *New York Times, LA Times, Chicago Tribune* and *San Francisco Examiner* produce weekly travel sections containing numerous travel agencies' ads.

LAND
Puglia and Basilicata's location means getting there overland involves travelling the entire length of Italy, which can either be an enormous drain on your time or, if you have plenty to spare, a wonderful way of seeing Italy on your way south. Buses are usually the cheapest option, but services are less frequent and considerably less comfortable than the train.

If you are travelling by bus, train or car to Italy it will be necessary to check whether you require visas to the countries you intend to pass through.

Border Crossings
The main points of entry to Italy are: the Mont Blanc Tunnel from France at Chamonix, which connects with the A5 for Turin and Milan; the Grand St Bernard tunnel from Switzerland, which also connects with the A5, and the Gotthard tunnel from Switzerland (which will have a new parallel railway tunnel, Gotthard Base Tunnel, possibly by 2015, which will cut the journey time from Zürich to Milan by one hour); the new Swiss Lötschberg Base Tunnel (opened in 2007) which connects with the century-old Simplon tunnel into Italy; and the Brenner Pass from Austria, which connects with the A22 to Bologna. All are open year-round. Mountain passes are often closed in winter and sometimes even in autumn and spring, making the tunnels a more reliable option. Make sure you have snow chains if driving in winter.

Regular trains on two lines connect Italy with the main cities in Austria and into Germany, France or Eastern Europe. Those crossing the frontier at the Brenner Pass go to Innsbruck, Stuttgart and Munich. Those crossing at Tarvisio in the east proceed to Vienna, Salzburg and Prague. Trains from Milan head for Switzerland and on into France and the Netherlands. The main international train line to Slovenia crosses near Trieste.

Continental Europe
BUS
Eurolines (www.eurolines.com) is a consortium of European coach companies operating across Europe with offices in major European cities. Italy-bound buses head to Milan, Rome, Florence, Siena or Venice and all come equipped with on-board toilet facilities. You can contact them in your own country or in Italy and the multilingual website gives comprehensive

TRANSPORT

details of prices, passes and travel agencies where you can book tickets.

From Italy

From Rome, **Marozzi** (www.marozzivt.it in Italian) offers a daily service to Bari, which also serves Matera in Basilicata, Brindisi, Lecce and Otranto. Alternatively, **Miccolis** (www.miccolis-spa.it in Italian) runs several services a day from Naples to Bari, Taranto and Brindisi. From Rome, **Liscio** (☎ 0971 5 46 73) serves destinations including Venosa and Potenza and connects Basilicata with Naples and Salerno. **CLP** (in Naples ☎ 081 531 17 06) also runs direct buses from Naples to Foggia in northern Puglia.

CAR & MOTORCYCLE

When driving in Italy always carry proof of ownership of a private vehicle. Third-party insurance is also a minimum requirement. Ask your insurer for a European Accident Statement (EAS) form, which can simplify matters in the event of an accident. A European breakdown-assistance policy is a good investment. In Italy, assistance can be obtained through the **Automobile Club Italiano** (ACI; ☎ 803 116, 24hr information ☎ 02 66 165 116; www.aci.it in Italian).

Every vehicle travelling across an international border should display a nationality plate of its country of registration.

There is an excellent network of autostrade in Italy, represented by a white A followed by a number on a green background. The main north–south link is the Autostrada del Sole, which extends from Milan to Reggio di Calabria (called the A1 from Milan to Rome, the A2 from Rome to Naples and the A3 from Naples to Reggio di Calabria).

There's a toll to use most of Italy's autostrade. You can pay by cash or credit card as you leave the autostrada; to avoid lengthy queues buy a prepaid card (Telepass or Viacard) from banks and ACI offices in denominations of €25, €50 or €75, which you can use throughout Italy. For information on road tolls and passes, contact **Autostrade per Italia** (☎ 800 269 269; www.autostrade.it in Italian).

Puglia is a popular destination for motorcyclists who take to the coastal roads of the Salento in spring and autumn. With a bike you rarely have to book ahead for ferries and can enter restricted traffic areas in cities. Crash helmets are compulsory. Unless you're touring, it is probably easier to rent a bike once you have reached southern Italy.

One interesting way to get around Italy is to rent or buy a camper van. Rental rates in high season can work out at as little as €15 per day, but if you are travelling for more than a few weeks, it is sometimes more cost effective to buy and then sell back the camper van. Check **IdeaMerge** (www.ideamerge.com) where you can lease or buy vehicles.

TRAIN

The *Thomas Cook European Timetable* has a complete listing of train schedules. The timetable is updated monthly and available from Thomas Cook offices worldwide for around €15. It is always advisable, and sometimes compulsory, to book seats on international trains to/from Italy. Some of the main international services include transport for private cars. Consider taking long journeys overnight as the €20 or so extra for a sleeper costs substantially less than Italian hotels.

If you're travelling to either Puglia or Basilicata from anywhere outside Italy you'll have to change trains somewhere along the line in Italy; the handiest place is Rome, although you may have to change again at Benevento, just south of Naples. From both Rome and Milan you should take an Intercity or Eurostar train to Potenza (Basilicata) and Bari (Puglia).

UK
CAR & MOTORCYCLE

Coming from the UK, you can take your car across to France by ferry or via the Channel Tunnel on **Eurotunnel** (☎ 08705 35 35 35; www.eurotunnel.com). The latter runs 10 crossings (35 minutes) a day between Folkestone and Calais year-round. You pay for the vehicle only and fares vary according to timing, season and advance purchase, but start at UK£49 each way.

For breakdown assistance both the **RAC** (☎ 0800 5722 722; www.rac.co.uk) and **Automobile Association** (AA; ☎ 0870 600 03 71; www.theaa.com) offer comprehensive cover in Europe.

TRAIN

The excellent passenger-train service **Eurostar** (☎ 0870 518 6186; www.eurostar.com) travels from London to Paris and Brussels. Alternatively, you can get yourself a train ticket that includes crossing the channel by ferry, Seacat or hovercraft. After that, you can travel via Paris and southern France or by swinging from Belgium down through Germany and Switzerland.

For the latest fare information on journeys to Italy, including the Eurostar, contact the **Rail Europe Travel Centre** (☎ 08708 371 371; www .raileurope.co.uk) or **Rail Choice** (www.railchoice.com).

Alternatively, log on to the website www .seat61.com – this man has surely been on every train in Europe!

SEA

There are regular car/passenger ferries cross the Adriatic Sea from Greece and Albania to Bari and Brindisi. Ferry prices are determined by the season and are considerably more expensive from June to September. In high season, all routes are busy and you need to book several weeks in advance. Fares to Greece are generally more expensive from Bari than those available from Brindisi, although unless you're planning on travelling in the Salento, Bari is the more convenient port of arrival and also has better onward links for bus and train travel. Bari is also served by ferries to Croatia and Montenegro.

Offices and telephone numbers for the ferry companies are listed in the Getting There & Away sections for the relevant cities. The search engine **Traghettionline** (☎ 010 58 20 80; www.traghettionline.net) covers all the ferry companies in the Mediterranean; you can also book online.

Blue Star Ferries (☎ 080 52 11 416; www.bluestar ferries.com) To Patras (8pm) and Igoumenitsa (8pm).

Hellenic Mediterranean Lines (HML; ☎ 0831 52 85 31; www.hml.it) The largest and most reliable of the Brindisi lines to Greece, Hellenic Mediterranean accepts Eurail and Inter-Rail passes. If you intend to use your pass, it is best to reserve in advance in high summer. It services Corfu, Igoumenitsa and Patras (April to October), Cefalonia (June to September) and the Ionian Islands (July and August).

Jadrolinija (☎ +385 51 666 111; www.jadrolinija.hr) A small ferry line offering services to Dubrovnik in Croatia.

Marmara Lines (☎ 0831 56 86 33; www.marmaralines .com) Runs a twice-weekly ferry from Brindisi to Cesme (Turkey).

Montenegro Lines (☎ 080 578 98 27; www.morfi mare.it) The only operator offering services from Bari to Montenegro, in the summer season only (April to September). Reservations should be made via Morfimare Travel Agency (see p63) in Bari.

Superfast (☎ 080 528 28 28; www.superfast.com) One of the biggest and best ferry operators with daily departures for varying destinations in Greece. It is also the only company that accepts Eurail, Eurodomino and Inter-Rail passes.

Tirrenia (☎ 199 12 31 99; www.tirrenia.it) This is the main company servicing the Mediterranean and all Italian ports. From Bari, it offers services to Durazzo in Albania.

Ventouris Ferries (☎ 080 521 76 09; www.ventouris .gr) To Igoumenitsa, Patras and Corfu. It has regular ferries. Also daily ferries to and from Durazzo (Albania).

Skenderbeg Lines (☎ 0831 52 54 48; www.skender beglines.com) Ferries most days from Brindisi to Vlore (Valona; in Albania).

SNAV (☎ 0831 52 54 92; www.snav.it) Ferries to Corfu and on to Paxos.

For sample fares to the above destinations see p69 and p142.

GETTING AROUND

The easiest way to get around Puglia and Basilicata is with your own car. Buses and trains will get you to most of the main destinations, but they are run by a plethora of private companies, which makes buying tickets and finding bus stops a bit of a bind. Furthermore, the rail network in the Salento is still of the narrow-gauge variety, so trains chug along at a snail's pace.

Your own vehicle will give you the most freedom to stray off the main routes and discover out-of-the-way towns and beaches. This is particularly the case in the Pollino National Park and in the Salento. The limited motorway (autostrada) system is toll-free, but only resembles a real motorway north of Bari heading towards Foggia and beyond. South of this you'll be using the state highways, which are generally fine, although the more popular routes (Bari–Taranto, Bari–Brindisi, Brindisi–Lecce) can be heavily trafficked as are the more scenic coastal roads during summer. Unlike much of Italy – where driving is only for the brave – driving in Puglia and Basilicata is a pleasant and stress-free experience. The only places where this isn't true is in Bari, Lecce and Foggia.

Easter and summer-only ferries operate to the Isole Tremiti off the Gargano Promontory. Outside of these times you'll need to negotiate passage with one of the local fishermen in Vieste or Peschici.

AIR

Helicopters fly twice daily in summer and around Christmas and Easter, from Foggia to the Isole Tremiti. Contact **Alidaunia** (☎ 088161 96 96; www.alidaunia.it).

TRANSPORT

TRANSPORT

BICYCLE

Cycling is a national pastime in Italy. There are no special road rules, but you would be wise to equip yourself with a helmet and lights. With good reason, you cannot take bikes onto the autostrade. If you plan to bring your own bike, check with your airline for any additional costs. The bike will need to be disassembled and packed for the journey. Make sure you include a few tools, spare parts and a bike lock and chain.

Bikes can be taken on any train carrying the bicycle logo. The cheapest way to do this is to buy a separate bicycle ticket (€3.50, or €5 to €12 on Intercity, Eurostar and Euronight trains), available even at the self-service kiosks. You can use this ticket for 24 hours, making a day trip quite economical. Bikes dismantled and stored in a bag can be taken for free, even on night trains, and all ferries allow free bicycle passage.

In the UK, **Cyclists' Touring Club** (☎ 0870 873 00 60; www.ctc.org.uk) can help you plan your tour or organise a guided tour. Membership costs £12 for under 18s and students, and £34 for adults. Locally, **Puglia in Bici** (www.pugliainbici .com) is a very good organisation that rents out good bikes and can also tailor-make itineraries throughout the region. You'll find its main office at the **NRG Bike Shop** (☎ 080 413 64 29; Via Sabin 1-5) in Monopoli. **Gargano Bike Holidays** (☎ 339 7175334; www.garganobike.com) in Vieste also specialises in cultural and scenic mountain bike tours, exploring the Gargano on half-day to weekly trips.

Cyclo-trekking is very popular in the Murgia and the Gargano Promontory and specialist operators and many hotels hire out bikes and offer guided itineraries in Matera, Laterza, Castellana Grotte, Ostuni and Vieste (see the Getting Around sections of the relevant regional chapters for more details). Cycling is also very popular in the Salentine cities of Lecce, Galatina, Gallipoli and Otranto. Rental costs for a city bike start at €10/30 per day/week

More challenging itineraries can be found in the Parco Naturale Gallipoli Cognato e Piccole Dolomiti Lucane (p186) and the Parco Nazionale del Pollino (p192)

Hire

Bikes are available for hire in most towns. Rental costs for a city bike start at €10 per day; a good mountain bike will cost around €25 to

€30. See Getting Around under the relevant cities in this guide for more information.

BOAT

Over Easter and between June and August several companies, including **Adriatica** (☎ 0884 70 85 01; www.adriatica.it) and **Navigargano** (☎ 0884 70 84 09) run boats from Vieste to the Isole Tremiti. At least one boat goes each day. Adriactic Tirrenia also operates a service from Manfredonia, stopping at Vieste on the way. At least one boat goes each day. Book tickets at local travel agents.

Outside these high season services you'll have to negotiate a ride with one of the local fishermen in Vieste or Peschici.

BUS

Bus services in Puglia and Basilicata are provided by a variety of companies. By utilising the local services, it is possible to get to just about any location, but it can be slow going, with limited services outside high season. Buses are usually a faster way to get around, if your destination is not on a main train line (trains tend to be cheaper on major routes). In the Salento, where the train network is very old, buses are the preferred mode of transport for long distance travel.

It is usually possible to get bus timetables from local tourist offices. In larger cities, most of the main intercity bus companies operate through agencies, which can be confusing for the first-time traveller. In some smaller towns and villages, bus tickets are sold in bars – just ask for *biglietti per il pullman* – or on the bus.

Services can be frequent on weekdays but, reduce considerably on Sundays and holidays – runs between smaller towns often fall to one or none. Keep this in mind if you depend on buses as it is easy to get stuck in smaller places, especially at the weekends.

Bus Operators

Major transport hubs are Potenza in Basilicata and Foggia Bari, Brindisi and Lecce in Puglia.

SITA (☎ 080 579 02 11; www.sitabus.it in Italian) is one of the largest bus companies operating in the region and covers most destinations in Basilicata as well as northern Puglia, with services linking Foggia with Canosa di Puglia, Trani, Bari and Manfredonia in the Gargano Promontory. Here the **Ferrovie del Gargano** (www

.ferroviedelgargano.com) bus and train operator takes over connecting all the smaller towns of the Gargano.

Further south, **STP** (☎ 0831 54 92 45; www.stp brindisi.it) connects Brindisi with the Valle d'Itria and the Salento.

Ferrovie Appulo-Lucane (FAL; ☎ 080 572 52 29; www .fal-srl.it in Italian) running between Puglia and Basilicata has direct buses from Bari to Matera and beyond. **Ferrotramviaria** (☎ 080 578 95 42; www.ferrovienordbarese.it in Italian), the bus fleet run by the Ferrovie Nord Barese (northern Bari train line), is the main link between Bari and the Terra di Bari, servicing towns like Bitonto, Ruvo di Puglia, Trani and Barletta.

Finally, buses operated by **Ferrovie del Sud-Est** (FSE; ☎ 080 546 21 11; www.fseonline.it in Italian) provide the main service south of Bari through the Valle d'Itria (including towns like Alberobello, Martina Franca and Ostuni) and the Salento.

Between 16 June and 9 September, FSE runs a special service called **Salento in Treno e Bus** (www.salentointrenoebus.it), which operates throughout the Salento, connecting all the smaller towns and beaches in the province. This makes life a whole lot easier for the traveller and enables those without a car to reach some of the more out of the way places.

CAR & MOTORCYCLE

The roads in Puglia and Basilicata are some of the most poorly maintained in Italy. Main roads, however, like the west–east autostrada, the A16, are generally fast. The A3 runs down the Tyrrhenian Coast from Naples to Reggio di Calabria, and is the fastest way to reach the Pollino National park. If you're driving across from Puglia the fastest route is along the SS106 (E90).

From Bari the A14 heads south to Taranto, although it narrows to single-lane traffic. For the Salento, the single-lane SS16 is the main arterial route although in summer this can be heavily trafficked.

To really explore the south, travellers will need to use the system of state and provincial roads. *Strade statali* (state roads) are single-lane highways and are toll-free; they are represented on maps as 'S' or 'SS'. *Strade provinciali* (provincial roads) are sometimes little more than country lanes, but provide access to some of the more beautiful scenery and the many small towns and villages. They are represented as 'P' or 'SP' on maps.

Automobile Associations

The ever-handy **Automobile Club d'Italia** (ACI; 24hr ☎ 803 116; www.aci.it; Via Colombo 261, Rome) is a driver's best resource in Italy. It has a dedicated 24-hour phone line for foreigners in need of emergency assistance, weather conditions or even tourist information.

To reach the ACI in a roadside emergency, dial ☎ 116 from a land line or ☎ 800 116 800 from a mobile phone. Foreigners do not have to join, but instead pay a per-incident fee.

Driving Licence

EU member states' driving licences are recognised in Italy. If you hold a licence from another country, you should obtain an International Driving Permit (IDP) too. Your national automobile association can issue this and it is valid for 12 months.

Fuel

The cost of fuel (petrol) in Italy is very high – ranging from around €1.12 to €1.2 per litre for unleaded petrol. Petrol is called *benzina,* unleaded petrol is *benzina senza piombo* and diesel is *gasolio*. There are plenty of petrol stations in and around towns and on national road networks.

Hire

With the advent of budget airlines flying into Puglia, the advent of the fly-drive package now provides some reasonably priced car rental. If you don't speak Italian, it is better to arrange car hire before you arrive. All the major car-hire outlets have offices at the airports, where you usually pick up your car and deposit it at the end of your stay. Agencies represented are as follows:

Autos Abroad (☎ 44 8700 66 77 88; www.autosabroad .com)

Auto Europe (☎ 1-888 223 55 55; www.autoeurope .com)

Avis (☎ 02 754 197 61; www.avis.com)

Budget (☎ 1-800 472 33 25; www.budget.com)

Europcar (☎ 06 481 71 62; www.europcar.com)

Hertz (☎ 199 11 22 11; www.hertz.com)

Maggiore (☎ 06 229 15 30; www.maggiore.it in Italian)

You can prebook a car before you leave home, but you can often find a better deal by contacting the agency directly. Check with your credit-card company to see if it offers a Collision Damage Waiver, which covers you for additional damage if you use that card

TRANSPORT

ROAD DISTANCES (KM)

	Altamura	Bari	Brindisi	Canosa di Puglia	Foggia	Gallipoli	Lecce	Santa Maria di Leuca	Manfredonia	Otranto	Taranto
Altamura	---										
Bari	45	---									
Brindisi	125	110	---								
Canosa di Puglia	85	85	195	---							
Foggia	140	135	245	55	---						
Gallipoli	170	190	75	260	310	---					
Lecce	160	150	40	250	280	35	---				
Santa Maria di Leuca	215	215	105	305	355	45	65	---			
Manfredonia	160	115	225	80	45	300	265	330	---		
Otranto	205	195	45	80	295	325	45	45	50	---	
Taranto	80	95	70	165	215	95	85	140	210	140	---

to pay for the car. Many car-rental agencies request that you bring the car back with the tank filled, and will charge you extra if it's not. Young drivers should call ahead, as many companies do not rent cars or bikes to drivers aged 25 and younger.

No matter which company you hire your car from, make sure you understand what is included in the price. It is also a very good idea to get fully comprehensive insurance to cover any bumps or scrapes that might happen. Note: many car-hire agencies will not cover you for theft in city centres like Foggia, Cerignola and Bari.

You'll have no trouble hiring a small motor-cycle such as a scooter (Vespa) or moped. There are numerous rental agencies in the cities and at tourist destinations such as seaside resorts. The average cost for a 50cc scooter (for one person) is around €25 per day or €130 per week.

Most agencies will not rent motorcycles to people aged under 18. Note that many places require a sizable deposit and that you could be responsible for reimbursing part of the cost of the bike if it is stolen.

Insurance
Third-party motor insurance is a minimum requirement in Italy. The Green Card, an internationally recognised proof of insurance obtainable from your insurer, is mandatory. Ask your insurer for a European Accident Statement form, which can simplify matters in the event of an accident. A European breakdown assistance policy is a good investment. In Italy, assistance can be obtained through the **Automobile Club Italiano** (ACI; 24hr info line ☎ 15 18, 06 49 11 15; www.aci.it in Italian).

Road Rules
In Italy, as throughout continental Europe, you drive on the right-hand side of the road and overtake on the left. Unless otherwise indicated, you must always give way to cars entering an intersection from the right. It is compulsory to wear seat belts if fitted to the car. If you are caught not wearing a seat belt, you will be required to pay an on-the-spot fine.

Random breath tests now take place. If you're involved in an accident while under the influence of alcohol, the penalties can be severe. The blood-alcohol limit is 0.05%.

The autostrade speed limits are 130km/h and on all nonurban highways 110km/h. In built-up areas the limit is 50km/h. Speeding fines follow EU standards and are proportionate with the number of kilometres per hour that you are caught driving over the speed limit, reaching up to €1433 with possible suspension of licence.

You don't need a licence to ride a moped under 50cc, but you must be aged 14 or more. You can't carry passengers or ride on motorways. The speed limit for a moped is 40km/h. To ride a motorcycle or scooter up to 125cc, you must be aged 16 or more and have a licence (a car licence will do). Helmets are compulsory. For motorcycles over 125cc you need a motorcycle licence.

On a motorcycle you will be able to enter restricted-traffic areas in cities without any problems. There is no lights-on requirement for motorcycles during the day.

LOCAL TRANSPORT

All the major cities and towns have good local (bus) transport systems, however, it's very unlikely that you'll have cause to use them.

Bus

City bus services are frequent and reliable. You must always purchase bus tickets before you board the bus and validate them once on board. If you get caught with a nonvalidated ticket, you can be fined on the spot, although this is highly unlikely in the south.

You can buy tickets at most *tabaccherie* (tobacconists), at many newsstands and at ticket booths. Tickets generally cost €0.80 for two hours.

Taxi

Taxis are generally expensive in Italy. If you need a taxi, you can usually find one in a taxi rank at train and bus stations or you can telephone taxi companies direct (numbers are listed in the Getting Around sections of the major cities). However, if you book a taxi by phone, you will be charged for the trip the driver makes to reach you. Taxis will stop when hailed on the street. For most journeys within a city you'll be looking to pay between €5 and €10.

TRAIN

Travelling by train in Puglia and Basilicata may be slow, but it is simple and cheap. **Trenitalia** (☎ 848 88 80 88; www.trenitalia.it) is the partially privatised state train system that runs most of the services to main towns like Foggia, Potenza, Bari, Brindisi and Lecce.

There are several types of train. Intercity (IC) trains are the fastest, stopping only at major stations. The *diretto, interregionale* and *espresso* stop at all but the most minor stations, while the *regionale* (also called *locale*) is the slowest of all, halting at every stop on the line.

Travellers should note that all tickets must be validated *before* you board your train. Simply punch them in the yellow machines installed at the entrance to all train platforms. If you don't validate them, you risk a fine. This rule does not apply to tickets purchased outside Italy.

As with the bus services, there are a number of private train lines operating throughout Puglia and Basilicata as follows:

Ferrovia Bari-Nord (☎ 080 578 95 42; www.ferrovie nordbarese.it in Italian) Services towns in the Terra di Bari, including Bitonto, Ruvo di Puglia, Andria, Trani and Barletta.

Ferrovie Appulo-Lucane (FAL; ☎ 080 572 52 29; www.fal-srl.it in Italian) As the name implies, this line links Bari province with Basilicata, with services stopping at Altamura, Matera, Gravina in Puglia and Potenza.

Ferrovie del Sud-Est (☎ 080 546 21 11; www .fseonline.it in Italian) The main network covering the Murgia towns and the Salento, stopping at tourist hotspots like Castellana Grotte, Alberobello, Martina Franca, Lecce, Gallipoli and Otranto.

None of these trains run on Sunday. Instead each operator runs a replacement bus service, which usually departs from the station.

Costs & Classes

Apart from the standard division between 1st and 2nd class on the faster trains (generally you can get only 2nd-class seats on *locali* and *regionali*), you usually have to pay a supplement for travelling on the fast Intercity trains.

TRANSPORT

Health

CONTENTS

HEALTH

BEFORE YOU GO

While Italy has excellent health care, prevention is the key to staying healthy while abroad. A little planning before departure, particularly for pre-existing illnesses, will save trouble later. Bring medications in their original, clearly labelled, containers. A signed and dated letter from your physician describing your medical conditions and medications, including generic names, is also a good idea. If carrying syringes or needles, be sure to have a physician's letter documenting their medical necessity. If you are embarking on a long trip, make sure your teeth are OK (dental treatment is particularly expensive in Italy) and take your optical prescription with you.

The major hospitals in Puglia and Basilicata can be found in Foggia, Fasano, Brindisi, Bari, Lecce and Potenza.

INSURANCE

If you're an EU citizen, arm yourself with the European Health Insurance Card, a handy piece of plastic, valid for two years, that entitles you to emergency treatment throughout the EU. Order through your local health office. This card supersedes the E111 form that previously entitled you to treatment within the EU.

Citizens from other countries should find out if there is a reciprocal arrangement for free medical care between their country and Italy. If you need health insurance, get a policy that covers you for the worst possible scenario, such as an accident requiring an emergency flight home. Find out in advance if your insurance plan will make payments directly to providers or reimburse you later for overseas health expenditures.

RECOMMENDED VACCINATIONS

No jabs are required to travel to Italy. The World Health Organization (WHO), however, recommends that all travellers should be covered for diphtheria, tetanus, measles, mumps, rubella and polio, as well as hepatitis B.

ONLINE RESOURCES

The WHO's publication *International Travel and Health* is revised annually and is available online at www.who.int/ith/. Other useful websites include www.mdtravelhealth.com (daily health recommendations for every country), www.fitfortravel.scot.nhs.uk (general travel advice), www.ageconcern.org.uk (advice on travel for the elderly) and www.mariestopes.org.uk (information on women's health and contraception).

IN TRANSIT

DEEP VEIN THROMBOSIS (DVT)

Blood clots may form in the legs during plane flights, chiefly because of prolonged immobility; the longer the flight, the greater the risk. The chief symptom of DVT is swelling or pain of the foot, ankle, or calf, usually, but not always, on just one side. When a blood clot travels to the lungs, it may cause chest pain and breathing difficulties. Travellers with any of these symptoms should immediately seek medical attention. To prevent the development of DVT on long flights you should walk about the cabin, contract the leg muscles while sitting, drink plenty of fluids and avoid alcohol and tobacco.

JET LAG

To avoid jet lag, try drinking plenty of non-alcoholic fluids and eating light meals. Upon arrival, get exposure to natural sunlight and readjust your schedule (for meals, sleep etc) as soon as possible.

IN PUGLIA & BASILICATA

AVAILABILITY & COST OF HEALTH CARE

If you need an ambulance anywhere in Italy, call ☎ 118. For emergency treatment, go straight to the *pronto soccorso* (casualty) section of a public hospital, where you can also get emergency dental treatment.

Excellent healthcare is readily available throughout Italy, but standards can vary. Pharmacists can give valuable advice and sell over-the-counter medication for minor illnesses. They can also advise when more specialised help is required and point you in the right direction. In major cities you are likely to find English-speaking doctors or a translator service available.

TRAVELLERS' DIARRHOEA

If you develop diarrhoea, be sure to drink plenty of fluids, preferably in the form of an oral rehydration solution such as Dioralyte. If diarrhoea is bloody, persists for more than 72 hours or is accompanied by fever, shaking, chills or severe abdominal pain, you should seek medical attention.

ENVIRONMENTAL HAZARDS
Heatstroke

Heatstroke occurs following excessive fluid loss with inadequate replacement of fluids and salt. Symptoms include headache, dizziness and tiredness. Dehydration is already happening by the time you feel thirsty – aim to drink sufficient water to produce pale, diluted urine. To treat heatstroke drink water and/or fruit juice, and cool the body with cold water and fans.

Hypothermia

Hypothermia occurs when the body loses heat faster than it can produce it. As ever, proper preparation will reduce the risks of getting it. Even on a hot day in the mountains, the weather can change rapidly, so carry waterproof garments, wear warm layers and a hat, and inform others of your route. Hypothermia starts with shivering, loss of judgment and clumsiness. Unless re-warming occurs, the sufferer deteriorates into apathy, confusion and coma. Prevent further heat loss by seeking shelter, warm dry clothing, hot sweet drinks and shared body warmth.

Bites, Stings & Insect-Borne Diseases

Italian beaches are occasionally inundated with jellyfish. Their stings are painful, but not dangerous. Dousing in vinegar will deactivate any stingers that have not fired. Calamine lotion, antihistamines and analgesics may reduce the reaction and relieve pain.

Italy's only dangerous snake, the viper, is found throughout Puglia and Basilicata. To minimise the possibility of being bitten, always wear boots, socks and long trousers when walking through undergrowth where snakes may be present. Don't put your hands into holes and crevices, and be careful when collecting firewood. Viper bites do not cause instantaneous death and an antivenin is widely available in pharmacies. Keep the victim calm and still, wrap the bitten limb tightly, as you would for a sprained ankle, and attach a splint to immobilise it.

Always check all over your body if you have been walking through a potentially tick-infested area as ticks can cause skin infections and other more serious diseases such as Lyme disease and tick-borne encephalitis. If a tick is found attached, press down around the tick's head with tweezers, grab the head and gently pull upwards. Avoid pulling the rear of the body as this may squeeze the tick's gut contents through the attached mouth parts into the skin, increasing the risk of infection and disease. Lyme disease begins with the spreading of a rash at the site of the bite, accompanied by fever, headache, extreme fatigue, aching joints and muscles and severe neck stiffness. If untreated, symptoms usually disappear, but disorders of the nervous system, heart and joints can develop later. Treatment works best early in the illness – medical help should be sought. Symptoms of tick-borne encephalitis include blotches around the bite, which is sometimes pale in the middle, and headaches, stiffness and other flu-like symptoms (as well as extreme tiredness) appearing a week or two after the bite. Again, medical help must be sought.

Leishmaniasis is a group of parasitic diseases transmitted by sandflies and found in coastal parts of Puglia. Cutaneous leishmaniasis affects the skin and causes ulceration and disfigurement; visceral leishmaniasis affects the internal organs. Avoiding sandfly bites

HEALTH

by covering up and using repellent is the best precaution.

TRAVELLING WITH CHILDREN

Make sure children are up to date with routine vaccinations and discuss possible travel vaccines well before departure as some vaccines are not suitable for children under a year old. Lonely Planet's *Travel with Children* includes travel health advice for younger children.

WOMEN'S HEALTH

Emotional stress, exhaustion and travelling through different time zones can all contribute to an upset in the menstrual pattern.

If using oral contraceptives, remember some antibiotics, diarrhoea and vomiting can stop the pill from working. Time zones, gastrointestinal upsets and antibiotics do not affect injectable contraception.

Travelling during pregnancy is usually possible, but always consult your doctor before planning your trip. The most risky times for travel are during the first 12 weeks of pregnancy and after 30 weeks.

SEXUAL HEALTH

Condoms are readily available, but emergency contraception is not so take the necessary precautions.

Language

Italian is a Romance language related to French, Spanish, Portuguese and Romanian. The Romance languages belong to the Indo-European group of languages, which includes English. Indeed, as English and Italian share common roots in Latin, you'll recognise many Italian words.

Modern literary Italian began to develop in the 13th and 14th centuries, predominantly through the works of Dante, Petrarch and Boccaccio, who wrote chiefly in the Florentine dialect. The language drew on its Latin heritage and many dialects to develop into the standard Italian of today. Although many dialects are spoken in everyday conversation, standard Italian is the national language of schools, media and literature, and is understood throughout the country.

Like most of Italy's provincial regions, Puglia has its own dialectal variants, each area reflecting a particular cultural history through the linguistic legacy that the various inhabitants (and invaders) have left. In the broader scheme of things, Puglia's two main dialectal groups fall under the banner of Neapolitan (in the north and centre) and Sicilian (in the south), but variation within these 'parent' groups is significant due to influences over millennia from other far-flung languages.

Regardless of the regional dialects within the province, Puglia today mirrors the rest of the country in using standard Italian as its universal (and official) language.

Italian has both masculine and feminine grammatical forms (in the singular they often end in 'o' and 'a' respectively). Where both forms are given in this guide, they are separated by a slash, with the masculine form first.

Lonely Planet's *Italian Phrasebook*, packed with practical phrases and simple explanations, fits neatly into your pocket.

BE POLITE!

You need to be aware that many older Italians still expect to be addressed in the third person polite form, *Lei* instead of *tu;* using *Lei* is a bit like using the terms 'he/she', rather than 'you' in English (you may hear something similar in historical dramatisations where a King or Queen is addressed directly, but in the third person).

It is also not good form to use the greeting *ciao* when addressing strangers, unless they use it first; it's better to say *buon giorno* (or *buona sera*, as the case may be) and *arrivederci* (or the more polite form, *arrivederla*). We've used the polite address for most of the phrases in this guide. Use of the informal address is indicated by (inf).

PRONUNCIATION

Vowels

Vowels are generally more clipped than in English:

a	as in 'art', eg *caro* (dear); sometimes short, eg *amico/a* (friend)
e	short, as in 'let', eg *mettere* (to put); long, as in 'there', eg *vero* (true)
i	short, as in 'it', eg *inizio* (start); long, as in 'marine', eg *vino* (wine)
o	short, as in 'dot', eg *donna* (woman); long, as in 'port', eg *ora* (hour)
u	as the 'oo' in 'book', eg *puro* (pure)

Consonants

The pronunciation of many Italian consonants is similar to that of their English counterparts. Pronunciation of some consonants depends on certain rules.

LANGUAGE

c	as the 'k' in 'kit' before **a**, **o** and **u**; as the 'ch' in 'choose' before **e** and **i**
ch	as the 'k' in 'kit'
g	as the 'g' in 'get' before **a**, **o**, **u** and **h**; as the 'j' in 'jet' before **e** and **i**
gli	as the 'lli' in 'million'
gn	as the 'ny' in 'canyon'
h	always silent
r	a rolled 'rr' sound
sc	as the 'sh' in 'sheep' before **e** and **i**; as 'sk' before **a**, **o**, **u** and **h**
z	as the 'ts' in 'lights'; at the beginning of a word, it's most commonly as the 'ds' in 'suds'

Note that when **ci**, **gi** and **sci** are followed by **a**, **o** or **u**, the 'i' is not pronounced unless the accent falls on the 'i'. Thus the name 'Giovanni' is pronounced jo-*va*-nee.

A double consonant is pronounced as a longer, more forceful sound than a single consonant.

Word Stress

Stress is indicated in our pronunciation guide by italics. Word stress generally falls on the second-last syllable, as in spa-*ghet*-ti, but when a word has an accent, the stress falls on that syllable, as in cit-*tà* (city).

ACCOMMODATION

I'm looking for a ...	Cerco ...	*cher*-ko ...
guesthouse	una pensione	oo-na pen-*syo*-ne
hotel	un albergo	oon al-*ber*-go
youth hostel	un ostello per la gioventù	oon os-*te*-lo per la jo-ven-*too*

Where is a cheap hotel?
Dov'è un albergo   do-*ve* oon al-*ber*-go
a buon prezzo?   a bwon *pre*-tso
What is the address?
Qual'è l'indirizzo?   kwa-*le* leen-dee-*ree*-tso
Could you write the address, please?
Può scrivere l'indirizzo,   pwo *skree*-ve-re leen-dee-*ree*-tso
per favore?   per fa-*vo*-re
Do you have any rooms available?
Avete camere libere?   a-*ve*-te *ka*-me-re *lee*-be-re

I'd like (a) ...	Vorrei ...	vo-*ray* ...
bed	un letto	oon *le*-to
single room	una camera singola	oo-na *ka*-me-ra *seen*-go-la
room with two beds	una camera doppia	oo-na *ka*-me-ra *do*-pya

double room	una camera matrimoniale	oo-na *ka*-me-ra ma-tree-mo-*nya*-le
room with a bathroom	una camera con bagno	oo-na *ka*-me-ra kon *ba*-nyo
to share a dorm	un letto in dormitorio	oon *le*-to een dor-mee-*to*-ryo

How much is it ...?	Quanto costa ...?	*kwan*-to *ko*-sta ...
per night	per la notte	per la *no*-te
per person	per persona	per per-*so*-na

May I see it?
Posso vederla?   *po*-so ve-*der*-la
Where is the bathroom?
Dov'è il bagno?   do-*ve* eel *ba*-nyo
I'm/We're leaving today.
Parto/Partiamo oggi.   *par*-to/par-*tya*-mo *o*-jee

CONVERSATION & ESSENTIALS

Hello.	Buongiorno.	bwon-*jor*-no
	Ciao. (inf)	chow
Goodbye.	Arrivederci.	a-ree-ve-*der*-chee
	Ciao. (inf)	chow
Good evening. (from early afternoon onwards)	Buonasera.	bwo-na-*se*-a
Good night.	Buonanotte.	bwo-na-*no*-te
Yes.	Sì.	see
No.	No.	no
Please.	Per favore.	per fa-*vo*-re
	Per piacere.	per pya-*chay*-re
Thank you.	Grazie.	*gra*-tsye
That's fine/ You're welcome.	Prego.	*pre*-go

| Excuse me. | Mi scusi. | mee skoo-zee |
| Sorry (forgive me). | Mi scusi/ Mi perdoni. | mee skoo-zee/ mee per-do-nee |

What's your name?
Come si chiama?   ko-me see kya-ma
Come ti chiami? (inf)   ko-me tee kya-mee

My name is ...
Mi chiamo ...   mee kya-mo ...

Where are you from?
Da dove viene?   da do-ve vye-ne
Di dove sei? (inf)   dee do-ve se-ee

I'm from ...
Vengo da ...   ven-go da ...

I (don't) like ...
(Non) Mi piace ...   (non) mee pya-che ...

Just a minute.
Un momento.   oon mo-men-to

DIRECTIONS

Where is ...?
Dov'è ...?   do-ve ...

Go straight ahead.
Si va sempre diritto.   see va sem-pre dee-ree-to
Vai sempre diritto. (inf)   va-ee sem-pre dee-ree-to

Turn left.
Giri a sinistra.   jee-ree a see-nee-stra

Turn right.
Giri a destra.   jee-ree a de-stra

at the next corner
al prossimo angolo   al pro-see-mo an-go-lo

at the traffic lights
al semaforo   al se-ma-fo-ro

behind	dietro	dye-tro
in front of	davanti	da-van-tee
far (from)	lontano (da)	lon-ta-no (da)
near (to)	vicino (di)	vee-chee-no (dee)
opposite	di fronte a	dee fron-te a

SIGNS

Ingresso/Entrata	Entrance
Uscita	Exit
Informazione	Information
Aperto	Open
Chiuso	Closed
Proibito/Vietato	Prohibited
Polizia/Carabinieri	Police
Questura	Police Station
Gabinetti/Bagni	Toilets
Uomini	Men
Donne	Women

EMERGENCIES

Help!
Aiuto!   a-yoo-to

There's been an accident!
C'è stato un incidente!   che sta-to oon een-chee-den-te

I'm lost.
Mi sono perso/a.   mee so-no per-so/a

Go away!
Lasciami in pace!   la-sha-mi een pa-che
Vai via! (inf)   va-ee vee-a

Call ...!	Chiami ...!	kee-ya-mee ...
	Chiama ...! (inf)	kee-ya-ma ...
a doctor	un dottore/ un medico	oon do-to-re/ oon me-dee-ko
the police	la polizia	la po-lee-tsee-ya

beach	la spiaggia	la spya-ja
bridge	il ponte	eel pon-te
castle	il castello	eel kas-te-lo
cathedral	il duomo	eel dwo-mo
island	l'isola	lee-so-la
(main) square	la piazza (principale)	la pya-tsa (preen-chee-pa-le)
market	il mercato	eel mer-ka-to
old city	il centro storico	eel chen-tro sto-ree-ko
palace	il palazzo	eel pa-la-tso
ruins	le rovine	le ro-vee-ne
sea	il mare	eel ma-re
tower	la torre	la to-re

HEALTH

I'm ill.
Mi sento male.   mee sen-to ma-le

It hurts here.
Mi fa male qui.   mee fa ma-le kwee

I'm ...	Sono ...	so-no ...
asthmatic	asmatico/a	az-ma-tee-ko/a
diabetic	diabetico/a	dee-a-be-tee-ko/a
epileptic	epilettico/a	e-pee-le-tee-ko/a

I'm allergic ...	Sono allergico/a ...	so-no a-ler-jee-ko/a ...
to antibiotics	agli antibiotici	a-lyee an-tee-bee-o-tee-chee
to aspirin	all'aspirina	a-la-spe-ree-na
to penicillin	alla penicillina	a-la pe-nee-see-lee-na
to nuts	ai noci	a-ee no-chee

| antiseptic | antisettico | an-tee-se-tee-ko |
| aspirin | aspirina | as-pee-ree-na |

condoms	preservativi	pre·zer·va·*tee*·vee
contraceptive	contraccetivo	kon·tra·che·*tee*·vo
diarrhoea	diarrea	dee·a·re·a
medicine	medicina	me·dee·*chee*·na
sunblock cream	crema solare	kre·ma so·*la*·re
tampons	tamponi	tam·*po*·nee

60	sessanta	se·*san*·ta
70	settanta	se·*tan*·ta
80	ottanta	o·*tan*·ta
90	novanta	no·*van*·ta
100	cento	chen·*to*
1000	mille	mee·*le*

LANGUAGE DIFFICULTIES

Do you speak English?
Parla inglese? — par·la een·*gle*·ze

Does anyone here speak English?
C'è qualcuno che — che kwal·*koo*·no ke
parla inglese? — par·la een·*gle*·ze

How do you say ... in Italian?
Come si dice ... — ko·me see dee·che ...
in italiano? — een ee·ta·*lya*·no

What does ... mean?
Che vuol dire ...? — ke vwol dee·re ...

I understand.
Capisco. — ka·*pee*·sko

I don't understand.
Non capisco. — non ka·*pee*·sko

Please write it down.
Può scriverlo, per — pwo skree·ver·lo per
favore? — fa·*vo*·re

Can you show me (on the map)?
Può mostrarmelo — pwo mos·*trar*·me·lo
(sulla pianta)? — (soo·la *pyan*·ta)

NUMBERS

0	zero	dze·ro
1	uno	oo·no
2	due	doo·e
3	tre	tre
4	quattro	*kwa*·tro
5	cinque	*cheen*·kwe
6	sei	say
7	sette	se·te
8	otto	o·to
9	nove	no·ve
10	dieci	dye·chee
11	undici	oon·*dee*·chee
12	dodici	do·*dee*·chee
13	tredici	tre·*dee*·chee
14	quattordici	kwa·*tor*·dee·chee
15	quindici	*kween*·dee·chee
16	sedici	se·dee·chee
17	diciassette	dee·cha·*se*·te
18	diciotto	dee·*cho*·to
19	diciannove	dee·cha·*no*·ve
20	venti	*ven*·tee
21	ventuno	ven·*too*·no
22	ventidue	ven·tee·*doo*·e
30	trenta	*tren*·ta
40	quaranta	kwa·*ran*·ta
50	cinquanta	cheen·*kwan*·ta

PAPERWORK

name	nome	no·me
nationality	nazionalità	na·tsyo·na·lee·*ta*
date of birth	data di	*da*·ta dee
	nascita	*na*·shee·ta
place of birth	luogo di	*lwo*·go dee
	nascita	*na*·shee·ta
sex (gender)	sesso	se·so
passport	passaporto	pa·sa·*por*·to
visa	visto	vee·sto

QUESTION WORDS

Who?	Chi?	kee
What?	Che?	ke
When?	Quando?	*kwan*·do
Where?	Dove?	do·ve
How?	Come?	*ko*·me

SHOPPING & SERVICES

I'd like to buy ...
Vorrei comprare ... — vo·ray kom·*pra*·re ...

How much is it?
Quanto costa? — *kwan*·to ko·sta

I don't like it.
Non mi piace. — non mee *pya*·che

May I look at it?
Posso dare un'occhiata? — po·so da·re oo·no·*kya*·ta

I'm just looking.
Sto solo guardando. — sto so·lo gwar·*dan*·do

It's cheap.
Non è caro/cara. — non e *ka*·ro/*ka*·ra

It's too expensive.
È troppo caro/a. — e tro·po *ka*·ro/*ka*·ra

I'll take it.
Lo/La compro. — lo/la kom·pro

Do you accept credit cards?
Accettate carte — a·che·*ta*·te kar·te
di credito? — dee kre·dee·to

I want to	Voglio	*vo*·lyo
change ...	cambiare ...	kam·*bya*·re ...
money	del denaro	del de·*na*·ro
travellers	assegni dee	a·se·nyee dee
cheques	viaggio	vee·*a*·jo

more	più	pyoo
less	meno	me·no
smaller	più piccolo/a	pyoo *pee*·ko·lo/la
bigger	più grande	pyoo *gran*·de

I'm looking for ...	Cerco ...	cher·ko ...
an ATM	un Bancomat	oon ban·ko·mat
a bank	un banco	oon ban·ko
the church	la chiesa	la kye·za
the city centre	il centro	eel chen·tro
the market	il mercato	eel mer·ka·to
the museum	il museo	eel moo·ze·o
the post office	la posta	la po·sta
a public toilet	un gabinetto	oon ga·bee·ne·to
the tourist office	l'ufficio di turismo	loo·fee·cho dee too·reez·mo

TIME & DATES

What time is it?	Che ore sono?	ke o·re so·no
It's (one o'clock).	È (l'una).	e (loo·na)
It's (8 o'clock).	Sono (le otto).	so·no (le o·to)
When?	Quando?	kwan·do
today	oggi	o·jee
tomorrow	domani	do·ma·nee
yesterday	ieri	ye·ree
in the morning	di mattina	dee ma·tee·na
in the afternoon	di pomeriggio	dee po·me·ree·jo
in the evening	di sera	dee se·ra

Monday	lunedì	loo·ne·dee
Tuesday	martedì	mar·te·dee
Wednesday	mercoledì	mer·ko·le·dee
Thursday	giovedì	jo·ve·dee
Friday	venerdì	ve·ner·dee
Saturday	sabato	sa·ba·to
Sunday	domenica	do·me·nee·ka

January	gennaio	je·na·yo
February	febbraio	fe·bra·yo
March	marzo	mar·tso
April	aprile	a·pree·le
May	maggio	ma·jo
June	giugno	joo·nyo
July	luglio	loo·lyo
August	agosto	a·gos·to
September	settembre	se·tem·bre
October	ottobre	o·to·bre
November	novembre	no·vem·bre
December	dicembre	dee·chem·bre

TRANSPORT
Public Transport

What time does the ... leave/ arrive?	A che ora parte/ arriva ...?	a ke o·ra par·te/ a·ree·va ...
(city) bus	l'autobus	low·to·boos
(intercity) bus	il pullman	eel pool·man
plane	l'aereo	la·e·re·o
train	il treno	eel tre·no

I'd like a ... ticket.	Vorrei un biglietto ...	vo·ray oon bee·lye·to ...
one-way	di solo andata	dee so·lo an·da·ta
return	di andata e ritorno	dee an·da·ta e ree·toor·no
1st class	di prima classe	dee pree·ma kla·se
2nd class	di seconda classe	dee se·kon·da kla·se

I want to go to ...
Voglio andare a ...   vo·lyo an·da·re a ...
The train has been cancelled/delayed.
Il treno è soppresso/   eel tre·no e so·pre·so/
  in ritardo.   een ree·tar·do

the first	il primo	eel pree·mo
the last	l'ultimo	lool·tee·mo
platform (two)	binario (due)	bee·na·ryo (doo·e)
ticket office	biglietteria	bee·lye·te·ree·a
timetable	orario	o·ra·ryo
train station	stazione	sta·tsyo·ne

Private Transport

I'd like to hire a/an ...	Vorrei noleggiare ...	vo·ray no·le·ja·re ...
car	una macchina	oo·na ma·kee·na
4WD	un fuoristrada	oon fwo·ree·stra·da
motorbike	una moto	oo·na mo·to
bicycle	una bici(cletta)	oo·na bee·chee·(kle·ta)

Where's a service station?
Dov'è una stazione   do·ve oo·na sta·tsyo·ne
  di servizio?   dee ser·vee·tsyo
Please fill it up.
Il pieno, per favore.   eel pye·no per fa·vo·re
I'd like (30) litres.
Vorrei (trenta) litri.   vo·ray (tren·ta) lee·tree
diesel
gasolio/diesel   ga·zo·lyo/dee·zel
petrol/gasoline
benzina   ben·dzee·na
Is this the road to ...?
Questa strada porta   kwe·sta stra·da por·ta
  a ...?   a ...
(How long) Can I park here?
(Per quanto tempo)   (per kwan·to tem·po)
Posso parcheggiare qui? po·so par·ke·ja·re kwee
Where do I pay?
Dove si paga?   do·ve see pa·ga
I need a mechanic.
Ho bisogno di un   o bee·zo·nyo dee oon
  meccanico.   me·ka·nee·ko

ROAD SIGNS

Dare la Precedenza	Give Way
Deviazione	Detour
Divieto di Accesso	No Entry
Divieto di Sorpasso	No Overtaking
Divieto di Sosta	No Parking
Entrata	Entrance
Passo Carrabile/Carraio	Keep Clear
Pedaggio	Toll
Pericolo	Danger
Rallentare	Slow Down
Senso Unico	One Way
Uscita	Exit

The car/motorbike has broken down (at ...).
La macchina/moto   la *ma*·kee·na/*mo*·to
   si è guastata (a ...).   see e gwas·*ta*·ta (a ...)
The car/motorbike won't start.
La macchina/moto   la *ma*·kee·na/*mo*·to
   non parte.   non *par*·te
I have a flat tyre.
Ho una gomma bucata.   o oo·na *go*·ma boo·*ka*·ta
I've run out of petrol.
Ho esaurito la benzina.   o e·zo·*ree*·to la ben·*dzee*·na
I've had an accident.
Ho avuto un incidente.   o a·*voo*·to oon een·chee·*den*·te

TRAVEL WITH CHILDREN
Is there a/an ...?
C'è ...?   che ...

I need a/an ...
Ho bisogno di ...   o bee·*zo*·nyo dee ...
   baby change room
   un bagno con fasciatoio   oon *ba*·nyo kon fa·sha·*to*·yo
   car baby seat
   un seggiolino per   oon se·jo·*lee*·no per
     bambini   bam·*bee*·nee
   child-minding service
   un servizio di   oon ser·*vee*·tsyo dee
     babysitter   be·bee·*see*·ter
   children's menu
   un menù per bambini   oon me·*noo* per bam·*bee*·nee
   (disposable) nappies/diapers
   pannolini (usa e getta)   pa·no·*lee*·nee (*oo*·sa e *je*·ta)
   formula (infant milk)
   latte in polvere   *la*·te in *pol*·ve·re
   (English-speaking) babysitter
   un/una babysitter   oon/oo·na be·bee·*see*·ter
     (che parli inglese)   (ke *par*·lee een·*gle*·ze)
   highchair
   un seggiolone   oon se·jo·*lo*·ne
   potty
   un vasino   oon va·*zee*·no
   stroller
   un passeggino   oon pa·se·*jee*·no

Do you mind if I breastfeed here?
Le dispiace se allatto   le dees·*pya*·che se a·*la*·to
   il/la bimbo/a qui?   eel/la *beem*·bo/a kwee
Are children allowed?
I bambini sono   ee bam·*bee*·nee so·no
   ammessi?   a·*me*·see

LANGUAGE

Also available from Lonely Planet:
Italian Phrasebook

Glossary

AAST – Azienda Autonoma di Soggiorno e Turismo; local tourist office

abbazia – abbey; also badia

ACI – Automobile Club Italiano; Italian Automobile Association

affittacamere – rooms for rent

agriturismo – tourist accommodation on farms

AIG – Associazione Italiana Alberghi per la Gioventù; Italian Youth Hostel Association

albergo – hotel (up to five stars)

alimentari – grocery shop, delicatessen

alloggio – lodging (cheaper than a *pensione* and not part of the classification system)

alto – high

ambasciata – embassy

ambo – pulpit, often elaborately carved

anfiteatro – amphitheatre

APT – Azienda di Promozione Turistica; regional tourist office

Apulia – same as Puglia

ara – altar

arco – arch

assicurato/a – insured

AST – Azienda Soggiorno e Turismo; local tourist office

atrium – (Latin) forecourt of a Roman house or a Christian basilica

autostazione – bus station or terminal

autostop – hitchhiking

autostrada – motorway, freeway

bagno – bathroom; toilet

baia – bay

bancomat – ATM

basilica – a rectangular building divided into three aisles by rows of columns; Roman Christians adapted it for their early churches

belvedere – panoramic viewpoint

benzina – petrol

benzina senza piombo – unleaded petrol

bicicletta – bicycle

biglietto – ticket

binario – (train) platform

borgo – ancient town or village, sometimes used to mean equivalent of *via*

calcio – football (soccer)

cambio – money exchange

camera – room

campanile – bell tower

campeggio – camp site

campo – field

canto – quarter

cappella – chapel

carabinieri – police with military and civil duties

Carnevale – carnival period between Epiphany and Lent

carta – menu

carta d'identità – ID card

cartoleria – paper-goods shop

caryatid – supporting pillar or column carved into a female form; male forms are called telamones

casa – house

castrum – Roman military camp, always rectangular in shape with straight streets and gates at the cardinal points

Catapan – the Governor of a province in the Byzantine world

cava – quarry (as in the pumice quarries at Campobianco)

centro – centre

centro storico – historic centre

chiesa – church

chiese rupestri – church carved out of the rock

chiostro – cloister; covered walkway, usually enclosed by columns, around a quadrangle

ciborium – casket or tabernacle containing the host

città – town, city

codice fiscale – tax number

colonna – column

comune – equivalent to a municipality or county; town or city council; historically, a commune (self-governing town or city)

consolato – consulate

contadino – peasant farmer

contrada – district

convalida – ticket-stamping machine

convento – a convent or a monastery

corso – main street, avenue

cortile – courtyard

CTS – Centro Turistico Studentesco e Giovanile; Centre for Student & Youth Tourists

cupola – dome

Daunii – ancient inhabitants of Puglia, a tribe of the Iapigi who came from the Illyrian (east) shore of the Adriatic

deposito bagagli – left luggage

diretto – direct; slow train

distributore di benzina – petrol pump

dolmen – a prehistoric monument (possibly a tomb) made up of two or more upright stones supporting a horizontal stone slab

duomo – cathedral

elenco degli alberghi – list of hotels
ENIT – Ente Nazionale Italiano per il Turismo; Italian Tourist Board
enoteca – wine bar
ente – organisation or office
Exultet – an illustrated scroll

ferrovia – train station
festa – festival
fiume – river
fontana – fountain
fortezza – fortress
fortino – fort
francobollo – postage stamp
frantoio – olive oil mill

gabinetto – toilet, WC
gasolio – diesel
Gnathian ware – a type of black pottery from Apulia (esp. Egnazia)
gola – gorge
golfo – gulf
grotta – cave
guardia di finanza – fiscal police
guardia medica – emergency doctor service

IC – Intercity; fast train
intarsia – inlay of wood, marble or metal
interregionale – long-distance train that stops frequently
ipogeo – entrance to underground cave or chamber
isola – island

krater – antique mixing-bowl, conical in shape with a rounded base

lago – lake
largo – (small) square
lavanderia – laundrette
lavasecco – dry-cleaning
lido – beach
locale – slow local train
locanda – inn, small hotel
loggia – open-sided arcade or gallery
lunette – semicircular space in a vault or above a door or window, often decorated with a painting or relief
lungomare – seafront road, promenade

mare – sea
masseria – fortified farmhouse
menhir – a single upright monolith, usually of prehistoric origin
mercato – market
Mesapii – ancient inhabitants of Puglia, a tribe of the lapigi who came from the Illyrian (east) shore of the Adriatic

mezza pensione – half board
monte – mountain
motorino – moped
municipio – town hall, municipal offices
museo – museum

Natale – Christmas
nave – large ferry, ship
necropolis – (ancient) cemetery, burial site
numero verde – toll-free phone number

oggetti smarriti – lost property
oratorio – oratory
ospedale – hospital
ostello per la gioventù – youth hostel
osteria – inn

palazzo – palace or mansion; large building of any type, including an apartment block
parco – park
passeggiata – traditional evening stroll
Pasqua – Easter
pedaggio – toll
pensione – small hotel, often with board
pensione completa – full board
Peucetians – ancient inhabitants of Puglia, a tribe of the lapigi who came from the Illyrian (east) shore of the Adriatic
pianta della città – city map
piazza – square
piazzale – (large) open square
pinacoteca – art gallery specialising in the exhibition of paintings
poltrona – airline-type chair on a ferry
polyptych – altarpiece consisting of more than three panels
ponte – bridge
porta – gate, door
portico – portico; covered walkway, usually attached to the outside of buildings
porto – port
prigione – prison
Pro Loco – local tourist office

questura – police station

rapido – fast train
reale – royal
regionale – slow local train, also called *locale*
rifugio – mountain hut
riserva naturale – nature reserve
ronda – roundabout (traffic)
ruderi – ruins

Sacra Corona Unita – Pugliese mafia
sagra – festival (generally dedicated to one food item or theme)

sala – room
saline – saltworks
Samnite – of/relating to an offshoot of the Sabines, an ancient ribe of south-central Italy
santuario – sanctuary
sassi – literally, rocks; i *sassi* – cave dwellings
scalinata – staircase, steps
sentieri – trails
soccorso stradale – breakdown service
spiaggia (libera) – (public) beach
stazione – station
stazione di servizio – petrol or service station
stazione marittima – ferry terminal
strada – street, road
supplemento – supplement, payable on a fast train
Swabian – of or pertaining to the period of rule by the Hohenstaufen dynasty (1194–1266)

taranta – a frenzied, ritualistic dance once thought to cure people of the poisonous bite of the tarantula
teatro – theatre
tempio – temple
terme – thermal baths
torre – tower

torrente – stream
trabucco – ancient fishing trap
traghetto – ferry, boat
Trenitalia – partially privatised state railway system, previously known as the Ferrovie dello Stato (FS)
treno – train
triptych – painting or carving on three panels, hinged so that the outer panels fold over the middle one; often used as an altarpiece
trullo (pl. *trulli*) – rural dwelling of Puglia, built without mortar of local limestone and usually whitewashed, with a conical roof formed of flat-pitched spiral courses of the same stone topped by a finial

ufficio postale – post office
ufficio stranieri – foreigners bureau
uffici – offices

via – street, road
viale – avenue
vicolo – alley, alleyway
vigili del fuoco – fire brigade

zona rimozione – vehicle-removal zone

Behind the Scenes

THIS BOOK

This 1st edition was researched and written by Paula Hardy, Abigail Hole and Olivia Pozzan. The book was commissioned in Lonely Planet's London office and produced in Melbourne.

Commissioning Editor Paula Hardy
Coordinating Editor Justin Flynn
Coordinating Cartographers Anthony Phelan, Valentina Kremenchutskaya
Coordinating Layout Designer David Kemp
Managing Editor Melanie Dankel
Managing Cartographer Mark Griffiths
Managing Layout Designer Celia Wood
Assisting Editors Kate James, Melanie Dankel, Judith Bamber
Assisting Cartographers Barbara Benson, Tony Fankhauser, Simon Goslin
Cover Designer Brendan Dempsey
Project Manager Rachel Imeson
Language Content Coordinator Quentin Frayne

Thanks to John Dabney for the Wine section in the Food & Wine chapter, Penelope Goodes

SEND US YOUR FEEDBACK

We love to hear from travellers – your comments keep us on our toes and help make our books better. Our well-travelled team reads every word on what you loved or loathed about this book. Although we cannot reply individually to postal submissions, we always guarantee that your feedback goes straight to the appropriate authors, in time for the next edition. Each person who sends us information is thanked in the next edition – and the most useful submissions are rewarded with a free book.

To send us your updates – and find out about Lonely Planet events, newsletters and travel news – visit our award-winning website: **www.lonelyplanet.com/contact**.

Note: we may edit, reproduce and incorporate your comments in Lonely Planet products such as guidebooks, websites and digital products, so let us know if you don't want your comments reproduced or your name acknowledged. For a copy of our privacy policy visit www.lonelyplanet.com/privacy.

THANKS
PAULA HARDY

I think I can honestly say that this book has been one of easiest LP titles I've ever researched, and that's due in no small measure to the warmheartedness of the Pugliese people I met on my journey. First and foremost, I'd like to thank our partners Angelo Pitro and Cristina Savia at EDT for sharing their knowledge and contacts. Thanks also to: Massimo Ostillio, Alfredo da Liguori and Stefania Manduria at the Ministry of Tourism; Cinzia at Slow Food; and Alessandro Laterza at Laterza publishing. And to the following people, who generously shared with me their knowledge and passion for Puglia: Berenice and Melanie de Bellis, Simona Melchiorre, Frederico Rubino, Amedeo Cosimi, Nancy Moscato, Gabriele Pellegrino, Francesca Bortone, Stefania Metta, Palma Colagiacomo, Giuseppe Barran and Rosalba Balestrazzi. Back in the office, thanks are due to Stefanie di Trocchio, Fayette Fox, Samantha Faccio and Imogen Hall, whose support of this project was much, much appreciated. Last, but never least, thank you so much to my fellow authors, Abigail Hole and Olivia Pozzan, for pounding the pavements of Puglia and Basilicata and coming up with so many great ideas and recommendations for this book.

ABIGAIL HOLE

Tante grazie a Anna, Marcello, Mum, Morag, Ganny Mo, Grandpa John e Ant per il loro lavoro di babysitting, e la famiglia Blasi per tutte le informazioni sulla Puglia. Special thanks to Marcello l'Oracolo for sharing all his knowledge about food and culture. Many thanks to John Dabney for his contributions on wine, Michele Cappiello at Ferula Viaggi in Basilicata for all his kind help, and to Alex for his input on *trulli*. Thanks so much to Paula Hardy and Olivia Pozzan for being such great co-authors, to Paula for making it all possible and to all the other people who worked so hard inhouse. Gratitude also goes to Antonio Carluccio, Sud Sound System, Alessandro Laterza, Simona Rocca, Deborah Grima, Gianni, Maria-Rita and Enzo for their interviews and assistance. Last but not at all least, thanks to Luca, who made me love Puglia in the first place.

LONELY PLANET: TRAVEL WIDELY, TREAD LIGHTLY, GIVE SUSTAINABLY

The Lonely Planet Story

The story begins with a classic travel adventure: Tony and Maureen Wheeler's 1972 journey across Europe and Asia to Australia. There was no useful information about the overland trail then, so Tony and Maureen published the first Lonely Planet guidebook to meet a growing need.

From a kitchen table, Lonely Planet has grown to become the largest independent travel publisher in the world, with offices in Melbourne (Australia), Oakland (USA) and London (UK). Today Lonely Planet guidebooks cover the globe. There is an ever-growing list of books and information in a variety of media. Some things haven't changed. The main aim is still to make it possible for adventurous individuals to get out there – to explore and better understand the world.

The Lonely Planet Foundation

The Lonely Planet Foundation proudly supports nimble nonprofit institutions working for change in the world. Each year the foundation donates 5% of Lonely Planet company profits to projects selected by staff and authors. Our partners range from Kabissa, which provides small nonprofits across Africa with access to technology, to the Foundation for Developing Cambodian Orphans, which supports girls at risk of falling victim to sex traffickers.

Our nonprofit partners are linked by a grass-roots approach to the areas of health, education or sustainable tourism. Many projects we support – such as one with BaAka (Pygmy) children in the forested areas of Central African Republic – choose to focus on women and children as one of the most effective ways to support the whole community.

Sometimes foundation assistance is as simple as helping to preserve a local ruin like the Minaret of Jam in Afghanistan; this incredible monument now draws intrepid tourists to the area and its restoration has greatly improved options for local people.

Just as travel is often about learning to see with new eyes, so many of the groups we work with aim to change the way people see themselves and the future for their children and communities.

OLIVIA POZZAN

I arrived in Basilicata to freezing conditions and unending rain, but the weather was no reflection of the incredible hospitality and assistance I found wherever I turned. A big thank you goes to: Michele Cappiello for his endless patience and helpful contacts (and a memorable date with the Addolorata); Giuseppe Cosenza for showing me the Pollino and the *pino loricato*, and answering a million questions; Susi Travisano for her friendly efficiency; Maria Minutiello, a big help after a long, wet and difficult day; and the Potenza APT. The tourist officials in Foggia were fantastic, showing me a side to the city I hadn't expected. In Manfredonia I found the organised, efficient, and warm-hearted Rosemary – and pray to find Rosemarys wherever I travel. A warm thank you to the beautiful people of the Gargano: Maria-Lucia for her lovely smiles, and for introducing me to the wonderful art of Michele Circiello; Francesca for finding nothing too much trouble; and Gino Fusco, the Vieste Rock Star. And lastly, to Tundra Gorza who shared the highs and lows – I really couldn't have done it without you – and to my commissioning editor, Paula Hardy, a stable rock throughout it all.

ACKNOWLEDGMENTS

Many thanks to the following for the use of their content:

Globe on title page ©Mountain High Maps 1993 Digital Wisdom, Inc.

Index

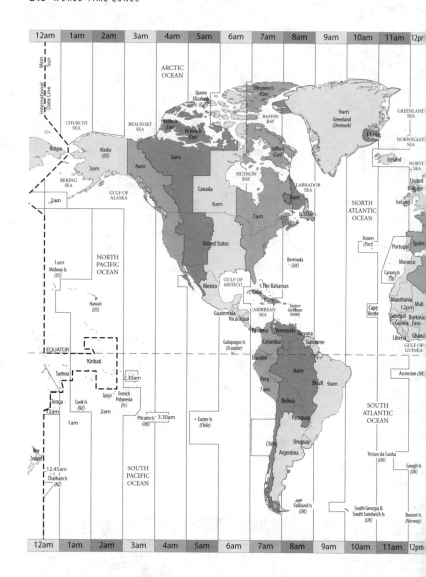

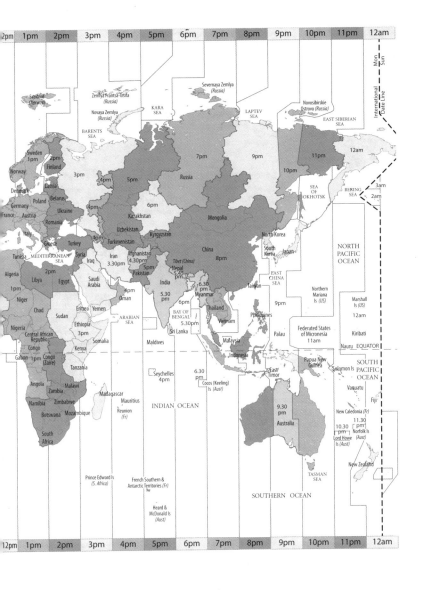

12pm 1pm 2pm 3pm 4pm 5pm 6pm 7pm 8pm 9pm 10pm 11pm 12am

Mon | Sun
International Date Line

Svalbard (Norway)

Zemlya Frantsa-Iosifa (Russia)

Severnaya Zemlya (Russia)

Novaya Zemlya (Russia)

KARA SEA

LAPTEV SEA

Novosibirskie Ostrovo (Russia)

EAST SIBERIAN SEA

BARENTS SEA

Sweden 1pm
Norway
Finland 2pm
Denmark
Latvia
Germany Poland Belarus
France Austria Ukraine
Italy Romania

3pm

4pm

5pm

Russia 7pm

9pm

10pm

11pm

12am

3am

SEA OF OKHOTSK

BERING SEA

2am

NORTH PACIFIC OCEAN

Tunisia MEDITERRANEAN SEA 2pm
Greece Turkey Syria
Algeria Iran
Libya Iraq 3.30pm
Egypt

4pm

Kazakhstan

Uzbekistan

Turkmenistan Kyrgyzstan

Afghanistan 4.30pm

Mongolia

China 8pm

North Korea
South Korea Japan

EAST CHINA SEA

Niger Chad
Sudan
Nigeria Eritrea Yemen
Central African Republic Ethiopia
Congo Kenya
Gabon 1pm Congo (Zaire)
Tanzania

1pm

2pm

Saudi Arabia

Oman

4pm

ARABIAN SEA

Pakistan 5pm

5.45pm
Nepal
India

5.30 pm

Tibet (China)

6.30 pm
Myanmar

6pm

Thailand
Vietnam

Taiwan

Philippines 9pm

Northern Mariana Is (US)

Marshall Is (US)

12am

3pm

Somalia

Maldives

BAY OF BENGAL

Sri Lanka 5.30pm

Malaysia

Palau

Federated States of Micronesia 11am

Kiribati

Nauru EQUATOR

Indonesia

East Timor

Papua New Guinea
Solomon Is

SOUTH PACIFIC OCEAN

Angola Malawi
Zambia Zimbabwe
Namibia Botswana Mozambique
South Africa

Madagascar

Mauritius
Reunion (Fr)

Seychelles 4pm

Cocos (Keeling) Is (Aust)

6.30 pm

INDIAN OCEAN

Australia 9.30 pm

Vanuatu

New Caledonia (Fr)

Fiji

10.30 pm
Lord Howe Is (Aust)

11.30 pm
Norfolk Is (Aust)

Prince Edward Is (S. Africa)

French Southern & Antarctic Territories (Fr)

TASMAN SEA

New Zealand

Heard & McDonald Is (Aust)

SOUTHERN OCEAN

12pm 1pm 2pm 3pm 4pm 5pm 6pm 7pm 8pm 9pm 10pm 11pm 12am

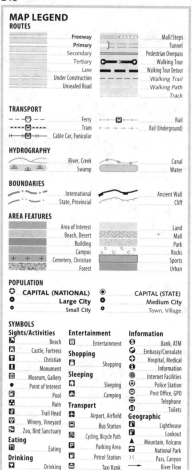

MAP LEGEND
ROUTES

Freeway	Mall/Steps
Primary	Tunnel
Secondary	Pedestrian Overpass
Tertiary	Walking Tour
Lane	Walking Tour Detour
Under Construction	Walking Trail
Unsealed Road	Walking Path
	Track

TRANSPORT

Ferry	Rail
Tram	Rail (Underground)
Cable Car, Funicular	

HYDROGRAPHY

River, Creek	Canal
Swamp	Water

BOUNDARIES

International	Ancient Wall
State, Provincial	Cliff

AREA FEATURES

Area of Interest	Land
Beach, Desert	Mall
Building	Park
Campus	Rocks
Cemetery, Christian	Sports
Forest	Urban

POPULATION

○ **CAPITAL (NATIONAL)**	◉ CAPITAL (STATE)
● **Large City**	● Medium City
● Small City	● Town, Village

SYMBOLS

Sights/Activities
- Beach
- Castle, Fortress
- Christian
- Monument
- Museum, Gallery
- Point of Interest
- Pool
- Ruin
- Trail Head
- Winery, Vineyard
- Zoo, Bird Sanctuary

Eating
- Eating

Drinking
- Drinking

Entertainment
- Entertainment

Shopping
- Shopping

Sleeping
- Sleeping
- Camping

Transport
- Airport, Airfield
- Bus Station
- Cycling, Bicycle Path
- Parking Area
- Petrol Station
- Taxi Rank

Information
- Bank, ATM
- Embassy/Consulate
- Hospital, Medical
- Information
- Internet Facilities
- Police Station
- Post Office, GPO
- Telephone
- Toilets

Geographic
- Lighthouse
- Lookout
- Mountain, Volcano
- National Park
- Pass, Canyon
- River Flow

LONELY PLANET OFFICES

Australia
Head Office
Locked Bag 1, Footscray, Victoria 3011
☎ 03 8379 8000, fax 03 8379 8111
talk2us@lonelyplanet.com.au

USA
150 Linden St, Oakland, CA 94607
☎ 510 893 8555, toll free 800 275 8555
fax 510 893 8572
info@lonelyplanet.com

UK
2nd Floor 186 City Rd,
London EC1V 2NT UK
☎ 020 7106 2100, fax 020 7106 2101
go@lonelyplanet.co.uk

Published by Lonely Planet Publications Pty Ltd
ABN 36 005 607 983

© Lonely Planet Publications Pty Ltd 2008

© photographers as indicated 2008

Cover photograph: Otranto, Giovanni Simeone / SIME/ 4Corners Images. Many of the images in this guide are available for licensing from Lonely Planet Images: www.lonelyplanetimages.com.

Printed by Hang Tai Printing Company.
Printed in China.